THE
MISADVENTURES
OF AN
AGEING MULE

THE
MISADVENTURES
OF AN
AGEING MULE

ANTHONY ASPINALL

ANDRE DEUTSCH

To the memory of E.M.D., without
whose gentle bullying I might not have told
so much of the truth about myself.

First published 1989 by
André Deutsch Limited
105–106 Great Russell Street
London WC1B 3LJ

British Library Cataloguing in Publication Data

Aspinall, Anthony, *1909-*
    The misadventures of an ageing mule
    1. Drug traffic – biographies
    I. Title
    364.1'77'0924
ISBN 0 233 98439 9

Phototypeset by Falcon Graphic Art Ltd
Wallington, Surrey
Printed and bound by
WSOY Finland

Contents

Foreword

I have changed certain details about many of my prison companions (especially personal names and occupations) in the hope of sparing them any embarrassment. Among the exceptions are my visitors from the British Embassy in Damascus (for whose kindness I shall always be indebted) and my few brief meetings with Alan Reeve in a Netherlands remand centre. The latter's case has acquired such notoriety over the years it seemed pointless to present him under an alias.

Throughout the book I have referred to prison officers – in both Syria and the Netherlands – as guards, because that is what we called them. I am aware that in the United Kingdom they are usually known as 'screws', but this was a term seldom used by even the tiny minority of British prisoners, most of whom had never been inside any of their own country's jails.

In conclusion I wish to express my gratitude to Sheila McIlwraith for her wise counsel and for pruning much of my over-exuberance from the original text.

SYRIA: HASHISH

THE AIRPORT

Damascus airport. It was half-past six in the morning and still dark, although as I got out of the taxi there was a faintly pink indication of dawn on the eastern horizon.

I was to catch a Lufthansa flight to Frankfurt. It was early March with a temperature only a degree or two above freezing. During the previous few days there had been heavy falls of snow, unusual in this ancient city where the heat in summer can be overpowering.

I paid the taxi-driver and surrendered my luggage to a porter who, in the darkness illuminated only by badly focussed headlamps from approaching traffic, looked like a Teddy bear. He picked up my two suitcases with visible ease, betraying no surprise at their exceptional weight. In spite of the cold he was wearing only a pair of old jeans, too small for him, and a grubby tartan shirt which barely covered his furry chest because most of the buttons were missing.

As he shuffled in plastic slippers towards the airport building, I grabbed the looped strap of my shoulder-bag and hoisted it into a position where I hoped it would not slip constantly down to my elbow. I followed him across the wide concrete driveway, still wet from the melted snow, towards a short flight of steps to the departure terminal. I turned up the collar of my sheepskin jacket against a cold wind, blowing strongly from the north – from Turkey and the Taurus Mountains.

It was an airport I had frequently passed through. Eighteen miles from the city, it had been created by flattening rocky, infertile land, typical of much of Syria to the east and south of its capital.

One was constantly being told the buildings were only temporary and, indeed, they looked it. In daylight it was possible to see, not far away, the half-completed new terminal, surrounded by a rubble of fragmented concrete. For some reason that was never explained, presumably shortage of money, work had been abandoned some time

3

ago. It had remained half-finished, deserted, pathetic. Meanwhile the ever-increasing number of passengers using the temporary building often caused chaos.

People everywhere were now getting out of cars and taxis; two overloaded airport buses had just arrived.

As I mounted the half-dozen steps, I was surrounded by a crowd who were obviously travelling to Frankfurt. Some were German business men, solitary and uncommunicative, clutching expensive briefcases; others were their much more genial Arab counterparts, clutching even more expensive briefcases with gold-plated frames and handles, many accompanied by womenfolk and a few by children.

Most of the Lebanese women looked as if they bought their clothes from the best Parisian couturiers but, as always, had failed to acquire French discretion in the art of make-up: in the chill light of dawn many looked like painted puppets. Their Syrian sisters were utterly different, most of them swathed, from head to toe, in layers of veiling, with dark-eyed, bewildered-looking children clinging to their skirts.

All of us were ruthlessly converging on the narrow entrance, determined to get out of the cold wind as quickly as possible. Two plainclothes policemen stood in the doorway taking a quick look at everyone's passport. Just as I was about to offer mine, an expensively-gloved hand, protruding from a wide sleeve of Russian sable, was thrust in front of me. The glamorous young woman waved her Lebanese passport imperiously under the nose of the surprised official, clearly feeling she should be given priority. She was given a frosty look of puritan disapproval and her importunate gestures were ignored. My passport was accepted instead. The policeman was one of those Syrians who look as if they prefer to shave only twice a week, with a blunt blade, and who openly consider all *mondaine* ladies no better than whores. Lebanese and Egyptian women unhesitatingly despise most Syrian males and regard them as a collection of donkeys.

The policeman flicked over the pages of my passport as the pressure of the crowd, including the now very cross lady in sables, increased all the time. The sight of my Syrian visa, with its whole page of dun-coloured stamps, convinced him I had not smuggled myself into his country. He handed the document politely back to me, indicating with a wave that I was free to enter the customs hall.

Holding my passport like a talisman in front of my chest (any action to avoid being mistaken for an American in an Arab airport is a wise precaution) I walked slowly towards the frustrating obstacle which all passengers, except the most privileged, have to cope with when leaving Syria: an often ill-mannered inspection of one's luggage by the customs. It was 1980 and 'scanners' had not yet been installed. All baggage had to be opened and its contents were usually left in a tangled mess. After this, permission was given for it to be trundled away for weighing, labelling and loading.

As I approached the long counter I saw the porter had placed my suitcases in a central position and was standing beside them. They were identical and of the type known as 'hard shell'. They were the biggest available. The product of an internationally well-known company, they could only be bought at the more expensive department stores of Europe and America. They were usually available in several colours. I always chose black.

Illuminated now by dozens of bulbs suspended on single strands of wire from the roof, they looked enormous and faintly sinister.

The sight of them produced within me, for the first time that morning, a nervous tension in the pit of my stomach. From this moment I became more and more uneasy.

For several years I, and those who were working with me, had been amongst the privileged passengers who knew they would be greeted with smiling courtesy by all airport staff, including customs.

The reason for this obsequious behaviour was that we were accompanied by a friendly senior officer of the Syrian police. His mere presence with us at the airport, or on the docks of several harbours, was a guarantee we would not be asked embarrassing questions by less exalted officials.

It was his habit in Damascus to meet whoever had been booked on a flight to Europe outside the departure terminal. Together they would stroll, chatting animatedly, through the customs hall. The staff would fall over themselves to scrawl chalk-marks on the unopened luggage and wave them graciously on towards the check-in. At the entrance to the departure lounge, our policeman would bid goodbye to his protégé.

Unfortunately, this most useful fellow was now on holiday in Paris, doubtless enjoying himself on the *douceurs* we had provided. He was not expected to return for some weeks and a replacement of sufficiently impressive rank had not been found.

A Canadian customer had been expecting a delivery for some time and was getting impatient. My partner had convinced himself that if I were to leave alone on the early morning flight to Frankfurt, the danger of trouble from the customs was hardly worth considering. At first, I did not share his confidence but the urgent messages he sent from Lebanon eventually won me over.

A middle-aged Czech had originally been engaged to take the suitcases as far as Barcelona, but it was now believed he could not be trusted. After all, I had previously agreed to take over all responsibility for the luggage when it arrived in Spain, and would then travel by a roundabout route involving ships, aeroplanes and trains, to British Columbia. Why should I baulk at the first hurdle, which would probably be the easiest to cope with?

The Syrian customs in the past had concentrated in a somewhat slap-happy fashion on the detection of small arms and ammunition. Anything else, especially if concealed by experts, was seldom discovered.

Experience around the world had taught me long ago that customs officials usually gave me an easy ride. Aided by a good tailor, a pair of hand-made brogues and a battered felt trilby, bought years ago from Locke's in St James's Street, I found it comparatively easy to assume the appearance and manner of an 'olde worlde' Englishman. It worked like a charm in most third-world countries and had been astonishingly successful in the United States.

However, on this cold morning I felt an unaccustomed lack of self-confidence, and hoped it could only be due to leaving without my usual cup of strong coffee.

I looked at the row of customs officers in khaki. Most of them were young and their stance seemed exaggeratedly macho. I hoped I would recognise some of them from previous journeys, but there was not a single familiar face. This time there would be no wreathed smiles of welcome – I was sure of that.

One moved suddenly towards my suitcases with almost military precision.

'Open,' he snapped in Arabic.

'Both?' I asked in English, still holding my passport in front of me, as if it would neutralise hostility.

'Both,' the young man replied, still in Arabic, and with what I felt to be a look of cold distrust he pointed to my shoulder-bag: 'That too.'

I obediently allowed it to slip from my shoulder and the porter laid it on the counter.

A second customs officer now joined his colleague. He seized the brown leather bag, pulling open its zip-fasteners and emptying it out. It contained the usual items to be found in any elderly man's over-night grip.

Slipping my passport into my coat-pocket, I took out a bunch of keys. The suitcases were upright, not more than an inch or two apart. With the porter's help I separated them until they were at least a couple of feet from each other.

I tackled the one on my left. The small key turned easily in both locks. I flicked up the safety-catches at each end, and, taking the greatest possible care, opened the suitcase as if it were a giant book, lowering each side very gently to the counter.

The customs officers joined forces to examine the contents, rumpling my neatly-packed shirts and underclothes without finding anything of interest.

As I got to work on suitcase number 2, I began to feel more confident – a confidence that quickly ebbed when one of the locks refused to open. It appeared to have become rock-solid. The key, hardly bigger than the nail on my little finger, would not turn in either direction.

This sort of emergency can be the subject of a smuggler's nightmare. When you wake you pray it will never happen to you in real life. It was happening to me and I knew I was in real trouble.

The porter, in an effort to help me, was doing his best to hold the suitcase firmly upright: he had already opened the safety-catches at each end. I, sweating with anxiety and using every ounce of strength in my fingers, made a final effort to get the fiddling little key to turn. Suddenly, I succeeded; the lock burst wide open, catching us both by surprise. The porter immediately released his hold, allowing both sides to fall open. I made a despairing effort to catch them as they fell apart, but failed. They hit the counter simultaneously with a noise like the explosion of a small bomb in a steel vault.

The sound seemed to bring the entire airport to a halt. A woman screamed and this was followed by a breathless hush. Crowds every-where in the terminal appeared to be gaping in my direction with shocked surprise.

The reaction of the customs men was different. Scenting something abnormal about my luggage, they got to work with the speed and controlled excitement of a couple of Jack Russell terriers above a fox's earth.

Quickly emptying both sides of the suitcase – throwing my clothes into an untidy pile on the counter – they prodded and sniffed at every inch of the interior, but were unable to detect any flaw. The blue nylon lining with decorative braiding was in perfect condition – there were no bumps or excrescences to be felt beneath it.

Still suspicious, they attempted to measure the depth of the interior with their fingers. To their annoyance both 'shells' seemed as wide and deep as they should be, with no trace of false bottom.

Irritation at their failure to find what they were looking for was becoming noticeable. Almost intuitively I realised the elder of the two was about to lift upright one section of the suitcase in order to compare the interior depth with the external shell. I quickly placed my hand on it, hoping the gesture would be interpreted as an old man's weariness. The manoeuvre was not successful. My hand was promptly knocked away and the side pulled up into a vertical position.

Its weight visibly astounded the young man, who shouted excitedly to his confrère. The two began to raise and lower each side repeatedly, like children who had discovered a new and exciting game. The intention to check internal with external measurements was forgotten. They were convinced the abnormal weight could only mean something *must* be concealed in my luggage. Of course they were right – but were they going to find it?

Their excitement began to communicate itself to the whole customs area. Many of their colleagues, ignoring the angry protests of waiting passengers, gathered to watch the little drama and give advice.

Now confident of ultimate success, the elder of the two produced a dangerous-looking clasp-knife from under the counter and made a small slit in the lining of one suitcase. He handed the knife to his colleague, inserted both forefingers into the hole and ripped the material wide open.

Had it not been for the highly charged atmosphere I would have laughed at the disbelief and astonishment reflected in the faces on the other side of the barrier ... for beneath the torn lining nothing could be seen but hard fibre, the inner shell of the suitcase.

Hardly able to believe their eyes, they ran their fingers over the smooth surface and stared resentfully at me.

I tried to look as if I expected an apology and began to wonder if I might yet get away with everything.

But a moment later, the younger man made the, probably unconscious, gesture that brought about my downfall.

In exasperation, he plunged the open clasp-knife blindly downwards in an effort to relieve his feelings ... the point of the blade penetrating the interior fibre wall by a fraction of a centimetre. He withdrew it with a half-apology, then stared in amazement at the result of his handiwork. The point had only just managed to penetrate the fibre, but there was now a black bubble, no larger than a pin-head, clearly visible.

Throwing away the knife he rubbed a finger over the bubble and held it to his nostrils. After the first sniff, he smiled delightedly and pushed the finger under his colleague's nose. The result was an immediate look of ecstasy on the face of the older man who, leaning across the counter, hissed in English: 'You carry hashish!'

He swung round, waving his arms like a ham actor, yelling in Arabic: 'Arrest him! Arrest him! He is a smuggler of hashish! There is hashish in his luggage!'

At the word 'hashish', pandemonium broke out, everybody began shouting. A policeman grabbed my passport from my coat-pocket while the porter tugged frantically at my sleeve, demanding his tip. Perhaps illogically, I found the porter's action exasperating, but gave him what he asked.

Two other policemen gripped me by the elbows and propelled me through the crowded airport. We were accompanied by a noisy retinue of customs staff. No less than four tottered along under the weight of my luggage like excited children, telling everybody within earshot I was a hashish smuggler who had been caught red-handed.

I will always remember the amazement and incredulity on the faces of those who had to make way for our cortège. I had never previously realised how far the human jaw can drop.

Eventually we came to a halt outside a small, empty office. The door was wide open. After a moment's pause, I was pushed inside and thrust roughly onto a small, hard chair. My left wrist was handcuffed to the steel leg of a large, flat-topped desk.

At least six customs officials followed me into the office. They put my luggage on a metal table and threw my clothes beneath it. They then set about the business of tearing the suitcases to pieces. As they

9

had been constructed by experts in the art of concealing every sort of contraband, this proved harder work than they expected.

A smuggler, opening his luggage at the end of a successful journey, usually needs special tools and never allows himself to be hurried. These young men had to make do with a clasp-knife, a pair of pliers and a variety of screwdrivers. It would have been easier if they had ever seen how much fastidious attention to detail is involved in the construction of luggage designed to prevent contraband being detected in its interior. However, they did not ask my advice and I was in no mood to tell them had they done so.

Our method was to 'cannibalise' two identical suitcases. From the interior of number 1 we would strip out everything – screws, rivets, clips, nylon-lining, the 'soft' division in the centre with its pockets – leaving two empty fibre shells attached to the hinges.

Into these shells, packets of hashish, mechanically pressed into small pancakes and sealed inside two layers of cellophane, were laid in neat rows. Using an exceptionally large suitcase it was possible to put as much as 5½ kilos on each side.

When this had been done it was time to get to work on suitcase number 2. With a small saw and a steady hand, the fibre shells on each side would be cut out, the hinges and surrounding metal frame thrown away. These two naked shells were fitted, after careful trimming, inside the shells of suitcase 1, completely concealing the hashish, now sandwiched between two layers of hard fibre.

After this came the lengthy job of replacing everything previously removed from the interior of number 1: the lining, with every little piece of decorative trimming, the soft pockets, every screw and rivet, every press-stud and clip had to be put meticulously in its former position.

The finished articles were so perfectly assembled customs officials all over the world had been deceived by them. There had even been an occasion when a British officer had, like his Syrian counterparts today, ripped a lining wide open. His confidence of being on the point of making an arrest received a rude shock when nothing except the inner-shell was revealed. Unlike the terrier-like Syrians, he pursued the matter no further. Crimson with embarrassment, he apologised profusely and a few minutes later my friend was on his way into London.

There were, however, always two very real dangers of discovery.

The first could be caused by a slight distortion in the suitcase's metal frame, brought about by the fitting of an additional shell on each side. This could make the locks difficult to open or shut. Care was taken to avoid this sort of damage, not always successfully. Customs staff often focus on luggage with temperamental locks and these suspicions can easily lead to a revelation of the second danger – excessive weight.

An extra 11 kilos (approximately 22 lb) makes an appreciable difference to the handling of any suitcase. We always did our best to prevent the customs noticing the effort necessary to lift them. At all costs we tried to look as though our luggage were filled with nothing heavier than feathers. It was particularly unfortunate that I, this morning, had fallen victim to both dangers within a few minutes.

The excited Damascenes took a long time, frequently getting in each other's way, to open up my luggage with their pathetically sparse collection of tools. By the time they had extracted every packet of hashish, the suitcases had been reduced to wreckage. Finally, yet another fruitless check was made of my shoulder-bag.

The hashish was put into a large cardboard box and taken away, presumably to be weighed. All the customs men and the police went with it and I was left alone, tethered like a dog to the immovable steel desk.

From time to time individuals would peer silently at me through the open door. Their expressions sometimes indicated mild hostility, sometimes amusement, sometimes smug satisfaction at the spectacle. Occasionally, amongst the younger *voyeurs*, I could discern a faint gleam of sympathy and, once or twice, a conspiratorial wink.

The time passed slowly, and twice the roar of aero-engines told me that flights, including my own, were taking off.

At last, what I assumed must be a senior customs official walked in and sat behind the desk.

He was about forty, slim, black-haired, with a closely-trimmed moustache above a mouth as thin as a hair-line fracture. His manner indicated peevishness at being summoned to deal with a displeasing situation. I felt sure my arrest must have interrupted his early morning session of small cups of gritty Arab coffee.

Dressed in a neatly pressed but shiny blue suit, he was wearing a vividly eye-catching heliotrope tie with a handkerchief to match.

He looked me over with weary distaste and, with a curiously furtive gesture, almost like a seller of dirty postcards, he produced my passport from inside his jacket.

11

In English, he asked my name.

I told him.

'And this is your passport?' He held it up.

I nodded, and then remembered that east of Greece a movement of the head closely resembling a nod is not an affirmative but a negative signal. So I answered quickly, 'Yes.'

He produced a pair of gold-rimmed specs and studied the document.

After turning the first page, he looked up in shocked surprise.

'You are seventy years old?' He was unable to keep the astonishment out of his voice.

I admitted this depressing fact.

He seemed to find it hard to accept. 'At your age, you carry hashish?'

I was tempted to ask if he considered there should be an age-limit for 'mules', but decided it was wiser merely to say: 'That is an accusation you'll have to prove in front of a *juge d'instruction.*'

He shrugged his shoulders and resumed his study of the passport, which soon provided another reason for excitement.

'I see,' he said, pointing to several heavily rubber-stamped pages, 'last year you bring motor car into Syria, and year before you do the same thing! What you do with them?'

'If you turn over a few more pages, you'll find evidence that I drove each car across your country into Jordan. After several weeks, I came back here for a short time and finally moved north into Turkey through your frontier station at Kassab.'

It took him a little while to check this. I did not feel it necessary to point out that the Ford and Mercedes registration numbers inked into my passport were not of cars but motor caravans.

'For what purpose,' he said at last, his eyes still focussed on the document, 'were you driving each time to Jordan?'

'I have a financial stake in tourism. I'm employed by a publishing house of international travel guides.'

Looking up at me again, he said acidly: 'You say nothing about your cars entering Lebanon, after leaving Jordan, but your passport shows each one was there for more than one month.'

The implication was obvious. The Lebanon is the supplier of most commercially-grown hashish in the Levant; Syria has none, neither has Jordan. My journeys to the Red Sea had always been made to camouflage my real intentions. Silently, I cursed the practice of inscribing a vehicle's engine, chassis and registration numbers in the owner's passport when crossing a frontier – a custom that begins when entering Greece and is repeated at every border-crossing further east.

'Part of my job is to make an annual check of living conditions for amateur archaeologists in Aleppo, Palmyra, Damascus, Jerash, Petra and in many other places of equal interest in Lebanon—'

'Such as Baalbek?' he interrupted meaningly.

This small town in the north of the Beka'a Valley is not only famous for its Greek and Roman ruins, but is also the centre of Lebanon's highly lucrative trade in hashish.

'Yes, Baalbek – amongst others,' I agreed, trying to sound casual.

'Many tourists visit Baalbek today?' His tone was derisory.

'Not many. But a medium-size hotel and two pensions remain open. Their owners live in hope that the horrors of the present situation will end before long. There is also a welcoming camping-site, if you should be interested.'

He gave a snort of disapproval and laid down my passport. 'Today you will be taken to the headquarters of the anti-narcotics brigade. It will be for them to decide if your travels in the past were as ...' he searched for the appropriate English word and failed to find it ... 'as you wish me to believe. This time we have much proof you carry hashish, yes?'

He opened a desk drawer and took out six buff-coloured forms. Inserting carbon-paper between each, he took up a ball-point pen and began writing down my answers to a seemingly endless series of questions. Not only my own full names, date and place of birth, but those of my parents; my schools, my university, my war service and as much as I was prepared to divulge about my working life.

I provided him with an easily verifiable account of a lengthy career of impeccable respectability, explaining I had only taken to crime in my old age. He obviously considered my attitude unforgivably frivolous and became more and more petulant as the interview continued.

All my answers were truthful. Later, when I discovered no one bothers to check such information, I regretted not having inserted a little spurious drama for my own amusement.

He had just come to an end of his questions when the uniformed staff burst in upon us again, carrying the box of hashish. Its weight, they declared, had been officially calculated at just over 22 kilos.

I was disappointed. I was hoping there was some truth in the

13

stories – freely circulating in Lebanon – of large-scale theft of hashish by Syrian customs for resale on the Damascus black market. Later, I learned that this can happen, but not to me.

They now began to stuff my clothes into the wreckage of my suitcases. The handcuff was unfastened and I was pulled to my feet. My arms were tugged behind my back and the bracelets snapped tightly round both wrists. We moved out of the office in procession, Heliotrope Tie leading. He was followed by two customs men, each carrying a suitcase. Another was holding the cardboard box in front of his chest as if it were the Holy Grail – an impression somewhat diminished by my shoulder-bag which dangled like a large puppet from his elbow. I brought up the rear with the rest of the uniformed staff who would doubtless have taken suitable action had I attempted to run away.

We marched to another small office, less than fifty yards along the corridor. I noticed military insignia over the door indicating it was the airport office of the Syrian Regiment of Gendarmerie.

It became obvious I was being handed over to this unit. My battered luggage was dropped in a corner. Heliotrope Tie briefly outlined the situation to a youthful, pink-faced sergeant who had risen politely to his feet; the box was placed reverently on the desk in front of him, together with my passport and the completed forms in sextuplicate. The customs staff then departed. Heliotrope Tie was the last to leave, and the mocking look in his eyes did not exactly endear him to me as I watched him go.

My wrists linked, I stood quietly and looked about me. The four gendarmes who had risen at the entry of the customs party were now gazing at me with what seemed to be half-smiles of genuine sympathy. They looked rather as Englishmen might, confronted by a lost animal.

There was a corporal who was older than the rest and might have been thirty; there were two private soldiers and a sergeant who could not have been more than twenty-five, and who was plainly in charge. All had neatly clipped moustaches except the sergeant.

With a jerk of his close-cropped curly head in my direction, the sergeant quietly gave an order to the corporal, who went to the door, locked it and put the key in his pocket. I wondered what they proposed to do with me. To my surprise and relief, the corporal gently removed the handcuffs.

The only comfortable-looking spot in the room was a large easy-chair with a floral-patterned, cretonne cover, in front of the sergeant's desk.

With a gesture, he indicated I was to sit in it. I was glad to obey. Then, seating himself, he asked in halting English if I would like some coffee, or perhaps tea. A wave of emotional warmth swept over me. Kindness, when one is apprehensive and miserable, has an extraordinary effect.

I said I would much appreciate a cup of coffee – could I be allowed to pay for everybody's coffee? My offer was refused with a smile. The sergeant gave an order to one of the privates, who picked up a tray of empty glasses and disappeared. The other two sat on a wooden bench under the window overlooking the main hall. They leaned back, tucking their big feet beneath them, and gazed at the sergeant and myself with a sort of benevolent curiosity.

The sergeant explained, in a mixture of English, French and simple Arabic, that he would have to write out another six copies of the personal details I had given customs. This time, it would be for the gendarmerie's own records.

For a little while all was quiet, but for the sound of the sergeant's ball-point as it moved across the forms, copying my replies to Heliotrope Tie.

The gendarme returned with a tray of tiny, clean glasses and a typical, Levantine coffee-pot made of aluminium and shaped like a wide-based, lidless saucepan with a long handle. After the customary pause to allow the dregs to settle the corporal filled five glasses, handing the first to me and giving my shoulder a friendly, reassuring pat as he did so.

The sergeant laboriously carried on with the forms, taking an occasional sip. It was taking a long time because, as he explained, his unit had not been issued with carbon paper.

I suggested he should borrow from Heliotrope Tie – I had noticed a stack in a drawer in his desk. The sergeant made a face, explaining there had always been a diplomatic coolness between the customs service and the gendarmerie, and he had no intention of risking an almost certain snub. He pushed an unruly quiff of hair back from his forehead – a gesture that showed a natural impatience with bureaucracy.

I did not mind how long the job took. The friendly faces of these four young men were wonderfully reassuring. I felt as if I had found sanctuary, even if it was temporary.

Possibly due to nerves and not the small amount of coffee I had drunk, I suddenly had an overwhelming need to pee. My request triggered off a discussion between sergeant and corporal. The corporal unlocked the door and beckoned to me to join him. When I did so, he linked his arm through mine and we walked out into the crowded terminal.

As we reached the gents' lavatory, some distance away and down several flights of stairs, he released me and waited at the entrance whilst I emptied my bladder with enormous relief.

After I had washed my hands, we entwined arms once more, and made our way back. No one, I suspect, was aware I was a prisoner under escort. I was grateful and knew it to be a privilege given only because of old age.

Back in the office, I looked at my watch and was surprised to see it was already after midday – and yet the moment when I was unmasked as a smuggler seemed aeons ago.

The feeling of being in a safe haven ended with a click, as the sergeant replaced the cap on his pen. He gathered the forms into neat piles, then placed them in two cardboard folders. He rose, confirming it was time to close the office. We were to leave for Damascus, where I would be handed over to the anti-narcotics brigade.

No sane man feels like ringing bells or waving flags when he knows he will be handed over to any Arab police force, many of whom have a reputation for excessive brutality. I remembered the fate of a young Canadian friend arrested in Morocco, accused of dealing in hashish. Today, years later, he still bears a lacework of small scars extending down both legs from groin to ankles: the result of cigarette burns while being interrogated.

My previous contacts with the lower ranks of the Syrian police had been for irreproachable reasons and I had always found them helpful and courteous. I guessed there would be a change in their attitude and braced myself to withstand the shock.

I guessed I would hear nothing more from the very senior officer who had been so happy in the past to escort me through customs. Now my 'cover' had been 'blown', he would only wish to widen the distance between us.

Before he picked up the box of hashish, the sergeant slipped the folders and my passport inside the lid. The corporal helped me into my sheepskin coat and picked up my shoulder-bag. He unlocked the door, again linked his arm through mine, and we walked through the terminal out into the open air, followed by the sergeant carrying the hash, and the two young gendarmes, striving continuously to prevent my clothes from falling out of the shattered cases. The sun was shining, but the wind, blowing more strongly than ever from the north-east, was still bitterly cold.

Their vehicle was in the carpark reserved for airport staff, a few hundred yards away. It was a Volkswagen mini-bus, not in the best of condition.

Someone pulled open the sliding-door. The sergeant put the hashish on a seat and, opening the near-side front door, slid along the bench-seat until he was behind the steering-wheel, pulling me after him. The corporal followed and slammed the door shut. The two younger men sat behind us.

It was some time before the engine could be persuaded to show any sign of life. But at last we moved forward with a series of bangs and hiccups towards the Damascus motorway, gradually picking up speed.

The country along this concrete highway is dull, flat and rocky. I gazed at it, hoping desperately it would not be long before I saw it again.

After eighteen miles of this desert landscape, enlivened only by an occasional monster-hoarding advertising a Damascus five-star hotel, we reached the scruffy outer suburbs. We drove on through heavy traffic to its modern centre, halting in front of an immense, grey office-block.

The Police Station

I knew the exterior well. It was almost within sight of the Damascus-Sheraton Hotel where I had often stayed. I had never suspected this building could contain a police station – and one of such significance to people like myself.

We got out of the little bus and, once again arm-in-arm with the corporal, I mounted the half-dozen steps to the main entrance. The others followed.

I was led down concrete stairs to an extensive basement illuminated by opalescent neon tubes, and taken into a large general office, where about a dozen young men, some wearing uniform, some in jeans and sweaters, some with the fashionable Zapata-moustaches, were lounging on leather *banquettes*. All were smoking and looked me up and down sardonically.

A sergeant in uniform – his moustache larger than any of the others' – suddenly got to his feet, strode across to a large desk and stood behind it expectantly.

My sympathetic sergeant of gendarmerie put the box of hashish, my passport and one of the cardboard folders in front of him, giving a short explanation of my presence. When he had finished he proffered an official-looking paper for signature – a receipt for delivering me safely into their hands.

Several policemen started to ask questions.

'Are you English?'

'Why d'you smuggle hashish at your age?'

'Where did you get it?'

'Did you bring it from Lebanon?'

A growl from the moustached authority silenced them. He signed the paper and handed it back to the gendarme who, after giving me several reassuring pats on the shoulder, left with his little team. The corporal paused in the doorway, pointing to my luggage against the wall. Before he disappeared, he grinned and gave me a thumbs-up sign.

The moustachioed sergeant told me to turn out my pockets. I did so, laying the objects on the desk. One of the sweater-and-jeans boys frisked me in a very casual manner.

Permission was given for me to retain my handkerchief, a bunch of keys and the Syrian coins from my trouser pocket. My airline ticket, my notecase containing several hundred Syrian pounds and four thousand Dutch florins in Fl.1000 notes were put inside the folder with the forms.

The sergeant, who had only half-a-dozen words of English and none of French, now pointed a stubby, nicotine-stained forefinger at my chest and then at the floor. This puzzling gesture was interpreted by one of his minions who said in English: 'He means you are to be taken to the cells – they are on the floor below.'

I realised I must now carry all my own luggage. This was not going to be easy because neither of the suitcases would shut. I tried holding them under my arms to prevent the contents from spilling, but they were too bulky and my arms were not long enough. My smirking audience offered no help. After some minutes of trial and error, I hung my shoulder-bag round my neck, pushing it behind me so it bounced cheerfully against my buttocks. With both hands free, I placed the suitcases one on top of the other, and held them in front of me like a butler carrying a tray.

I was led down two short flights of stone stairs. We halted in front of a small steel gate set into a concrete wall. Apparently forged from intertwined metal bars, it looked like a product of a giant Meccano set.

A shout from my escort was answered by a thin, sour-looking man in his forties with hollow unshaven jowls. He thrust an enormous key into the old-fashioned lock and pulled the heavy gate open. I shuffled across the threshold with my awkward burden and he slammed it quickly shut.

Muttering imprecations, he indicated with an impatient wave that I was to put my luggage into a large wall-cupboard at the entrance of a narrow cul-de-sac about twenty yards long. This passage was lined on one side by a row of cells. They varied in size; each had walls on three sides but was separated from the corridor by steel bars extending from floor to ceiling, like cages in a zoo.

The jailer, wearing badly stained trousers and a torn sweater, beck-oned me to follow him. He opened a narrow door fitted between the bars of one of the cages, pushed me inside and locked it. Still muttering discontentedly under his breath, he trotted back to his own comfortable quarters near the main entrance. I was alone.

I was very much alone. The oppressive silence all around indicated I must be the only prisoner in this small enclave. My cell seemed bigger than the others, an impression I later found to be correct. It was about twelve feet by eight, completely empty apart from a wooden dais at one end. This was not more than two inches from the ground, covering only a small area of the grubby concrete floor. It was made of matchwood and part of it was badly broken. A folded blanket had been left lying on it. I held it up to shake out the folds, but it was so caked with dirt, had I put it against the wall it would have stood upright without support.

At the other end of the cell was a thin, curved cement screen, just over six feet high, concealing a wc of the type familiar to travellers in Mediterranean countries: the kind where you squat over a hole. This hole smelt strongly of decomposing excreta. There was also a defective shower which had been installed with the off-handedness common among Arab plumbers: immediately above the dark hole. It leaked a continuous fine spray of ice-cold water, impossible to stem, over everybody using the privy.

I sat down wearily on the dais and remembered I had been told that Syrian courts, like those of Turkey, habitually sentence hashish smugglers to long terms of imprisonment, fifteen years or more. At my age I could hardly expect to live that long. The absence of daylight, the grey concrete walls, the steel bars, the noxious smell of human ordure all combined to produce considerable gloom and pessimism.

Half an hour later the jailer reappeared. Beside him was a boy of about sixteen who explained in simple Arabic that he was a 'runner' for a local snack-bar.

Was I hungry? If I gave him money he would bring me something to eat.

I realised I was ravenous. I had eaten nothing all day and it was already late afternoon. I took a few coins from my pocket – enough for a sandwich. The boy's bright cheerful face made me feel ashamed of myself, and I decided an empty stomach was at least partly responsible for my self-pity.

He returned after ten minutes with an object about twelve inches long, wrapped in greaseproof paper, which he pushed through the bars. It was a typical Middle Eastern sandwich – salami and goat's cheese encased, tubular fashion, in a large, circular slab of unleavened pitta bread.

I ate slowly and was just finishing what was to be my only meal of the day, when the jailer returned, opened the door, gestured me to follow and handed me over to two uniformed policemen who escorted me back to the large general office.

This time the atmosphere was different. The desk had been pushed close to the wall furthest from the door, and behind it were five obviously senior police officials, all wearing civilian suits, except for an impressive figure in the centre. This character was in uniform, wearing the insignia and red tabs of a full colonel; he was clearly going to preside. The jeans and sweater brigade seemed to have vanished.

The colonel appeared to be a few years short of fifty. Slim, with a toothbrush moustache, dark hair becoming pepper and salt over the temples, he looked almost indistinguishable from any British senior soldier and might well have been a product of Sandhurst.

He looked at me intently for a few moments, as I stood in front of him. When he said courteously: 'Will you please sit down, Mr Aspinall,' pointing to a chair in isolation in front of the desk, I was not surprised he did so in English.

I obeyed, noticing several policemen were now sitting on each side of the door behind me.

The colonel continued to speak to me in English. Only rarely did a misplaced inflection betray he was not speaking his native language.

'Tomorrow,' he said, 'we shall be asking you many questions about your criminal activities in this country.'

I realised an interval was necessary while they scraped together any evidence against me from the staff of my Damascus hotel, and elsewhere in the city.

'This afternoon,' he continued smoothly, 'we should like to find out more about your personal background.'

I immediately demanded to be put in touch with the British Embassy.

'Not until we have your full statement. Later tomorrow I will personally telephone your embassy.'

'Am I allowed a lawyer?'

'After you have given us an acceptable statement, yes. In a day or so, you will be taken before a judge of instruction – I believe the nearest British equivalent is an examining magistrate – who will decide what charges are to be brought against you. You may then employ a lawyer, but I must warn you their fees are high in Syria. We are a poor country and do not have the legal aid system you have in Great Britain.'

I saw my passport and airline ticket on the desk, but no notecase.

He picked up the ticket, saying: 'You have obviously missed your flights to Frankfurt and Barcelona and are in no position to collect a refund. You will not object if we do this for you?'

I naively assumed this offer was intended to be helpful and agreed at once. It was never hinted that if the police obtained the refund it would be confiscated. Fortunately, Lufthansa's Damascus office refused to hand over a single piastre, insisting payment would only be made to an accredited official of the British Embassy acting on my behalf. I have naturally had a warm affection for this airline ever since.

The colonel's questions ranged over a much wider field than those of Heliotrope Tie. He seemed to be obsessively interested in my origins and my life as a young man. Having discovered I was the son of a regular soldier, he started a discussion of the wars in which my father had been involved, ranging from South Africa to Flanders. I then had to give an excessively detailed account of my own experiences in World War Two. I was puzzled by his curiosity and remain so. However, the room was pleasantly warm, the colonel was friendly; I began to feel almost relaxed.

The junior officials on each side of him were clearly bored by his idiosyncratic method of questioning. They all had an absent, drifting expression and were not paying much attention to our gossipy dialogue. There was no interpreter and their knowledge of English was, in many cases, not sufficient for them to follow it.

The only reference the colonel made to my smuggling was when he expressed surprise I should be doing this at over seventy.

Still undecided about what form – if any – my defence should take, I just shrugged my shoulders.

When the time came to take me back to my cell, he asked if I had any personal requests.

I told him the exceptionally cold weather made me shivery and could I collect a heavy wool jersey from my luggage.

Permission was granted.

As I was led out of the office, I remembered a paperback biography in my shoulder-bag and asked if I might have that too. He assented, and gave the necessary instructions to my escort.

This was relayed to the sour-faced guard downstairs, who grumbled continuously as I searched amongst the tangled mess of my belongings.

As he opened the cell gate, I asked if I might have tea or coffee. The enquiry brought a storm of Arabic abuse on my head: I was told to quench my thirst with cold water from the leaking shower. I then asked for a cup or glass, which provoked another outburst.

He hobbled away calling upon Allah to witness I was an intolerable old infidel. A minute later he came back to throw an empty Pepsicola tin through the bars.

I took off the jacket of my grey flannel suit and put on the jersey and my sheepskin overcoat.

Sitting with my back to the wall, on the unbroken section of the dais, I concentrated on Lauren Bacall's autobiography. I found, to my surprise, I could do so without much difficulty. The contretemps of starting out on a stage career thirty years ago in New York, which she describes so vividly, were comfortingly remote from my present situation.

After a time I heard the gate open and shut. This was followed by footsteps growing fainter and fainter as they ascended the stairs. My jailer was going off-duty.

I read for a long time. Tiredness began to make my eyes ache. I folded my jacket into a reasonably neat package with the lining outside, stretched out on the dais with the jacket as a pillow, and tried to sleep. I was totally unsuccessful. The cell seemed to become colder and draughtier every minute. In addition, the neon light was almost blinding.

I shivered in the silence for several hours, then suddenly heard somebody descending the stairs and the gate opening and shutting. I assumed Sour Face must have returned.

I was mistaken. A youthful, pleasant-looking police official, who had been sitting near the colonel during my interview, came and looked at me.

'Tonight, I am duty-officer,' he said hesitantly in heavily accented English. 'You are all right?'

I sat up, saying: 'I'm cold – very cold.'

He raised his arms in a gesture of helplessness.

'The heating – always at night, no heat.' He looked at me with what seemed like genuine sympathy.

'Tomorrow morning – no, I mean this morning – it is after one o'clock – there will be heat again.' He pointed towards the ceiling. 'Above there are many offices – empty at night – no heat. But in a few hours it will come back. Not often so cold in Damascus.'

'Must I wait until eight o'clock before I can get warm?'

'Sooner than that. Six o'clock, perhaps. You are not sick, I hope?'

'No, just cold.'

'I am sorry. I wish I could help you.'

'Could you get me another blanket? There's one in the cell, but it's horribly dirty.'

'I would like – but the guard, he take his keys when he goes off-duty.'

Plainly the blankets were locked away. There did not seem anything more to be said. There was something very apologetic about the young man's manner as he turned away, saying: 'I hope the day will come quickly for you. Goodbye.'

A moment later I heard the gate shut with a decisive click. He had gone.

Never since the Second World War had I spent so miserable a night. I got up frequently and marched up and down to keep my blood circulating. When I lay down I drifted from time to time into semi-consciousness, only to have an uncontrollable bout of shivering bring this to an end in a few seconds.

About half-past six the temperature slowly began to rise. Soon after seven, Sour Face reappeared, seeemingly in a better mood, for he astonished me by asking if I would like tea. I accepted enthusiastically. About twenty minutes later he returned with a small glass of hot, milkless, heavily-sweetened amber liquid, which is the customary method of serving tea everywhere in the Middle East.

As I was sipping this nectar, the young 'runner' rattled the bars, asking if I wanted something to eat. I counted my change and was glad I had enough for a sandwich.

Shortly after he had gone, voices could be heard descending the stairs. Sour Face came into view, herding two prisoners. He opened my door and waved them inside.

The elder was about thirty-five, his face brown and unusually lined for his age. He was lean and long-limbed, wearing jeans, a crimson shirt and a black blouson of imitation leather.

The other was a boy of eighteen; a robust muscular youth who seemed on the point of bursting out of corduroy trousers and a torn, green jersey, worn over a clean, but equally torn, white vest.

24

Both greeted me with broad smiles and handshakes, the elder introducing himself as Hisham, the younger murmuring his name was Aziz.

Hisham, who had a few words of English and French, began at once, with the addition of simple Arabic, to ask questions. What was I doing here? How long had I been here? Why had I been arrested?

I answered with one word: 'Hashish!'

His eyes sparkled. 'Me too! How much?'

'Twenty-two kilos.'

He whistled with surprised appreciation and said he had been caught with a mere fifteen grammes.

Sour Face, who was apparently still feeling benign, approached with two small glasses and a steaming aluminium teapot. He handed glasses to Hisham and Aziz, then refilled mine.

The 'runner' was soon back with my breakfast sandwich of fetta cheese and honey. He enquired hopefully if the other two were hungry. They both said no – Hisham saying his wife would be bringing plenty of food every day. There would be enough for all of us, he insisted generously. He volunteered that he had served several prison sentences since his marriage twelve years ago. His wife, he said, always brought more food than he could possibly eat, and Aziz's mother would also be doing her duty by her son.

Having spent a good deal of my life in North Africa, I knew it was customary to allow families constant access to prisoners. They were encouraged to bring food, the basic diet in many jails being insufficient to keep inmates alive. In police stations there was nothing except what a detainee could afford to buy from a snackbar. Foreigners like myself, and others far from home, were always grateful for the charity of our fellow prisoners.

Suddenly, a series of peremptory commands were shouted with exceptional lung-power from the floor above. The only word I could recognise – and it seemed to hang menacingly in the air – was the name AZIZ. I was shocked to see that the boy looked thoroughly frightened.

There were more threatening shouts; Sour Face bustled along the passage, flanked by two uniformed policemen. He leered unpleasantly at Aziz and ordered him out of the cage.

The boy was plainly scared. His trembling hands had spilt tea over the crutch of his corduroys and on the floor. Hisham squatted

25

beside him and spoke softly. What he said was apparently reassuring, for the boy got reluctantly to his feet and walked slowly, almost as if sleepwalking, out of the cell.

A policeman jerked his arms behind his back, clipping his wrists together with a handcuff.

He was pushed roughly towards the exit of our little ghetto and we heard them climbing the stairs.

I felt bewildered. 'Why is Aziz so frightened?'

'Because they will beat him,' was Hisham's cool reply.

'Beat him? Do they beat people?'

My naivety must have astonished him. He explained patiently that the police beat everyone they suspected of withholding information. He had never met Aziz until last night when they had been locked up in the same cell in a small station in an outer suburb. Both had been arrested during the afternoon, accused of possessing small quantities of hashish. A couple of ready-made joints had been found in Aziz's pockets and he was still refusing, after several interrogations, to say where he had got them. The police, Hisham assured me, could become almost paranoid in their efforts to nail the supplier of those caught with even the smallest amount. There had been cases where a single 'joint' had led to the arrest of more than thirty people. Success in this sort of sleuthing always increases a policeman's chances of promotion.

'Couldn't Aziz say the joints were given to him by a stranger in a coffee house?' I asked.

'Better not mention a coffee house,' he insisted. It would be raided at once, and if the 'stranger' could not be identified they would probably grab the owner and many of the customers. These could sometimes prove dangerous enemies. It was safer to say the deal had been arranged in the street – one couldn't be too careful ...

Hisham was interrupted by a voice from the floor above. It was Aziz, protesting violently. His protests almost immediately changed to screams of pain. We could hear, and almost feel, the rhythmic throb of the beating they were giving him, while his agonising cries grew louder and louder.

I fought back a compulsion to put my fingers in my ears, while my companion clicked his tongue in disapproval that Aziz had not given the police the answers they wanted. In a matter-of-fact way, he explained the technique of the bastinado now being inflicted. He would have been thrown to the ground, and laid on his back with his legs pulled up through the centre of an old motor tyre. His shoes and socks would have been removed and at this moment upwards of a dozen policemen would be taking turns at bashing the soles of his feet with wooden staves.

Threatening voices were questioning Aziz incessantly. After a while the cries became choked by sobs which slowly – very slowly – began to subside.

Hisham and I stared miserably at each other, hoping desperately the painful sounds would not suddenly begin to get louder again.

A door opened upstairs, followed by a hubbub of voices gradually getting nearer. Someone was weeping, softly but uncontrollably.

Sour Face, looking like a shabby cockerel and smirking at us, opened the cage door and stood beside it. The two policemen came into view, holding upright by his armpits, as if he were a giant rag-doll, a limp, sobbing Aziz.

They were about to let him drop heavily to the concrete floor when Hisham and I seized the trembling boy and laid him gently on the dais.

Sour Face, who had been carrying Aziz's pathetically worn shoes and socks, now hurled them contemptuously at the back wall. The whole party withdrew.

Hisham knelt beside Aziz and we looked anxiously at his feet. They were bleeding quite badly and any visible skin beneath the gore was either purple or blue.

Hisham probed the insteps and ankles with a feather-light touch. Aziz yelped in pain. Hisham spoke soothingly to the boy and persisted.

After a moment he said: 'No break – no break. That is good.' He clapped his hands just above the boy's feet. 'Tomorrow they will be like two big footballs – much swollen!'

Aziz wiped his tears with a clenched fist and made an effort to smile.

The door opened behind us. Sour Face and the two policemen were there again. The colonel, I was told, was waiting for me.

My morale was not at its best as I mounted the stairs, unshaven, unwashed, with two policemen treading on my heels. At the top we passed a room where I could see a tyre suspended, about three feet from the ground, by short lengths of rope from two hooks in the wall. Seeing me glance at it, the policemen sniggered.

We entered the large office which was already familiar to me. Again I was told to sit on that lonely chair in front of half-a-dozen officials.

But in view of what had happened during the last quarter of an hour, the impression they created was a good deal more sinister than it had been.

There were two new faces beside the colonel. One was cadaverously thin with a narrow head, prominent nose and small eyes set wide apart. He resembled two profiles of a bird's head pasted together.

The colonel introduced him: 'This is our official interpreter. I'm sure you'll agree it is better there should be two of us who have some understanding of your language?'

Bird Profile smiled, revealing misshapen brown teeth, and explained it would be his function to translate the proceedings into Arabic for the official statement. 'It will also,' he said, 'be helpful for my colleagues and essential for Mister Zayed' – he indicated the other new face: a pale young clerk next to him, almost obscured by an enormous, old-fashioned typewriter. 'It will be his duty to type every word of my translation.'

In spite of his polite manner, I wondered how long it would be before they threw me on the floor and beat my feet.

The colonel opened his cross-examination. 'Mr Aspinall, we know you entered Syria on a Swiss–Air flight from Athens to Damascus five days ago. Do you wish to deny this?'

'No.'

He selected a scarlet pencil from a full pen-tray on his desk and used it, occasionally, to doodle elaborate flowers and leaves on a small pad of yellow paper.

'We know you arrived in the evening and were driven by taxi to the Meridien Hotel, where you were given room 285. It was a double room and you booked it jointly with a Mr Kevin Morton who had *not* travelled with you from Athens. Where did you meet?'

'At the Meridien.'

'This Mr Morton – is he your partner in the business of exporting hashish?'

'No. I'd never seen him before.'

'Was he a stranger – or were you expecting him to be there?'

'I was expecting somebody.'

'How did you recognise him?'

'He recognised me. He had been told my age and that I'd be wearing a grey flannel suit and a blue shirt and tie. I was the only Englishman in the foyer who fitted the description.'

'Why was he there?'

There was a pause; I watched the colonel draw the outline of a flowering yukka. During a sleepless night I had decided any attempt to avoid admitting my guilt would be useless. I was anxious, however, not to implicate those who had been working with me. To succeed, I would have to be somewhat devious.

'He was there as a messenger,' I said quietly.

'From whom?'

'From the Benami brothers.' I said this with a deliberately casual shrug.

At the mention of this name it was as if an electric current had passed through everybody in front of me. Eyes that had been half-closed in boredom opened wide.

'So you know the Benamis?' The colonel's tone suggested that contact with this family was the modern equivalent of supping with the Borgias.

This was a notorious Lebanese family of Shi'ite Muslims who claimed to have extensive business interests ranging from merchant banking to the construction of skyscraper office-blocks in cities all over the Middle East. Some of these buildings had been known to collapse even before being completed. They were a clan more than a family and were dominated by seven brothers; the youngest just over twenty; the eldest a little more than fifty. Many of their so-called business interests were merely a façade for the prodigious cultivation of hashish over many hundreds of acres.

The Benami brothers were a phenomenon, powerful enough to maintain their own private army which a succession of weak and divided Lebanese governments could not oppose. It was well-trained and armed with the latest Kalashnikov assault rifles and Czech-made Skorpion sub-machine-guns. These weapons, they claimed, had been acquired in exchange for hashish from an agency in Sofia sponsored by the Bulgarian government. From the Lebanese army, they succeeded in capturing a tank. This force was invaluable in guarding convoys sent by road from the Beka'a Valley to coastal ports.

The Syrians had been bright enough to realise, when their army entered Lebanon in 1977, that the hashish-growing areas of this long and beautiful valley would have to be held on a very light rein. Here, the Benamis and several families of almost equal importance, some Christian, some Muslim, would remain a dominating influence.

Without their tacit support there would be constant disruption. The position of the 'hash barons' was impregnable.

'Would you describe the Benamis as your partners?' There was a noticeable eagerness in the colonel's voice.

'No, I would not.'

'Then you work for them – you are one of their runners?' This idea obviously pleased him.

I had speedily discovered the Benamis' lack of scruple in dealing with those outside the clan. On their behalf I made several solo journeys with large motor-caravans from Lebanon, through the Balkans and East Germany, to Sweden. These trips required me to cross many high-risk frontier checkpoints: sometimes as many as thirteen or fourteen. Frequently, customs would inspect every cranny and crevice, inside and outside my vehicle, with a hammer in one hand and a chisel in the other, often accompanied by sniffer-dogs whose incompetence, fortunately for me, was only equalled by that of their masters.

After each expedition, the Benamis presented me with ingenious excuses for failing to pay the rate for the job; this, as they well knew, should never be less than ten per cent of the profit made from the run.

I had long ago ceased to work for them, although remaining on friendly terms with those not personally involved in trying to cheat me. I was convinced, because of the Syrian attitude towards the hash barons, my accusations could do my allies no harm; and I guessed the police would be delighted with the capture of a self-proclaimed Benami 'mule' and the expressions on the faces in front of me already confirmed this.

My decision to implicate the family was not, at this stage, inspired by malice but by my anxiety to protect my partner, a young Canadian whose identity was as yet unknown to the Syrians. Later, however, when the news reached me of the murder of an Iraqui friend in the garden of Baalbek's principal hotel – the brothers had accused him of 'poaching' an important customer – I wished my evidence could have proved really damaging.

'You are one of the Benami runners?' insisted the colonel.

With another deliberate shrug I said: 'I suppose there's no point in denying it.'

'But the Benamis export their product by the ton. Suitcases by air – even of the finest quality hashish – is surely not usual?'

I began to wonder if he was going to be the pushover I had hoped.

With tongue well-concealed in my cheek, I said: 'Perhaps they thought it wise to trust a beginner only with small stuff.'

'Judging from the many visas and scores of frontier control-post stamps in your passport, you can hardly claim to be a beginner.'

'Let me remind you I work for an international publishing house specialising in travel guides.'

'You must forgive our suspicions that most of your recent travelling has been at the behest of the Benami brothers.'

'Can you prove that?'

His candid answer was a surprise and a relief. 'No – and to attempt to do so would be a waste of our time. Frontier guards of many nationalities failed to catch you, and it's not up to us to do their work for them. We shall therefore concentrate on your latest sortie from the Beka'a Valley which came to an ignominious end at our airport yesterday. This time there is no doubt we shall be able to supply sufficient evidence to convict you.' He paused to add the finishing touches to what appeared to be an elaborate cactus flower. 'This young colleague of yours – or perhaps I should say this young messenger you claim never to have met before – according to our information he had no luggage with him when he contacted you at the Meridien Hotel.'

'He intended to return to Lebanon that night.'

'Why didn't he?'

'It was snowing so heavily he was unlikely to find a taxi willing to take him across the frontier. (A journey of about two and a half hours over mountainous country.) There was an extra bed in my room, so he stayed the night.'

'But when he came back the day before yesterday he had some very noticeable luggage, hadn't he? Two exceptionally large, heavy suitcases – identical to those you had brought with you. The hotel staff have good reason to remember, for they carried them up to your room. An hour later, this young man used your telephone to ring the hall porter for a taxi. During the interval, the suitcases had apparently become as light as air, for he carried them out of the hotel without any need of assistance.'

'You should congratulate the Meridien's staff. They must be as inquisitive as cats!'

He ignored my comment. 'The luggage Morton brought to the hotel – it contained the hashish?'

'Of course.'

31

'It had come from Lebanon?'

'Yes.'

'With this Kevin Morton?'

I said quickly: 'No, the suitcases were already in Damascus. All he had to do was pick them up, bring them to me and switch them with the two I'd brought from Amsterdam.'

'You must be joking. Why should he cross the frontier just to do that?'

'Because someone had to deliver those suitcases to me and he is the sort of young Englishman who can walk about a good hotel and not look as if he would be more at home in a youth hostel. His aura of upper-class respectability normally excites no comment from hotel staff. This time it obviously didn't work!'

'Where in Damascus did he pick up this luggage?'

I knew he was expecting an evasive answer, so I decided to surprise him by telling the truth. Very casually, I said: 'Oh, in that public car park not far from the Semiramis Hotel – the one that's used a great deal by the service taxis from Lebanon.' I knew this information could no longer harm anybody.

'Then who did bring these cases into Syria?'

'I've no idea. I never ask unnecessary questions.'

Although I had not asked, I knew it would have been a group of Syrian NCOs. Many army units in Lebanon had long ago found the rewards of transporting hashish between the two countries a lucrative addition to their meagre pay.

To my surprise, the colonel did not press me on this point. He asked if Kevin Morton had returned to stay with the Benamis after our meeting, and was he still there. This hint of possible extradition did not impress me. I knew, if attempted, it would fail.

'Sitting here,' I said, 'I'm hardly in a position to say what anybody is doing in the Beka'a Valley.'

Actually, Kevin had never met a Benami. He was an adventurous youngster who had been given the job of delivering my Canadian partner's giant American sports car from Amsterdam, via the Balkans and Turkey, to a mountain village in Lebanon. After that, he had made himself generally useful, running errands, bagging-up and pressing hashish. He was anxious to work as a mule but my partner considered him too young. Customs officers nowadays have a built-in distrust of everyone under forty-five. A youthful appearance is a constant liability for any smuggler, especially in Europe and the United States.

Kevin had brought me two messages in Damascus. The first concerned the suitcases then being assembled in Baalbek: they would not be ready for another four days. The second referred to the Czech 'mule' engaged to take the luggage as far as Barcelona, who was now considered 'unreliable': my partner had convinced himself that in the usual confusion of Frankfurt airport, the Czech would disappear, taking the luggage with him. There had been moments during the last twenty-four hours when I regretted he had not been given the opportunity!

I was sure the news of my arrest would by now have reached Baalbek. Although telephone calls were restricted, the hashish fraternity had their own methods of communication. Kevin did not have the protection of the Benamis, but I was sure my partner would have sent him somewhere safe from snooping or extradition. It was of course unfortunate, but inevitable, that his full name and passport number would have been eagerly supplied by the Meridien and communicated to Interpol; but this would only be a minor irritation, for no police force, even in another Arab country, would take action on such trivial evidence emanating from Syria. Several months later, when Kevin was landing in England, he was momentarily halted by passport control who said, 'Laddie, be careful – don't go back to Syria – they seem to want you there and we don't think you'd like it!'

The colonel had been gazing at me with a puzzled frown wrinkling his high forehead. 'You are frankly admitting,' he said, 'you knew you were carrying hashish?'

'It's hardly possible for me to deny it.'

'Surely you could have disclaimed all knowledge of what was in your luggage?'

'Would you have believed me?'

He gave me a broad grin. 'No!'

'Then why should I waste your time, and mine?'

'Because it's usual. I can't remember ever interrogating a smuggler who didn't insist he knew nothing about whatever contraband he was carrying.'

At this moment the proceedings were interrupted by a policeman with tiny cups of coffee for everyone.

We all sipped the sugary, almost boiling liquid in silence, until the colonel said, 'You're a most unusual smuggler, aren't you?'

'In what way – unusual?'

'Your age and appearance are so very unlike someone who makes his living outside the law. Yet Interpol tell us they have had many reports of an elderly Englishman being involved in the Lebanese hashish trade. They'd never managed to establish his identity until we did it for them – yesterday!' He seemed as pleased as a dog with two tails.

I was not surprised rumours about me had reached Interpol. Before joining the criminal classes in my old age, I imagined drug-traffickers to be menacing, tight-lipped characters who spoke only in grudging monosyllables. I now knew them to be a collection of extroverted chatterboxes, eager to tell everything.

The colonel was encouraging me to imitate them. 'Won't you tell us your reasons for getting involved with hashish,' he cajoled. 'You will seldom have a more interested audience!'

After a few more sips of the burning coffee, I said: 'Basic reason, I suppose – fear of being old and poor. Having lost all my capital when I was well over sixty, I had to go on earning my bread. The smuggling of hashish can be lucrative and I consider its illegality a nonsense. I don't regard myself as a menace to society. To me, such drugs as alcohol and tobacco are more dangerous. Soft drug users never indulge in those explosions of irritability, anger and physical violence common amongst heavy drinkers. I have no apologies to make for what I've been doing.'

There was a pause. The colonel raised his eyebrows as if he expected me to continue.

'There isn't much more I can say ... except I was probably influenced by a writer whose books were published nearly half a century ago.'

'A writer?' There was curiosity in his voice.

'Yes, a writer – Henri de Montfried – whose books were a mixture of travel and autobiography, now considered minor classics in France. *Les secrets de la mer rouge* and *Aventures de mer*; there was another called *Hashish*! He was sent out to work in a Djibouti office when a young man, and so loathed his bourgeois French colleagues he bought an Arabian dhow and spent the rest of his life fishing for pearls off the Farsan Islands, running guns into Abyssinia and carrying a variety of cargoes up and down the Red Sea. He continuously outwitted every police force and customs service between Suez and the Horn of Africa. I bought all his books when they were first published and they seemed then, as they do now, to be compelling descriptions of what would have been, for me, an ideal lifestyle. Various responsibilities made this impossible, but I continued to envy de Montfried and when it was suggested – at what must be almost the end of my life – that I could save myself from penury by becoming a hashish 'mule', I didn't hesitate for a second. Although, I grant you the circumstances were different – and there was no dhow!'

Bird Profile's translation of what I had said caused some friendly amusement.

'Can you sail?' asked the colonel.

'Ever since I was a small boy.'

'And you get on well with the African people?'

'I like to think so.'

There was a long silence while he looked at me with a half-smile. Then he said: 'Pity about the dhow!' He now switched to Arabic and the session was brought to an end. Some of the staff left the room, others stood about, smoking and talking quietly.

The colonel remained seated while the interpreter carefully checked the typewritten record. When he had finished it was given to the colonel who signed each page with a tremendous flourish. That done, he threw the typescript and a ball-point pen across the desk, telling me to sign below him on every page. As there were more than twenty sheets of foolscap, this took some time. Without asking permission I wrote NOT UNDERSTOOD above each of my signatures.

When I handed the papers back he stared at what I had written, raising his eyebrows but saying nothing.

A policeman tapped me on the shoulder, indicating I was to return to the cells.

As I got to my feet, the colonel said: 'You asked to be put in touch with the British Embassy. I telephoned their consular department this morning. They will be coming to see you tomorrow.'

I thanked him and was taken down again to my cage, where Hisham was sitting cross-legged on the floor, surrounded by cardboard plates on which quantities of food had been stacked. There was a pile of mutton chops, a salad of sliced tomatoes and onions, a great platter of *homus*: one of the staple dishes of every Middle Eastern country, a purée of crushed chick-peas mixed with sesame oil which looks like soft beige cement but tastes delicious.

Hisham was tearing a slab of pitta bread into small pieces. These he dipped into the *homus* and gave to Aziz who was lying close by, still a bit tear-stained but no longer sobbing.

'Come eat – come eat!' said Hisham excitedly. He loaded a plate with the choicest titbits and pressed it upon me. 'My wife, she bring food while you upstairs.'

The smell of fresh food made me realise how hungry I was. Using only my right hand, I clumsily tore bread into small pieces and ate voraciously.

Hisham was a flamboyant but kindly scamp, genuinely glad I had been treated decently. Since childhood he had made his living within the criminal world of Damascus. Burglary, particularly of radio and television shops, and the sale of small quantities of hash in overcrowded coffee houses, were his chief sources of income. It was always, he told me, the hash that got him into trouble.

I was grateful for the food he so generously shared. Towards the end of the meal he produced a large box of *halva* as a bonne-bouche. *Halva* is a somewhat cloying sweetmeat, a mixture of crushed sesame seeds and honey, normally too sugary for my taste. Today I was glad to accept a large piece.

Feeling deliciously full, I settled down to read. Hisham and Aziz chattered away, every sentence liberally sprinkled with the phrase *Insha' Allah*. This insistence on the omnipotence of God was continually on their lips. '*Insha' Allah*, if God wills, I will do so and so.' 'Tomorrow, my wife will bring me torch batteries, *Insha' Allah!*' Resignation to the will of God is the very essence of Islam. It is no good making plans as if you had free will. No Muslim would consider trying.

An hour later, when Hisham was summoned for interrogation, Aziz and I naturally wished him luck, and I was careful to interject as many *Insha' Allah*s as possible into my good wishes. As he left he winked at Aziz, saying *he* was not going to play the silent hero – any information the top brass wanted they would get!

While he was away, poor Aziz suddenly had a pressing need to evacuate his bowels. His feet had become shapeless lumps of raw meat and it was agony for him to walk. I did my best to help by putting my arm around his waist and pulling his across my shoulders. We staggered a few paces towards the lavatory like a couple of drunks, but the pain was too much and he begged me to let him drop to the ground. He dragged himself the rest of the way on hands and knees.

There was an empty 2-litre petrol-can behind the partition that screened the wc from the rest of the cell. I filled this with water and left it beside him as he bravely made ready to squat over the dark hole, which must have been desperately painful for the boy.

The Muslim religion condemns the use of lavatory paper which is considered insanitary. Only water (or small pebbles in the desert!) may be employed for this purpose.

Time passed. Aziz could be heard trying to stifle his groans. There was a sound of splashing water and, after another interval of even louder groaning, he emerged, still on hands and knees, and crawled back to the dais.

About an hour later, Hisham returned, looking tired and depressed but glad no one had expressed a wish to beat him.

Sour Face, from time to time, meandered about his little ghetto-kingdom muttering imprecations against us under his breath. He did, however, grudgingly provide glasses of tea after we had finished the remainder of the food; and before going off duty he condescendingly presented each of us with a blanket. All were dirty, although not as saturated with filth as the one I had found in the cell.

We bedded down, although 'bed' probably gives a false impression. There was only room for two on the broken, matchwood dais and Hisham insisted it should be occupied by Aziz and myself, while he stretched out on the concrete floor. He had tried to persuade Sour Face to allow each of us an extra blanket, but his pleas, like my own on the previous evening, had failed.

Mercifully, the weather seemed to have turned warmer. When the heating diminished, I shivered less than on the preceding night, perhaps because I now had a full belly and human companionship.

The night passed peacefully enough. Poor Aziz groaned occasionally and Hisham snored loudly. Owing to the hard surface beneath me, my hip-bones ached painfully, but in spite of this I managed to achieve several periods of uneasy sleep.

The next day was Sour Face's day off. His stand-in was a hefty young man with a Zapata moustache, glistening with heavily scented pomade, above a mouthful of excellent teeth and a heart-warming smile. Unlike Sour Face, he allowed us to keep our blankets during the day and we loved him for it.

That morning I was taken to an upper floor where a little man wearing steel-rimmed spectacles pinned a large white card to my chest on which he had scrawled a number with an indigo felt pen. He photographed me from every angle with an old-fashioned, quarter-plate camera.

The card was then snatched from my jersey and I was taken to be fingerprinted. I found it difficult to overcome a strong feeling of revulsion as the fingers and thumbs of each hand were pressed, singly, on to an ink-pad and then on to sheets of a special white paper.

There was a basin with running water in the room and I asked if I could wash the stains off my hands. This simple request made my two escorts giggle. In spite of the language difficulty they made me understand at least ten copies of each print were needed: any attempt to clean myself at this stage would be a waste of time.

When the job was finally completed I was allowed to wash and was still rubbing my fingers with what appeared to be dog-soap when a voice was heard, shouting from below, that two visitors from the British Embassy had arrived to see me.

I was taken to a large private office which I realised must be the colonel's private sanctum. Big leather easy-chairs were distributed around the room. There were several windows through which a warm sun was shining.

The colonel was seated behind a large desk in the corner furthest from the door. Two strangers who appeared to be in their mid-thirties, wearing light-weight suits and ties, were occupying armchairs on each side of him.

All three were talking animatedly when my escorts interrupted, pushing me firmly into the room. The colonel quietly ordered the policemen to remain outside.

One of the strangers came quickly towards me. He insisted on shaking my still damp, ink-stained hand, and guided me (I suspect deliberately) to an armchair as far as possible from the desk. He sat down next to me, positioning himself so that I was effectively screened from the colonel's line of vision. I had the impression he did this because he thought I might launch into a vociferous denunciation of police behaviour: a frequent reaction of Europeans arrested in Arab countries. He may well have been surprised when I did not do so.

He was tall and slim, with a neatly-trimmed Vandyke beard, and radiated a sort of quiet confidence that I found wonderfully reassuring.

He pushed a visiting-card into my hand saying: 'You'd better hang on to this – it gives our address and telephone numbers. If you find yourself in a real emergency you can sometimes get one of the senior staff – if you're lucky and kick up sufficient fuss – to ring us.'

The card was printed in English on one side and in Arabic on the other. The English side told me this was Richard Lyne, Third Secretary and Vice Consul.

'How are they treating you?'

'After seeing what they do to their own people, I don't feel I have much to complain about. I'm not one of those tedious Englishmen who, if they get into trouble through their own fault in a foreign country, assume the British Embassy can perform miracles on their behalf.'

'Miracles, no – but we can be of some help.'

'All I really need at the moment is some information about my future – my future as a prisoner in this country.'

'About what will happen to you?'

I nodded.

'I expect you already know you'll be taken to the law courts where you'll be kept until you've been interrogated by what we would call an examining magistrate. Have you had any experience of the continental system of justice?'

'Never as a prisoner, but I've lived most of my life outside England and I was at school for some years in France.'

'Then you obviously know the form well enough, which should be a help.' He was evidently relieved I would not need to be guided through the complexities of Syrian law. 'From what I've been hearing about your case,' he said, 'I don't think there's much doubt the *juge d'instruction* will send you for trial by the high court. When he's made a decision you'll be taken from the law courts to the civil prison which is in the Old City.'

'Whereabouts?'

'In the Citadel – that seventh-century stone castle not far from the Omayed Mosque, close to the Street Called Straight.'

'Good God!' I said, 'I've often looked at the outside and wondered what it was used for.'

This amused him. 'Well now you'll find out – at close quarters!' He became more serious. 'I must warn you, everything connected with the law in Syria works very slowly indeed, at least as slowly as it does in England. You mustn't expect your case to come up in the high court for probably six months, and it may be longer.'

My mind had concentrated so much on the length of sentence that might be inflicted upon me, his suggestion of a six months' waiting period before the hearing hardly seemed to matter. I gripped the arms of my chair and put the question I had been anxious, yet afraid, to ask ever since my arrest. I took a deep breath, and said in a very strained voice I hardly recognised as my own: 'I was told, not long ago, one could get fifteen years in this country for smuggling hash – is that so?'

To my unspeakable relief he shook his head. 'I can contradict that at once,' he said. 'The last Englishman to be caught carrying hashish in Syria – he had a car and a good deal more of the stuff than you had – was sentenced to three years.'

I found it impossible to say anything. I had never previously felt choked by feelings of relief, but I was now.

'Your predecessor finished his sentence just over four months ago. You're more than twice his age and had less than half the quantity of hashish. With luck, you'll get a slightly shorter sentence.'

He must have noticed surprise mixed with relief on my face, for he said quickly: 'I don't suppose there'll be much in it because they're getting tougher all the time with you people. Whatever you get, you'll be entitled to a remission of a quarter of its length for good behaviour. This isn't granted automatically, as in most European countries, it has to be applied for, but is seldom denied to foreigners. I doubt if there'll be any difficulty in your case.' He looked quizzically at me and said: 'Have you had much experience of Arab countries?'

I found my voice at last. 'I lived for some years in Morocco, and I've frequently spent months at a time in Lebanon.'

'So it's hardly necessary to warn you that being a prisoner in an Arab country can be a fairly rugged experience.' He waved his hand towards the other stranger who was talking in Arabic with the colonel. 'Before you were brought in here, my colleague and I – he's one of our Syrian staff – were discussing your case with the colonel, and I'm glad to say his attitude is not unsympathetic. He feels you've probably been the victim of an unscrupulous family of Lebanese hash growers. Is this true?'

I shook my head. 'No, it isn't! I knew exactly what I was doing.'

My reply obviously amused him. 'I appreciate your frankness,' he said quietly, 'but I'd let your captors keep their illusions for as long as possible.'

He took a notebook and silver pencil from his pocket, saying: 'Let us now discuss practical matters. I'm afraid there's nothing much we can do for you until you've been sent on to the prison. As soon as they let me know you're there – this will take several days, in spite

40

of the distance between us being less than two miles – I'll come and see you. After that, I'll try to visit at least once a fortnight during the initial stages of your imprisonment. Later, because I'm a busy man, I'll probably cut the visits down to once a month, or even less.' Then, almost without a pause, he said: 'Have you any money?'

'Only a few Syrian coins. I was carrying three thousand dollars and several hundred Syrian pounds – all of it in banknotes. Shall I ever see that money again?'

'Unlikely. It'll almost certainly be confiscated by the court.'

'How do I pay for a lawyer?'

'You don't. A lawyer's not necessary until nearer the time of the trial.'

'How about coping with the *juge d'instruction*?'

'You'll do just as well on your own.'

'You're sure?'

He nodded confidently and asked: 'Have you any friends in Damascus?'

'A few dubious acquaintances but no friends.'

'How about Lebanon?'

'Yes, I have friends there.'

'Will they be willing to send you cash?'

'It's possible – when they find out how to do it.'

'I'm asking,' he said, with a faint touch of irony, 'because this country calls itself the Socialist Democratic Republic of Syria yet its prisons are operated on distinctly capitalist lines. Even some of the basic necessities have to be paid for.'

'How do the Syrians manage?'

'Usually their families rally round.'

'Is there no work in their prisons?'

'Not much. What there is is more like occupational therapy. You can buy coloured beads to make handbags, purses, key-fobs, costume-jewellery or whatever. The authorities will buy them at prices that barely cover the cost of the materials. I advise you to ask your friends in Lebanon, or elsewhere, for financial help – and use the embassy as a post-box for inward and outward mail. You've got my card – tell your friends to address your letters care of me. You'll find I'm a more reliable postman than those employed by the prison services!'

At this point his Syrian colleague broke off his talk with the colonel and came across. Richard Lyne introduced him, and the young man's pale features, unusually ascetic for an Arab, softened into a pleasant smile

41

as we shook hands. He turned towards Lyne, saying in English with only the slightest of accents: 'The colonel's been telling me Lufthansa won't hand over to the police a refund on Mr Aspinall's ticket. The airline insists the money will only be paid to somebody from the embassy, acting on his behalf.'

Richard Lyne's expression indicated this was good news. 'That can be a little job for you this afternoon!' To me, he said: 'You've been lucky. If the police had got hold of it, they'd have confiscated it with the rest of your cash. It was a ticket to Barcelona via Frankfurt, wasn't it – what did you pay for it?'

'About the equivalent of four hundred pounds sterling.'

'Splendid! When we get our hands on it your financial problems will be over for some time. If you're reasonably economical it should last you for months.'

Meanwhile, the colonel had walked slowly across and opened the door. He was now standing beside it, smiling courteously – but it was a clear indication the interview must be brought to an end.

As I said goodbye to the embassy officials, I did my clumsy best to thank them adequately. Richard Lyne's tactfully expressed friendliness had given me back the confidence I needed to face the future. Ever since my arrival a small knot of anxiety had lodged under my breast bone and had become almost a physical pain. Now it had gone and I was grateful.

In the months ahead I was often to remember Richard Lyne's words as I left the office. Very quietly, he said: 'If things get really unpleasant, don't forget we shall always be on your side.'

The rest of the day passed without incident. Hisham's wife and Aziz's mother – both had careworn, middle-aged faces and were swathed from head to foot in soft-coloured, clinging draperies – brought quantities of food which they insisted on sharing with me.

It was early evening when our tranquillity was interrupted by the clatter of hob-nailed boots. The four gendarmes from the airport lined up outside the cell and grinned at me through the bars. Our jailer, astonished at this invasion, opened the door and they all burst in, exuberantly shaking my hand, patting me on both shoulders, enquiring if I was being well-treated and whether I needed anything.

Before I had time to answer, they fell about with laughter and all shouted at once, telling me another hash smuggler had been caught that afternoon at the airport. They had just brought him in.

The sergeant, after making an effort to quieten his troop without much success, explained the new prisoner was German, and very young. 'But he speak good English,' he said. 'We tell him you here and he very glad!'

After briefly chatting with Hisham and Aziz and making further enquiries about my general condition – assuring me I should be far better off in the civil prison – they stamped upstairs, the corporal giving me his favourite thumbs-up signal as he did so.

In less than half-an-hour, our jailer ushered a young Siegfried into the cell. Kurt was six feet five inches tall, very slim with flaxen hair, cornflower-blue eyes, good teeth and an engaging smile. An expensive tweed jacket and cavalry-twill trousers could not disguise the embodiment of the Germanic hero. He was indeed very young, having celebrated his twentieth birthday only a few days before.

We sat him down on his 'issue' blanket and Hisham and Aziz pressed him to eat from their still considerable stock of food.

He spoke English fluently with scarcely a trace of an accent. As I got to know him better I discovered he had an exceptional gift for languages: his French was excellent and he picked up Arabic remarkably quickly.

We talked a great deal on that first evening, and I soon learned that he had been working for neighbours of mine in Amsterdam. The pattern of his arrest and the reasons for it were similar to my own. He told me the airport customs were now hacking every hard-shell suitcase almost to bits, especially the widely advertised Korean product sold by the more expensive department stores.

They had told him the hash concealed in his two cases had been assessed at 14 kilos. As he knew beyond doubt they had contained a total of $15^1/_2$, he wondered which service at the airport had thieved the missing $1^1/_2$ kilos. I told him he should be glad it had disappeared and wished some of my 22 kilos had also been stolen.

Kurt was a Bavarian, the son of a broken marriage; he had an adoring mother and two younger sisters; well-educated, he had travelled all over Europe during school holidays. Disliking the idea of military service, he had convinced the medical board that he was a 'junkie' when, in fact, he had never experimented with hard drugs. He was, of course, thrown out as unsuitable material for the German army. He combined an abundance of charm with a total lack of scruple in cheating authority.

As the evening wore on, he complained several times about the diminishing heat in the cell. When our agreeable temporary jailer came to wish us goodnight (Sour Face never bothered with such courtesies) Hisham asked him, without much hope, if we could be allowed extra blankets. Much to our amazement this was treated as a perfectly reasonable request, and we were given a pile of bedding.

When he had gone, Kurt started to complain about the blankets being dirty. I hastily told him to be thankful for something to keep out the cold and to stop expecting Teutonic standards of hygiene in a Syrian police cell. He accepted my rebuke with good humour.

Feeling guilty because I had occupied a privileged place on the dais for two nights, I suggested we should now take turns to sleep on the thin layer of matchwood. My idea was rejected by Hisham and Kurt. I insisted the floor would seem no harder to my old bones than the dais, but neither would listen.

We cocooned ourselves in the grubby blankets, having first wrapped a couple around the suffering Aziz, who was now beginning to manage an occasional smile in spite of his tortured feet. My blankets smelt pungently of sour milk which I did my best to ignore. Kurt was less successful, and I heard him constantly swearing in German under his breath, before I managed to fall into a fitful sleep.

The next morning I was once again taken up to the colonel's office, where he told me I should be leaving within the hour for the Law Courts.

There was a Syrian banknote for one hundred pounds (roughly £9 sterling at that time) on the blotter in front of him. He pushed it towards me, saying: 'It's possible you may be kept at the court for some time, if a judge isn't immediately available to hear your case, so, on my own initiative, I'm giving you this.'

Good manners seemed to demand I should thank him for giving me back a small fraction of my own money, and I did so.

Looking more than ever like a product of the Staff College, he surprised me by standing up to shake my hand and wish me good luck and goodbye. I could not help liking him.

Aziz and Hisham had been told they would be leaving with me, but Kurt, of course, would not, as he had yet to be interrogated by the colonel. He made no secret of his regret about this. I assured him that European prisoners would almost certainly be kept together in prison, and it would not be long before we met again.

It was nearly eleven o'clock when a posse of policemen came

down to supervise our departure. Aziz was still unable to walk and, as Hisham and I were doing our best to help him, he was seized and hustled roughly up the stairs.

I was taken to pick up my baggage. Hisham started to help me, they slapped handcuffs on his wrists and pushed him away. So, as before, I slung the shoulder-bag round my neck and, putting the distorted wrecks of suitcases on top of each other, I carried them gingerly up the stairs, not wishing to leave a trail of multi-coloured underwear.

At last, with aching muscles and very much out of breath, I emerged into the open air and tottered towards a rusty old Peugeot delivery-van, whose rear doors had long ago been broken off, or deliberately discarded. It was doing duty as a Syrian 'black maria'.

Naturally, there were no seats. Hisham was sitting on the spare wheel, casually dumped inside the vehicle; Aziz was lying beside him. Pushing my luggage ahead of me, I clambered in. Two policemen jumped on the back and stood, holding on to its roof, in the fashion of delivery boys in the England of my distant youth. The police driver and a young sergeant were already in their seats. The engine had been ticking over and I barely had time to drop to the floor before our journey had begun.

It was a fine, sunny morning and the streets of Damascus were crowded, but no one appeared interested in a dilapidated van with policemen clinging to its roof like monkeys and a trio of dissimilar prisoners within.

The Law Court was a beige, weather-beaten building, resembling any small French *palais de justice* built during the first twenty years of this century. After passing its façade, the driver swung down a narrow sidestreet and halted outside the most modest of all the entrances to the courts.

THE LAW COURTS

The police hustled us out of the van and down an endless circular staircase to the basement. The steps were of stone, many badly worn, some broken. I was reminded of a descent inside a lighthouse. Carrying my inconvenient luggage, I found it a hazardous business and was glad to reach the bottom with my ankles intact.

A left turn at the foot brought us into a corridor, about forty feet by ten. On the right were the office, messroom and sleeping-quarters for the police guard. The left of the corridor was occupied by three cages, with the customary steel bars, six inches apart, from floor to ceiling. Each cage was separated from its neighbours by a plaster wall, once white, now grey with dirt.

The cage closest to the staircase was the smallest and cleanest and contained half-a-dozen women, wearing head-scarves and various forms of *kaftan*. Most were quite young; one was continuously wiping away her tears; another, dry-eyed, gazed at us with heart-rending despair; the remainder looked at us speculatively, occasionally putting out their tongues and making mildly obscene gestures.

'Whores!' snapped Hisham. 'Dirty womans!'

Aziz, who had been helped down the stairs by the police, was now sitting on the floor. He made no male chauvinist comments.

The second cage was slightly larger and was occupied by four or five boys in the twelve to fifteen age-group. Showing a great interest in everything, they had lined up facing the corridor, pushing their noses as far as possible between the bars.

The third cage took up all the remaining space and was larger than the other two put together. It was crowded with adult males, most in their twenties and thirties, all talking at once.

The noise made by two dozen Arabs exchanging reminiscences or giving advice is ear-splitting. A few were chatting to visitors who lined the corridor, some were seeking last minute advice from their lawyers,

46

others were being greeted by their families who, in some cases, had brought babies that cried indignantly: these were constantly being held up for fathers or brothers to kiss between the bars.

On the right of the corridor, well above eye-level, was a single window, hermetically sealed of course. Through the grimy glass it was just possible to glimpse the grey stone walls of the small basement courtyard. The sky was so far above, only a glimmer of daylight could insinuate itself down to our level.

Without several meagre strips of tubular lighting, the place would have been in semi-darkness, even at midday. The only ventilation was provided by accidental draughts of dust-laden air down the circular staircase. In the corridor ceiling was an electric fan with large blades, which the police would switch on for short periods, usually when the concentration of cigarette-smoke (most Arabs are chain-smokers) began to hurt their eyes. The sole effect of the slowly revolving fan was, however, to push the stale air lazily in circles.

A police sergeant, shouting and gesticulating to make himself heard above the clamour, ordered me to stack my luggage against the wall under the window. He removed Hisham's handcuffs, unlocked the narrow gate between the bars of the big cage and told us to carry Aziz inside. We did as we were told, but had some difficulty finding a space on the crowded floor where we could make the boy reasonably comfortable. However, Hisham was accosted by several old friends who helped us find a suitable spot.

While they recalled previous prison experiences, I looked around for a lavatory. This did not take long; had I been stone blind my nose would have guided me to it. The effluvium increased in strength as I moved towards the box-like shanty against the wall dividing our cage from the boys'. In spite of my affection for many Arab countries I have often wished my natural functions could be temporarily suspended while travelling in them. I pushed open the door and peered into almost total darkness. I felt for the light-switch – there was none. As my eyes grew accustomed to the gloom, I could just discern the circular outline of a faecal-encrusted dark hole. Beside it, also at ground level, was a continuously dripping tap. Previous users had obviously suffered from a poor sense of direction: it was necessary to be careful where one put one's feet.

When I emerged from this malodorous experience I was subjected to a barrage of questions. They were intensely curious to know why

I, a European, was there. When I told them, they asked how many kilos of hash I had been carrying; where had I been arrested; had I been beaten by the police; was I married; did I have children; how old was I. My truthful answer to the last brought cries of disbelief. Few Syrians, they assured me, lived to the age of seventy. Several spoke some French or English and translated my answers for those who only knew Arabic.

Half-a-dozen policemen began to clear the corridor of visitors. They only had to shout for the majority to obey. One or two elderly women clung to the bars, anxious for a few final words with husband or son. They were seized and pushed, roughly, towards the stairs.

When they had gone, the sergeant, reading from a millboard, began calling out names. Nearly twenty prisoners responded and were made to line up, two by two, facing the exit to the corridor; each couple linked by a single handcuff. It became a colourful 'crocodile'. A few of the older men were wearing the long flowing cloak known as a *sillam* over their even longer *galabiehs*. Most of the middle-aged were dressed in ill-fitting suits, the younger generation in blue jeans and cheap blousons.

Hisham explained the party was going to the high court, somewhere above us. All of them had been sent from the civil prison early this morning. They were marched off in quasi-military formation up the winding staircase.

Innocently, I asked if they could all be guilty of the same offence.

'Of course not,' was the astonished answer. 'Some will be accused of theft or raping a woman or, perhaps, a boy. Others, like ourselves, of dealing in drugs and a few, probably, of murder.'

'But will they all be put in the same dock?' I was incredulous.

Hisham plainly found my attitude difficult to understand. Of course they would be kept together in court. The president would question each individually and would listen while the prisoner explained himself. If the man had a lawyer, he would argue with the president and make speeches, while the others waited their turn. Was that not how it was done in my country?

I began to feel mildly apprehensive about the administration of Syrian law.

From time to time the sergeant would reappear and shout a name. The man would be handcuffed to a policeman and taken upstairs. About fifteen to twenty minutes would elapse before they returned.

These were prisoners who were being interrogated by an examining magistrate.

I asked if our names would be called soon.

'*Insha' Allah!*' said Hisham, but he doubted if this would be possible. The morning was nearly over, and neither courts nor magistrates ever sat in the afternoon.

How many magistrates were there?

He didn't know, but thought there were two.

Did he think we would have to stay in this awful cage overnight?

He thought it probable – especially in my case.

Why was that?

Because an interpreter would be needed, and it might take time to find one.

It was nearly two hours before those who had been taken into court returned. The guttural sounds of Arabic rose to a crescendo as they discussed, with big dramatic gestures, what had taken place in court.

Against this barrage of sound I suddenly heard someone shouting a distorted version of my name. A young man in a light overcoat was in the corridor, beckoning.

My immediate hope that he had come to take me in front of a magistrate was quickly dashed. He had just enough English to explain he was a clerk in the office of the *juge d'instruction*. He had, he said, some bad news for me, but looked rather smug about it.

I braced myself.

It would not be possible, he said, for his boss to see me today, and tomorrow would be equally impossible because it was a Friday. Nothing, of course, would function on the Muslim holy day.

'You mean I'll have to stay here until Saturday?' I was appalled.

'Longer,' he said complacently; Saturday was a national holiday and I would therefore be kept in this cage until Sunday, when it should be possible to take me in front of what he called 'the judge'.

I badly wanted to protest but knew it would be a waste of breath. So I thanked the young man, I hope politely, for bringing me this unwelcome information, went back to my patch of floor and reported to Aziz and Hisham. Living night and day under artificial light had made all of us suffer from a kind of amnesia about the passage of time. They had also forgotten tomorrow was Friday and the day after a celebration of Syria's national independence. Hisham cursed the anti-drug squad for not sending us to the law courts earlier.

The sergeant reappeared, a roll was called and a majority of prisoners left. They were being sent back to the prison, with the addition of a few new arrivals who, during the morning, had been interviewed by an examining magistrate. They were kept waiting in the corridor, and there was quite a lengthy exchange of good-humoured, mildly obscene badinage with the police, before they were led away. Fewer than ten of us were left behind.

The police chucked a couple of long-handled brooms at two of the youngest and told them to sweep the stone floor. Soft brooms could do little to remove ingrained layers of dirt, but the cage looked slightly less squalid when they had finished.

For everyone except myself, most of the afternoon was taken up by short visits. In addition to large quantities of food, the visitors all brought bedding: in most cases, a quilt, a pillow and multi-coloured rugs. Those whose visitors arrived early laid claim to all space along the outer edge of the cage, showing they intended to sleep at right angles to the corridor with their heads almost touching the bars.

At the police station, bedding from outside sources had been expressly forbidden, but here, where blankets were never issued, it was encouraged. It was essential, unless you were prepared to sleep on cold stone – a fate I thought all too likely to be mine when I refused to deprive Hisham and Aziz of any of their few bed-clothes, although they pressed me to. I did, however, allow myself to eat some of their food. In return I was able to keep them supplied with frequent glasses of tea and coffee from a local sandwich-bar.

Just as I was wondering if I could persuade the police to loan me a blanket as a special favour, two prosperous-looking young prisoners seized my arms, talking both at once in very broken English, insisting, as I was a lonely foreigner, I must allow them to supply all my needs. Still gripping my elbows, they led me firmly to a colossos of a quilt on which were piled half-a-dozen folded rugs. They insisted it was amply big enough for all three of us. I was only too happy to agree.

Karim and Tariq were brothers, Iraquis from Baghdad, but in daily contact with cousins in Damascus. Both were in their early twenties, small and lithe as cats with a fragile bone-structure that could have been the envy of any flat-racing jockey. Quick-witted, warm-hearted and unimpressed by authority, there was an endearing sparkle about them. They specialised in the robbing of jewellers' shops, which they clearly felt placed them amongst the aristocrats of theft. I shall never forget them.

I decided to make an effort to clean myself up, although the idea of using the tap in a lavatory ankle-deep in excrement (our only water supply) made me shudder. Unnatural conditions, however, soon become natural to most prisoners, and it was not long before I stopped being so fastidious and began to use that water not only for washing but also for drinking.

The sergeant who had greeted us when we arrived had gone off-duty. His successor was a younger man with red hair, a fair skin and eyes of so pale a grey, they were almost white. His profile – a prominent nose combined with a thin-lipped mouth and fly-away chin – gave an immediate impression of a fox. Hisham had obviously got to know him on previous occasions for they were talking through the bars. I waited patiently until their conversation seemed to be over, then asked if I might be allowed to collect towel and wash-bag from my luggage, which was still in the corridor. Hisham interpreted. To my surprise, the sergeant barked at an underling who promptly handed me my shoulder-bag.

I began the first of many efforts to clean some of the grime from my face with a flannel moistened from the tap. Afterwards I removed my incipient beard with a battery-shaver and became the focus of amused interest.

It had been agreed with Karim and Tariq that I should occupy the left-hand side of their enormous quilt which they had placed against the wall at the furthest point from the nauseating lavatory. On my right, Aziz lay on the bedding his mother had brought, his feet still badly swollen, although he assured me they were less painful. Hisham was just beyond him.

My shoulder-bag made an acceptable pillow, and seemed to provide a reassuring link with the world outside, like a 'comforter' in a baby's mouth.

During the next three days time crept forward in slow motion. On Friday no visitors were allowed to interrupt the monotony, even the runner with tea and coffee was absent because his sandwich-bar was shut. We had nothing but water from the tap. Food, however, was no problem; such generous quantities had been brought the previous day, no one went hungry. All insisted I must eat with them, whether a small snack or a full-scale meal. I had to use all the tact of which I was capable to refuse some of these invitations, otherwise I should have ended each day feeling like a Strasbourg goose.

Despite the padding in the quilt, my old bones ached at night and I never managed to get much sleep. The cage was never cold, doubtless to provide comfort for the nightwatch. Those of us trying to sleep with our heads to the plaster walls regretted we had not been amongst the lucky few alongside the bars. They were not kept awake by the shower of bugs that dropped from the upper area of each wall, in hundreds, every night. These obnoxious objects, flat, dark brown and about the size of a fingernail, fell like rain on our faces and scuttled away to hide under every quilt and blanket. When caught and crushed, their smell was sickening.

Every night there was at least one disturbance, sometimes three or four, created by the arrival of drunks arrested for disorderly behaviour. Most of them subsided quietly into a dark corner, but a few would shout and sing, staggering about for an hour or so, often treading on us. This could lead to angry protests and sometimes to serious fights. Occasionally, one of the drunks would get knocked out.

The police normally ignored these contretemps, but once they did react, and with exceptional violence. A young man wearing an expensive suit, silk shirt and sober tie, was brought in. At first he appeared only mildly drunk, then suddenly began to beat a tattoo with his fists against the bars – he chose the gate because the noise was greater – and launched into a stream of abuse against the entire Damascus police force. This verbal assault continued for what seemed like minutes, and all around I heard murmurs of admiration at his extensive vocabulary of insults. It would have been kinder if they had told him to shut up.

The reaction of the police was savage. All four rushed out of their sleeping-quarters, each carrying a heavy wooden stick, about the width and half the length of a cricket bat. They seized the offender, dragging him roughly away to their office. A sickening noise began, of heavy blows slugging a soft object we knew to be a human body.

The young man cursed each one of them, but as the blows increased in speed and ferocity, the shouts of contempt gradually changed to screams of pain. The beating went on until sobbing appeals for mercy could be heard as they continued to hit with savage violence. At last they stopped, obviously out of physical exhaustion, not concern for their prisoner. There were several minutes of silence before they reappeared, dragging an apparently unconscious body along by its feet. They opened the cage and threw the limp figure contemptuously inside, chucking his shoes after him.

The young man struggled to his knees and then, very slowly, to his feet. The skin of his forehead had been split, and blood was dribbling down his face and on to his jacket which had been badly torn. He made no sound except for an occasional sobbing intake of breath as he stumbled towards the lavatory. He reached the door, pushed it open and, doubtless because the haemorrhage from the head-wound was partly obscuring his sight, slipped and fell, head first, into the unspeakably filthy hole.

Several of us wearily pushed our blankets aside and went to help him. We stood him on his feet and did our best to clean him up with water from the tap and our bare hands. Then we left him alone for a few minutes. Defecating and urinating are very private matters to every Muslim.

When he came out, blood was still oozing from the gash in his forehead and we discovered several other open wounds concealed by his curly hair. His hands and feet were badly bruised and the skin broken in many places. I remembered there were a couple of clean white handkerchiefs in my shoulder-bag which Hisham, who had been a medical orderly during his military service, tore into strips and used for bandaging the young man's head. He was silent and hardly seemed aware of our efforts to help him. Still suffering from shock, he lay down against the wall at the back of the cage. He was obviously in considerable pain, many of the blows he had received had been directed at his groin. Offers of blankets were firmly waved away, but he did not reject a pillow.

By mid-morning he had made a remarkable recovery and came to thank everybody who had tried to help him. The Arab capacity for absorbing the heaviest of physical punishment never ceased to astonish me. He was twenty-three years old, the son of a prosperous landowner from north of Aleppo who had sent him to the best schools in Syria. Recently he had quarrelled with his father who had been deeply shocked by the drinking habits he had acquired from American friends, part of the United Nations small HQ in Damascus. The generous allowance he had received since he was eighteen had been cut off and this had created problems for him. He had become accustomed to a good deal of social drinking in the bar of the Damascus-Sheraton, something he could no longer afford. Nevertheless, he had gone there early the previous evening and, for a time, had been drinking with friends. Just before eight, these companions had left. He had remained on his own, and for three hours had steadily consumed double whiskies. The chief barman, no doubt realising his customer was approaching alcoholic coma, had at last presented him with a bill. With a deliberately contemptuous gesture he had flung it back across the counter saying: 'I've no money at all – you'd better send for the police!'

That, of course, is precisely what he did.

I asked why he had been so angry with the police.

He shrugged his shoulders. 'They are all animals – I hate them. When they arrested me I was most polite, but when they got me into their horrible van, they threw me on the floor and kicked me. They are corrupt, every one of them.' He suddenly smiled seraphically at the recollection of something. 'I was sick over all their boots,' he said, dreamily, 'I enjoyed that!'

Another of my companions under the law courts was a distinguished-looking middle-aged Mexican whose attitude towards us was a mixture of hauteur and condescension. Night and day he wore an overcoat of superb Spanish leather that reached almost to his heels; the sort of garment one sees in the windows of those very expensive men's shops in Madrid or Barcelona. He kept very much to himself which I found surprising, as his mother had been Syrian and he spoke Arabic fluently. He naturally spoke Spanish and also French, which we spoke together. He told me he had been arrested because of matrimonial troubles. He had married a Syrian girl some years ago and wished to divorce her. This was being opposed by her family who had succeeded, with the help of an expensive lawyer, in getting him taken into custody on trumped-up charges. How much of this was true, I never found out, but only a few weeks were to elapse before his release. He was splendidly scornful when he learned I was a hashish smuggler. Why did I burden myself, he asked, with a substance so heavy, so bulky, so easy to detect? If I wished to become a smuggler – which he clearly regarded as a sensible method of earning a living – why did I not do as he did and smuggle precious stones? He travelled regularly between South America and Spain, carrying a small collection of uncut emeralds, obtained from black market dealers in the wilds of Colombia. He wrapped them in tissue-paper and slipped them into his notecase; the profits were substantial, the risk practically nil. I pointed out that the ability to

judge the quality of a jewel, especially in its uncut state, required years
of experience, whereas the capacity to distinguish good hashish from
bad could be acquired in a very short time. After some argument I
succeeded in persuading him I was too old a dog to learn new tricks.

On Saturday afternoon, while I was absorbed in Lauren Bacall's
moving account of Humphrey Bogart's slow death from lung cancer,
I heard my name called. A police sergeant was standing in the corridor
waving an envelope at me. Totally baffled, I accepted the letter he thrust
through the bars. I had no idea who, at this most unusual moment of
my life, could have written a note to be delivered by hand. When it
was explained that the sergeant was on the staff of the civil prison, and
was delivering the letter for a prisoner, I was even more baffled. On a
thin sheet of paper, somebody had written quite legibly, but in a hand
more accustomed to Arabic script than the Roman alphabet:

Dear Tony,

Maybe you remember me. We often used to meet in Baalbek.
I believe you don't know I have been a prisoner in the Citadel for
almost a month. Yesterday I was told of your arrest by my wife
when she visited me. Please be careful not to say to anyone that
you brought the hashish into Syria yourself. Say it was somebody
else – anybody else.

There will be no problems for you when you get here.
I will look after you as if you were my father.

Good luck!
Rachid Benami.

I knew the writer well enough, but the news of his imprisonment
astounded me. Rachid Benami was not a blood relation of the infamous
Lebanese family. He was a Syrian, a captain in the army, who had
married one of his Lebanese namesakes. But he was also not merely
a Syrian, he was an Alouite, a member of the same small, powerful
clan as President Hafez Assad. Ever since I had known him, Rachid
had claimed to be a member of the personal staff of the President's
younger brother, Rifa'at Assad, who at that time was the ruthless
commander of Syria's military intelligence. Knowing something of
Rachid's background, I was astonished to learn he was in prison,
particularly a civil prison. With the important influences he had behind
him, I would have thought it possible to get away with any crime in

the book. Selfishly, I was glad he was there. Although never a crony of mine, the news that he would be waiting for me made the prospect of prison less alarming.

At last Sunday arrived, and early in the morning, long before it was necessary, everyone folded up their bedding in piles against the walls. The floor received its indifferent brushing. I shaved and put on a jacket, hoping I did not look as dishevelled as I felt.

Soon after eight o'clock a party of twenty or more from the civil prison shuffled in. The corridor began to fill up with visitors.

The first call from a magistrate was for Aziz. The boy's feet were a lot better and he could hobble without assistance. I was glad to see the police made no attempt to hustle him and gave him as much support as the obligatory handcuff would allow. Shortly afterwards, Hisham received a similar summons, and I began to wonder if I should have to remain in the cage for another twenty-four hours. Was the difficulty of finding an interpreter going to cause more delay?

I had just about given up hope when I heard my name. A handcuff was clipped on and I was hurried up the staircase, through swing-doors and across the marble floor of the immense central hall, crowded with lawyers and their hangers-on. The spectacle of an elderly Englishman being towed by a policeman was a conversation-stopper; voices were stifled in mid-sentence as my escort pushed a path through the animated throng.

We halted in front of a solid mahogany door. The policeman knocked and nervously pushed it open, revealing a narrow office with a large desk in front of a single window at the far end. Behind the desk, the outline of an overweight, middle-aged male in a light-coloured suit could be seen against the bright sunshine. Close by in an armchair was a much younger, slimmer figure whose skin was as black and shiny as polished anthracite. The paunchy character gave a curt order to my escort who unlocked the handcuff and pushed me forward. The office was sparsely furnished with metal filing cabinets along one wall, a small table and chair beside the desk and, occupying almost the whole length of the other wall, a narrow banquette, uphol-stered in black leather.

The young black looked up at me from his armchair and said in English: 'You'd better sit down. We shall have to wait for the judge of instruction's clerk before you can be cross-examined.'

Obediently, I sat on the banquette and scrutinized the other occupants. I was surprised by the black skin of the interpreter, who was talking with the magistrate in lively, colloquial Arabic. Syrians are an amalgam of many ancient races but, unlike in Egypt, or the rest of North Africa, black skins are rare.

I was resisting the temptation to break into their conversation and ask where he came from when a pale, bespectacled young Syrian walked in. He was carrying a typewriter with a box of foolscap balanced precariously on top. He shut the door with his heel, bowed obsequiously to the magistrate and put his machine on the table. He sat, inserted a sheet of paper into his old Olivetti and, fingers poised over the keyboard, looked up expectantly at the treble-chinned, unsmiling face.

The magistrate's obesity reminded me of ultra-conservative officers in the Egyptian army in the time of my youth, who used to consider the cultivation of a paunch essential if promoted to major or above. I wondered if this habit had been retained by the Syrian judiciary. In spite of his girth, his feet, protruding through the knee-hole of the desk in crocodile-leather shoes, were tiny. So were his hands, heavily weighted with gold rings, with which he made great play as he asked the many questions that had to be relayed by the interpreter whose English, fortunately, was excellent.

The questions were merely a repetition of everything I had been asked at the airport. As the young typist hammered out the Arabic translation, my replies become more and more mechanical. During my cross-examination by the colonel, I had often been conscious of a tenuous sort of rapport with him: there were moments when we almost winked at each other. Such reaction was not possible with this corpulent representative of Syrian bureaucracy.

The examination ended as I knew it would, with the pronouncement that I must be sent for trial in the high court and, until this took place, I was to be detained in the city's civil prison. Bail for foreigners has no place in Syrian law. My lack of emotion at the magistrate's dictum seemed to irritate him.

'The judge wishes to know if you understand the seriousness of your situation?' asked the interpreter.

'I know it to be a serious offence in Syria.'

'And also in England?'

'I haven't lived in England for years. My home is in the Netherlands where smuggling hashish is a matter only for police courts, and generally regarded as less important than the non-payment of a dog licence.'

This statement was, of course, not well received and the magistrate appeared on the verge of apoplexy. However, he restrained himself sufficiently to instruct the stenographer to hand the typescript of my evidence to the interpreter for checking. He kept glaring at me as if I were the source of a peculiarly unpleasant smell.

As soon as the interpreter expressed himself satisfied with the translation, it was handed to me for signing at the bottom of each page. The young black assured me, with a friendly smile, it was as accurate a translation as he could make it. Nevertheless, as in the police station, I carefully wrote NOT UNDERSTOOD before signing. The magistrate made no comment; he may have thought it an adjunct of my signature.

The young clerk left us, bowing again to the magistrate. He looked mildly startled when I opened the door for him. My police escort could now be seen in smiling conversation with a pretty girl some distance away. When he realised he was under observation, the smile vanished and he advanced towards us looking sheepish, extracting handcuffs from his hip-pocket.

I shook hands with the interpreter, thanking him and congratulating him on his easy fluency in English.

'It's really my second language,' he said.

'Then you're not a Syrian?'

'No, I'm Sudanese – from Khartoum.'

What was a Sudanese doing as an interpreter in a Damascus court? I never had a chance to find out because our brief moment of friendliness did not please our plump magistrate who squawked at my escort, who snapped on the handcuffs and tugged me unceremoniously from the office.

Back again in the cage with its pungent atmosphere of stale sweat, urine, excrement, bed-bugs and cigarette smoke, it was obvious the high court was in session because the crowd which had descended upon us earlier was absent.

Hisham was there and, like everyone else, was delighted a magistrate had quashed the case against Aziz, who had been set free. The young man who had drunk too much in the Sheraton bar had not been released but was undismayed. He was confident friends in Damascus would settle his drink bill and, if so, he would be discharged within the next few days. The blood-encrusted gash on his forehead was beginning to heal.

Karim and Tariq were gloomy, having been told they would be deported back to Iraq. Not wishing to pry, I never knew what infringement of the law had, this time, brought about their arrest; but they were hopeful no action would be taken against them on their return to Baghdad.

About an hour later, the party who had been in court clattered in again. There was a further delay of at least an hour before we were told to line up in the corridor. Those of us on our way to prison for the first time were ordered to the tail-end of the crocodile.

When I had gathered up my battered suitcases, I found my partner in the queue was the debtor from the Sheraton. My impedimenta made it impossible to link us like the others, so the sergeant decided, after some argument with his staff, that my bar-fly companion was to have his wrists handcuffed together and I would depart as I had arrived, with nothing to restrict my freedom except my own luggage.

It was not easy, but I managed to ascend the twisting stairs without falling too far behind, and without dropping anything.

A 15cwt truck, with a metal roof and no rear doors had been backed up to the entrance reserved for prisoners. This was a routine practice adopted by police drivers for the dual purpose of screening us from spectators and restricting the opportunity for escape.

When I reached the exit everyone had already clambered into the truck. Many hands, in spite of their shackles, reached out to take my luggage and help me up. Dishevelled and out of breath, I made the necessary effort to crawl into this congested mass of humanity.

Within a few seconds our driver was forcing his way ruthlessly into one of the city's main arteries, with the customary brace of policemen standing at the rear, holding tightly to the roof. For a short distance we joined the stream of traffic travelling north; then, after making a sharp right-angle turn, we entered the narrow lane that divides, under a high roof, the two sections of the Omayed *souk* devoted to the sale of leather goods and luggage. We emerged from the semi-darkness of this market – old, even at the time of Christ – on to a large parade ground, encircled by eucalyptus trees. In the fading afternoon sunlight several platoons of soldiers were engaged in squad drill on the crushed black cinders. The truck swung through an arc of ninety degrees, so violently that if we had not been so tightly packed some of us would have been thrown out. It reversed along a rutted track, coming to a halt in front of an impressive edifice rising towards the sky like a grey stone mountain. We had arrived at the Citadel: built in the seventh century AD and now the civil prison of Damascus.

THE CITADEL

The policemen dropped to the ground and were joined by their colleagues from the driving cab. The rest of us scrambled out in their wake, and were again told to line up like animals about to enter the ark. Once more, I took up a position on the end of the queue.

The ancient castle, a primitive colossus, soared above us. We were in front of its only entrance: an enormous archway with a solid iron gate, painted an unpleasant cobalt blue. In its centre was a small door, just wide enough to pass through in single file.

It was suddenly opened from within, and an order given for us to get moving. Those at the front of our crocodile began to squeeze through; each couple having to manoeuvre crabwise. My luggage made it difficult but, after one abortive effort, I succeeded.

We were in a small courtyard surrounded by stone walls fifty feet high. There was a wooden hut, painted the same shade of blue as the gate, which served as a small office.

Syria has no special service of prison warders. The jails are staffed by ordinary members of the police force assigned, for a period, to prison duties; and all wear the same uniform – blue in winter, khaki-drill in summer.

Between this small front courtyard and the main area of the prison was a giant stockade: a line of upright steel stakes, six inches apart, at least twenty-five feet high, stretching from wall to wall. There was a gate in the middle, which was really a section of the stockade constructed to pivot on its hinges. It was now wide open and standing beside it were several guards looking, as always, somewhat scruffy. There never seemed to be any compulsion for them to clean their boots! The most noticeable of the bunch was an aggressively masculine, middle-aged sergeant: a thick-set bull of a man with a black moustache. Later I was to learn his name was Abou Taïeb, and he

60

was usually in charge of all entries and exits through the inner and outer gates.

Prisoners who had been to the law courts or elsewhere, had on re-entry to stand by the stockade gate, legs apart and arms aloft, to be frisked from head to toe before being allowed to return to their quarters. Naturally, new arrivals had to submit to the same treatment, to prevent such articles as knives, drugs and even small arms from being smuggled in.

Abou Taïeb almost always carried out the frisking operations himself, seldom delegating the job. He was an acquisitive character; if his groping hands detected cigarettes or chocolate (given to a man by his family while waiting to appear in court) he would often find an excuse to confiscate them. The younger and better-looking prisoners also resented his frequent practice of undoing their belts when their arms were raised, allowing their trousers to drop while he thrust probing fingers under their shirts to search for contraband which he claimed might be hidden in their briefs. They all knew of his unabashed sexual interest in young men and boys.

It was as our first frisking began that I noticed a tall figure in a white sweater and fawn corduroy trousers standing beside the sergeant. This apparition seemed to be waving in my direction; not merely waving, but beckoning. It was Rachid Benami. He was using the Greek/Arab gesture for summoning anybody: the hand is held palm-downwards, with the forearm extended – the action resembles a cat digging with its front paw. Seeing I had noticed him, Rachid's signals became increasingly imperious, making me an object of curiosity. So I decided to obey, picking up my luggage and advancing towards the 'stockade', wondering if my queue-jumping would be greeted with cries of outrage. There were none.

Rachid said something to the sergeant who told me to put my luggage just inside the gate. I did so, then stood with my arms raised. The queue was held up while the sergeant frisked me in so genteel a fashion I could have entered the Citadel with knives and packets of hash in every pocket. Meanwhile, Rachid had seized my stuff and stacked it neatly against a wall, and now gave me the traditional greeting between friends in the Arab world: as I took his hand, he pulled me against him, giving me a bear-hug and kissing me on both cheeks.

This member-in-law of the Benami tribe was twenty-eight years old, tall, with a fair skin. His eyes were slate-grey and his hair the shade Germans describe as *dunkel blond*: a colouring I believe to be fairly common among Syrian Alouites. His good looks had been marred by a blow which had flattened his nose while training as a commando. The injury had been clumsily repaired. The nose had been straightened but was thicker than it should have been, giving him a slightly wolfish air.

I thanked him for his letter and asked how his wife had known of my arrest.

'She is staying with her father while I'm here,' he said. 'Our baby son is with her. The news of your trouble reached most of your friends in the Beka'a Valley within twenty-four hours.'

Rachid had rich parents and had been educated in Egypt – at a school which claimed to be modelled on an English public school. Middle East old hands were apt to consider it a melting-pot of snobbery and sodomy. I doubt if there was ever much truth in these slanderous opinions. Rachid had imbibed Alouite arrogance at his mother's breast and would have been just as autocratic had he been sent to his local village school. As for sodomy, he had a strait-laced almost nineteenth-century distaste for any suggestion of homosexuality. Several times during the following weeks he was to take me to task for being friendly with prisoners whose morals had incurred his disapproval. I ignored his reproaches.

His school had certainly taught him good English: only an occasional misplaced inflexion showed he had not been brought up in the company of Sloane Rangers. He now explained my luggage would have to be examined by Abou Taïeb and his minions; but this was unlikely to happen for at least an hour and, anyway, I was not to bother because he would supervise the operation himself. Meanwhile, he felt sure I would be glad of a cup of tea.

He linked his arm with mine and guided me through several large inner courtyards of the old castle in the gathering dusk. It felt good to be in the fresh air after days in the fetid miasma of police station and law courts.

As we walked, I brought Rachid up to date with what had happened since my arrest. He was glad I was not going to be charged with importing the hashish, personally, into Syria. Smugglers convicted of this, he assured me, always got heavier sentences than those who could prove it had been delivered to them after they had entered the country. Later, I found this to be accurate, but never discovered why.

I was surprised we did not pass any other prisoners on our way to this cup of tea, only an occasional guard who would look at me with obvious astonishment but, seeing Rachid, say nothing and pass on. This made me ask if the prison was almost empty, which made him laugh. 'There are more than twelve hundred at the moment!' he said.

'Where are they then?'

'Locked up in their rooms.'

'You mean cells?'

'No, I mean rooms – big rooms. Perhaps I should say dormitories? Cells here are only for punishment. Everyone will be let out tomorrow morning from eight o'clock until two in the afternoon – it's compulsory to be outside during that time.'

I could not resist saying: 'What exactly are you dong here?'

'Like you, I'm a prisoner.' His tone seemed deliberately bland.

'But they don't lock you up like the rest?' I persisted.

He smiled. 'Sometimes – but I have influence,' was his reply; and I never doubted its truthfulness.

He led me down two short flights of steps, through a wide stone archway and into the interior of the castle. I expected to be confronted by the sight of prisoners behind bars, but instead we entered a large, brilliantly lighted hall, with a wide apron-stage under a proscenium arch occupying one end of the immense space. Small tables and chairs stood along each wall and above them were rows of paintings, most of them in oils, far more vivid in their use of colour and violent in their realism than the work of most European amateurs. Representations of small arms and Israeli flags trampled in blood hit me between the eyes wherever I looked.

In front of the stage was a table covered with official-looking papers and, behind it, a slim figure was busily writing. I was so bemused by the astonishing 'picture gallery', I sensed rather than saw the young man leave his chair and pump up the flame of a primus stove. It was a question from Rachid that brought me out of this trance. 'You speak French, don't you, Tony?'

I admitted the fact.

'Good! You'll be able to talk to each other!' He pointed to the figure, now ladling sugar and tea into an aluminium teapot. 'Yussef speaks no English, I speak no French and you have hardly any Arabic, so we obviously can't all talk at the same time!'

Yussef, smiling and rather bewildered by Rachid's volubility, introduced himself in stylishly formal French; he was delighted to meet me and would I please sit down. Surely I must feel half-dead after so many days at the police station and under the *palais de justice*? He switched momentarily into Arabic, telling Rachid to bring up a chair for me.

He extinguished the primus and placed the boiling teapot on a metal tray beside half-a-dozen glasses. I now saw he was not as young as I had first thought: early thirties, not mid-twenties. He had delicate-looking limbs, a narrow head with a pale, ascetic face and a finely chiselled mouth. This was crowned by an aureole of abundant black hair, prematurely flecked with grey. He gave an immediate impression of almost feminine fastidiousness which contrasted with the pelt of tightly-curled grey-black hair on chest and forearms, revealed by his open-necked, white woollen shirt with sleeves pulled up to the elbow. He poured the tea. Rachid said in English: 'I've explained we've been friends for a long time. He knows you were at my wedding and in my father-in-law's house when my son was born there.' To any Arab these are important factors and make for a binding friendship.

Yussef seemed to sense what was said, for he broke in to tell me in French that my name had long been known to him. Although he lived and worked in Beirut, his family were from the Beka'a Valley.

'From Baalbek?' I asked.

He mentioned a village about twenty kilometres further north. I knew it well. I once had the interior of a motor caravan entirely rebuilt in a workshop there.

He smiled. 'I'm sure I know the mechanic who did it. Was it well done?'

'No!' I answered. 'As I was driving north through Yugoslavia, the interior of the roof suddenly opened up and packets of hashish began dropping in a cascade around my head!'

'Had you much further to travel?'

'About fifteen hundred kilometres – through four more countries.'

'What happened?'

'It was between Belgrade and Zagreb. I drove off the *autoput* and found a quiet spot in what I thought was a wild, uncultivated part of Croatia. I was just starting to repair the roof when two military policemen poked their heads through the cab windows. They told me, almost apologetically, I was trespassing in an area reserved by the army for tank training! Fortunately, they were simple peasant boys whose homes were not far from the Austrian frontier. Both spoke German and accepted my story of being a tired old man who merely wished to find a place to rest and cook a meal. No attempt was made to examine the vehicle. I drove immediately on to Zagreb and repaired the roof in an almost deserted, tree-lined suburban street!'

They laughed. Rachid had heard my account of this incident soon after it happened, but it still amused him. He had guessed what I was saying from the words Yugoslavia and Zagreb. 'You must have wished the Damascus customs had been equally unobservant!' he snickered.

The name of Yussef's village had told me two facts about him. It was high in the mountains, its inhabitants exclusively Maronite Christian. Most owners of palatial villas in the surrounding countryside had made fortunes out of the cultivation of hashish. His family name was well-known to me. I had friends all over Europe who had been dealing with them for years. I was curious to know why he had been working in Beirut.

'Teaching,' was his answer. 'I got a good degree in French at the university ten years ago, and I am now a permanent member of the staff, or I was' – here he gave me a wry smile – 'until the *déplaisant contretemps* that brought me to this place.'

'It was your – family business,' I said, meaningly, 'that brought you in here?'

'Of course. My wife and I were going to Paris for the summer vacation – she is French, from Montpellier. I decided to take some of our good quality product hidden in a suitcase to pay for our trip! Unfortunately, neither of us got nearer to France than Damascus airport.'

'What happened to your wife?'

'I insisted she knew nothing, and they let her go in a few hours.'

'How long a sentence did they give you?' I braced myself for his reply.

'Two years.'

'For how many kilos?'

'Five.'

'I had twenty-two.'

He turned to Rachid. '*Vingt-deux kilos – c'est plus serieux, tu pense?*' he said. Then, remembering his friend's lack of French, repeated his question in Arabic.

'The courts in Damascus,' said Rachid, 'don't seem much concerned about the amount. If it's between five and fifty kilos, the penalty is usually from two to three years. In the north it's different – especially in the port of Latakia. There you can get five years if your breath smells of pot!'

'Do you always get remission?' I asked. 'What I've been told is called "quarter time" – for good behaviour?'

'Good behaviour is not as important as a good lawyer, and money,' said Rachid.

'And if I have neither?'

'*You* will still get it. You're a foreigner and no longer young – you'll be given preferential treatment. Your embassy will help. The British and Americans are good at helping people in here. The other countries don't give a damn!'

As Rachid and I sipped the traditional three glasses of tea, Yussef tidied his papers. I asked if he were doing some sort of administrative job.

He laughed. '*C'est plutot l'administration de la cuisine – c'est moi qui surveil le distribution de la nourriture tous les jours!* If they find out you can read and write, you get pushed into clerical work. But I don't mind, it allows me more freedom to move about than most prisoners – except for Rachid, of course – he just does as he pleases!'

Rachid demanded to know what was being said about him.

'Yussef was saying you do as you please in this place!'

'If that were true I would have walked out within ten minutes of my arrival,' he snapped, banging his fist impatiently on the table. 'I should never have come here at all!'

I was strongly tempted to ask why he was here, when he thwarted my curiosity by getting up and saying: 'It's time we did something about collecting your luggage before the guards grab everything worthwhile. And I must take you to the admin offices – they'll be wanting your thumb-print on a few documents.'

'My thumb-print?'

'Yes, thumb-print. Oh, they'll know you can write, even if you can't do so in Arabic. But many prisoners are illiterate, so in here, the thumb-print is the usual form of signature.'

I thanked Yussef for the tea. I had not yet begun to appreciate that this young don and small-scale smuggler was one of the most considerate and humane men I have ever met. He was respected throughout the prison; always prepared to listen patiently to those in any kind of difficulty, giving advice that was invariably wise and objective, and as much comfort and support as possible. His job brought him constantly in touch with the governor and his deputies, and there were many occasions when his tactful intervention alleviated the harshness or unfairness of an action contemplated by the 'top brass' against a prisoner, or even a member of the staff.

It was almost dark as Rachid and I retraced our steps through the centre of the Citadel, dimly illuminated by electric lamps, enclosed behind oval glass frames with metal borders. These, set apparently at random into the stone walls, resembled an irregular chain of ships' portholes.

He led me into a narrow cul-de-sac where the light was somewhat brighter, most of it emanating through the windows and open doors of two small adjoining offices, carved out of the rock wall on one side of the little enclave. Here, leaning against the stone buttresses or sitting uncomfortably on broken pieces of masonry, were those who had come with me from the law courts. I had felt guilty when I left them to accept tea and sympathy, and was glad to find none seemed to have resented my behaviour. I was often to notice how Arabs, by European standards, are remarkably lacking in the vice of envy. Never once did I hear that familiar cry: 'If we can't have it, why should they?'

Rachid left me, saying he would return shortly with my luggage.

I was talking with my two Iraqi friends when the bibulous habitué of the Sheraton bar joined us, complaining bitterly that his beautifully styled hair-do had been so roughly shorn with clippers that his head looked like an old clothes-brush. He exaggerated slightly, but I could see what he meant. Tariq and Karim had suffered the same fate, but less noticeably because their hair had been shorter. Trying hard not to laugh, they pointed to a young guard; the ground at his feet looked as if he had been stripping a goat – most Syrian goats are black – and I realised this carpet of hair could only be the curls and quiffs of my fellow prisoners.

The guard was waving his clippers in my direction and, feeling I must not claim any more privileges, I surrendered to his blunt, unsympathetic instrument. There was no chair, so I bent my head to allow him to shear away my few remaining white hairs and watched as they gently floated down to join the curly black stubble at my feet.

My meek submission to this primitive barbering was greeted with vociferous protests of 'Aib!' (Shame) shouted so loudly, that the clippers faltered then stopped altogether. Having no wish to be left with a half-shorn skull, I insisted he should finish his work.

Shortly afterwards, I was summoned into one of the offices where a sergeant was gazing at a sheet of paper which, apparently, told him nothing except my name and the charges against me. Once again I had to go through the rigmarole of supplying full names of parents, date and place of birth, marital status and so forth. The sergeant, who had a few words of English, asked the questions. The answers were written down by an underling. About half-way through this catechism, Rachid bounced in unannounced. To my surprise, his arrival caused no comment, neither did his fierce protest at my loss of hair. When I convinced him my life had not been blighted by a prison haircut, he quietened down and interpreted for me, which speeded up the questioning.

When it was over everyone got ready to be marched off to their allocated quarters. The Citadel was divided into two main areas. To the east was *el Abraaj* (the Tower), occupied by short-term prisoners and those unlikely to be sentenced to longer than six months. The western side was known as *el Kalaa* (the Castle) and housed the medium-to-long-term offenders. I was surprised but relieved to learn Rachid was an inmate of *el Kalaa* (I wondered for how long) which was to be my destination. His dormitory was full, but he had used his influence to get me the last available bed in the one next door. Every dormitory in *el Kalaa* was overcrowded – he would explain why later. He had already asked someone in this room to look after me. I remember receiving this news rather ungraciously. I had no wish to be 'nannied' by someone pressured to do so.

I was the only new prisoner picked out for *el Kalaa*. The job of escorting me there was given to Rachid. My companions from the law courts were all earmarked for *el Abraaj*. I was now to be separated from those who had shown me so much kindness and this was painful. I asked quickly if I should see them again or would this be a final goodbye. I was assured we would meet often in the days to come. This was true for Hisham and a few others, but I was never to see Tariq and Karim again, nor was I ever to discover what had happened to them. There were rumours suggesting they had been transferred to another prison, others that they had been extradited to Iraq. Their disappearance remained, to my eternal regret, a mystery.

As we left the little office-enclave, I was startled to see Yussef, and two young men carrying my luggage, waiting for us. The men were 'service staff': prisoners who earned a small wage as porters and general handymen for the guards. They were always willing to fetch and carry in their spare time for those who had sufficient *baksheesh* to employ them.

The sight of my luggage reminded Rachid to tell me the guards had agreed to let me keep my nail-scissors and shaving-mirror. Normally these were confiscated because of the supposed danger of their being used as weapons. This was a bureaucratic nonsense because there were so many objects freely available in the prison capable of destroying human life – as was demonstrated all too frequently during my time there. Rachid said, tactfully, this concession was due to my being a foreigner, and my age. I felt sure the real reason had been *baksheesh*.

We approached the *Kalaa* by the only available route. With Yussef leading we ascended, in single file, a rickety steel staircase, bolted to one of the massive interior walls of the fort at an angle of forty-five degrees. The steps were narrow, badly worn and quivered alarmingly under our feet. On the outer edge was a fragile metal balustrade, broken in several places. We climbed to about sixty feet and followed a broad pathway along the top of the wall for several hundred yards. From this vantage point there was a splendid view over Damascus, whose lights seemed to twinkle away into infinity. I was not surprised to be told that prisoners had killed themselves by jumping from this spot into the depths of the courtyard.

Our descent into the *Kalaa* was easier: down a gradual slope to a long flight of steps; across the roof of what had been, centuries ago, the stables of the Citadel; a sharp left-turn to yet another descent, this time a short flight of stone steps ending in front of a white door in a wooden, one-storey building.

The door led to a small anteroom where, if one turned right – which was strictly forbidden – one entered the sleeping quarters of the *Kalaa* guards: half-a-dozen narrow steel bedsteads, usually buried under a clutter of rough, grey army blankets. A left-turn led to the guardroom and brought one immediately under the critical gaze of the duty-sergeant and his normal staff of four. This was the only method of gaining entry to the *Kalaa* courtyard and its dormitories.

The sergeant on duty at the time of my arrival was Abou Jaouar, a chubby little roly-poly of a man with shining dark eyes and a big black moustache. He leaned across the desk with a bright smile saying: '*Ahlan wa sahlan!*' and shook hands. He then began an animated conversation with Rachid and Yussef who took turns in translating bits into English

69

or French. Abou Jaouar wanted to know if I spoke Arabic. I told him my total vocabulary consisted of twenty words of *M'grebi* (North African) Arabic which few Syrians could understand. He asked if I liked Arabs. I said yes I did, but preferred not to be their prisoner. He laughed and went on to question me about the growing and marketing of hashish. I was to discover that many members of the Syrian police are eager to become involved in the import-export of this commodity.

The life I had led for the last few days had depleted a good deal of my nervous energy. Yussef, who had a sympathetic eye for human frailty, had noticed this, and suggested it was time to get me settled in.

One of the junior guards picked up a metal ring, almost the size of a child's hoop, with half-a-dozen huge keys suspended from it. After bidding Abou Jaouar goodnight, all of us, including the two young porters, trooped out into *Kalaa's* immense courtyard, illuminated by unmanned searchlights at the four corners. There was also a good deal of light from the barred windows of the many dormitories surrounding the court, all of one storey and built within the last thirty years against the walls.

We followed the guard, jangling his enormous keys, to the covered entrance of a dormitory. It bore some resemblance to a church porch, except it was made of metal and beneath it were twin gates, one behind the other, forged from steel bars. The inner gate had been amateurishly covered by a wide sheet of transparent plastic to protect those inside from winter weather.

While both gates were being unlocked, many of the room's inhabitants gathered to take a look at the new arrival. Some were wearing jeans, a few wore *galabiehs*, but the majority were in pyjamas. The spectacle of an elderly Englishman becoming one of their number was an obvious surprise but did not, for one moment, make them forget their natural good manners. Cries of '*Ahlan wa sahlan!*' 'Welcome! Welcome!' greeted me from all directions; and there were continuous exchanges of '*Salaam aliekum!*' and '*Aliekum salaam!*' with those who were with me.

As I walked apprehensively into this concentration of jet-black eyes, bright with curiosity, against a background of two-tier bunks arranged in rows, a tall, slim young man with a thin, faintly saturnine, face pushed through the crowd to shake hands with me. He smiled, revealing teeth as white and strong as an animal's.

Rachid, standing beside me, introduced him: 'This is Fahdi. He's

Lebanese and comes from Baalbek. He speaks no English but claims to know a little French. He'll do his best to look after you.'

Yussef and Rachid wished me goodnight, Rachid promising he would come in early the next morning. The porters had dumped my luggage inside the entrance and the small party went on its way.

Fahdi now told me in deplorable French (he was proud of his small knowledge and did not like to be corrected) how he had often seen me in Baalbek and knew me well by sight. He mentioned several of my friends and told me where he lived. I knew the neighbourhood well. It was on the northern outskirts, within sight of the big white villas of several important hash barons.

He seized my luggage and led me along the long, narrow room between two rows of bunks. Most prisoners had hung coloured sheets or towels over the frames of their bunks, presumably to give some illusion of privacy. Even the occupants on top had, with the aid of fine wire or string drawn tightly between the metal pillars at the corners of each bunk, draped material over these flimsy supports, tucking the ends under their mattresses. These formed a low screen for those lying flat on their backs and could be a protection against draughts, even if they could not isolate the occupants from the prison atmosphere.

Many were now lying or sitting on the bunks, reading books or newspapers. Some were listening to transistor radios, many tuned to different stations but all with the sound turned up as loudly as possible. A few were playing chess, many more were playing *dama* or draughts. As Fahdi and I walked past, they nearly all looked up and smiled, saying: 'Welcome! Welcome!'

He turned into the narrow space between two sets of bunks and, pointing to the upper berth on the right, said it was to be mine. There was a mattress, three neatly folded blankets and a pillow with a clean white cover. Fahdi explained that the pillow and one of the blankets were his, the rest had been provided by Rachid. Tomorrow, he said, he would take me over to *el Abraaj*, where I would be issued with blankets from the prison's supply. He had not been able to get them for me because it was a rule that one had to make a personal application and sign for whatever had been issued.

When I thanked him, saying I hoped he had not stripped his own bed for me, he told me not to worry. He had been three years in jail and had inherited several pillows and blankets from released prisoners.

I promised to return his property in the morning but he insisted I

71

must keep the pillow, because they were never supplied. Embarrassed by his generosity and shocked to hear he had been a prisoner for three years, I asked how long it would be before he was released.

Not for another three years, he told me. He had been caught by the customs in Latakia with 200 kilos of hashish in the truck he was taking to Cyprus. He was still angry with his employers for not paying enough in bribes to ensure his safety. He had been given five years and a fine of two hundred thousand Syrian pounds. Of course, he said, it was impossible for him to pay such a sum; he would have to spend an extra year in jail to purge his debt under Syrian law.

At the mention of fines in addition to prison sentences, I felt a chill of apprehension. Had I not been so weary, I would probably have asked more, but when Fahdi turned to introduce the bearded young man lolling on the berth beneath mine, working out a mathematical problem with a pencil, I did not pursue the subject.

Zayed was a Kurd, convicted of fomenting Kurdish opposition to the authorities in his native village north of Aleppo. It was difficult to believe him guilty of revolutionary activity; gentle in manner, with delicately expressive hands and a disconcerting cast in one eye, he took advantage of all the educational opportunities offered by the Syrian prison system.

He insisted on taking my luggage from Fahdi and put it on a wide shelf about six feet from the ground; these shelves extended almost the entire length of each wall; it was here that prisoners in top bunks kept most of their possessions. A window high above our heads, with a badly-fitting wooden frame, provided more fresh air on chilly nights than either Zayed or I appreciated.

Fahdi showed me a sink with a cold water tap close by; it was the only one in the room, to be used for all purposes. The lavatory was also not far away and was shared by all fifty of us. Its exterior resembled a yellow telephone-box with a small window of frosted glass. Built into an inner corner, it was kept surprisingly clean.

Everybody seemed to have their own primus stove and many were now brewing up tea or coffee. Zayed was doing so, and while I was reaching up, on tip-toe, to make my bed, he insisted on giving me several glasses of tea. He had a few words of English, but I had to use mime to make him understand how tired I was. I clambered awkwardly into my bunk: it was, I am afraid, some time before I acquired sufficient expertise to do this without making poor Zayed feel our two-tier combination was about to fall apart. He was very tolerant.

I relaxed on the comfortable mattress and pulled off all my clothing bar underbriefs, for the first time since my arrest. I stacked it on the shelf behind my head, and wrapping the blankets around me with a sigh of contentment, I composed myself for sleep.

At this moment Fahdi's face reappeared. '*Viens manger spaghetti avec moi et mes amis!*' He then added '*Tamam!*' – which can be roughly translated as '*très bon!*'

I thanked him for his kindness but said I was just too tired to eat. He offered to bring a plateful to me, but I begged him not to, saying all I needed was sleep. He said he understood and hoped I would sleep soundly. I closed my eyes and even all those portable radios could not keep me awake.

When I awoke the sun was shining through every window. I heard a murmur of voices and a rattle of keys as a small group of guards made their way round the square, opening the double-gates of the dormitories. A few of my neighbours seemed to be stirring; but the majority showed no sign of life.

Suddenly a hand reached up and seized one of mine. It was Rachid, wearing white silk pyjamas with a heavy blue jersey slung round his neck, his bare feet encased in soft, yellow leather *barbouches*.

'Would you like a shower?' he asked in almost a whisper.

'My God – yes!'

'Then come with me.'

I struggled into my trousers, slipped on my dirty shirt and dropped to the ground as gently as I could. Hastily, I collected clean clothes from my cases, as well as a towel and sponge-bag.

I followed Rachid across the courtyard to a low, tomb-like, windowless concrete building in the north-east corner. We were greeted by gusts of hot air and the low hum of an oil-fired boiler. Ahead was a corridor with five shower cubicles on each side, each concealed by long, greyish-white canvas curtains hanging from wire runners. Plaster walls, about seven feet high, separated the cubicles. All were occupied and the atmosphere was not unlike the steam-room of a Turkish bath.

A brown-skinned young man with shoulders like a bull and a noticeable limp, wearing jeans and an arsenic-green shirt so transparent it did nothing to conceal the abundant hair on his chest, emerged from the steam at the far end.

Rachid introduced him: 'Meet the bath-house boss! His name is Anwar and I know he'll be delighted if you talk to him in English. He speaks it quite well, himself.'

Shyly, Anwar gave me a bone-crushing handshake.

Putting his hand on the attendant's heavy shoulder, Rachid said: 'Mister Tony is an old friend of mine – always see he gets one of the good showers with plenty of hot water!' To me, he said: 'Anwar wants to become a student at the University of Damascus. Prisoners are allowed to do this if they pass the necessary examinations, and of course English is an important subject.'

Anwar, looking embarrassed, asked a question in Arabic.

Rachid, moving towards the door, replied in English. 'Not now, I'll have my shower later – and let Mister Tony settle down in our lovely holiday camp before you start bullying him to help you with your examinations!' He looked back at me. 'When you've finished come and join me in room 8. I'll have some orange-juice waiting!'

Anwar surprised me by speaking English with all the correct vowel sounds, contrasting strangely with his almost Quasimodo-like appearance and native Arabic growl. 'Please take no notice of what Rachid said about me. He talks much nonsense. I am sorry to keep you waiting, but the water is hotter and the jets are more powerful in the showers furthest from the door. One will become vacant in just a moment.' He pointed to a bright scarlet, three-legged plastic stool which he kept in the corridor for his own use. 'Please to sit down.'

I said I was quite happy to stand, and congratulated him on his English.

'It has always been my ambition to go to England,' he said, 'that is why I wish to make special study of your language.'

We were interrupted by a voice from one of the showers asking for something.

Anwar opened a metal box, the sort that normally contains household tools, and took out what appeared to be an old safety-razor and a much-used blade. He fitted the one into the other, limped along the passage and halted in front of a shower-curtain. This was pulled aside, just enough for a hand to emerge and accept the razor with a murmured '*Shukran*'.

Arabs who observe the commandments of the *Koran* regularly shave their pubes and armpits. In prisons, where the possession of a razor-blade is forbidden, the chief bath-attendant is allowed to loan them, together with a razor if needed.

This simple method of keeping the body free from lice is hardly necessary now the majority of Arabs are no longer nomads in waterless deserts. But the habit remains among those who take their religion seriously. The practice has the advantage of almost totally eliminating body odour.

An elderly, bearded Syrian wearing a blue and white *galabieh* came out from one of the cubicles carrying a plastic soap-box and a safety-razor. He fumbled for a moment with the razor, extracting the blade which he presented to Anwar together with a couple of coins (Syrian pounds). Anwar thanked him, and carefully placed all these objects into different compartments in his precious box. He now seized a long-handled mop, swabbed the walls and floor of the vacated shower, and ushered me into it with the grave dignity of a major-domo, saying: 'Please excuse me for having detained you. I hope you will have a good shower.' He insisted I take his stool into the cubicle.

In spite of Anwar's swabbing, the grey walls still looked unpleasantly slimy. There was nowhere to hang clothes or towel except over the wire holding up the curtain. I was glad to put my clean underclothes on the stool. There was no place for the soap, so I balanced it on the tap. However, the water was gloriously hot, and to wash away the sweat-impregnated filth of the last seven days was a wonderful sensation.

I could hear Anwar limping up and down between the showers, mopping up in each as it became vacant, selling small tablets of soap for 50 piastres and handing out razor-blades, insisting on the return of the latter before the borrower was allowed to leave the bath-house.

I was to find out that our bath-attendant was a Palestinian, a country boy born in a small village near Hebron. His family had been deprived of their land by the Israelis and had taken refuge in Syria. Doubtless due to that capacity for violence that can so quickly rise to the surface in any Arab community, he had, at the age of nineteen, when alone in his parents' house, hurled a grenade out of a window into a crowd of people he assumed to be enemies of his family and about to attack him. I was told the explosion killed two and injured more than half-a-dozen. Anwar himself never mentioned this event to me and I was too reticent ever to question him about it. The damage done to his right foot was a permanent legacy of this affair. Everybody knew he had been sentenced to life imprisonment which, in Syria, means twenty-five years.

When he had arrived in *el Kalaa* seven years before, he was unable to read or write a word. He had made such good use of the prison's educational facilities, he could now not only read Arabic, but write it so well he had become almost a professional scribe for illiterate prisoners. Even more surprising was his extensive vocabulary of English, doubtless due to the help of a young English smuggler only recently released after almost three years in *el Kalaa*.

The feeling of relief at being clean again and rid of the clothing that had glued itself tightly, night and day, to my aged flesh for nearly a week, was marvellous, and a sensation I had not experienced since the end of the Second World War. I tried to press a couple of Syrian pounds (at that time the equivalent of forty pence) into Anwar's hand. He firmly refused it, saying he never took money from friends and hoped I would, in time, consider him a friend. He explained every dormitory was officially assigned a day a week for a visit to the bath-house. But the rules were not rigorously applied and whenever I wanted a shower he would do his best to fit me in. 'In summer,' he said, 'you will want two showers every day!' And, of course, he was right.

I thanked him and walked out into the mild, bland sunlight. The snowstorms of the previous week seemed hardly believable. The courtyard was no longer empty. At least fifty prisoners, most in couples or groups of up to half-a-dozen, were taking an early morning stroll up and down the yard. It was the custom in the *Kalaa* to take one's exercise in straight lines, never in circles.

I noticed for the first time that the topmost branches of several eucalyptus trees in the parade ground outside were just visible across the wall at the southern end of the courtyard. Something about their yellow-green foliage gave me a feeling of reassurance, possibly because I had spent much of my childhood in a Provençal garden where such trees grew all round the perimeter. I stood still, looking up at them and sniffing the fresh air which that morning bore a hint of spring.

Suddenly I was aware of a lone figure coming towards me. Apart from myself, he appeared to be the only prisoner in the courtyard who was on his own. He was lean and long-limbed, the outline of his body showing clearly through the clinging folds of his *galabieh* which seemed to be soaking wet. As he approached I noticed his eyes – intensely unhappy and almost sightless with concern for himself. He was obviously suffering some sort of mental breakdown. He had no intention of speaking to me, his loose mouth was busy talking to himself. He did not even see me, I just happened to be in his path. I moved aside and as he came almost level with me, I saw he was holding something … it looked like a small box … it was a small box … a box of matches …

He was alongside me when his fumbling fingers struck a match. There was an instantaneous explosion as if a giant gas-jet had been ignited – the man immediately became a flaming torch, the heat singeing my eyebrows. An overpowering smell made it obvious his *galabieh* had been soaked not in water, as I had assumed, but in paraffin.

I expected a scream. There was none. He dropped to the ground with no sound save a sort of stifled sob, the blue flames continuing to hiss and flutter for a brief moment as the charred body lost its resemblance to flesh and blood.

There were immediate shouts of alarm all around the square and men rushed from dormitories with blankets and rugs which they wrapped swiftly and gently around the scorched object. It was useless. There was no longer any sound or movement from what had been, only a moment ago, a living, breathing human being. Everyone in the yard gathered round, clucking like barnyard fowls inspecting a juicy cabbage-stalk. Two junior guards approached. No doubt the incident had been seen through the big windows of the guardroom which overlooked the yard. They made no effort to hurry. Behind them sauntered a couple of service staff, one carrying a folded canvas stretcher.

Strong fingers gripped my elbow. 'There is nothing we can do to help,' said Rachid's voice. 'Come and drink that fruit juice!'

After dumping my dirty underwear on my bed I followed him into his room. Now wearing the blue jersey with a pair of immaculate white jeans, he pointed to two large glass jugs on a collapsible metal table beside his bed. One was filled to the brim with orange juice, the other with apple juice. I chose the orange. He handed me a large tumbler-full.

Sitting opposite Rachid was a pear-shaped, middle-aged man, wearing an eye-catching suit in a draught-board check pattern. Rachid introduced him as the chief of the room – an expression I had not heard before.

The chief favoured me with a brief flash of gold-studded teeth before exchanging a few sentences with Rachid – the subject was obviously the self-induced funeral pyre whose paraffin smell was still in my nostrils. Neither seemed very concerned about it. When he had gone I asked if this sort of suicide happened frequently.

'Not every week – not even every month – but several times a year, perhaps.'

'I could see from the man's expression he was suffering from a mental breakdown. He should have been in hospital.'

'It's possible he was better off in here.'

I felt this might be an implied criticism of Syrian hospitals, so I did not pursue the subject. 'Where did he get the paraffin?' I asked.

'Several litres are issued to each prisoner every month. How otherwise could we keep our *barbouas* alight?' With the toe of his slipper he pointed at a primus stove, just visible under his bed, and to the big metal can, nearby, which clearly contained fuel. 'Almost everybody has a *barboua*. Without them we shouldn't be able to cook or keep warm.' He pointed to the bunk the chief had just vacated. 'Do sit down.'

I suggested the chief might object to my sitting on his bed which produced a snort of contempt.

'What is he? Just a government official caught with his hands in the till! Don't worry about him, we much prefer wicked old smugglers like yourself! Anyway, the bed is Yussef's, who apologises for his absence, but he had to go to work early this morning.'

I expressed regret at missing him, then said: 'I didn't know these dormitories had chiefs. Are they similar to the 'capos' in German concentration camps?'

'Possibly. Remember I wasn't born at the time of the last world war. All the rooms have chiefs. They're responsible for seeing everything is kept clean and tidy. They're also supposed to keep order and prevent fights. If they keep having to call the guards to support them they quickly lose the job.'

'Has my room got a chief?'

'It has indeed. He was in the crowd at the entrance last night. Elderly, pale and flabby – but much tougher than he looks, usually wears a striped *galabieh*. Speaks quite good German – worked there for some years and has never forgiven the British or the Americans for defeating Hitler. You can guess why!'

Mention of Germany reminded me at once of Kurt who must now be languishing under the law courts. When I told Rachid about him he said, 'I will find out when he'll be arriving and we'll go to the main gate and meet him.'

My thanks were brushed aside. 'He was carrying hashish obtained from my in-laws – of course I shall do all I can to make things easier for him.'

He suggested we take a walk before eating. In the courtyard every trace of the fiery immolation had gone. It might never have happened.

This great open rectangle was about seventy yards long by thirty wide. The jerry-built one-storey dormitories encircling it had been erected during the early years of this century, and appeared to have been neglected ever since. Rachid confirmed almost every roof leaked in several places. It was fortunate Syria has a dry climate.

The rooms were numbered clockwise from 1 to 10. They varied in size. Some were occupied by fewer than twenty prisoners, others by as many as 140 or more. The only exceptions were three small rooms in the south wall. Instead of bunks, these contained school desks and a blackboard, and were in daily use as classrooms.

The guardroom was in the north-west corner, a kind of buffer state between rooms 1 and 10. Behind it was a small open space containing a trio of punishment cells. These looked more like cages in an inferior zoo than places for human habitation. Syrians do not confine the inmates of prisons in small cells except as a punishment for breaches of regulations. Well-behaved offenders are always kept in large barrack-like rooms which combine the functions of day-room and dormitory.

In the centre at the northern end of the yard were two free-standing market stalls, very close together. One was operated by a butcher who was allowed to keep his refrigerator plugged into the prison's unreliable electricity supply. His meat was usually goat; occasionally there would be a small quantity of liver from an unspecified animal, so stringy and fibrous it was more suitable for repairing shoes than for eating. The other stall was mainly a greengrocer's where one could buy fruit and vegetables, also eggs, and such things as cheap quality towels, plastic sandals, cotton pyjamas, inferior writing paper, ball-point pens and Syrian-made flashlight batteries so lacking in power they provided, even when new, only a meagre glimmer of light for a torch and refused absolutely to operate an electric shaver.

There was also a laundry, run by a trio of prisoners, in a small basement between rooms 3 and 4. It was equipped with two ordinary domestic washing-machines and an electric iron. The method for drying anything was to hang it from wires criss-crossing the yard. For nine months of every year in the Syrian climate, washing hung up outside will dry within an hour, so this was no problem.

A few yards from the southern end was a very insecure-looking shanty, commonly referred to by those who spoke English as the cafeteria. Whenever there was a high wind, part of it could be guaranteed to fall down. It had counters on two sides from which hot and cold drinks were dispensed. It was surrounded by an extensive clutter of green and orange plastic chairs, but seldom enough for its many customers who, if they were wise, would bring their own camp-stools or cushions. Prisoners would sit and talk here all morning while quaffing tumblers of apple or orange juice, heavily sweetened with sugar. Only eccentrics like myself preferred their drinks unsweetened, and I had to issue firm instructions when ordering. These fresh fruit drinks were too expensive for many. The less well-off would consume an endless sequence of 'sludge' coffee or syrupy tea served in tiny cups without handles, costing only the smallest of piastre coins.

As we walked, Rachid explained the laundry, the market stalls and the cafeteria were all leased to individual prisoners by the authorities. The leases were due for renewal or transfer every six months. To obtain one it was necessary to put down a sizeable deposit and to guarantee that a stipulated percentage of the takings would be paid into the coffers of the Ministry of Justice every week. Failure to do so would mean the sum would be deducted from the deposit when the tenancy ended. Permission to take over these enterprises was usually given only to prisoners of proven solvency. Foreigners, and those convicted of drug offences, were ruled out.

To give the advantage of running a small business to a minority of well-heeled convicts seemed strange; especially in a country which takes pride in referring to itself as a democratic socialist republic. I said so to Rachid, who shrugged.

'We are a poor country and cannot finance welfare schemes out of taxation as you can in Europe. The average salary in Syria is too low for any sort of income tax to be imposed upon it. So we encourage small businesses and take what we can from them.'

More prisoners had now come into the sunshine. Those who were not around the cafeteria took up positions along the western wall, having brought rugs and cushions to add to their comfort. To sit in the direct rays of the sun was a pleasant experience during the winter months, and would remain so until the beginning of May.

After that, the increasing heat drove us in a body to the very limited shade on the other side – shade which grew less each day as the sun rose higher in the summer sky. In July and August this was reduced to a strip not more than six inches wide that vanished altogether soon after 9 AM. From that moment onwards, if there was no room under the flimsy cafeteria awning, one was compelled to roast in the savage Syrian sun, which could be a real hazard even for hardened Arab skins.

I realised I was an object of considerable interest, especially to those at the side of the yard, many of whom were making small objects with brightly coloured beads. But as Rachid had drawn my arm through his as we walked – a typical Arab gesture of friendship – they were too well-mannered to break in to what they obviously regarded as a private conversation.

Their clothing varied enormously, from *galabiehs*, usually white, but sometimes in pale blue or green, or striped, to jeans with shirt and sweater, usually brilliant in colour. A small minority wore city suits, sometimes complete with tie and waistcoat, and a few always carried a walking-stick. On their heads many wore the ubiquitous *keffieh*: that all-purpose square yard of Manchester cotton in a black-and-white or red-and-white check, usually with bobbles at the edge. It can be put to a variety of uses. It can be wound round the head like a turban; a length can be pulled across the eyes and nose if sand should be blowing; it can be wrapped round the neck as a muffler with the ends trailing below the waist; it can be taken off and used as a tablecloth or folded to make a pillow. Most wore plastic sandals; others preferred the soft yellow *barbouches* that wearers always convert into 'mules' by crushing the back of the heel under their feet.

As Rachid and I paced up and down he fed me gobbets of information.

Rooms 7, 8 and 9 he explained (I was in 9, he in 8) were normally occupied only by those taking advantage of the educational opportunities. To enable them to go to their classes (between 9 AM and 1 PM) the rooms were left open all morning. Prisoners in the other rooms were thrown outside soon after 8 AM and had to remain in the open air until early afternoon. Only the chief of each room, and not more than two of the room's service staff (responsible for cleanliness, distribution of rations, etc.) were allowed to remain inside, or to come and go. The only exceptions were those with a medical certificate from the prison doctor – never easy to obtain – which permitted them to spend the morning on their beds.

Everyone else was locked out until just before 2 PM when the duty-sergeant, flanked by two junior guards, would conduct a roll-call at the entrance to each room. It was the custom to line up in single file and answer to one's name on re-entering. Those who had been longest in the room were the first to have their names called, recent arrivals were always at the tail-end of the roster. On rare occasions when there was a heavy downpour of rain or, as had happened the previous week, a blizzard had blotted out the landscape for several hours, permission was given by the governor for all rooms to be opened up.

Once the roll-calls were over and all gates locked (and this included the privileged rooms 7, 8 and 9) prisoners would not be allowed out again until the following morning. The few exceptions were members of the volleyball or basketball teams and those who had the governor's blessing to practise karate.

I asked Rachid why I had been allocated a bed in room 9. Surely nobody thought I was a candidate for education? Privately, I wondered what *he* was doing in 8.

'You're there because the whole accommodation plan in *Kalaa* has been temporarily upset by extensive repairs to the roof of room 2 – the room reserved for hashish offenders, which is where you should be. At the moment, it's empty. For months, big lumps of masonry have been falling from the ceiling, causing minor injuries. While it is being repaired all the occupants have been assigned to other rooms. Most of them are sleeping on the floor.'

'In that case why have I got a bed?'

He grinned. 'Because you're an old man – and a foreigner!'

I guessed his influence and probable *baksheesh* were more likely reasons.

'Room 2 is unique in this prison,' he went on, 'because all the others are referred to by their numbers. Room 2 is known to everyone as *Hofra*.

I had not heard this word before. I asked its meaning.

With a single snort of a laugh, he said: 'It means the Pit! Come – I'll show you why.'

We were approaching the northern end of the courtyard. Instead of turning, Rachid continued ahead. I followed him through an archway; the steel twin-gates beneath it were wide open. We descended two short flights of narrow, badly worn steps into semi-darkness. We felt our way along a short tunnel with a roof so low we had to bend almost double to get through. Rachid straightened up and halted. I stood beside him.

So this was *Hofra* – the Pit. We had emerged into the centre of a dimly-lighted subterranean vault, about a hundred feet long and less than twenty wide. It occupied all the space below the north wall. The only illumination came from a dozen or so bulbs suspended on long single strands of wire from the curving roof at least twenty-five feet high. There were three square holes in this roof, one at each end and one in the centre. Each hole was only just large enough to contain a medium-size metal extractor-fan, which obscured almost all the meagre amount of daylight that might otherwise have penetrated. I was later to learn only one of these fans ever worked and even it often broke down.

Half-a-dozen workmen in plaster-splashed *keffiehs* and overalls were mixing cement by hand and carrying it up rickety ladders to thrust into cavities in the stone buttresses supporting the roof. Quite large boulders had obviously fallen out of these crumbling *points d'appui* and dropped more than twenty feet on to prisoners. It was surprising there had been no serious injuries.

'What d'you think of it?' Rachid was gazing around. 'They say there used to be a large entrance at the western end, but it was blocked up when the fortress became a prison. A thousand years ago this was probably a giant stable.'

'I wouldn't like to keep my horses here.'

'You'll be here yourself before long!'

He called out something to a workman aloft, who answered briefly. 'He says it should be finished in about two weeks. When they've completed the repairs they're going to whitewash the whole place.'

Extending for about seven feet from the walls towards the centre-line of this tubular cavern were two platforms of solid concrete, about eighteen inches high, leaving only a narrow pathway along the centre and a small gap on the south side for the entrance.

I asked Rachid if bunks were placed on the top of these raised surfaces.

'No. No bunks are allowed in *Hofra*. Just a row of mattresses, each touching its neighbour. There will be just room for your luggage against the wall behind your head. Such things as plates, dishes and a *barboua* can be kept in orange boxes at your feet.'

'Where does one get the boxes?'

'From the greengrocer's stall. Take your pick – they throw them away every day.'

I looked at *Hofra*'s vast, gloomy emptiness and wondered how I would survive when it was filled with characters to whom I might be as strange as a visitor from Mars.

I noticed there were two taps above a low earthenware sink, jutting out from the wall at the eastern end. I guessed this would be the only water supply. I did not know then that one tap would be frequently out of order! Close by was a windowless, metal cabin, to which one gained access up some steps and through a rusty door. I knew at once this would be the one and only wc.

'How many of us will be in here?'

'Never less than a hundred, usually more. If the number goes over 120, the new arrivals have to doss down along the central passage until there is a vacancy on either platform.'

It was a relief to crouch down once again and follow Rachid through the short tunnel and up into the sunshine.

I think it was at this moment I first noticed the catwalk along the top of the walls surrounding the courtyard. Policemen with small, Czech-made sub-machine-guns slung casually over their shoulders were sauntering about on it. Two were sitting on the parapet overlooking the yard, gazing down upon us with expressions of glassy-eyed, bored indifference. On the higher ramparts to the north-east were more armed police. They had a watching brief over the whole Citadel. The majority of prisoners having been locked out of their rooms, there were now about five hundred in the yard.

Because of an obvious distaste for the crowd, Rachid insisted we return to his room. As we entered we passed a small, gnome-like prisoner on his knees washing the floor. Rachid gave him a peremptory command to make us coffee. The little man hastily dropped his floor-cloth into the bucket and hurried away. We heard a primus stove being primed and lighted.

Having spent many months up-country in Lebanon over a period of several years, I was accustomed to getting up early and consuming an endless succession of tiny cups of coffee, alternating with large tumblers of fruit juice, until about ten o'clock when I would sit down with my host and his family to the first meal of the day.

Apart from the gnome, room 8 appeared to be empty. It was obvious the school classes had begun. I looked at Rachid, sprawling comfortably on the bunk opposite, and wondered again why he was here. In many ways he seemed to be just another prisoner and yet the guards were almost reverential towards him.

Having no previous experience of jail, I wondered if it would be a breach of prison etiquette to ask. My curiosity got the better of me and I chanced a leading question.

'How long,' I said, 'will you be remaining here?'

He frowned. 'Only a few more weeks.' His hands played nervously for a moment with the hem of his jersey. 'Have you seen my wife's family recently?'

'Not during the last two months.'

'Then you didn't know I'm here because of a misunderstanding?'

Puzzled, I raised my eyebrows.

'Yes, it has all been a big mistake and I shall be released before the end of the month.' He looked about the room uneasily, as if to make sure there were no eavesdroppers. The only sound was the hiss from the *barboua*.

Almost in a whisper he said: 'You know I work for military intelligence, don't you?'

'You told me so yourself – a long time ago.'

'You won't speak about it to the others?'

'Of course not.'

He looked relieved. 'Some day, maybe, I shall be able to tell you why I am here.'

'I'll look forward to that. For my own sake I'm naturally – selfishly, of course – glad you're here.' I was obviously being told not to pry any more.

'There should be just enough time for me to see you comfortably settled in *Hofra* before I go.'

'Is it possible for anybody to be comfortable in *Hofra*?'

'Who is talking about *Hofra*?' A strange voice was calling in English with what sounded like the faintest of French accents. A pale young man of hardly more than twenty advanced towards us.

Rachid's expressive eyes surveyed the newcomer without enthusiasm. 'Jean-Pierre, you can always be guaranteed to appear immediately I've asked the service staff to make coffee!'

The new arrival ran immensely long fingers through his close-cut blond thatch. '*Mon cher* Rachid, I know you to be a most hospitable man and I, of course, am naturally lucky!'

'You weren't so lucky when the police caught you with fifty kilos of hash in your car!' Turning to me, Rachid said: 'Meet Jean-Pierre, who was not a customer of my wife's family but of one of their competitors in the Beka'a Valley. At present the only European, apart from yourself, in this prison.'

'It may be selfish of me,' said Jean-Pierre, as we shook hands, 'but I am simply delighted to see you here.'

'Perhaps you've already met in Baalbek?' said Rachid.

'Unfortunately, no,' said Jean-Pierre, 'but I heard much about Monsieur Tony while I was in the Valley.'

'You are a Frenchman?' I said confidently.

'Yes. I am *Niçois*.'

'Nice,' I said, 'is a city I've known since I was five years old. My mother worked there for the French Red Cross during the First World War, and I was with her. Afterwards, until the outbreak of the Second World War, she made her home near Vence.'

His eyes widened with surprise. 'Then you speak French?'

Rachid interrupted: 'Yes he does – but don't encourage him, because it cuts me out of the conversation – something I experienced last night when I introduced him to Yussef!'

'Ah, Yussef!' exclaimed Jean-Pierre, settling himself on a stool conveniently placed between the bunks. 'A most charming person – so civilised, so different to the majority in this prison.'

Rachid said irritably: 'Haven't the majority always treated you with the consideration we usually give to foreigners in our midst?'

Before Jean-Pierre could answer, the gnome-like man reappeared with a tin tray.

Rachid poured some of the cardomom-scented coffee into one of the cups and handed it to the gnome with a gesture of dismissal. As he handed cups to us, he said again to Jean-Pierre: 'Most people have been helpful to you, surely?'

'We always have with us those whose method of settling an argument is to batter their opponent's head with a flaming *barboua*!'

'Not many.'

'Too many. In every room there are those who behave like that, and in some they are in a majority.'

Rachid poured coffee for himself. 'Jean-Pierre, rightly or wrongly, you've got yourself a reputation for taking everything that's offered to you and giving very little in return.'

'What else can they expect? I am poor!'

'It's not a question of money – it's your attitude towards us. Over and over again you can be heard using the expression *les indigènes*. I admit my knowledge of French is poor, but even I can understand the enormous contempt implied by that word.'

'It is not an insult – it is an exact translation of the English word native.'

'In French it has much more offensive implications.'

'You are over-sensitivie. Why do you think I have been attending classes for months with *les indigènes* who have never been to school? Because I want very much to learn your language.'

With a half-smile, Rachid said: 'For commercial advantages! When you're released you hope to get a well-paid job in the Gulf States.'

'Is that a criticism?'

'No. As long as you don't pretend it's because of your wish for a greater understanding of the Arab peoples!'

'Your trouble, Rachid, is your inability to forget I am a Frenchman and the French were once masters of Syria.' He turned towards me, saying: 'How have you been treated up to now? Did they beat you at the police station?'

'No. Did they beat *you*?'

'Every day – until I was taken to the *palais de justice*.'

'Why?'

'To make me confess where I had bought the hashish.'

'But you bought it in the Lebanon. Why didn't you say so?'

'Because I denied knowing anything about it. I said I was only interested in the Greek and Roman ruins in such places as Palmyra and Baalbek.'

I remembered how I'd reacted to Heliotrope Tie at the airport. 'Too many of us have tried that sort of gambit,' I suggested.

'I considered my story a good one. I said my car had never been garaged at night – always left unguarded in cities and in villages. You must know car theft here is not the problem it is in Europe. I insisted the hashish must have been hidden in the car, by strangers, without my knowing anything about it.'

'How were these mythical strangers supposed to reclaim it?'

'By following me back to Europe where they would remove it without my knowledge. I told them I had been followed everywhere by a white Peugeot 504!'

'And they didn't believe you?'

'Unfortunately, no. They went on beating me in the hope of finding out the truth. I never told them.'

'Where were you caught?'

'Here in Damascus.'

Rachid gave one of his sudden snorts of laughter. 'Can you believe it? He'd stuffed some of the hash inside the casing of the windscreen-wiper's motor! And there was a lot more behind the inner lining of the doors. He admits it wasn't too well wrapped. The weather was hot and you could even smell the stuff from outside the car! A traffic-cop put his head through the driver's window during a traffic jam and was almost stoned on the spot! Yet this boy went on claiming he didn't know what was hidden inside.'

Looking sheepish, the young Frenchman shrugged his shoulders. 'I had no experience of transporting hashish – I did not know what else to say. But there were twenty more kilos, welded professionally, between the luggage boot and the back seat. This, I believe, has still not been discovered. When I was sentenced, the judge insisted the car must be confiscated. I am told it is now being regularly used by senior police officers here in Damascus.' He laughed. 'Fat chief inspectors are being driven about the city, unaware of the twenty kilos of hash behind them. '*Ah, ils sont tous des conards!*' This outburst seemed to restore his good humour.

'When were you arrested?' I asked.

'On the tenth of July, last year.'

'And you've been to court – your trial is over?'

'I was sentenced just a month ago.'

'And for how long?'

'Two and a half years – which means twenty-three months if I am lucky and get what everybody calls "quarter time".'

'Why should luck play a part in getting you remission if you're legally entitled to it?'

He gave me a pitying smile. 'Syrian bureaucracy and their willingness to accept *douceurs* is the reason. If you have money and know the right people, you will get it. If you haven't either of these *avantages*—' He broke off, looking defensively at Rachid, who obviously did not feel it was a statement worth disputing.

I said: 'Fahdi told me, last night, it's possible to get a heavy fine as well as a prison sentence. Did that happen to you?'

Jean-Pierre shook his head. 'No, but it might still happen. A separate *tribunal* is operated by the customs service who occasionally – not always, but from time to time – summon people like ourselves months after we have been sentenced. They then impose a heavy fine, claiming it to be customs duty on the hashish we imported into Syria.'

'But why accuse us of *importing* the stuff? It was only in transit through this country. Surely none of us intended selling it here?'

'*Bien sûr*, but that seems to make no difference. The fines are always enormous and, if you cannot pay, it means an extra year on your sentence.

'I'd never heard about these fines until last night when Fahdi mentioned—'

Rachid interrupted, saying: 'Fahdi was sentenced in Latakia, where these fines seem to be automatic. In Damascus, it's a gamble whether the customs get hold of you or not.'

I felt the workings of Syrian-type socialism were distinctly odd, its legal set-up being so much kinder to the rich than to the poor.

Fahdi, as if on cue, thrust his head through the entrance to tell me breakfast was ready next door, and would I please come and eat.

As I got to my feet, Jean-Pierre said to me: 'As I came in here I heard you say something about *Hofra*. Believe me, it is not so terrible down there. I am temporarily in one of the smaller rooms at ground level, and I don't like it so well.'

I was far from confident I would ever share his opinion of life in that great tomb, but was grateful for his attempt to reassure me.

I followed Fahdi to room 9 where I learned he always ate in the company of three friends and insisted I must join them for all my meals. Their 'dining area' was the small space between their bunks; these were tucked in a corner against the rear wall.

A white, soft plastic tablecloth, with a printed border of improbable-looking scarlet daisies was laid over a small square of beige carpeting, on which all five of us sat to eat, cross-legged.

The carpet belonged to Badr, a sinuous, flashing-eyed gipsy jailed for theft. He was a warm-hearted youth who always had plenty of money; very much a dandy and the possessor of many lightweight suits in pale blue, cream and lime green; often changing his clothes several times a day. He took great care of his extensive wardrobe, which he kept, neatly folded, between layers of tissue paper in cheap brown fibre suitcases.

It was generally known that Badr's wealth was provided by his six sisters who, wearing headscarves and long, flowing skirts of dazzling colours, regularly gyrated around the area of the Damascus central post office, thrusting their upturned palms at everybody, imperiously demanding money. Men of my age they normally addressed as *Hajji* – a form of deference inferring that the prospective giver of alms had made the pilgrimage to Mecca. If, however, a modest coin was not forthcoming, their attitude would change abruptly – the hand would become a predatory claw, seizing the *Hajji*'s sleeve and shaking it with such ferocity, the stitching would sometimes burst open.

Of the other two members of the Fahdi quartet, one was Sultan, a Lebanese in his early twenties with large, soft brown eyes and a full sensual mouth. He had a splendid collection of rainbow-coloured shirts, which he left lasciviously unbuttoned as far as his navel, revealing an ivory smooth chest, surprisingly hairless for an Arab. He had been arrested at the frontier of the Beirut–Damascus highway, with a small quantity of hashish taped to his body. He had been the victim of a much older man who had persuaded him to take the risk for a very small reward. The boy had never received the promised cash because the customs noticed a suspicious bulge around his slim waist and this had resulted in a sentence of eighteen months.

The other member of the coterie was Nasir, a tall, immensely dignified Palestinian of nearly thirty. A reserved, undemanding man who usually spoke only in monosyllables, he spent much of his time gazing at snap-shots of his four children, and playing with the olive-wood beads of his *mousbaha* (worry beads). Nasir had been – it was whispered confidentially in my ear – accused of espionage. I never discovered the details of his case and on this first morning I was still much too innocent to appreciate the awful implications behind this statement. I failed to realise they were telling me a hangman's noose was, metaphorically, suspended over Nasir's head.

I squatted on the floor with these companions and gazed hungrily at the food. There was a large, deliciously runny omelette, a lot of smaller dishes containing goats' cheese, sardines, homus and honey, and a great pile of pitta bread, every piece approximately the shape, size and colour of a large English pancake.

Realising they had waited for me, I helped myself quickly to bread and broke off pieces with my right hand, using them to scoop up tiny portions of the omelette. Most Arabs, unless Europeanised, scorn knives and forks and, anyway, such potential weapons were not permitted. Spoons, however, were allowed, and often in the early days of my imprisonment were pressed upon me by those who assumed I had not yet mastered the art of using fingers and bread. I detected relief amongst Fahdi's friends when they saw they would not have to give me lessons in Arab table manners.

Having eaten, we queued for the room's only tap, where we washed our hands and used our fingers to clean our mouths and teeth.

We returned to our corner where Fahdi, while we were eating, had placed a teapot on a lighted *barboua*. He was now heaping spoonfuls of tea and sugar into the boiling pot. Arabs do not make tea in the British fashion by pouring water on dry leaves. They put the tea and sugar (far too much of the latter for most European tastes) directly into the boiling water and brew it for several minutes. In North Africa they frequently infuse mint into the mixture, but this seldom occurs in the Middle East.

After a few minutes, Fahdi turned out the primus, stirred the contents of the teapot with a long-handled spoon and poured sticky-sweet liquid into glasses. Meanwhile, the rest of us gathered up the uneaten food and put it carefully in a wooden box with ventilation holes in its lid. The bread was put in a plastic carrier-bag. Our dirty dishes were piled up ready for the service staff (there were two) to collect for washing.

As we sipped, I thanked Fahdi – who could be said to combine the functions of mess secretary and cook – for allowing me to join his group.

I was soon to discover this young man had a streak of vanity which took the unusual form of wishing to be considered better educated than, in fact, he was. He had impressed on his close companions in *el Kalaa* – none of whom spoke a word of any language except Arabic – his exceptional fluency in French. This was a bluff. He had a very small vocabulary and was always reluctant to admit, especially if his friends were nearby, that he hadn't understood something said to him in this language. Although this sometimes led to misunderstanding between us, I always had the most amicable feelings towards him from the moment he welcomed me so hospitably on my first evening. He treated me with a sympathetic consideration few young Englishmen would give to a stranger of my age; but to those of his own generation – Arab or European – he was capable of baring his teeth in a tigerish fury that could be alarming.

He was one of many children of a farm worker and had been brought up in a small, single-storey cottage on the northern outskirts of Baalbek; today, in spite of its fascinating history, little more than a large dusty village, clustered around the splendid ruins of its Greek and Roman temples. Its situation, however, is magnificent – between two mountain ranges whose peaks I have seen snow-capped at midsummer. His education consisted of little more than a sporadic attendance, for a few years, at a Koranic village school. Nevertheless, his intelligence, capacity for hard work, good looks and, possibly animal magnetism, had helped him become a trusted employee of a Valley landowner whose chief interest was the cultivation and marketing of hashish.

Fahdi was ambitious and wanted to buy land. He had been delighted to be given the task of driving secondhand cars across the Lebanese frontier to Latakia. Here, they were loaded into ships usually destined for Barcelona, where the attitude of the Catalonian customs towards vehicles arriving from Levantine ports was, from my personal observation, casual beyond belief. Unfortunately for poor Fahdi, the Latakia customs became suspicious of his frequent appearances, always with a different car or truck for export. One day they pounced, took the vehicle to pieces, and found what they were looking for. Fahdi had, unwisely, assumed the *baksheesh* his boss was paying would guarantee his safety. Unfortunately, it proved insufficient.

Over tea, I questioned him about how much I should contribute towards the cost of the food. I was anxious to pay my share and also needed advice about how much I should tip the servicemen.

When Fahdi, at last, understood my questions, he explained that the eggs for the omelette had been supplied from prison rations; the homus and honey were gifts from visitors; only the tin of sardines had been bought from the courtyard stall. He added that Rachid had given him more than enough to cover any expense on my behalf for the next few weeks. This did not entirely surprise me. The Lebanese mafia has the habit of looking after its own. He also reminded me that our group would shortly be broken up because three of us would be moving into *Hofra*. Badr and Nasir, not being guilty of a hashish offence, would remain in 9. As for the service staff, they received a weekly salary of a few piastres from the authorities, but it was customary to give each about five Syrian pounds at the end of each week. I made a mental note to remember that, in Muslim countries, the week ends on a Thursday, not a Saturday.

92

During the next few days I discovered Fahdi had a remarkable talent for producing an appetising meal from the most unlikely ingredients. Although I enjoy good food, years spent at English boarding schools still enable me to eat almost anything without complaint.

Bread, great quantities of it, was delivered to each dormitory every morning soon after 7 AM. The servicemen distributed it immediately: the official ration was two slabs, but it was always possible to get more if you were really hungry.

Just before 2 PM – immediately after we had been locked up after exercise – the only hot meal of the day, supplied by the kitchen in the *Abraaj*, would be brought in giant, lidless pails. Once again the contents would be dished out by the service staff who would move slowly up and down the room, ladling the food into our receptacles – usually cheap tin bowls.

There was an awful monotony about these midday meals. Rice (such glutinous white rice) was the basis; cooked in heavy oil and mixed with either broad beans, lentils or dried peas, it was certainly filling. On about every third or fourth day we were given meat: usually goat, which if well cooked (preferably grilled over a wood fire) can be very good indeed. Unfortunately, it was always in a stew so liquid it resembled thin soup, to which a few chopped carrots, sliced aubergines and a vast quantity of tomato paste had been added.

As no evening meal was provided, food for later in the day was delivered with the bread: corned beef (one tin between two) or sardines (one tin each); eggs – about four per week; yoghurt, which was delicious, usually twice a week; homus about as often; sometimes, on a Friday, a piece of sweet *halva* for everybody.

Towards the end of my imprisonment, Fridays became noteworthy for a parboiled half-chicken that was given to us all. Syrian chickens are dreadfully skinny: even those served in five-star hotels are undersized, and those provided for the inmates of the Citadel were just wizened little bags of bones. They had always been carelessly plucked, with large clusters of wet feathers adhering to their pathetically meagre little carcasses. To be rendered edible, they had to be boiled for some time. All dead flesh, human or animal, putrefies quickly in the Syrian climate, and the effluvium from thirty to fifty fiercely boiling saucepans – each atop a smoking *barboua* – produced a sickly-smelling miasma that lingered for hours.

Those too poor to buy anything extra were never in danger of starvation. Many, in fact, put on weight eating so much starch, and almost all were brought good things from the world outside.

Later that morning I took my dirty shirt and underwear to the small laundry in a basement room behind the bath-house. Writing my name in indelible ink on my shirt tail presented something of a problem to the young prisoner who ran the place. After several attempts, he achieved a hieroglyph that he assured me was the closest he could get to the sound of Anthony in Arabic.

My craving for fresh air and sunshine had not yet been assuaged, so I returned to the courtyard. After exchanging friendly greetings with Hisham, I walked slowly up and down on my own.

I noticed Jean-Pierre emerge from a dormitory. He stood still for a moment, one hand fingering some post-adolescent acne on his cheeks, then came to join me, asking if I had had a good breakfast. I said it had been very good.

'Was it Rachid who arranged for you to eat with Fahdi and his friends?' he asked.

I made an affirmative noise.

'I find that surprising. In Baalbek – did you meet Fahdi, perhaps?'

'No. But he claims to have seen me there from time to time.'

'*Vraiment je n'aime pas ce garçon,*' he said, kicking a small stone irritably from his path.

I was surprised at his vehemence and said so.

'We have been together in *Hofra*, you know. He had been there ever since he transferred from Latakia. When I first arrived we were quite friendly.'

'He seems to like the French and tries hard to speak your language.'

With a derisive twist of the mouth, Jean-Pierre said: 'He has other interests that disgust me. *Je n'ai pas les yeux dans la poche, vous savez*!'

'What did you see that upset you?'

'It was a cold morning, last November. I got permission to go down into *Hofra* to get a sweater. Fahdi had not come out because he was one of the service staff, yet at first I thought the room was empty. The chief was at a weekly meeting with the governor. Then, suddenly, I saw Fahdi. He was lying on a bed astride the Lebanese boy, Sultan, who was extended, face downwards, beneath him. They ignored me completely and were quite shameless.' He leaned towards me, as if imparting an important secret, and snorted: 'At home he has a wife and two children!'

'He seems to fit the French expression, *à voile et à vapeur*!'

Jean-Pierre blinked in surprise. 'Ah, so you know the French slang for bisexuality?'

'And a few other expressions,' I said, smugly.

'Fahdi – c'est un *queutard*! You know what that means? I do not like such people.' He gave an old–maidish sniff.

Before I had time to express an opinion about Fahdi's morals and Jean-Pierre's view of them (I guessed the latter was the result of a cloistered French-Catholic upbringing) we were accosted by a short, alert-looking man in his fifties who had a neatly-trimmed grey beard. His manner was so brightly perky he reminded me of a frosted robin on a Christmas card. He wore an expensive leather blouson over a thin, pale blue suit, and a skull-cap knitted in blue, white and red stripes.

This apparition seized my hand with a fearsome grip, saying: 'Why, hullo there! Ever since they told me there was a Limey in the can, I've been just crazy to get to know you!'

I detected a slight chill in Jean-Pierre's voice as he said grandly: 'Permit me to introduce Abou Mustapha ... Monsieur Tony.'

'Gee, I never knew Englishmen were called Tony! To me it sounds kinda like a Wop bootblack! But don't get me wrong, Mister, I like Englishmen. I served with the British in Egypt during World War II – a mighty fine bunch of guys!' (I subsequently learned he had been one of a number of youthful Arab 'auxiliaries' employed by the Pioneer Corps.) Were you with the 8th Army?' he asked.

I murmured something about that distinction having been denied me.

'The subject of the Second World War is of great interest to Abou Mustapha,' said Jean-Pierre in the sort of tone he might have used to describe a child's interest in a model railway.

'It sure is!' The little man glanced contemptuously at the Frenchman. 'Of course this kid wasn't born at the time – and, anyway, I guess in his country they never got real excited about that war.'

Noticing Jean-Pierre's ominous expression, I said quickly: 'I doubt if the last world war is of much interest to the younger generation in any country.'

'Then it should be,' said Abou Mustapha fiercely. 'I sure don't like their attitude.'

'You're an American?'

'You betcha sweet life, I am!'

'But born in Damascus,' interjected Jean-Pierre.

'Sure I was born here, and in a pretty fancy neighbourhood, too. But I'm no longer a Syrian. Never was one, really. My pa's family came originally from Turkey, several generations back, and Momma was a Circassian. But I've lived and worked in the States for almost thirty years and for more than twenty of 'em I've been an American citizen.'

'What sort of work were you doing?' I asked.

'I settled in Trenton, New Jersey, in 1952. In less than five years I had my own high-class diner – ten years later, I had six of 'em, all over New Jersey.'

'Who's looking after those diners now?'

'My sons. I have three sons and two daughters by my first marriage.'

'All still in New Jersey?'

'Yeah. Oh, they keep in touch – they write, sometimes.'

'Why did you come back to Syria when you'd been so successful in America?'

He twisted the broad gold wedding ring on his left hand, suddenly very tense. 'I used to come back on vacation every few years. When my first wife died, I married again – somebody I'd met over here, a much younger woman who never really settled in the US. Always crazy to come back to see her parents – well, that's the story she always gave me. Two years ago, we brought my big Caddy over by ship. I was plannin' to drive up into Turkey and find the spot my grandfathers came from.' He looked at me sadly. 'We never made the trip – and I've never been States-side since that summer.'

'You decided to remain in Syria?'

He thrust his chin upwards – a frequent Arab gesture signifying a negative. 'I didn't decide nothin' – I found out my wife was two-timing me.'

Not knowing what to say, I said nothing.

'Yeah,' he continued, 'so I shot her dead. For the last two years I ain't been nowhere, just here.'

I was silent, and felt ridiculously embarrassed.

Then Jean-Pierre said: 'You still hope the court will only give you seven years?'

'Gee whizz, I wish I knew.' There was pain in his eyes.

'You haven't yet been sentenced – after two years?' I was shocked.

'It sure is a heck of a time, but my lawyers – and they're the best and brightest this country's got to offer – are still tryin' to blind the

prosecution with science. I get taken to court every month and this
guy who defends me gets up and makes long speeches. He objects to
this and objects to that – after about two hours the judges get fed up
and the president of the court says to bring me back in six weeks. The
attorneys insist these delays work in my favour and, if I'm lucky, I'll
only get seven years.'

'You've already served two,' said Jean-Pierre.

'Sure thing! And with quarter-time I could be almost on my way
out of here!' His breezy self-confidence was returning.

It sounded as if he had been guilty of a *crime passionel* and I
wonder if the Syrian attitude to this sort of murder differed from the
French.

'I guess you're here because of hashish,' he said to me. 'Except
for truck-drivers who run down jay-walkers, you seem to be the
only kinda European to get busted in Syria! It'll mean they'll put
you in *Hofra* as soon as that slammer is opened again.'

'I was given an escorted tour of the dungeon earlier this morning.
It didn't raise my spirits.'

Jean-Pierre could barely conceal his impatience. 'There is too much
condemnation of Hofra,' he said sharply. 'It is terrible, yes – but so
are conditions in most of the rooms. Where I am now is not good
either.'

'Where's that?' asked Abou Mustapha. 'Room 1?'

Jean-Pierre nodded.

'*El Kalaa*'s most exclusive collection of army deserters and big-
time criminals! There are twenty of you – am I right?'

'I am the twenty-first – sleeping on the floor.'

'There are guys from Hofra sleeping on the floor in every room.
Is that what's got up your nose?'

'No, that I do not mind. It is the ambiance of the room I do
not like – the moral atmosphere.'

'Come again?' said Abou Mustapha. I suspected his failure to understand was deliberate.

'In *Hofra*,' explained Jean-Pierre, 'nothing can be hidden because it
is impossible for the beds to be screened. Almost everybody, therefore,
behaves decently. In the other rooms there are bunks and almost all
have curtains. They are supposed to be a protection from *courants d'air*,
but they are also an encouragement for indecency to take place where
it can be hidden from public view.'

Abou Mustapha gave me an amused wink. 'Indecency, eh?' he said. 'I get you. What you're sayin' is twenty beds are occupied during the day but only ten at night! Am I right?'

'You exaggerate, of course,' admitted Jean-Pierre. 'But there are other things – less important – I do not like.'

'What sort of things?' I asked.

'The restrictions imposed by the chief of the room. It is not permitted to do this, it is not permitted to do that – *cela me gêne beaucoup!* It is forbidden to light a *barboua* in the room. If you wish to make tea or coffee, or to cook at all, you have to do so in the adjoining kitchen.'

'What's wrong with that?' said Abou Mustapha. 'It keeps the fumes out of the livin' quarters.'

'The kitchen is no bigger than a small cupboard, so everybody gets in each other's way. Because of this people lose their tempers and there are constant fights. It is also forbidden to do your own washing–up. This must be done by the service man. There is only one and he is jealous of his privileges and very slow.'

'And you're such a tightwad you begrudge that poor cat a few small coins for doin' the job?'

'Why should I pay for something I am willing to do for myself?' snapped Jean-Pierre. 'And we have another stupid regulation forbidding us to wash our own clothes, even in the precious kitchen. I am now forced to use the laundry which is expensive and bad.'

'Why d'you have to be so gosh–darned careful with your money?' persisted Abou Mustapha.

'Because I have very little.'

'But you're the son of a rich guy – director of a big international corporation.'

'My father does not know I am in prison.'

'Jesus! Why not!'

'Because my mother decided it would be wiser not to tell him. He would be angry and spend much time cursing me. I am a good photographer and he thinks I am free-lancing in the Near East for French illustrated magazines.'

'You're not worried he might hear from somebody else?' I asked. 'The consulate staff at the French Embassy, for instance?'

Jean-Pierre said scornfully: 'No one from my embassy has ever bothered to come and see me since my arrest. Since they seem not to care if I am alive or dead, I feel there is no danger of their writing to my father. There was nothing in the French newspapers about my arrest or trial – nothing in the Syrian papers, either. They never report hashish cases, so no one knows anything about us unless we tell them. I go along with my mother's pretending because it makes life easier for her. She sends me all she can afford and I will not ask for more.'

'Gee whizz!' said the abashed Abou Mustapha. 'Pardon me.'

It was getting close to midday. Young men were unrolling long strips of cheap carpeting under the eastern wall. Prisoners were discarding their shoes, leaving them in two great piles. They then lined up three or four deep along the carpet, having first washed their feet under one of the two taps. They stood in silence waiting for the amplified sound of the muezzin's call to prayer from the nearby Omayed Mosque.

Our chubby little robin of a man said suddenly: 'I'll have to ask you to excuse me. It's time to pray. I must go wash my feet.'

'You're still a devout Muslim,' I said, 'in spite of all those years in America?'

He smiled and shrugged. 'I guess a little prayer can't do any harm!' As he walked quickly away he called: 'It's been just great talkin' with you. Hope to see a lot of you while you're here!'

As we watched his retreating figure, Jean-Pierre said: 'Surprising – do you not agree?'

'That he should pray?' I asked as we continued to walk.

'No – that after so many years in New Jersey he should still speak English like a character out of Damon Runyon. He knows so little of your language except a few set phrases and routine wise-cracks.'

'From my limited experience of New York and the West Coast, many elderly immigrants speak as he does. They only feel comfortable in the language of their birthplace, so they live in ghettos of their own nationality and emerge only to earn their living. It's different for the children – they go to school and quickly become one hundred per cent American.'

'A "diner" is a small restaurant, yes?'

'Sort of – small tables and a long counter.'

'I wonder if he really owns six diners in New Jersey?'

'I expect so. Syrians have had a lot of success in the fast food business all over the world.'

'I noticed your surprise when he told you he had killed his wife!' There was a hint of malice in Jean-Pierre's smile.

'I've had no experience of being told that sort of thing! Give me time – if it often happens, I'll get better at it! Is he right to think he'll be given seven years?'

Jean-Pierre's smile vanished and he shook his head severely. 'No, he is being stupid and deceiving himself. If it was only his wife he had killed, things might be different … '

'Were there others?'

'Oh yes. He shot her lover, his mother-in-law and the chauffeur. *C'était un massacre!*'

'All dead?' I said, incredulously.

'Every one of them.'

'But it's so extraordinary. Such a harmless, genial little man.'

'Wait until you see him lose his temper. I have several times. It can be frightening. He has no control at all.'

'Do they hang people for murder in Syria?'

'No. Only for crimes against the state.'

'Do they recognise such a thing as a *crime passionel*?'

'They recognise the right of a husband to kill his wife's lover, but they seem to disapprove of wife-killing. In a country where divorce – for a man – is so simple, this is the accepted way to dispose of an unfaithful wife.'

'It's for fathers and brothers to kill an adulterous woman?'

'Exactly. And for a man to kill not only his wife, but his mother-in-law and the family chauffeur as well, *cela c'est un peu trop*! In addition, the dead wife's relations are rich and powerful as well as strong supporters of the government. They are doing their best to see he gets the ultimate penalty – life imprisonment.'

'Does that really mean for life?' I asked.

'It means twenty-five years – unless there is an amnesty, which could cut it by half.'

Abou Mustapha had now taken his place along the eastern wall. The reverberating call of the muezzin had just begun. I watched his rotund little body as he knelt in unison with his companions, positioning his hands on the ground in order to bend forward repeatedly, touching his forehead to the earth and thrusting his solid, blue-trousered bottom upwards into the sunlight.

'Are amnesties often given?' I queried.

'In the last thirty years I think there have only been two. When this country linked with Egypt at the time of Abdel Nasser there was a general amnesty. The coming to power of President Assad was the reason for another.'

'When this happens – sentences are cut in half?'

'For most prisoners, yes. Those guilty of small crimes are released immediately.'

I asked hopefully when he thought the next one was likely.

'Not in our time, you can be sure of that,' said Jean-Pierre. 'And remember there were two categories excluded from the last amnesty – political prisoners and drug offenders!'

At that moment I stopped hoping for miracles and decided I must settle down to several unproductive years in *Hofra*. Jean-Pierre appeared to be doing so with highly commendable common sense. 'I gather you recommend *Hofra*?' I said.

'Recommend, no. I was really saying I find it easier to live the sort of life I prefer in that cellar than in the other rooms. It is, of course, much too big – there are too many people – the ventilation is terrible – but its size is a protection from the propositions I am always receiving in the smaller places.'

'Because so many are sexually *capable de tout*?'

'Too many. It may surprise you, but I am most envious of your age! I can never walk alone in this yard. As soon as I leave my room, someone will attach themselves to me. Even if they do not mention the subject, I know instinctively what is in their minds.'

I soon found out I could not walk alone, either. This was not due to my physical charms but to the anxiety of so many to practise their English!

I looked at Jean-Pierre and wondered if his instincts were infallible. With his small, pale eyes, bad skin and thin, ungainly body with large hands and feet, I felt he might be overestimating his allure. Although many Arabs are susceptible to blond hair in either sex, I did not feel the Frenchman's light-mouse fleece, cut *en brosse*, was sufficient to change him into a sex-symbol. My impression was later confirmed when we were joined in *el Kalaa* by several other youthful Europeans, all considerably better-looking than Jean-Pierre, who rarely found themselves subjected to sexual advances.

Meanwhile Jean-Pierre was continuing to give modified praise to *Hofra*. 'One has a wider choice of friends,' he was saying. 'In so big a place it is possible to assemble a little community around you and to ignore the rest.'

At this moment there was an outburst of shouting, almost powerful enough to drown the Call to Prayer. Two middle-aged men had seized plastic stools and were attacking each other, each apparently determined to break the skull of his opponent. The younger was already bleeding profusely from a cut over his eye. Those at prayer calmly went on with their devotions and ignored the uproar. At least a dozen prisoners, yelling loudly, were making strenuous efforts to pull the combatants apart.

Three guards ran towards the fracas, elbowing through the crowd. After a short struggle they wrenched the stools from the prisoners. The elder allowed himself to be quietly led towards the guardroom. The other, uttering short sharp screams like an amorous dog-fox, rushed to the cafeteria, seized a glass and lunged at the nearby wall, scraping the rim against the rough concrete, converting it into a jagged weapon. He remained with his back to the wall, panting, blood flowing from the cut above his eye, his *galabieh* torn away from his heaving chest, revealing a tangle of bloodstained black hair.

The two remaining guards had now been joined by the sergeant who had approached the scene in a more leisurely fashion. All three were standing casually, hands clasped behind their backs, obviously hoping to diffuse the heat from the situation, while the prisoner, in between gasps, was threatening to cut in pieces anyone who approached him.

The sergeant, Abou Talal, was a tall man of twenty-six with an impressive brushed-up moustache. I learned later he had married at seventeen and was already the father of six. He began talking quietly to the frenzied man. At first his gentle efforts were greeted with incoherent shouts of fury, but he persisted with a flow of soothing comment and gradually the man's demoniac violence seemed to subside and a note of pleading crept into his responses. A few moments later, the glass dropped from his hand. He stumbled forward almost blindly and there was a sigh of relief from those watching. At a barely perceptible gesture from the sergeant, the guards took him gently by the elbows and led him, now weeping, to the office.

'You will soon become accustomed to these fights,' said Jean-Pierre. 'Sometimes there will be half-a-dozen during a single morning.'

'What will happen to those two?' I asked.

'The one who stopped fighting at once will probably be given a sharp rebuke and sent out here again. He might get a slap across the face, but Abou Talal does not usually hit people.'

'What about the maniac with the broken glass?'

'He may get twenty-four hours in what they call "the single cell". In English I think the expression is "solitary confinement". Here, they are more like cages than cells. No toilet facilities, just a bucket into which to piss and shit. The service staff wash the cages out once a week with a powerful hose, and in winter everything remains soaking wet for days. At night it can be bitterly cold and you are only allowed one blanket.'

Prisoners were given this punishment for a variety of reasons, some being kept in the single cells for weeks. Many assured me being alone was harder to bear than anything. Almost all Arabs dislike solitude. From their earliest infancy they are part of a community, and loneliness in adult life is something to be avoided at all costs. For Europeans, the lack of privacy in Arab households, particularly in country districts, with those families who have no inclination to be what they call *moderne*, can often be disconcerting. Bedrooms, virtually, do not exist. One's host, if he decides you are tired, will seize a palliasse which has been rolled up against the wall, cushions and a coverlet from the room's inevitable *banquette*, press these into your arms and expect you to settle down to sleep on the floor. He will do the same, a few feet away. The sexes tend to separate at night, but the children, who never seem to need sleep at all, wander blithely from room to room and are welcomed with as much affection by the menfolk as by the women.

From my experience of these households it is rare for husband and wife to sleep together unless they have very recently been married. As soon as children arrive, they sleep apart. If a man feels in need of sexual intercourse – and the Koran says 'Women are your fields. Go then into your fields when and how you will' – he will join his wife on her palliasse and perform the act without undressing and with practically no sound. Afterwards he will return to his sleeping place in another room, the whole operation having taken little more than five minutes. Arab women are not romantic and have been brought up to expect this treatment. They expect husbands to give not love, but children. Romance hardly ever seems to enter into it.

After the fight Rachid joined us and we finished the morning outside the cafeteria, gossiping and drinking coffee. I noticed the two men behind the counter treated Rachid with a sort of nervous deference: an attitude most people seemed to adopt towards him.

Soon after half-past one, Abou Talal and his guards began herding us back into our rooms. The schools had finished for the day and almost the entire population of *el Kalaa* was in the courtyard. In order to make himself heard above the hubbub, he had to use a portable loud-hailer.

It was the custom to leave until last the closure of the room whose personnel had, that day, had official access to the showers. Even so, there were always those who would delay taking a shower until nearly zero hour and then rush, damp, flustered and trailing wet towels, across the yard to answer their names. Some guards became so irritated by this they would propel the offenders back into their room with a well-directed boot.

Today, the locking-up began with room 1, Jean-Pierre's temporary abode. So, after typically Gallic handshakes with Rachid and myself (this habit is still universal in France's former colonies) he left us, promising to rendezvous with me the next morning. As we watched him manoeuvre through the crowd, his spring-heeled walk more noticeable than usual, Rachid made a face, saying: 'You will have guessed he isn't much liked here?'

'He's very young,' I said, 'and seems afraid many people have amorous intentions towards him!'

'Just his dirty imagination,' said Rachid, contemptuously. 'He's a fool, and has far too much of the French *de haut en bas* attitude towards the whole Arab race. He is also exceptionally mean. Did you notice how he let you and me pay for the coffee this morning?'

'He has very little money.'

'How can that be? His father is a well-known French industrialist.'

'His father doesn't know he's here.'

Rachid looked astonished. 'I don't believe that. If you're in trouble, the first person you tell is your father.'

'European family relationships are prone to the kind of stress I suspect you know little about.'

He was unconvinced. 'It isn't just a question of money,' he said, 'he has an ungenerous spirit. Many here have almost nothing, but they invite him for tea or coffee, or to join them in some snack they have cooked. He always accepts but never returns this hospitality – it wouldn't cost him anything – he never shares his food with anyone.'

'You've explained traditional Arab behaviour?'

'Frequently – perhaps too frequently. It falls on deaf ears.'

'He assured me this morning he would share everything when we are moved into *Hofra!*'

A grin spread over Rachid's face. 'Well, he has the best *barboua* and collection of cooking-pots in the prison! He inherited them from an Italian and an Englishman who were released last autumn. Notice how Europeans always stick together in this place! But, in spite of such advantages, I'm afraid you'll have quite a few problems with our young friend ... '

A voice behind me suddenly interrupted in French, saying: 'I am sorry to have seen nothing of you this morning, but I have been absurdly busy. How have you been getting on?'

I turned; Yussef, smiling, held out his hand. Shaking it, I said I had been getting on fine.

'No sense of shock – no deep depression?' he asked sympathetically.

I shook my head. 'That will probably come later!'

Rachid burst into an eloquent flood of Arabic. The only word I understood was the constant repetition of Jean-Pierre's name. This diatribe obviously amused Yussef, who laughed and said: 'He gets much too worked up about that young Frenchman who is quite harmless – *justement un peu egoiste!*'

Fahdi, who had just shaved and showered, joined us and chatted animatedly in Arabic, having first presented me with a large orange.

All too soon it was time to be locked up. Fahdi and I watched the occupants of room 8 answer their names and disappear inside. Rachid, a recent arrival, was at the end of the queue. As he approached the doorway he turned, saying: 'I usually come out for a breath of fresh air at about half-past four – would you like to join me?'

'Very much,' I said.

'I'll see if it can be arranged. See you later!'

Today, our hot meal consisted of broad beans, black in colour, mixed with the usual lumps of oily rice. This was followed by liberal helpings of goat's cheese from Fahdi's special store, eaten with pitta bread. We finished, as always, with tea. As soon as it was over, Badr, our young gipsy, produced a draughtboard and, cross-legged on his precious piece of beige carpet, challenged Nasir, our political prisoner, to a game of *dama* – a game that closely resembles draughts and is popular throughout the Levant.

The doe-eyed Sultan climbed into his bunk, above Fahdi's. He sat at the foot and began threading multi-coloured beads on short lengths of string. Fahdi climbed up with him, sat at the opposite end and began converting the beaded strips into hideous purses.

I went to my own bunk, wondering if I could sleep for an hour or so with radios all round me. It was not the transistors that kept me awake, but my neighbour in the adjoining upper berth.

In every room the rows of bunks were placed in pairs, almost touching – never more than an inch between the two. If you were in a right-hand 'twin', access to either bunk (upper or lower) was only possible from the right; vice versa if your bunk was in a 'twin' on the left.

My neighbour, in an unscreened upper-berth, looked like an ageing all-in wrestler; fortyish, with wavy hair as regular as a stage wig and an exceptionally loud, gravelly voice. His pear-shaped curves reminded me irresistibly of a male character in a Thurber cartoon. He was serving a two-year sentence for dealing in substantial quantities of hashish. Paradoxically, he was a most devout Shi'ite Muslim and a *Hajji*, having made an unusually youthful pilgrimage to Mecca. The Koran expressly forbids the consumption of alcohol but makes no mention of drugs. There are many like my *Hajji* neighbour who intone their devotion to Allah five times a day, and believe themselves not guilty of even the most minor peccadillo when engaged in the sale of every illegal narcotic from hashish to heroin.

I had already been made vaguely aware of my neighbour's religious fervour when, soon after 4 AM, my bed had been shaken as if by a minor earthquake. Half-conscious, I dimly realised that the *Hajji*, having spread a prayer-mat over his bunk, was performing the ritual prostrations to Allah to the muted accompaniment of the muezzin from the Omayed Mosque.

This afternoon it was not his devotions that kept me awake, but his insistence on showing me a large collection of colour photographs of his children. It seemed surprising that this creature with the body of a whale could have produced such attractive moppets, most between the ages of two and six. Hovering in the background of several snap-shots were two rather sad-faced young women. Hoping I was not transgressing Islamic good manners, I pointed to the elder of the two, asking if she were his wife. He beamed acknowledgement and then, pointing his stubby finger at the younger, told me proudly she was also his wife. This explained why so many of his brood were approximately the same age.

I was later to discover a good many prisoners had more than one wife, although few had acquired – or could afford – the permitted maximum of four.

I did my best to make the right appreciative noises, doubtless overworking such Arabic words as *muzien, quiess* and *tamam* (beautiful! splendid! wonderful!). Finally, the exhibition came to an end and I was able to close my eyes and doze for a little. I was dimly conscious of the gates being opened and a call being made for those whose names had been accepted by the sports committee for volleyball practice, and much more conscious of the noise of their game in the courtyard for the next hour. After they returned from the showers there was a short period of comparative peace, apart from the radios. The gates were then again unlocked and my name was called.

Rachid was waiting. The guard who had let me out left us to walk in the deserted yard. I never discovered if Rachid obtained this privilege – and many others – because he was officially still serving in the army and a protégé of the President's brother, or because of the 100-pound notes (slightly less than £10) he showered upon the staff like a paper snowstorm. He called for me almost every evening and we would walk together for about an hour.

To vary the monotony, Rachid would occasionally insist on our strolling through the guardroom (there was never a murmur of protest) and up over the ramparts of the Citadel, descending into the *Abraaj* which was equally empty of prisoners. Sometimes we dropped into the theatre to talk with Yussef, often working late on the balance sheets of his catering job.

In spite of Rachid's comments about daily incidents in our enclosed world, I soon realised the subject of hashish smuggling was usually uppermost in his mind. It was clear his interest was in its promotion, not its prevention! His wife's family had long ago found the cultivation and export of hashish extremely lucrative. On our evening walks he would return to the subject again and again, seeking my opinion about every conceivable method of smuggling. I asked if he intended to quit the army and take it up 'professionally'. He smiled enigmatically: 'Isn't there an English maxim about having two strings to one's bow?'

When we returned to our rooms it was usually quite dark, there being no lingering twilight in the Middle East. In room 9, Fahdi and Sultan, who had been working for most of the afternoon making those awful purses, would now cook our evening meal. Sometimes it was an

107

egg dish, eaten with lots of bread; often it was spaghetti, mixed with a small quantity of corned-beef and lots of sliced onions. Occasionally, if one of us had received money, there was meat from the butcher's stall; Fahdi would add potatoes, carrots, sliced aubergines, parsley and olive oil, presenting us, an hour later, with a bubbling *tajine* (casserole), heavily flavoured with garlic.

After our meal it was usually time for the black-and-white television set, belonging to a prisoner, to be switched on. The majority would then grab their stools and seat themselves in neat rows in front of the 'box'. Every night except Friday provided a lengthy episode of a crime serial. All these soap operas had been made in Egypt especially for television. Most of them were incredibly amateurish, poorly acted and badly photographed. It amazed me that the audience could find them so compulsively viewable. On Fridays there was nothing except religious programmes which seldom attracted more than half-a-dozen. Some Fridays the set was not switched on.

In the morning after my first evening walk with Rachid, the courtyard was unusually crowded at an early hour. It was visiting day. Tuesday and Thursday mornings were allotted to *el Kalaa* for this purpose; on Mondays and Wednesdays it was the turn of *el Abraaj*. Male visitors only was the rule for Tuesdays, women and children were restricted to Thursdays. Exceptions were sometimes made for families who had travelled long distances. Decisions about these cases seemed quite arbitrary and to depend on the state of the governor's liver on the day.

Surprisingly, the loud-speaker system was never used to let prisoners know their visitors had arrived. Instead, long lists of names would be telephoned from the main gate to our guardroom. These names would be scribbled on slips of paper and announced to an anxiously waiting crowd through a portable loud-hailer.

When a prisoner heard his name, he would punch his way through the throng, his identity would be briefly checked by the sergeant (mistakes often occurred because of the similarity of Arab names) and he would make his way quickly to the main courtyard of *el Abraaj*, where the visits took place.

Later that morning I was able to see the arrangements for myself. Fraternization between *Kalaa* and *Abraaj* was expressly forbidden to the majority, but Jean-Pierre was permitted to go to and fro because his talent for painting naif pictures had impressed the governor. He was allowed – with several other amateur artists – to use the theatre as a

makeshift studio when it was not needed for staff meetings. The sergeant
on duty was easy-going and raised no objection to my accompanying
Jean-Pierre to draw my ration of blankets from the store in the *Abraaj*
courtyard (Fahdi had promised to meet me there).

Access to the *Abraaj* courtyard was through a creaking iron gate,
set into a high stone wall. It was reached by climbing a dozen steps
that had probably been there since the seventh century. The yard itself
– smaller than *el Kalaa*'s – was on a sort of plateau between the inner
and outer walls of the castle. It was not (unlike *Kalaa*) encircled by
living accommodation. *Abraaj* prisoners were distributed over a wide
area, most in dark caverns hewn out of rock, well above ground level.

As Jean-Pierre and I approached the steps, my eardrums began
to vibrate with the pressure of sound from a crowd of voices behind
the high wall in front. I was reminded of cocktail parties given by
over-hospitable minor diplomats in very small drawing-rooms.

Along the whole length of the yard's western and southern bounda-
ries was a wall about three feet high. Behind it were two tall screens
of fine-mesh wire, supported at intervals by steel posts, embedded in
concrete. The screens were about five yards apart, the inner screen
being only a few feet away from the lofty courtyard walls. It was in
this narrow space, behind the second screen, that the visitors had been
crushed together.

Any communication between prisoners and visitors could only be
achieved by shouting. Many were to tell me it was often impossible
to exchange a single coherent sentence during a visit of half-an-hour
(the imposed time limit), every word being swallowed up in the
encompassing ear-splitting clamour.

The area between the two screens was kept empty, apart from
the guards standing, apathetically, about twenty yards apart.

Both screens had a small gate at the northern end of the yard.
These were for an interchange of baskets, not people.

Visitors could only enter or leave the courtyard through a space
in the castle wall, immediately behind the gates. Before pushing along
the narrow path, they would halt to hand over a straw basket or plastic
carrier-bag to the guards. Inside would be all kinds of food, especially
fruit; clean underwear, soap, cigarettes, etc.

To prevent smuggling, the contents would be carefully examined
then whisked across the five yards between the screens to a prisoner
who had been patiently queueing by the outer gate.

In exchange, the man would hand back the bag or basket brought on a previous visit. It would usually be empty except for dirty laundry. As these bags and baskets were often identical, the interchange would frequently lead to mistakes and sometimes to angry altercations.

When I complained of the noise to Jean-Pierre, he said scornfully I should be thankful it was not a Thursday, the day for women and children, when the sound would be a great deal higher on the decibel scale!

Apart from the phalanx of *el Kalaa* prisoners, the courtyard was empty. On those mornings reserved for *Kalaa* visitors, *Abraaj* prisoners were kept locked up until after mid-day, then allowed out until four in the afternoon.

In spite of the absence of surrounding dormitories, the yard was very similar to *el Kalaa*'s. The bath-house was in almost exactly the same spot. There was an even bigger cafeteria and a large market stall, under a rickety canopy, selling meat and vegetables. On the eastern side was a line of small shops, recessed into rock. All profitably operated by prisoners, they included a tailor, a grocer and a cobbler. Here, also, was the blanket store where Fahdi, having said goodbye to a visiting brother, was waiting.

I was issued with the regulation three blankets; rust-coloured and excessively grubby. One was so riddled with cigarette burns Fahdi insisted it be changed for another. All three smelt pungently of stale tobacco and human excreta. I hardly needed Jean-Pierre and Fahdi's advice to give them at once to the *Kalaa* laundry. Unfortunately, the smell was to linger for months, in spite of frequent immersions in boiling detergent and being hung out to dry in almost tropical sunshine.

As we left the yard, Fahdi seized the blankets from me, slinging them over his shoulder, saying – as he disappeared before I had time to protest – he would take them immediately to the laundry.

Walking along the broad path between high stone walls that linked the eastern and central areas of the Citadel, Jean-Pierre and I passed the surprising (to me) sight of a small, two-storied villa, faintly baroque in style, faced with peeling white stucco; so typically French of the first decade of this century, it might have been lifted, seventy years ago, from any of the smaller side-streets near to the *Promenade des Anglais* in Nice – leaving behind a patch of yellow cannas and pink oleanders – and dropped from the heavens on to its present incongruous site. Amid the towering remains of a seventh-century fortress, this relic

110

of French colonialism could not have looked more astonishingly out of place. The ground floor, Jean-Pierre explained, was used as offices by the governor and his deputies.

We descended into the theatre, which I now realised was almost as deep below ground as *Hofra*, but square instead of oblong and far more brightly lit. We found Yussef busily pressing the buttons on his pocket-calculator and writing down the results. Rachid was sitting on the desk, swinging his well-shod feet lazily. Yussef looked up with a welcoming smile, immediately offering to make tea. We begged him not to bother.

The only other occupant of the theatre was a heavily-built young man at an easel, painting a large, meticulously realistic picture of a hand with its forefinger on the trigger of a Beretta 38 pistol. His pink tongue was pressed against his upper lip in concentration. The sight of his lovingly executed daub increased my exasperation with the Lebanese and Syrian obsession with firearms. I was reminded of the splendid homes of my friends in the Beka'a Valley, where the doors of every cupboard and the space under every *banquette* and easy-chair conceals an armoury of weapons and ammunition.

Hamoudi, the young painter, was just twenty years old; he had the most heavily muscled shoulders and the smallest hips I have ever seen. His eyes were dark amber, heavy-lidded, serious: but his smile was brilliant. He was Syrian, brought up in Beirut, and had worked from a tender age as an assistant in a keep-fit gymnasium, hence the superbly developed torso; he had a black belt in karate. He was one of the few Arab prisoners to whom Jean-Pierre never condescended, chiefly because he was fascinated by all forms of ju-jitsu and wanted to learn as much as possible. Hamoudi had been called up for army service and was now a prisoner because of a gross miscarriage of justice perpetrated by court martial. He had an astonishing ability to tell fortunes by examining the grains at the bottom of coffee cups, and was constantly pestered by prisoners and staff to do this. He would often refuse, saying he was not in the mood. When he did agree, his predictions were about ninety per cent accurate; to me, a mind-blowing achievement.

This morning Hamoudi and I exchanged few words, but enough for me to realise he spoke passable English. Later, despite the enormous difference in our ages, he was to become one of my most constant companions during the hours in the courtyard.

While he and Jean-Pierre were criticising – in English – the quality of Syrian oil paints, and Rachid and Yussef were deeply involved in an Arabic discussion of an accounting system, I climbed the steps at the side of the proscenium arch and walked to the centre of the stage. I stood gazing around and sniffing the curious smell of acrid dust that seems to emanate from the stage of any theatre in the world. My musings were interrupted by Jean-Pierre: 'Why do you stand on the spot where they hang people?'

'Hang people?' I repeated, wondering if I had heard correctly.

'Yes – hang people! Exactly where you are standing at this moment!'

Stupidly, I looked up in the air and down again, as if expecting to see a noose above my head and a body at my feet. 'I thought capital punishment had been almost abolished,' I stuttered.

Rachid broke off his discussion. 'For murder, yes,' he said, 'but not for traitors.'

'He means political prisoners,' said Jean-Pierre acidly.

This remark plainly irritated Rachid. 'I do not mean political prisoners,' he snapped. 'Only those convicted of helping the enemies of this country are executed.'

'And they're hanged right here on this stage?' I asked.

'Not as a spectacle for an audience, I can assure you.' Rachid was now standing below me. 'They hang traitors here because it is out of sight and earshot of the rest of the prison.'

'Such a thing cannot be hidden,' insisted Jean-Pierre. 'It would make no difference if it took place in one of the courtyards. Everybody knows what is going to happen as soon as the special hanging squad arrive early in the morning with their gruesome apparatus – that cannot be hidden. The news circulates with the speed of light.'

'Have there been any hangings since you've been here?' I asked him.

'Of course. And they chose a very special day – Christmas Eve!'

'Did you know them – those who were hanged?'

'Naturally. Condemned prisoners are not kept apart until their last few hours. There is no death row in a Syrian prison. They are taken from their rooms at about nine in the evening and put into special single cells, no bigger than cupboards – just outside, over there – ' He pointed towards the theatre's entrance. 'They are usually hanged soon after midnight.'

I jumped down from the stage, not wishing to stand where others had waited to have life choked out of them. Hamoudi said nothing, but looked up at me as if he understood.

Rachid said impatiently: 'They were all traitors to this country. If you knew the facts you would have no sympathy for them.'

Jean-Pierre was examining small sheets of dusty white plasterboard, hoping to find something suitable for the picture he intended to paint. 'The mechanical device for hanging a person – how do you say that in English?' he asked.

'A gallows – a gibbet?'

'The gallows they bring enables them to hang four persons at a time. But last Christmas there were only two poor devils.' In the same casual tone he would have used when offering a lollipop to a child, he said: 'When we leave I'll show you the doors of the cells where they keep them waiting.'

I felt a need for fresh air. 'If you don't mind,' I said, 'I'll go back right away to *el Kalaa*.'

Waving his selected piece of plasterboard at me, Jean-Pierre said: 'Will you not stay and tell me what you think of my talent?'

I shook my head. 'Someone who can't draw the outline of a jam-jar has no business criticising others.'

'You and I must share a lack of artistic talent,' said Rachid, smiling.

As I walked towards the exit I said I would be seeing them all before lock-up.

'Remember to be ready at four this afternoon,' Rachid shouted after me. 'The young German you met at the police station is arriving. We will go to meet him together.'

I called out my thanks and went on up the staircase, fighting the inclination to avert my eyes from several narrow steel doors on either side, emerging with relief into the midday sun.

Shortly after four o'clock Rachid and I were a few inches from the giant stockade separating us from the small courtyard that formed part of the prison entrance. Guards were leaning indolently against the blue hut, obviously awaiting the arrival of a new batch of prisoners. While Rachid talked with the notorious sergeant, Abou Taïeb, I kept my eyes on the door at the base of the huge main gate.

There was the muffled sound of an approaching vehicle, a pause and then the small door burst open and a policeman carrying a millboard walked briskly into the hut. The guards stood up straight. A line of prisoners entered, shuffling clumsily under the burden of diverse luggage. They all looked bleary-eyed and unkempt. The last was a slim youth twice as tall as anyone else who had to sink almost to his knees to get through the door. When he stood up, a shaft of evening sunlight illuminated his pale gold cap of hair. It was, of course, Kurt.

He was so instantly recognisable it was unnecessary to point him out. Rachid did so for the sergeant's benefit. Abou Taïeb shouted to a minion, who gave the Germanic hero a gentle push in our direction. Kurt had not yet noticed me and glared resentfully at the guard as he stumbled towards us. I waved energetically and beckoned to him. Suddenly he recognised me and almost ran the last few yards to the gate.

He was looking desperately weary. His chin sprouted a pale fluff, the colour of a young chicken. His eyes were dull, the corners encrusted with yellow discharge; his face pale and sweat-stained, his hair heavily streaked with dust; but he had not neglected his excellent teeth, for his smile as he said: 'Hullo – nice to see you again!' was as brilliant as ever.

He was holding a large leather suitcase as if it were a baby, both locks having been broken by the customs. He put this down to allow Abou Taïeb to frisk him. Due to Rachid's presence and, doubtless, to *baksheesh*, this was performed in a very restrained manner.

Rachid seized the suitcase, placing it against an inner wall, saying: 'I'll come back for that, later.'

I introduced them, explaining how I had met Rachid some years ago in Lebanon. The customary guided tour for novices followed.

We went first to the theatre where Yussef, as always, played the generous host and insisted on making tea. Poor Kurt looked as if he needed a stronger stimulant, unavailable in our present surroundings. I was agreeably surprised to discover he spoke French fluently. I learned later he had a natural gift for languages; like so many young Germans he had spent his summer holidays from school camping all over Europe.

After twenty minutes of tea and gossip, Rachid went off to pick up Kurt's luggage and to supervise its inspection by the guards while I guided the new prisoner to the admin offices, just as the lights were being switched on throughout the Citadel. There were fewer prisoners than on the day of my arrival. Kurt had only a few minutes to wait before being called into the office.

As he came out, Rachid reappeared with his suitcase, able to confirm that none of its contents had aroused the guard's acquisitive instincts.

The young man who did duty as a barber on these occasions waved his clippers commandingly at Kurt.

'Rachid said quickly: 'Take no notice – I'll fix him!'

Kurt hesitantly ran his fingers through his tarnished locks, saying: 'It's so very dirty, perhaps I'd better have it clipped off ... '

'You can get several brands of shampoo in the prison shop,' I said.

'There are shops – in this prison?' He sounded incredulous.

Meanwhile, Rachid had walked over to the clipper-waver and clasped his free hand in both his own, shaking it gently. I was sure a banknote was being pressed into his palm. The guard promptly slipped that hand into his pocket.

Rachid picked up the suitcase and, with a jerk of the head, commanded us to follow him. At the bottom of the steps to the pathway over the inner wall, he handed the bag to a waiting serviceman who took the lead up the quivering iron staircase towards the night sky.

Kurt and I stopped for a moment at the highest point to look down at the lights of Damascus. Rachid was now some distance ahead. The young German whispered: 'Your Syrian friend – is he a prisoner, or one of the staff?'

'He's a prisoner.'

'But he does as he likes – how is that?'

'I don't know. I doubt if anybody knows, except the governor – and perhaps he doesn't know, either!'

'But you know him well – can you not ask?'

'I have – and just get evasive answers. I've decided not to probe any more – just to be glad it amuses him to play godfather.'

'Long may it continue,' said Kurt.

'It won't. He tells me he's leaving quite soon.'

Rachid was calling to us to hurry up. We obeyed.

The sergeant on duty that evening was the same Abou Jaouar, the roly-poly with a heavy moustache who had greeted me on my arrival. '*Wallah!*' he shouted, 'what a height the boy is – at least two metres! (Kurt was just under 1m 90) Isn't it cold up there!'

Rachid managed to extricate our young Teuton from the little sergeant's over-eager interest and it was not long before we were locked into our respective dormitories.

The gates of room 9 barely had time to clang shut before Fahdi was advancing upon us. The entry of this blond giant was the cause of universal excitement. There were loud cries of: '*Ahlan wa sahlan!* Welcome! Welcome!'

While drinking tea in the theatre, Kurt had been given a brief summary of the basic features of life in *el Kalaa*. He was told he would have a mattress (thanks to Rachid) which would remain his property. There would be blankets on loan until they could be replaced from the stores. Unhappily, there would not be a bed until the next prisoner in room 9 was released. Kurt said the comfort of just a mattress would seem like paradise after almost a week on the pitilessly hard floors of the police station and law courts.

The buying and selling of mattresses was a minor racket. They were supposed to be issued to every prisoner, but were always in short supply. On the rare occasions when the stores had some in stock, they were given only to those who could provide substantial *baksheesh*. Most prisoners relied on family or friends to provide some sort of palliasse. When they left, they usually took these with them, rolled up like a giant swiss-roll, with their possessions piled into the centre. A few, however, sold them to other prisoners and fewer still gave them away.

Fahdi suggested that Kurt should sleep in the corner where we took our meals. The mattress was already there, blankets folded beside it.

Kurt admitted he was so weary he would be thankful to sleep anywhere. Would we mind if he bedded down immediately?

Fahdi and I started to make up the bed, while Kurt stripped off jacket and shirt, pulled off shoes and socks and, with towel, soap and toothbrush, went off to the tap.

A moment later I was gently pushed aside by Nasir and Sultan, who took over. I knew better than to protest. To allow an elderly man to take part in any physical activity, if there is someone younger present capable of performing the task, is a serious breach of Arab good manners. The trio quickly finished their work, Nasir insisting on loaning a pillow.

Kurt returned, towelling his broad neck and muscular chest, shaking beads of water out of his much cleaner hair; his gentian-blue eyes were clear and some of his vitality seemed to have revived under the cold tap.

'Everything is so dirty,' he complained. 'My clothes, my towel, everything – can I wash them somewhere tomorrow?'

I told him he could use the laundry or, if he needed to save his piastres, he could heat water on a *barboua*, beg a handful of detergent powder from the service staff and wash the stuff himself. What was forbidden in room 1 was freely permitted in 9.

He said angrily: 'Those bastards at the police station grabbed all my dollars and Deutschmarks and left me nothing but a few worthless Syrian coins!'

'Will your friends or family send money?'

'My friends will, yes. But shall I be allowed to receive it?'

'I'm told there are no regulations to stop you, but it's safer to have it sent via the consular department of your embassy. Didn't the colonel at the police station give you a small "donation" from your funds before you left for the courts?'

'Not a pfennig! Did he give you something?'

'One hundred Syrian pounds.'

'You lucky old sod!'

Kurt had remained stripped to the waist, his chest looking as if it had been carved in ivory under the strip-lighting. He was now about to take off his trousers, and as he began to unzip his fly I felt it necessary to utter a word of warning.

'Kurt!' I yelped, 'don't do that!'

'Do what?' He paused, obviously puzzled, his hand suspended over his crutch.

'What are you wearing under those trousers – just briefs?'

Still puzzled, he said: 'Yes – why? What does it matter?'

'It matters,' I insisted, 'because if you take off your trousers you'll be naked apart from your briefs. If they should get even slightly displaced, you'll be in serious trouble.'

'In trouble – why?'

'Because the Arab attitude to a bare body is very different to ours. If this was Europe you could walk about starkers and no one would bat an eyelid. Here, if you stand about, even for a few moments, in the barely perceptible underwear worn by most of your generation the younger men will believe you guilty of shameless sexual provocation and the older generation will consider themselves insulted by deliberately whorish behaviour.'

'You're not serious?'

'Indeed I am.'

'Then how can I remove my trousers?' he said desperately.

'Put on a shirt before you do so.'

'But that is crazy –'

'I know. But I advise it just the same. Or you could lie on your mattress and take them off under a blanket.'

'They must be paranoid about sex and every one a *wärme Brüder*!'

'Not at all. They just have a totally different ethos to ourselves.'

Kurt zipped up his flies again, saying: 'As you're an old Arab hand I will accept your advice, but God in heaven, it's going to make life most difficult!'

He turned to those who had prepared his bed and thanked them warmly in French. They understood little of what he was saying, but knew he was expressing appreciation because he instinctively touched their shoulders with his fingertips. Arabs have no phobias about physical contact, using such gestures a great deal to demonstrate pleasure or gratitude.

Kurt solved his problem by slipping a clean T-shirt over his head, lying down and covering himself with a blanket. This was followed by a great deal of squirming and body contortion, until the trousers were flung into the air with a flourish. I seized them, folded them and put them on the suitcase at the foot of his bed. He protested sleepily: 'Don't touch them. They're filthy – haven't had them off for a week!'

'We all arrive here in the same condition. Tomorrow I'll take you to the bath-house for a hot shower.'

'Sounds wonderful,' he murmured, 'but don't wake me too early. I feel as if I need to sleep forever … ' He closed his eyes.

'*Il va dormir sans rien manger*?' said Fahdi sadly.

'Never mind. Tomorrow he'll appreciate your cooking so much more,' I consoled him.

Room 9 was noisy that evening and reverberated until after midnight with television, radio and the inevitable arguments over *dama* and chess. Kurt slept through it like a hibernating animal, remaining unconscious even while the five of us sat eating and talking beside his bed.

The next morning he was still sleeping so deeply I did not have the heart to wake him. I went across to shower and explained the situation to Anwar, who promised to let Kurt take precedence in the queue, an accepted custom for new arrivals.

Soon after half-past-eight, while I was strolling with Jean-Pierre, one of the younger guards rushed up to me and, patting me on the shoulder, said just one word: '*Safara.*'

Jean-Pierre translated. 'It means embassy,' he said. 'Somebody from the British Consulate is waiting to see you.'

'Where do I find them? In that awful place in the *Abraaj*?'

'No. In the governor's office – that rococo villa.'

118

I was soon outside the small building that looked more like a home for *la belle* Otero than the office of a prison governor. I was confronted by two doors, side by side in the centre of the ground floor, each protected by a fine wire fly-screen. A guard was lounging on the half-dozen marble steps leading to the entrances. He pulled a hand out of his pocket and pointed to the door on the left, miming that I should knock. When I did so, he smiled, giving me a thumbs-up sign.

I could hear no answer, so I pushed the door open, only to discover I was not, as I had expected, in an entrance hall or anteroom, but had bounced directly into the Persian-carpeted office of the governor himself. Contrasted with the stone cellars and dilapidated, roof-leaking shanties of the prisoners' quarters, it seemed startlingly luxurious if, perhaps, in questionable taste. Against each pale green wall was a line of small, mahogany-framed armchairs with cane backs and seats of lemon-yellow leather. Beside almost every chair was a glass-topped, pedestal table. The room had three large windows, heavily draped with beige nylon-velvet curtains, fringed with huge chocolate bobbles. The governor's immense desk was at right angles to the window opposite the door. On it – the first object I noticed as I pushed open the door – was a big table-lamp, fashioned out of cheap pottery in the shape of an improbable female wearing a crimson crinoline and holding aloft a frilly, arsenic green, silk shade.

The governor, sitting at the desk, showed no surprise at my sudden appearance. Impassively, he pointed at the two other occupants of the room, who sat with cups of coffee in front of them. One was Richard Lyne, the other a young Syrian member of the British Consulate staff.

This governor was the first with whom I came into contact and the highest in rank, a brigadier. He was also the least outgoing: a sad, sunken-eyed, taciturn man, astonishing in a Syrian who are like most Arabs, a volatile people.

During my time there were many changes at the top; no governor occupied the post for longer than four or five months. Educated Syrian prisoners assured me the frequent changes were made to prevent any governor having time to get involved in large-scale corruption when handling the prison's financial assets and the bulk-buying of food. If the rumours circulated by the junior staff were to be believed, most of them managed to line their pockets fairly substantially during their brief tenure. Was it perhaps significant that all of them were without previous experience of governing a prison before being appointed to the Citadel, one of the largest in Syria?

The majority held the rank of lieutenant-colonel, but towards the end of my time a mere major was appointed. He retained the job for as long as any of his more elevated predecessors; small, chubby and boisterous, he spoke excellent German; worshipped the memory of Hitler; and like his predecessors was capable, at times, of much kindness and, at others, of considerable brutality.

They all made a point of carrying on with their work while prisoners were visited by embassy officials; busily reading documents and signing them with a flourish of gold-plated fountain-pen; discussing problems rather too loudly with their deputies; cross-questioning prisoners who had made a formal complaint. These men were usually handcuffed to two guards; all too often the interview would degenerate into a slanging match between prisoner and governor, ending with the wretched man being dragged from the office, both parties screaming with rage.

But on this sunny March morning, everything was quiet and orderly. From the beginning I found these visits from the embassy staff a pleasurable experience and looked forward to them.

Never having been a prisoner in any country, I was uncertain of the diplomatic protocol. I seemed to get things right, however, by shaking hands with the governor before turning to greet my visitors.

I shall always be grateful to the young Syrian who accompanied Richard Lyne on this occasion. He acted as my interpreter throughout the many stages of my trial in the high court. His ability to switch from Arabic into English and back without a second's pause was remarkable. His easy fluency in colloquial English was also astonishing and convinced me that his mother must have been English. This, I soon discovered, was not so; he had, in fact, only spent a few weeks of his twenty-eight years of life in England.

Much of these visits was taken up with mundane, practical matters of immediate importance to me. The first item was the news of Lufthansa's refund of the cost of my flight. I now had approximately £400 to my credit. It was suggested the consulate should keep a 'float' of £100 to pay for articles I would need from outside. I agreed, and Lyne handed me the remaining cash in Syrian currency.

I explained I was sleeping on a borrowed mattress and resting my head on a borrowed pillow. Could I now please be supplied with my own. These requests were written in a notebook, and I was asked if I also needed blankets. I said I was prepared to put up with those issued. I asked for a small transistor set with good short-wave reception. Without wishing to add to the general cacophony, I wanted to keep up to date with what was going on in the world.

They warned me that the summer recess of the law courts would almost certainly delay my trial until the autumn. During July, August and September, the Damascus high court sits for only two weeks each month, which creates a backlog of cases seldom disposed of before Christmas.

Lyne asked if I wanted to employ a lawyer, warning me that fees, especially for those with good reputations, could be very high indeed.

I said that decision would have to wait until I knew how much financial support I would get from friends. As I had been caught red-handed it was difficult to believe even the most brilliant of barristers could do anything for me unless they were masters in the art of bribery. Neither visitor contradicted me.

When they got up to go I gave them a packet of letters to post. I had been keeping them for this moment in my shirt pocket. Simultaneously, they presented me with two very full carrier-bags. Inside, I found writing-paper and envelopes (previously I had to borrow from Rachid), slabs of milk chocolate, fresh fruit and a wonderful selection of English newspapers, magazines and paperbacks. I felt like a child given two Christmas stockings. I had mentioned my voracious appetite for newsprint to Richard Lyne at the police station, indicating my tastes inclined towards the 'posh' rather than the 'popular'. With every visit the embassy staff brought me many issues of *The Times*, *Guardian*, *Sunday Times* and *Observer*; there would also be copies of the *Spectator*, *Economist* and *New Statesman* and that short-lived 'technicoloured' weekly of James Goldsmith called *Now*, so much abused in the columns of *Private Eye*, but which I thoroughly enjoyed. I also enjoyed Richard Lyne's own copies of *Private Eye* which he was kind enough to pass on.

During the seemingly endless afternoons and evenings when there was so little to do except lie on our beds, I read every one of these publications from first page to last, often several times – including the classified advertisements. It would be impossible to over-estimate their importance to me.

The mattress and wireless set were delivered a few days later by an embassy driver. There was a note from Lyne saying the mattress was a spare from the embassy's store and I would not be charged for it. It was a splendid gift – its interior springs became the envy of everyone in *el Kalaa* who was allowed the privilege of sitting on it. Doubtless because of my age, the staff made no protest about its width: instead of the regulation two feet it was three inches wider than the space normally permitted in *Hofra*.

The small transistor set was a good one, but I found batteries something of a problem, and also for my German shaver. Those of good quality for sale in Syria had always been Iraqi-made; because of steadily increasing antagonism between the two countries, they were no longer imported. The local product, on sale in the prison, lasted only a few hours. I much appreciated the efforts made by the Syrian staff of the British Embassy who appeared to ransack most of the souks in Damascus in search of hidden or forgotten stocks of the excellent Iraqi batteries.

As far as wireless reception was concerned, I soon discovered the short-wave transmissions of the BBC World Service were too often subjected to maddening atmospheric interference; their signals a good deal weaker than those from the Soviet Union and other eastern bloc countries broadcasting in English. I therefore became a constant listener to the Israeli transmissions on medium wave from Jerusalem. I found their news bulletins as accurate as those of the BBC and their current affairs programmes surprisingly impartial, often outspokenly critical of action taken by their government at home or abroad.

Damascus Radio also broadcast daily bulletins in (imperfect) French and English, but these consisted of little but crude, inaccurate propaganda.

The delivery of the wireless was held up by one of the deputy governors; presumably he wished to make sure hashish had not been substituted for batteries. I was never sure if the staff really believed the British Embassy might be capable of this sort of narcotic smuggling. Paradoxically, they made no attempt to examine the mattress which could easily have contained many kilos of the stuff.

Every item a prisoner received during a visit was supposed to be checked by the *el Kalaa* sergeant and his minions before he was allowed into the courtyard en route for his own room. In my case they seldom bothered to inspect anything. I would hold up my carrier-bags and utter the magic password, '*Safara*', which was usually answered with a smile and a gesture to go straight through.

Most guards were between the ages of twenty and forty; sturdy, thick-set, hairy-chested bulls. The majority were basically good-natured, but even the gentlest would not hesitate, if provoked, to make a physical assault on a prisoner. No one considered this surprising, except, perhaps, a few youthful Europeans who arrived later. A tactless question or a remark considered impertinent, or merely inopportune, could result in a resounding slap across the face from a hand as hard as teak. An upwards thrust of the knee or toe of a boot into the groin was also a possibility.

Colonisation by France and Turkey of much of the Levant and North Africa has probably encouraged this tradition. Although a lover of France since earliest childhood, I must admit to occasionally being sickened by the public spectacle of *les flics ou les vaches à roulettes* beating some inoffensive youth into a pulp before throwing the unconscious body into a *pannier à salade*. There was no suggestion of deliberate sadism in the guards' attitude: no visible evidence of sexual pleasure being derived from the slappings and kickings. They obviously looked upon such behaviour as a normal function of the job. They seemed to feel they must establish, at almost any cost, a macho image, otherwise the prisoners might mount a serious revolt and destroy them. It was true their physical safety was sometimes in danger and, occasionally, their lives could be at risk.

The hazards of being a prison guard in Syria, and in other Arab countries, are greater than in a similar European establishment, where the staff is never far from a spot where a recalcitrant prisoner can be locked speedily – often electronically – into a single cell. Prison officers, even in England where jails are out of date and overcrowded, seldom have to deal with a mob that cannot immediately be isolated.

The smallest so-called cell in *el Kalaa* contained twenty men and the numbers occupying the remainder varied between fifty to one hundred and fifty. There were, of course, the single punishment cells, tucked away behind the guardroom, but in order to get hold of special offenders there was no option but to enter these dormitories – usually never more than two guards together, like a couple of Daniels – and brave the collective antagonism of the guilty prisoner and his friends, all of whom might be there for crimes of violence, even murder. Every guard carried a small pistol in a leather holster on his belt, but I never saw them use these; they relied on their ability to threaten and to use their fists and feet.

A few days after the visit from my embassy Rachid left us. Early one morning I heard his name over the tannoy system to go to the governor's office. About quarter of an hour later he was back in the courtyard and, taking me by the elbow, propelled me inside room 8, where he started to fold up his clothes. He grabbed a suitcase from a shelf above his head, saying, 'As you have no doubt already guessed – I'm leaving.'

'Immediately?'

'Yes. My lawyer is here with the necessary papers and my wife is outside in a Baalbek taxi. I'm only taking my clothes and a few personal things. Everything else is for you. If you don't need the *barboua* and all the pots, give them to somebody who does. Jean-Pierre, I know, has everything he needs, but the young German can probably use the blankets and pillows.

'You're very kind. We shall all miss you.'

'*You* have nothing to fear – except for the terrible waste of some of the last years of your life. The staff like you and I'm sure you'll cause them no problems. You've reached an age deserving of respect, and I'm sure you'll get it.' He began to put his clothes into the case. 'Next week you'll be moving to *Hofra*. The man who was chief of the room before the reconstruction is almost at the end of his sentence and doesn't want the job any more. I have therefore used my influence with the governor to allow Fahdi to take over. I wanted to be quite sure you had somebody to look after you.'

He then snapped his luggage locks shut, sat on the bed and looked at me seriously: 'I wish I could take you with me, but that isn't possible.'

'Of course not.'

Then, almost in a whisper, he said: 'But if you're unlucky enough to be given a long sentence, I'll help you get out.'

'How … ?' I was genuinely puzzled.

'You must make an official application to be transferred to Latakia prison. Tell the governor you wish to go there because it's smaller and less crowded than *el Kalaa* and the sea air will be good for your health – the prison is right on the beach.'

'Are such transfers possible?'

'They take place all the time. The governor will have to refer your application to the Ministry of Justice for approval, but that's a formality.'

'And how would a transfer to Latakia help you to get me out?'

'When you get there you'll have to pretend to be ill. Either give yourself a real illness or fake something serious enough to get you a bed in the hospital, next door to the prison. It has a special ward for prisoners and an absurdly poor security system – I could bust the place wide open in no time. As soon as I know you're there – that will be no problem, several of the prison staff are my friends – I'll collect half-a-dozen men from my unit and we'll have you out in a couple of minutes. In less than an hour we shall have put you across the Lebanese frontier and you'll be a free man!'

I found it difficult to show much enthusiasm for this idea. 'It sounds a bit dicey,' I said doubtfully.

'Rubbish! My men would look upon it as an amusing way to spend a winter's evening. We should operate in plain clothes, of course.' He got up and slapped me on the back. 'But let's hope you get a short sentence so it won't be necessary.'

He called the servicemen, telling them to gather up everything he was leaving and hand it to their opposite numbers in room 9. 'Tell them everything is for Monsieur Tony,' he said. He tipped them generously and shook their hands. Picking up the suitcase, he linked his arm through mine, saying: 'Come with me while I say goodbye to everybody.'

There was much shaking of hands and one or two close embraces for special friends. We finally arrived at the guardroom where he gave me an Arab bear-hug, kissing me on both cheeks. 'This is not goodbye,' he said, quietly, 'I'll return to see you as often as I can. Let me be the liaison between you and your friends in the Beka'a Valley.'

I watched him bid a brief farewell to the guards and disappear towards the long flight of steps that would lead him to freedom.

Kurt and Jean-Pierre were now standing on each side of me. Speculation about the reasons for Rachid's imprisonment began again.

'So our guardian angel has left us,' said Kurt. 'Some people will be glad.'

'I remember the day he walked in here and the rumours that began circulating immediately,' said Jean-Pierre. 'Everybody was whispering the new prisoner in room 8 was not a prisoner at all, but a spy sent by Riffa'at Assad.'

'What evidence did they have?' I asked.

'Oh, none. Just one of the political prisoners knew Rachid had been in military intelligence. You know how they gossip – they were sure he had been sent to listen to somebody and report on them.'

'Who?' I said.

'They did not know – and they still don't. He seemed to take no interest in political prisoners.'

Kurt poked me in the ribs. 'You walked with him almost every afternoon. Did he never tell you why he was here?'

I shook my head.

'Did you ask him?' said Jean-Pierre.

'Only once. I was politely told to mind my own business. We spent most afternoons discussing methods of transporting hash by the ton to Europe and America.'

'Because he hoped to learn how to put a stop to such traffic?' queried Jean-Pierre.

'On the contrary – he hoped to take an active part in promoting it!'

'Interesting,' said Kurt, cheerfully. 'I hope he keeps in touch – he could be useful to us in the future.'

Jean-Pierre said seriously: 'Not for me. I have had enough of this sort of life.'

Kurt looked at him with surprise. Then, turning to me, said: 'I suppose you know your special friendship with Rachid has caused a lot of gossip?'

I shrugged. 'I suppose that was inevitable – in a closed community nobody has much to do except speculate about each other.'

Kurt grinned. 'Did you know several people warned me against you on my first day here?'

This did surprise me. 'What sort of warning?' I asked.

'Oh, they told me to be careful of what I said to the old Englishman. They were uneasy because it's clear you've known Rachid for some time and they didn't know if your association was based on hashish or politics – it's the politics that had them worried.'

I had not realised I had acquired a mildly sinister reputation which was going to take me some time to live down.

Jean-Pierre sniffed contemptuously. 'What have these stupid people got to hide and why are they so – so *craintif*? Why did they not make more of an effort to find out Rachid's reasons for being here? They hardly ever opened their mouths to him, except to say, 'Yes, *sidi* – No, *sidi*!' In a French prison a similar character would have been threatened, perhaps killed. But here *ces indigènes* just rush into corners and whisper rumours – so typical!'

126

Rachid's name was not often mentioned thereafter. When he disappeared up those steps it seemed as if he faded from everyone's memory but mine. From time to time he came to see me as he had promised, always in uniform with a parachute emblem on his left breast, bringing news of friends, and money from those with whom I had been working. These visits took place, like embassy visits, in front of the governor or one of his deputies. Their manners on these occasions showed signs of a suppressed apprehension not noticeable when they were exchanging pleasantries with foreign consular staff, as though Rachid were a time-bomb ticking away in their office.

HOFRA: PART 1

There were, of course, postponements before those accused or convicted of drug offences could be moved into *Hofra*. The cement used to reinforce the weaknesses had, at the last minute, been found to be hardly stronger than cold porridge. It had to be scooped out of the buttresses and replaced with tougher material. But in the end, the inescapable took place, and we had to move.

We had been warned to be ready, with all our effects, to move into our new home at two in the afternoon. Dead on time, all one hundred and twenty-three of us – some from every room in *el Kalaa* – lined up in single file. The queue extended from *Hofra*'s stone-tunnel entrance down the length of the courtyard; each of us surrounded by an untidy pile of baggage. The spectacle reminded me of scenes I had witnessed in the defeated Germany of 1945: those pathetic groups of humanity, waiting for a repatriation train or entry into a DP camp.

Fahdi, with his newly-acquired authority as chief of the room, flanked by a couple of guards to help him, was already in our tubular cellar, allocating living space, just wide enough for a palliasse, to each prisoner as he stumbled, clumsily, through the low entrance. From the sounds that travelled up into the yard, few seemed satisfied with what they were given.

Although we Europeans had already been told of the places assigned to us, we had to line up with everybody else in order of length of time in the prison. Jean-Pierre, after eight months, was well up towards the head of the procession; Kurt and I were definitely parts of its tail. Our progress was slow, about one yard every ten minutes, as we pushed or dragged our impedimenta along. We were occasionally halted for longer by the bitter disputes about *placements*.

When Kurt and I finally reached the steps, the protests and complaints from below were suddenly annihilated by a voice raised to such a high pitch of fury it blotted out all other noises: It was Jean-Pierre who

128

had clearly and completely lost his temper. His tirade was quickly interrupted by a demonic outburst from Fahdi. This exchange of violent insults was interwoven with gruff interruptions from a guard, supporting Jean-Pierre's claim to the space immediately on the right of the entrance. This was being sharply contested by Fahdi who considered this the ideal vantage point from which to exercise his authority as chief.

As neither would give way, the duty-sergeant was summoned to mediate. After listening patiently to both sides, he came down firmly for Jean-Pierre. By the time Kurt and I had dragged our mattresses etc. down the last few steps and through the tunnel, Jean-Pierre was established just inside the gates and smirking in triumph at Fahdi's discomfiture.

Fahdi, deeply conscious of a serious loss of face on his first day as chief, was silent: but his expression suggested Jean-Pierre would have an uneasy ride in the months to come.

Kurt and I arranged our chattels within the tiny space allotted. I laid my mattress on the platform next to Jean-Pierre's (Kurt having hissed in my ear that he would rather sleep in the corridor than next to the 'old-maidish, Gallic hen'!) and wondered how to make best use of the nine-inch gap between the foot of my mattress and a drop of two feet into the corridor. Was it here I was supposed to put the stuff that had previously filled two suitcases? I had crammed all my clothes into the least-damaged one and discarded the other; but there were cups, plates, saucepans, forks, spoons and a teapot inherited from Rachid, and the precious *barboua* which had never left my hand.

Now even Kurt had to be grateful to Jean-Pierre. His previous experience of the troglodyte life in *Hofra* proved of great benefit. He demonstrated the best place for a suitcase – upright against the wall behind our heads. Also, like most prisoners who had been in *Hofra* before, he had collected half-a-dozen orange-boxes from the greengrocery stall, and now arranged them in a row along the open space below our feet. Here, they performed as platforms for *barbouas*, as makeshift cupboards for domestic utensils and as tables.

Before locking us up, the sergeant bellowed that we were not to deface the newly whitewashed walls in any way: no nail or hook must be allowed to mar their pristine perfection. This order was greeted with derisive laughter. Jean-Pierre explained this was the sort of instruction the staff never attempted to enforce for longer than a few days; and he was right – within a week a forest of hooks had sprouted above the beds. Suspended from them, on metal hangers, was an amazing variety of multi-coloured clothing: everything from overcoats to nylon underwear. Later, Jean-Pierre, Kurt and I hung our suitcases on such hooks, with the aid of piano-wire wound round the handles. This gave us space for a sizeable library of books and magazines behind our heads.

Fahdi, deprived of the position he coveted, decided nevertheless to establish himself with us on the dais reserved by tradition for foreigners. He unrolled his palliasse alongside Kurt's. It had been obvious for some time that he was susceptible to Kurt's good looks. This had aroused a certain amount of lip-curling from Jean-Pierre, who I knew would soon start making snide remarks. I wondered if Fahdi would be unwise enough to instal the odalisque-like Sultan on his other side, but discretion prevailed and the boy was given a place in a far corner. The lad was also given the job of *Hofra*'s junior serviceman.

Another vacancy remained in the foreigners' section and Fahdi chose to give this – doubtless because of Arab deference to age – to a little Syrian nearing sixty. Abou Khaldoun was a gentle soul who spoke excellent French and quickly became a friend to us all. He had an exceptional gift for getting on with the younger generation and both Kurt and Jean-Pierre became extremely fond of him. His appearance can be easily described. As he said of himself: '*Je suis bien comme le Père Noel, n'est pas!*' and this was true. With his abundant snowy locks and *bouffant* white beard, he did look like a diminutive, twinkling-eyed Santa Claus.

The ventilation of *Hofra* was a farce. The single, slowly revolving extractor-fan high above us was incapable of clearing the clouds of tobacco smoke, often infused with hashish, puffed continuously into the air from a hundred chain smokers. (The wide publicity in the Western World about the danger to health of cigarette smoking has never been emulated by the media in Arab countries, the majority of whose citizens smoke incessantly.) Jean-Pierre and I were the only non-smokers in *Hofra*: this was looked upon as European eccentricity. Happily, the smoke never caused me any difficulty in breathing, but my eyes would often feel gritty and mildly painful.

Another constant source of pollution were the *barbouas*, most of them never properly cleaned and allowed to emit giant flames followed by clouds of heavy black smoke. Our exodus each morning would produce a temporary improvement but, by late afternoon, it was possible to stand at one end of *Hofra* and see nothing of what was happening at the other.

Apart from the single, inadequate ventilator, there were two small rectangular holes in the roof, each partly blocked by a broken fan. Some smog would escape through these during the night, but many prisoners did not sleep well and when they could not sleep they smoked.

These gaps in the roof were also our only source of daylight, but even in the brightest weather they did little to disperse the semi-darkness. All other rooms in *el Kalaa* were illuminated by tube-lighting, but *Hofra*, buried deep in the ancient Citadel, was more primitive and we had to be satisfied with a dozen naked bulbs suspended on thin wire from the centre of the roof. They had to be kept switched on night and day and, being of local manufacture, they did not last long. A form-filling bureaucracy made replacements slow to arrive, so we considered ourselves lucky if half of them were working at one time.

We became accustomed to the frequent failures of electricity common to the majority of Levant countries. Most power-cuts were fairly short. I remember only one occasion when the lights were deliberately switched off during the night. This was the handiwork of a prisoner – who was also the jail's official electrician – deciding to make a getaway. Being a privileged 'trusty', he managed to gain access to the Citadel's master control-panel at about 2 AM on a dark night, just prior to a new moon. He removed a number of important fuses and cut several cables, plunging the entire prison into total blackout. Combining the abilities of a cat-burglar and rock climber, he scaled the ramparts and got clean away. He was never recaptured.

Although *Hofra*'s skylights were too small to provide much light, being devoid of glass they were big enough to admit large quantities of rain. Between November and early May it can often rain in Damascus, sometimes quite heavily; occasionally, as at the time of my arrest, it can snow.

During the winter our central passage would sometimes become flooded to a depth of several inches. Perhaps surprisingly, this did not worry us unduly unless we had more than our usual number of prisoners. If we were suffering from one of our periodical bouts of overcrowding, it could make conditions exceptionally unpleasant.

New arrivals in *Hofra*, even in fine weather, usually had to put up with a period of acute discomfort, having to sleep in the corridor. Sometimes there would be as many as twenty men sleeping, head to

131

toe, below our feet, leaving a space no wider than a single shoe for those making their way to the tap and lavatory.

Heavy rain would quickly turn this passage into a canal, and many of us privileged to have a tiny area on one of the platforms, had to share this with the poor wretches who were about to be submerged. This, naturally, caused appalling discomfort and made sleep virtually impossible, until the rains abated and the flood could be swept down the only drain, under the taps.

Unfortunately, the rain did not confine itself to the central passage: a good deal would splash over a wide area on each side, depending on the direction of the wind. Those whose beds were immediately under the holes suffered more. These included Kurt, Jean-Pierre and myself. We were induced by Jean-Pierre to buy several yards of a transparent, man-made material, for sale in the *Abraaj*. At one end we stitched small loops of string to the two corners. At the onset of a rainstorm, we would attach these loops to hooks well above our heads, and tuck the other end under our mattresses. The result was a sort of lean-to type of tent, and was surprisingly successful in keeping our beds dry.

Many protests were made to a succession of governors about conditions in *Hofra*, always in vain. On one occasion my own protest was strongly supported by the British Embassy, but to no avail. Apparently it had been decreed long ago by the Ministry of Justice that all prisoners accused or convicted of drug offences should be confined within this elongated dungeon and, seemingly, no power in all Syria was going to alter this dictum, in spite of vacant spaces sometimes available elsewhere in *el Kalaa*.

Our only lavatory was in a kind of giant metal box at the western end, perched on a concrete platform. To enter, it was necessary to walk up three or four steps, duck under the lintel and open a rusty iron door whose hinges screamed like tropical birds.

The lavatory was the kind where you squat over a dark hole. A defective brass tap, set, surprisingly, into the right-hand wall, about eighteen inches from the ground, provided a continuous trickle of water. A narrow gully below the tap allowed the water to flow into the hole: obviously installed for washing the left hand and flushing the 'loo', the dribble it provided was scarcely adequate for either function. It had presumably been fitted on the right because *Hofra*'s pipes had been installed on that side long before the construction of our giant box, and must have caused a good deal of inconvenience to our Arab

132

companions who are commanded by Islam to use only the left hand for such functions. As they are reticent about these things, I refrained from asking embarrassing questions. Jean-Pierre and Kurt, who had no experience of an Arab community, were surprised to discover that many of our middle-aged and elderly colleagues, plus the young fundamentalists, always peed squatting. To do so standing up is frowned upon by Islam, because of the danger of spray from the urine defiling one's clothes.

The privy was certainly whiffy; it could hardly have been otherwise with over a hundred regular customers, but did not give off the lung-penetrating stench common to others in the prison. This was mainly due to Fahdi's insistence on the service staff flushing out the box every day with a rubber hose attached to an adjacent tap through which there was, mercifully, an exceptionally strong pressure of water.

The water from these two taps was the only substance obtainable in the entire Citadel which could be accurately described as delicious. Its source was a spring beneath the old city of Damascus: clear, sparkling, filled with oxygen; even in high summer, with a shade temperature of over 100°F it always remained delectably cool.

Also at this end of Hofra were half-a-dozen metal dustbins, filled to overflowing by the end of each day with stale food, empty tins, rotting vegetables and fruit-peelings, until they disappeared under a mountain of garbage. Every morning, they were emptied into a refuse-cart manhandled over the ramparts. The bins were always washed before being replaced, but this never prevented their contents from having a magnetic attraction for a legion of large black rats.

I was surprised at how speedily I became totally indifferent to these creatures. In order to wash, brush my teeth and use the 'loo' without having to queue, it became customary for me to get up earlier than anybody else. I would slip out of bed soon after six and, clutching towel and sponge-bag, stumble along the central passage as quietly as possible. During our overcrowded periods it was like walking a tight-rope. At this hour the bins would be covered by a sort of undulating, grey-black carapace. As one approached it became obvious this rippling sheath was an almost solid mass of rats, gorging themselves on the *Hofra* refuse.

My appearance would be a signal for some to break away, up the steps into the privy – the hole was their sole means of entry or exit. Others would continue stuffing themselves until I waved my

133

towel threateningly at them. There were always a few macho types who never stopped eating until the service staff beat them away with broomsticks.

As I got used to squatting nonchalantly over the hole, it amused me to realise how impervious I had become to these big rats as they scampered in and out between my legs and over my, often bare, feet. For a time after I left the Citadel, it seemed strange to perform my natural functions without them sprinting to and fro beneath me.

I was told of an Englishman, in *Hofra* the previous year, who liked to amuse himself by holding a large plastic bag over the black hole as a snare to trap rats as they emerged. He would then take the bag and beat the animal to death against the lavatory wall, splashing blood in all directions. This did nothing to reduce their numbers. He would throw the battered corpses into the dustbins, where they were promptly devoured by their relatives. I made no attempt to emulate my predecessor.

The rats seldom strayed far from the bins. Only occasionally would one or two decide to explore. Several times, on hot summer nights, I felt furry whiskers investigating my bare toes; but this was a rare event and they made no attempt to bite.

Only once was a serious effort made by the prison staff to put an end to the rat infestation. They actually succeeded in locating the spot where the rats gained access to our main drain, and plugged it – and for at least a week there were no rats to be seen. They must have steadily gnawed away the barrier for, on the eighth day, they were back in larger numbers than before and as hungry as ever.

Those of us who had been in dormitories where the gates were open all morning, had to forfeit that privilege. By ten to eight there was a long queue waiting to use the lavatory and wash face, hands and feet (as laid down by the Koran): a misery I avoided by my Spartan early rising.

Fahdi, as chief of the room, would be moving up and down the passage, tweaking the toes of those still asleep, determined to get them up in time to scramble into their clothes and fold their bedding before the arrival, soon after eight (Arab punctuality is elastic) of the guards. These uniformed young toughs would crash into the vault, shouting with Rabelaisian good humour, using their batons to tap the feet of those who had not yet stirred.

It would usually take about ten minutes to clear the place, expelling everyone except Fahdi, the service duo, and the exclusive few in possession of a doctor's certificate. The inner gates to *Hofra* were then left open, but those at the top of the steps were locked until the general roll call at about 1.30 PM. Fahdi and the servicemen were permitted to move in or out when their work made this necessary. Getting out was sometimes a problem; they had to attract the attention of somebody in the yard and ask him to call a guard to bring keys. This was our morning routine for six days out of seven: on the seventh both gates were left open all morning to enable everybody to go to the bath-house.

Immediately on re-entering *Hofra* in the afternoon, most of us would change into pyjamas before settling down to a hot meal. These garments, long ago discarded by the young and even the middle-aged of the Western World, have not suffered a similar decline in popularity among the Arab races of North Africa and the Middle East. If you are invited to dine *en famille* with old friends in these countries, it is always possible that your host, and other male members of his household, will be wearing pyjamas. In the stuffy atmosphere of *Hofra* they proved sensible and were worn by all who could afford them. Even Kurt and Jean-Pierre, who had slept 'raw' almost from childhood, succumbed to the habit.

As we were members of an almost exclusively Muslim community, apart from a few Lebanese Christians, it was necessary to observe yet another Islamic convention: always to wear briefs, slips, or underpants under our pyjamas. In view of these prudish taboos, I found it surprising that in the exceptional heat of high summer, when trousers only were *de rigueur*, many of the younger men would wander around with the cord of these garments deliberately encircling not their waists but their hips, low enough in some cases to display an inch or two of pubic hair and the beginnings of the cleft between their buttocks.

The inmates of *Hofra* tended to be rougher and tougher than in other rooms. Abou Mustapha from New Jersey expressed it best: 'Hash-smoking in Europe and the States is kinda high class – in Syria it's just sumthin' for the bums!'

Some of these Syrian 'bums' used to insist it was their country who had populated the Levant before Islam, before the Jews, before the Christians; that they were the first scientists, writers and mathematicians; that their history gave them the right to claim Lebanon, Jordan, Iraq, Israel and Cyprus for their own, and that the frontiers of Syria should extend from Paphos to Basra and from Kurdistan to Sinai.

135

They varied in age between eighteen and the mid-fifties, none being anything like as old as myself. In spite of their toughness they were usually genial and good humoured. Hostilities, when they did break out between individuals could, however, escalate quickly into a savage battle, each trying to strangle or gouge out the eyes of the other. Knives were forbidden but were often smuggled in in food parcels. It was also possible, with a pair of pliers, to fashion a razor-sharp knife out of a corned beef tin; Kurt and Jean-Pierre made several during their time in jail, for cutting meat and vegetables. Others were less scrupulous in their use.

If the antagonists were some distance apart when the row began, war would sometimes be declared by one hurling his blazing primus at the other. I remember one incident when I was caught in the cross-fire, the blue flames from this domestic rocket singeing my fringe of white hair, just above the right ear, as it whistled past. To my surprise everybody turned furiously on the youth who had thrown the *barboua*, shouting: '*Aib! Aib!*' (Shame! Shame!) His plea that it was an accident and he intended no harm to me did not mollify them. 'You should be more careful,' they chorused, 'remember the respect due to an elderly foreigner!' In the ensuing slanging match, the original quarrel was forgotten.

Whenever two prisoners or more attempted to settle an argument by force, the friends of the belligerents would always make a sustained effort to tear the pair apart before they had time to injure each other. When the fighting couple were surrounded by a crowd anxious to restrain them, it would become a sort of giant, whirling rugger-scrum, trampling across beds up and down the room, smashing everything in its path; overturning litres of cooking oil, cans of paraffin and crushing crates of eggs and tomatoes by the dozen; reducing the orange-boxes to splinters. When peace was restored many had to send blankets to the laundry or wash them ourselves.

Fahdi was always quick to try and halt these human maelstroms. When they were over he would leap to the entrance-gate and bang the huge padlock against a crossbar. The noise usually penetrated to the guardroom who would send one of their number down to investigate. It was generally accepted that whoever had struck the first blow would be locked in solitary confinement for twenty-four hours. If the culprit was a frequent troublemaker, he might be kept in solitary for several days then have his head shaved before being returned to his room.

More successful than anyone at soothing those who lost their temper and restraining belligerents, was *Hofra*'s chief serviceman. Fahad had been a junior NCO in the Syrian army. He was only twenty but, to European eyes, looked a good deal older. Tall, with wide shoulders, muscular torso tapering to a slim waist and hips, he resembled a mixture of Italian bronze with Turkish wrestler. His dark eyes seemed to survey the rest of us with quiet amusement; his wide, generous mouth, surmounted by a closely-trimmed, black moustache, radiated a benevolent good humour which a single missing front tooth seemed to accentuate. He was not only good-looking but tough-looking, tough inside, and yet very gentle. His sentence was for two years for the possession of hashish. The amount of the drug had not been large, so there was much speculation about why he had been given so long a term by a military court with a reputation for leniency in such cases. Fahad's reaction was merely to smile, shrug and answer evasively those who felt he must have been involved in some additional illegal activity. The prevailing rumour was that he had been discovered indulging in minor sexual dalliance with young army conscripts and had attributed these indiscretions to the influence of hashish.

This, indeed, was the sort of excuse made by many accused of much more serious sex offences. Amongst us we had a party of eight middle-aged agricultural workers from a village on the Lebanese-Syrian frontier, all gnarled and wizened by years of toil under a blazing sun. They had been convicted of gang-raping a seven-year-old boy by tying him to a tree and sodomising him repeatedly until the child died from an uncontrollable haemorrhage. They, too, had pleaded their behaviour was the result of being 'stoned'. Such prisoners were always assigned to *Hofra*, where they often spent years living alongside a succession of those sentenced to perhaps six months for no crime but possessing a very few grams of the drug.

In *Hofra*, unlike the other rooms, the service staff were not responsible for washing up: there were always at least a dozen impecunious prisoners to do the job for those who could afford a small amount of *baksheesh*.

Fahad and Sultan distributed our rations and were busily employed keeping the place reasonably clean and tidy: no easy task in the bowels of a crumbling fortress among a crowd of Arabs, endowed by nature with superb dignity, but also an ability to create slummy disorder quicker than almost any other race. Any object they no longer need is thrown to the ground, the floor swiftly becoming a carpet of dog-ends, orange-peel, empty sweet- and cigarette-packets, yesterday's newspapers and much else. Yet it was always the most untidy who complained loudest about conditions.

Fahad and Sultan did their best to share out the food fairly. The so-called hot meal was brought over from the *Abraaj* kitchens by the service staff employed by the guards. Our own couple, usually assisted by Fahdi, would ladle the contents (never more than lukewarm) into the bowls we held out as they almost ran up and down the corridor.

It resembled a scene from Dickens with Levantine overtones. There were always prisoners certain to complain they had been given smaller helpings than their neighbours. There was also a minority who disdained anything brought in a bucket because they could afford to buy most of their food from the stalls, and have the remainder provided by visitors. Often, they employed poorer prisoners to cook their meals.

The distribution of bread, sugar, tea, eggs, tins of sardines and corned beef – also paraffin, for which we had to pay – afforded fewer opportunities for friction and did not normally provoke our malcontents into squawking they had been victimised. Fahad, fortunately, had a natural ability to soothe ruffled feelings, but there was always a small percentage even he could never appease.

Fahdi, whose appointment as chief had been due to Rachid's influence, was never much of a success in the job. I always felt an acute sense of responsibility towards him, because I knew he had been given the post for what had quickly become an unnecessary task – looking after me.

He was far too young and immature to have the necessary authority over some of our sharp-witted city-slickers. Also, his being Lebanese made him an automatic target for criticism from many Syrians who accused him of favouring the few Lebanese amongst us. This, I believe, was untrue, but those deprived of liberty can often become obsessed by fancied grievances.

All forms of gambling were forbidden; cards, dominoes, even backgammon, were officially banned; but chiefs of rooms would often turn a blind eye if they could be sure those taking part would give them a 'cut' from their winnings: a custom Fahdi was quick to adopt.

His behaviour with regard to hashish was similar. He gradually allowed himself to become involved with the principal traffickers in our *Hofra* community. He never smoked the stuff himself but slowly, over several months, became one of the chief suppliers: an acknowledged link-man between the prisoners and a minority of the guards who were willing to supply as much as anybody could afford, at a considerable profit.

I would smoke an occasional joint if one was offered but never bought the stuff for myself. Kurt and Jean-Pierre never took a single puff while in jail. Other Europeans, who arrived later, seldom stopped doing so.

From the beginning of our time in *Hofra*, there was little amity between Fahdi and Jean-Pierre but, for the first few months, he and Kurt were practically inseparable. Some thought it the beginning of a romantic friendship, but I was not one of them. Living in enforced intimacy with both, I saw this association was chiefly founded on Kurt's appreciation of good food and Fahdi's expertise as a cook. Kurt spent most evenings encouraging our Lebanese chief to prepare a splendid meal over a couple of *barbouas* while he sniffed the aroma appreciatively.

Fahdi's attitude was different. He had clearly been mesmerized by Kurt's good looks. It is not unusual for Arabs to become infatuated with fair-haired Europeans of either sex. Kurt was as heterosexual as it is possible for a human male to be; perhaps even more girl-crazy than most men of his age. Nevertheless, he often mentioned when talking about his home, Bavarian friends with whom he had grown up who now declared themselves 'gay'. They had, he said, understood he had no physical interest in them and was glad they remained friends. This frank expression of his feelings shocked some of his Syrian and Lebanese listeners, accustomed to conceal their bisexual proclivities under layers of dissembling. Sniffs of disapproval also emanated from Jean-Pierre.

The break-up happened not because Fahdi began pinching the German's bottom but because Kurt failed to understand that Arabs tend to become possessive even in the most innocent friendship. Kurt had an outgoing temperament and a gift for languages that enabled him to become reasonably fluent in Arabic with surprising speed – fluent enough to enjoy exchanging accounts of triumph or disaster with our companions, and to play *dama* or chess with them.

Fahdi could not conceal his jealousy and protested Kurt was associating with the lowest of the low. Kurt replied he found the 'low' very entertaining and had no intention of foregoing their company. Finally, there was a complete split when Fahdi took up his bed and established himself alongside Sultan at the western end of our 'pit'. His place was taken by a succession of Syrians until the arrival, about two months later, of two Italians.

There was also constant friction between Kurt and Jean-Pierre. Sandwiched between them for month after month, I often felt as if a Franco-German war had broken out across my inert body. It was a clash of personalities and in no way due to a dislike of each other's country.

Jean-Pierre was nit-pickingly tidy; anything not in use must be folded and put away. Kurt preferred a more chaotic life-style – his bed perpetually unmade, the area at top and bottom of his mattress always in a state of clutter. He did not take kindly to the Frenchman's strictures on the importance in communal life of method and self-discipline.

I will always remember Jean-Pierre telling us, quite seriously, that when he married it would be to *une petite paysanne*. 'The women of my social milieu are much too opinionated,' he declared. 'If a girl hasn't much education it will be easier for me to mould her to my own ideas.' This astonishing remark from a twenty-year-old reduced Kurt and myself to helpless laughter. This was not well received.

Washing up also caused continuous dissension between my companions. If it were Jean-Pierre's turn, he would heat a kettle immediately we had finished a meal and, piling our dirty dishes on a tray, join the queue that was always waiting to use the taps over the badly cracked, floor-level earthenware sink. When he finally got there he would wash and dry every item most carefully and stack them neatly in our orange-box cupboards.

Kurt, if it was his turn, would often ignore the chore for hours while he chatted, played several games of *dama* or chess or, possibly, went to sleep for an hour or two. Finally, he would often thrust everything into the hands of some needy Syrian delighted to earn a few piastres. Jean-Pierre would seethe with not always silent frustration.

In an effort to establish a more peaceful atmosphere I volunteered to do all the washing up myself. This did indeed produce concord but not the kind I intended. They ganged up against me, insisting I was far too old to crouch in front of the sink, coping with a small kettle of hot water and a load of greasy pots. I retorted that, although undeniably ancient, I was not yet doddering. They still rejected my offer but, as a concession, allowed me to wash the cups and glasses.

Although the Franco-German 'war' was to continue for a long

time, both were always wonderfully patient and tolerant in their attitude towards me. It cannot have been easy for these very young men, or for those who came later, to be compelled to live for months on end squashed like sardines with a man older than their grandfathers; but they managed to do so without a word of complaint and without ever making me feel I was a nuisance or a bore. I shall always be grateful.

As May gave way to June, the heat became more and more intense. Each day the ribbon of shade on the eastern side of the courtyard became narrower until, long before noon, it would vanish altogether. Those of us from dormitories locked all morning had difficulty in finding shelter from the pitiless sun, except under the broken awning of the overcrowded cafeteria. The shade temperature had now begun to fluctuate between 90° and 100°F. I tried to keep cool by wearing only a light shirt, cotton trousers and a pair of plastic flip-flops from the shop. The only exposed bits were my forearms and head. Having lived for a time in Morocco, I was sure the leathery texture of my facial skin would not burn, however hot the sun – but I did find some protection necessary for my bald pate. I was therefore delighted when Abou Mustapha, our Syrian from New Jersey (whose fringe of hair was even less abundant than mine) crocheted a pair of skull-caps in thick, white, cotton thread. These were most effective. Mine caused a good deal of leg-pulling from those who accused me of deliberately cultivating a resemblance to Pope John-Paul II. I found Abou Mustapha's dexterity with a crochet-needle surprising in one so sturdily masculine, whose English appeared to be culled from an old-fashioned gangster movie.

(This could be the moment to explain the word *Abou*, frequently employed throughout the Middle East as a prefix to a man's name. *Abou* means 'Father of'. Abou Mustapha = father of Mustapha. Abou Talal = father of Talal. When a man becomes father of a son, his own name seems to disappear into limbo except on official records. Even his wife will call him by this title and no longer use his name even in the closest intimacy. This custom does not extend to the Arab races of North Africa. There, it is the son who – for official purposes only – adds his father's name to his own: like my good friend Ahmed ben Boulaid, meaning Ahmed, son of Boulaid.)

I was later to discover my confidence in the toughness of my face was misplaced. A small crack in the skin below my left eye, which I

141

had attributed to nothing more serious than dry skin, revealed itself during a second summer to be something less pleasant.

My efforts to help Anwar with his English allowed me to sit in partial shade outside his *hammam* for an hour or so every morning. He shared the universal craze to learn our language, which was regarded as the key to success in every walk of life. I did my best to help as many as I could, although my lack of Arabic was always a disadvantage.

I think it possible that I was of some real use to Anwar because he had already acquired a considerable understanding of English and all that was really needed was polish.

Whenever there was a slack period in his bath-house, he would limp in search of me and ask, with almost excessive politeness, if he might read to me. I repeatedly told him just to shout whenever he wanted help with his books, but he apparently felt this would show lack of respect for my age.

We would sit on three-legged stools while he read aloud passages from the works of English writers chosen by the University of Damascus for their entry examination. These included Shakespeare's sonnets, the poetry of Marlowe, Milton, Keats, Shelley, Byron and Wordsworth, but nothing more recent. There were also novels such as *Pride and Prejudice, The Mayor of Casterbridge, Anna of the Five Towns* and *Lord of the Flies*; also one play, a translation of Ibsen's *Enemy of the People* which seemed to have been thrown in as an afterthought.

I cannot claim to have had much success in interpreting the subtleties of Jane Austen to a young Bedouin! I hope I did better with Thomas Hardy, Arnold Bennett and William Golding.

In between paragraphs, Anwar would constantly leap up to supply a bather with soap or a razor-blade or to swab out a cubicle.

He could read English exceptionally well; only occasionally did I have to correct his pronunciation and sometimes explain the meaning of a word or phrase he had failed to understand. Like all Arabs, he hated to lose face and was not always prepared to admit he had not grasped something. As I grew to know him I developed a sort of intuitive awareness of those moments when he read something faultlessly yet failed to comprehend what he was saying.

From the bath-house steps we could look across the great crowd milling in the yard, but Anwar always insisted on placing his stool where, whenever he looked up from his book, the passage between the showers would be directly in his vision. At times he seemed to glance into his steamy domain after every full stop, the muscles under his hard, black eyes occasionally becoming rigid with suspicion.

For a poor Bedouin, the job was a sinecure and he was determined not to give the authorities any cause to throw him out of it. He not only received a modest weekly salary, but the *baksheesh* must have added up to a pleasant total, although I never once heard him ask for a tip and he often refused to accept one.

Anwar accepted the bisexuality of some of his countrymen as a fact of life and was well aware that many *hammams* in the Levant and elsewhere are rendezvous for those attracted by their own sex. He had resolved not to allow his bath-house to acquire a similar reputation. This was not because of high moral principles – he was young, lusty and, with the prospect of spending the next twenty years without women, had a notoriously roving eye for a good-looking youth – but he never forgot that if rumours of indiscreet behaviour in the showers were to reach the governor he would lose his precious job.

Only once did I see two men attempt to shower together. Anwar threw both culprits into the yard, still draped in their towels, hissing they ought to be transferred to the special dormitory in the *Abraaj* reserved for those convicted of homosexual offences. This little epi-sode was greeted with a good deal of ribald laughter by the crowd and ignored by the guards.

Richard Lyne and a Syrian employee of the embassy paid me a second visit about a month after my arrival. Amongst other things, they brought a packet of mail – the first since my arrest. I was naturally delighted, but the delight began to fade when I noticed that an envelope addressed in my partner's handwriting had a Swiss stamp and had been posted in Geneva. This startled me, because I was sure he would now be in Amsterdam. I tore it open at once – excusing myself perfunctorily for doing so – and read of my young friend's arrest while crossing the Austro-German frontier and of his extradition by the Swiss police because of a little *contretemps* that had taken place at Geneva airport on the previous Christmas Eve; an event triggered off by an informer in Lebanon who must have felt he had a score to settle with both of us.

The mini-drama took place at the end of a direct flight from Beirut to Geneva. The aeroplane, when it landed, was surrounded not only by police but also by a detachment of troops with armoured vehicles. Passengers and crew were taken into custody and not released until they, and all luggage and freight, had been searched. A total of eighty-six kilos of hashish was found in four suitcases.

Due to some curious oversight or, perhaps, plain stupidity, the Swiss police never realised until too late that my partner was the passenger responsible and the employer of the English 'courier' they did arrest.

Because of the delay, many passengers had missed their connecting flights, my partner amongst them. In his case they apologised most humbly, installing him for the night, at their expense, in one of Geneva's nicest five-star hotels. The following morning he took the first train to Paris and rang me from the Hilton (I was still in Beirut) to tell me the story.

The Swiss police took some time to discover the identity of the man they had let slip through their fingers and four months elapsed before the German police grabbed him on their behalf as he was returning from a weekend with his Viennese girlfriend.

His Swiss lawyer had warned him to expect a sentence of not less than four years. His assets had been frozen and would almost certainly be confiscated. As we shared a joint account and investments, this meant I was now as poverty-stricken as he was.

I explained the position to my visitors, emphasising I could no longer afford to employ any lawyer, let alone one with sufficient legal and political clout to bend the penal code.

Lyne assured me there never had been much chance of getting one of their star barristers. 'They all dislike smuggling cases,' he said, 'and usually refuse them. Most of you are caught redhanded and that leaves little room for subtle legal manoeuvres.' He smiled reassuringly. 'The colonel at the police station told me you reacted quite impressively to his cross-examination. We'll give you a good interpreter and I think you'll do all right for yourself.'

He thrust his hand into one of the two shopping-bags containing newspapers, fruit and chocolate. They were on a chair beside him and I remember they both had *Boutique au Petit Bonheur* emblazoned in puce lettering. He extracted a substantial pad of A-4 paper, waving it at me before replacing it, saying: 'Although your trial won't take place for some time, I want you – whether you employ a lawyer or not – to write us an account of your life ... '

'All seventy years of it?' I interjected.

He grinned. 'Perhaps some things would be better left out – but please be careful to mention briefly all the creditable episodes. What is needed is an aide-memoire of a few pages to be translated and sent to the Ministry of Justice for inclusion in your police file before it goes to the law courts. In this country these things take time – all embassies have to channel everything through the Syrian foreign office – we're not allowed to deal directly with any other ministry. That's why I want you to have it ready for our next visit. Write it carefully, because if something important gets missed in cross-examination, the judges will have it in front of them in black and white.'

I promised I would do my best.

Jean-Pierre and Kurt appreciated these visits almost as much as I did. They could both read English and all books, magazines and newspapers were, of course, shared between us. They envied the neutral sympathy shown me by the embassy. Jean-Pierre had been a prisoner more than eight months and had recently received a sentence of two and a half years, yet nobody from the French Embassy had ever paid him a visit, either at the prison or during his many court appearances.

'Perhaps they don't know you're here?' I suggested.

He snorted indignantly. 'Of course they know! If a foreigner is arrested in this country his embassy is notified within days. Besides, my mother went to see them just before Christmas. They kept her waiting a long time and she was then received by some *couille molle* with frigid politeness. Oh yes, they were well aware I was in the Citadel, but it was not their policy to interest themselves in the conditions in which any Frenchman was being held if he had been involved in the wicked crime of smuggling hashish. *Je me'en fou de ces conards*, but the guards tell me a Frenchman who was here two years ago suffered very much because of their attitude. This man had a serious mental breakdown – he began to suffer from persecution mania, convinced everyone was trying to poison him. You know how Arabs believe if you are suffering this sort of illness you have been touched by Allah? He was liked. They were sorry for him, and eager to buy him fruit drinks, coffee, tea. They even prepared special food to tempt him to eat, but these efforts always made him rush to the guardroom screaming they were trying to poison him. This continued for months, until he had become a sort of crazy skeleton. He was eating nothing and hardly drinking. Finally, the governor persuaded the Ministry of Justice to bring pressure on the French Embassy and get him sent back to France.'

'Could he not have been shamming, to achieve just that?' I asked. There was usually someone in *Hofra* attempting to get his sentence quashed by similar tactics.

'The guards are sure his breakdown was genuine, and you know they are not easily deceived. Even if his illness was faked, I think he deserved to get away with it.'

Although his embassy ignored him, Jean-Pierre's prison life was not entirely devoid of local visitors. His mother was Italian by birth and while visiting her son had been most hospitably received – owing to some distant family connection – by the matron/mother superior of the city's Italian hospital. This private *ospedale* accepted patients of all faiths, the nursing being entirely in the hands of nuns. After his mother's return to France, a small group of this nursing order, their great white wimples fluttering in the gritty Syrian winds, began to visit him regularly, always bringing some very welcome tinned food, fresh fruit and chocolate; often slipping little coloured medallions of the saints and the Virgin Mary into the parcels. Jean-Pierre stuck them on the wall behind his head, until there were so many his living-space looked like one of those market stalls for trinkets outside the Grotto at Lourdes. He always referred to his visitors with a sort of proprietary condescension as '*mes religieuses*'.

Later in my imprisonment, a nun from Southern Ireland joined the staff of this hospital. When told there was an old Englishman incarcerated in the Citadel, she would sometimes, when her work as a ward-sister allowed, join her colleagues on their visits. Although totally lacking a belief in a personal God and devoid, since infancy, of any religious feeling, I always enjoyed seeing her. Sister Bridget was a gentle, sweet-faced young woman with a considerable sense of humour, who always brought with her much of the warmth and charm of her native country and awakened memories of my Anglo-Irish godfather's household where life seldom stopped imitating the fiction of Somerville and Martin Ross.

The reception of *les religieuses* by the authorities varied from governor to governor. A few accorded them honorary diplomatic status and welcomed them into their private sanctum to talk to Jean-Pierre and me. Others were openly hostile and had them thrust into the 'battery-hen' shanty for visitors in the *Abraaj*. This was certain to be the treatment after some particularly frightful act of terrorism committed by the Lebanese Christian Phalange.

The British, American, Dutch and Scandinavian embassies in Damascus showed a friendly concern for the health and welfare of their imprisoned nationals. The French, as I have already indicated, preferred to ignore compatriots in trouble, as did most diplomatic missions accredited to the Syrian government. There was, however, one particularly offensive exception – the Germans.

The behaviour of the German Embassy towards Kurt was uniquely unpleasant. They visited him every five or six weeks and behaved as if they were virtual appendages of the German police; two unsmiling, charmless young consular officials with shaven upper-lips, wispy blond beards and, like so many Teutons, no backs to their heads. They questioned him incessantly about his contacts in the international drug scene (he had very few) and repeated, like ventriloquists' dummies, questions obviously inspired by the Bavarian anti-narcotics squad. They never showed a flicker of interest in the problems of an intelligent youth of twenty with no previous criminal record. When Kurt refused to respond to their vindictive cross-examinations, they resorted to threats. They warned him they would give the Munich police an adverse report on his 'lack of co-operation' and this, they insisted, would lead to his immediate arrest when he returned to Germany, no matter how long a sentence he might have served in Syria. Incredibly, this was to prove no empty threat.

Their malice even extended to refusing Kurt permission to use the embassy as a forwarding address. His letters had therefore to be subjected to the caprices of the prison staff, some of whom were capable, unless their palms were frequently crossed with sizeable coins, of delaying letters indefinitely or losing them altogether. During his first six months his embassy never brought him a single newspaper, magazine or book: nothing whatever while he was waiting to come up for trial. After that, they relented slightly, possibly because Kurt had constantly mentioned the different attitude of British and American counterparts towards Abou Mustapha and myself. Although still pretending to be unimpressed, they now brought him an occasional out-of-date copy of *Die Welt*, impressing upon him that no German previously held in a Syrian prison had been so pampered!

★

For several months, we three were the only Europeans in the Citadel, except for three brief intervals when our unique status was interrupted by the arrival of two TIR intercontinental truck drivers and one owner-driver of a small car. All had to spend a short period in custody because they had been involved in road accidents causing death or injury.

The first was an Austrian who, while returning from Baghdad to the car-ferry port of Tartous, had killed an elderly jay-walker on the main road from Damascus. Being hardly more than a boy and on his first trip to the Middle East, he panicked – instead of stopping, he stamped on the accelerator in an absurd attempt to reach the ferry for Greece before the accident was discovered. With more than a hundred and fifty miles to cover, this was a vain hope; it was not long before the police cars caught up with him. He occupied my former bunk in room 9 for about two weeks. A tough, blond youth, who looked as if born to wear *Lederhosen*, he spoke with so strong a Graz accent even Kurt had difficulty understanding him. His effort to avoid responsibility for killing, however accidentally, an elderly pedestrian – which would have resulted in serious charges against him in almost any other country – was, in Syria, completely ignored. As soon as his embassy obtained confirmation that he and the vehicle were correctly insured and compensation paid to the victim's family, he was released. His lorry was handed back and, within an hour or so, he was once more on his way to Tartous.

Our second truck-driver was a Greek who had also knocked down an old man with fatal results close to the Syrian frontier with Jordan. He wisely stopped immediately and summoned the police himself.

Anyone who has driven in the Middle East will appreciate how difficult it can be to avoid accidents. To a Westerner, ninety per cent of the population appear utterly devoid of traffic sense and apt to saunter in front of rapidly approaching traffic without warning.

Spiro was a typical macho Greek in his mid-thirties with a heavy moustache, splendid teeth and the habit of keeping his shirt always open to the navel, demonstrating an abundance of black chest-hair already showing flecks of grey. He spoke English fluently and had an extensive fund of ribald stories about the American, German and Scandinavian girls he had bedded every summer on his own island of Poros, and at other times of the year in the car-ferries between Greece and Syria. He was not with us long; his embassy quickly supplied the

necessary confirmation about insurance and secured his release. We were
sad to see him go.

Our third short-term prisoner was a young Frenchman, an architect
employed by the Syrian government on the construction of the new airport buildings. Married with two young children, he had rented a house
in the embassy quarter. He had killed no one, but while driving in the
area around the new terminal – amongst the cement-mixers, builder's
rubble and piles of sand, he had collided with a youth on a bicycle. The
boy had spread-eagled himself across the bonnet, breaking a leg and a
collar-bone. While he had been rushed into hospital, the Frenchman had
been rushed, equally quickly, into *el Kalaa*. Under Syrian law a driver in
this situation must be kept in custody not only until his insurance cover
has been checked, but also for the injured party's physical condition to
be assessed by the hospital. The Frenchman accepted the situation with
patience and good humour. He made many friends before his release,
especially among the Lebanese hash-smugglers, whose company he
obviously preferred to the supercilious Jean-Pierre.

It became more and more difficult to believe there was another sort
of life going on outside the Citadel. Any changes in routine, however
temporary, engendered feelings of mild apprehension.

This was certainly true of a brilliant morning in early June when
Kurt and I received an urgent summons to the admin offices. There we
were handcuffed together without a word of explanation and handed
over to a grizzled, morose sergeant, who was equally unforthcoming as
he led us through the main gates to a much-battered Japanese mini-bus.
(Hundreds of these vehicles have been used for years by the Syrian
army and police. The majority appear to be held together by wire and
string.)

The sergeant pulled open the sliding door. Kurt and I manoeuvred
ourselves along a bench-type seat, taking care not to spear our buttocks
on the broken, rusty spiral-springs emerging through the leatherette
upholstery. The sergeant locked us carefully inside, pocketed the key
and got in beside the driver.

With the usual crashing of gears we lurched past a soldier rigid in
the shade of his sentry-box, through the dimly lighted *souk* and out
into the tumultuous Damascus traffic. We shot past the law courts
in a fast moving stream of traffic, dodging the tiny, white-painted,

three-wheel, Japanese delivery-vans that zoom along every street in the city like a cloud of gnats.

Our failure to stop at the law courts surprised both of us; we had begun to assume this unexpected jaunt must be due to some whim of an examining magistrate.

'D'you think they are taking us back to that *entsetzlich* police station?' said Kurt.

A few minutes later, after our driver had turned right in front of the railway station and left at the corner by the offices of Air France, I said gloomily: 'I think we're being taken to the customs.'

Kurt, who had been gazing with smiling lechery at the pretty girls strolling freely along the pavements, now turned to me as if stung. 'God!' he said, 'are you sure?'

'Somebody in *Hofra* told me they were now in a new building not far from the Sheraton – that's where we seem to be heading.'

We were almost in sight of the hotel, still travelling westwards along a wide avenue lined with pepper trees, when the driver made a sudden U-turn into the forecourt of a new, white concrete office-block. He halted close to its ostentatious entrance flanked by mock-Corinthian pillars.

The door of the mini-bus was unlocked; Kurt and I dragged ourselves out of the vehicle. The driver stood watching, obviously ready to help the sergeant if we ignored the handcuff linking us and made a bolt for freedom. If I had only been a few years younger I think we might have made the attempt. We would probably have been shot dead while doing so – all Syrian policemen are armed and reputed to be good marksmen.

Instead, we meekly followed the sergeant into the building where all floors appeared to be made of marble and all walls lined with mosaic murals in doubtful taste. The attempt to create a grandiose impression was marred by layers of dust and a top-dressing of butt-ends and discarded cigarette packets.

The sergeant led us up two flights of a wide but excessively grubby staircase and along a corridor lined by open doors revealing a succession of offices where clerks were tapping away at typewriters. As we passed, many of them gaped in surprise, their fingers freezing over the keyboards.

We were ushered into a large room where an enormous desk took up most of the space in front of two windows, through which the morning sun was shining directly. Behind the desk sat an obese little man in a dark, silk suit, wearing a shirt of such flamboyant black and white stripes (with a tie to match!) he only needed a banjo to resemble a leader of an old-fashioned minstrel show. Apart from a few steel cabinets and a row of chairs against one wall, there was no other furniture in the room.

The handcuff was removed and Kurt and I were told to sit down against the wall. The sergeant and driver stood just outside the open door and lit cigarettes.

There was a silence that seemed to go on forever while Striped-Shirt gazed at us through half-closed eyes. I began to wonder, not for the first time, why a race usually so lean and muscular as the Syrians seem to swell like Strasbourg geese when they achieve responsibility in an office job.

The silence ended when a young man in jeans and a sports-shirt, heavily stained with sweat under the arms, hurried breathlessly into the office. He was carrying two large ledgers; one of them, covered in vermilion plastic, slipped from his grasp and fell with a crash, raising a cloud of dust. Smothering a groan, he retrieved it, placing it almost reverently in front of Striped-Shirt, obeising himself with frantic apologies while the patches of sweat under his arms extended noticeably.

Both ledgers were opened up on the desk. Striped-Shirt studied them for a few minutes while the young man stood behind him, mopping his brow with a dirty white handkerchief. From time to time he would lean forward and point to some item which, I suspected, referred either to Kurt or myself.

Suddenly, Striped-Shirt looked up and made a downward, scooping gesture with his right hand – summoning me to stand in front of him. I obeyed and he began asking questions in Arabic.

I interrupted, saying: 'I don't understand. I need a *turguman*.'

He seemed incredulous. 'No *Arabie*?' he squawked.

'No *Arabie* – I need an interpreter. *Turguman*!'

He leaned slightly sideways, focussing on Kurt sitting behind me. 'No *Arabie*?' he called, almost plaintively.

Kurt said tersely: 'Nix!'

I doubt if Striped-Shirt understood the word, but the tone in which it was uttered supplied the answer. He pointed a stubby finger at me, saying: '*Ingles*?'

I admitted the fact.

Again he leaned slightly to starboard, asking Kurt the same question.

Kurt had plainly decided to be uncooperative: '*Nein, ich bin deutsch,*' he snapped.

Striped-Shirt shouted peremptory commands at the hovering young man who bounded from the room. After a moment's pause, we could hear his voice as he entered office after office along the corridor. A constant repetition of the word *turguman* showed he must be searching for someone who spoke English or German.

Before long, high heels could be heard tapping towards us. The sweating youth reappeared, and a pretty girl with luminous dark eyes, wearing a simple, yellow cotton frock and bright green shoes. She hesitated in the doorway, smiling nervously. Striped-Shirt beckoned her towards him. After a brief exchange of courtesies, she turned to me saying, in a barely audible voice: 'I speak a little English.'

I said irritably: 'A little is not enough. I need an official interpreter. Will you please ask somebody to phone the British Consulate . . . ' Pulling out my notecase I extracted Richard Lyne's card with the necessary telephone numbers. Knowing Damascus well, I was aware the embassy and consulate were less than quarter of a mile away.

The girl understood and began translating what I had said, but before she had time to complete a couple of sentences, Striped-Shirt's chin began a series of upward jerks which, anywhere in the Greco/Turkish/Arab world, means no.

'Tell him,' I persisted, 'the British Consulate has promised to provide a fluent interpreter whenever I need one.'

She made another attempt to translate. This made the fat little man thump the ledgers with both fists. He began shouting: '*La! La! La!*' (No! No! No!), with steadily rising inflections.

What I really needed, of course, was not so much an interpreter as the reassurance of a friendly embassy face. However, I had learned long ago the futility of opposing Arab bureaucrats without several aces up my sleeve. This time I had nothing, so I shut up.

Striped-Shirt had now quietened down and was pressing his short, blunt fingers on the buttons of a pocket-calculator. It apparently refused to work for he suddenly flung it, with a yelp of impatience, into the waste-paper basket. He then produced a gold-plated fountain-pen (seemingly an indispensable adjunct to every senior Syrian civil servant) and made a number of simple calculations on paper. When he had finished he sat back, looking at me with a smugly confident expression that boded no good.

He snarled a question at the girl who turned towards me with a frown, obviously concentrating on how to say something in a language not really familiar to her. 'You bring twenty-two kilos of hashish into Syria, yes?' she said at last.

I jerked my chin quickly upwards in what I hoped would be recognised as denial.

It was. The poor girl looked bewildered, and Striped-Shirt started shouting and thumping again.

Recoiling from the noise, the girl said: 'You have the hashish in your luggage when, at the airport, they arrest you?'

'Certainly. But I was leaving your country, not entering. Even your police agree I wasn't responsible for bringing it here.'

Sandwiched between protagonists who must have seemed bent on refusing to let her finish any of her carefully formulated sentences, she looked more and more unhappy as she tried to interpret the ill-tempered epithets her boss was bellowing.

I realised that my plea that the hash had merely been 'in transit' and should not be subject to customs duty was getting me nowhere. I asked if they considered themselves above the law which had, so far, made no effort to convict me. This stung the little man into shrieking that I was now standing before a court – a customs court – and I had better be quiet and listen while I was told the sum demanded of me for excise duty, plus a fine for importing an illegal substance.

He read out some of his figures. Arabic numerals were familiar to me; he was quoting astronomical amounts in Syrian pounds. The total he eventually claimed was more than half a million in local currency: at that time approximately sixty thousand pounds in sterling.

I had heard rumours of prisoners, heavily fined for drug offences, who had succeeded in negotiating a much lower penalty than the sum originally demanded. Apparently, to do this successfully, it was necessary to employ a member of the small, diamond-studded circle of Damascus lawyers, preferably one who had close contacts with the upper echelons of the Assad government. Sadly, I remembered my bankrupt state – my partner, now in a Swiss jail – there would be no help from that direction, and my small capital had doubtless already disappeared into the over-filled coffers of that country. Nevertheless, I decided to play for time.

Assuming an arrogance I was far from feeling, I said: 'You will, I suppose, allow me time to discuss this matter with staff from the British Consulate and, perhaps, their lawyers, before expecting me to make any definite arrangements for the transfer of so large a sum to this country?'

To my surprise, Striped-Shirt raised no objections, appearing to consider this a perfectly normal request. I began to breathe almost freely again. This concession would allow me to put off the evil moment when I would have to face up to that extra year on whatever sentence was given me. I was even favoured with a bleak smile, revealing a set of porcelain teeth, far too white and far too regular, saying something in Arabic in a normal tone of voice.

There was definite relief in the girl's widely-spaced eyes. 'You will be given three months in which to pay,' she said. I felt she was almost as relieved as me.

My interrogation was obviously at an end. I thanked her for the brave effort she had made to help me and sat down again.

It was now Kurt's turn in front of the desk, like a schoolboy being questioned by a master. He now agreed he understood English well enough to be questioned in that language. It was obvious any insistence on a German/Arabic interpreter would do nothing except delay the disclosure of how much would be claimed from him in fines and duties; whoever they dug up to translate would probably be worse than the pleasant young woman.

Unfortunately, she was less successful than she had been with me. Distracted, perhaps, by his blond-Aryan looks, her English, at times, tended to disappear altogether. Kurt, spoiled by pretty women from birth, did not help matters by being unnecessarily brusque. Having listened to what had been said to me, he had no illusions about his fate.

Accused of bringing fourteen kilos of hashish into Syria he, like me, denied the accusation, but admitted to having that amount in his luggage when arrested at the airport. He made no mention of the one-and-a-half kilos that had vanished while his suitcase was en route to the police station, although I could sense he was aching to do so.

The total demanded of him was slightly more than half the amount claimed from me. He smiled ruefully, simultaneously pulling out the linings of his trouser pockets to demonstrate their emptiness. 'I am just a poor student from a university,' he said, 'I have no money.'

Striped-Shirt greeted this with a disdainful sniff and a shrug of the shoulders. The heavily sweating young man in the background continued to dab his forehead. The girl gazed at Kurt with a woebegone expression. The atmosphere seemed heavy with the implication that Kurt and I would be spending an extra year in jail. Striped-Shirt made a few notes in each ledger. When he had finished, these huge account-books were reverently carried away by the young man with the over-active pores.

Five minutes later Kurt and I, handcuffed together once again, were locked inside the mini-bus which was nosing its way through the undisciplined midday traffic.

When we re-entered *el Kalaa* and told our friends about our experience, they were puzzled. Even those who had been in jail for some years had never known a demand for customs duty to be made, or a fine imposed, until after conviction. Jean-Pierre, who had been carrying more hash than either of us, and was already convicted and sentenced, had not heard a word from the customs. Unhappily for him this state of affairs did not last forever.

It was seriously suggested that the customs chose their victims by sticking a pin into a list of names, for more than two thirds of those convicted of hashish-smuggling by the Damascus courts were ignored. Those sentenced in Latakia and Tartous were not so lucky. In these ports the customs pounced immediately on every convicted smuggler and imposed such enormous fines every one had to serve an extra year. This method of penalising the poorer smuggler seemed a strange paradox in a country which calls itself the Socialist Republic of Syria and has close links with Soviet Russia.

At the end of three months Kurt and I expected to be summoned again for an interview with Striped-Shirt or, perhaps, informed in writing of the consequences of our failure to pay up; but nothing happened. Neither of us heard another word from the customs service. Apparently they forgot about us. But from this time until our eventual release, we never entirely lost the feeling that one day something, or someone, would jog their memories.

My insistence that I was not responsible for bringing the hash into Syria was, of course, the truth; although there had been many occasions in the past when I could have been lying through my teeth.

It had become my habit to fly to Damascus from a variety of European cities; preferably those with a reputation for not being involved in the drug scene. On my arrival, I would pick up one of Rachid's friends, all junior officers in the Syrian army, and drive north for seventy miles. We would then turn off the main Aleppo highway and follow a succession of mountain tracks with appalling surfaces, sometimes blocked, in winter, by snowdrifts. Our vehicles had to be tough. Only Land Rovers, Mercedes, Volkswagens or Peugeot 504s could stand up to the gruelling treatment. After forty miles of severe jolting we would emerge into the northern area of the Beka'a Valley. There were no customs posts or passport control on these trails, seldom used except by donkeys.

As we descended, usually as dawn was breaking, into the great valley, we would pass an occasional Syrian army command-post but, with a uniformed companion beside me, their only reaction was a deferential salute.

These tracks were also used by vehicles travelling in the opposite direction. Cars, trucks and motor caravans, if they were sufficiently well-built, would often make this journey from Lebanon into Syria, laden with hashish en route for Tartous or Latakia, or to begin the long, overland trek into Europe through Turkey. This method of avoiding passport and customs control was operated by those hash-growing co-operatives who had close ties of either blood or friendship with the more adventurous members of the Syrian SAS. Each car or truck required a uniformed escort, preferably with pips on his shoulders, although stripes on the sleeve, especially if he were the driver, could also guarantee safe conduct.

I came to know these high-altitude bridle-paths so well I could navigate their entire length on a dark night without lights, and without prompting from my companions. I used these bone-shaking methods to avoid having a Lebanese visa or any of that country's frontier control stamps in my passport. The stamps were bright blue and tiresomely noticeable, as were the visas, because of at least one very large postage-stamp they always stuck, strategically, in the centre of a page: invariably a highly-coloured facsimile of Lebanon's national emblem, the cedar tree (nowadays impossible to find except in a single, remote mountain area). These stamps could be guaranteed to catch the eye of any passport control official, sparking off suspicions that the possessor might be involved in the world of guns or hashish smuggling.

★

Shortly after the depressing little excursion to the customs house, Richard Lyne paid another visit. The embassy had not been told of any demands made by the customs and pointed out that such matters lay outside their jurisdiction, although they would have been willing enough to supply an interpreter. His advice was to do my best to forget the incident. Several years of coping with Syrian bureaucracy had conditioned him in the belief that most of its members failed to implement their threats as often as they did their promises.

He brought me letters and a large parcel of books despatched from Hatchards by a generous friend. This evoked such feelings of pleasure and gratitude, I felt a momentary sting in my tear-ducts. I realised soon after my arrest that almost any sort of kind action directed towards a prisoner ignites a feeling of emotional warmth in the recipient, sometimes out of proportion to the value of the kindness. This time, I knew the books would have been chosen with meticulous care for my personal taste by someone who could ill-afford such generosity, and I was genuinely grateful.

On this visit Lyne was accompanied not only by a Syrian colleague but also by the chief of his department, the British Consul, who was on the point of leaving Damascus for another appointment. I am ashamed to admit I have forgotten his name but I remember a leonine head and a personality that radiated calm, unprejudiced sympathy: an attitude reflected by all the staff of this embassy with whom I came in contact. In return, I always tried my best to avoid shocking them, for they could all be described (my tongue, for once, is not in my cheek) as decent chaps – and I had discovered, before I reached puberty, that decent chaps were dumbfounded when confronted by someone as amoral as myself: so many of my opinions and actions are met, even today, with bewilderment and anxious frowns of incredulity.

But on this occasion it was the governor who brought frowns to the consul's face. Our tall, laconic brigadier had left us and been replaced by an almost dwarf-like lieutenant-colonel with a resonant voice all too often raised in acrimony.

He followed the accepted habit of working at his desk and, if necessary, interviewing prisoners while embassy visitors were chatting to their nationals. He was one of those – we had several – who kept a thin, wooden lathi near to hand. When faced by an argumentative prisoner, they would seize the stick and whack the man, almost casually, over the head and shoulders while continuing to harangue him.

This sort of behaviour was responsible for a minor melodrama during the consul's visit. The governor had been haphazardly using the lathi to hit a truculent prisoner, when a sudden, sharp blow on the nose – possibly breaking the bone – precipitated a stream of blood down the front of the man's white *galabieh*. Instant uproar: the moans of the victim, who fell to his knees, bleeding profusely over the carpet, mingled with the governor's yells of alarm and fury.

The consul was visibly appalled. He stood up and remained for a moment silently shaking his head, as if undecided what form of protest to make. Then, turning his chair deliberately through ninety degrees, he sat down again to resume our conversation, keeping a disapproving back towards the governor.

I shall always remember the anxiety on his face when he bade me goodbye. 'I simply hate to leave you here,' he said, as we shook hands. I was touched by his concern and did my best to reassure him.

HOFRA: PART 2

It was inevitable that most of my friends in *el Kalaa* had a smattering of French or English. I always regretted my inability to achieve any real conversational fluency in Arabic, a language said to be, apart from Chinese, the most difficult in the world.

One young man, ignorant of any language but Arabic, decided it was his duty to provide me with a basic knowledge. This was Sulieman, a Palestinian accused of treachery, or worse, against the Syrian Republic. I never fully understood the reason for his arrest, except that it had something to do with the perpetual antagonism between certain factions of the PLO and the Syrian government. He had been charged with being a traitor to the Arab cause.

He was chubby, clean-shaven – when he troubled to shave, in his middle twenties, with a bullet-shaped head, deeply-set, widely-spaced eyes and thick, black eyebrows. His teeth were splendid and so was his heart-warming smile.

During our morning exercise periods he delighted in seizing hold of me as if I were on wheels and pushing me about the courtyard, pointing to objects and making me repeat, again and again, what they were called in Arabic. I am unlikely ever to forget the words for wall, window, door, pane of glass, sky, clouds, sun, chair, table; all very useful, but not much help in promoting brilliant conversation.

Nevertheless, I became extremely fond of this beefy young tough who took an endearing pride in my ability to memorise a few simple words. His friendliness towards me was demonstrated by his greeting each morning; our shaking hands always had to be conducted with considerable brio. The Latin habit of shaking hands is universal in Arab countries, but in Syria and Lebanon there are subtle differences. The strength of the feeling of friendship is shown by the vigour of the slap as the hands are joined – the warmer the relationship, the noisier the smack. When two really great friends greet each other, each right hand takes a wide encircling sweep through the air and they are brought together with a sound like a report from a gun. It was in this fashion that Sulieman and I greeted each other.

Another of my constant companions was the young Hamoudi whom I had first met skilfully painting an absurdly lifelike impression of a man's finger on the trigger of a Beretta 38.

Hamoudi spoke remarkably good English in which he took justifiable pride. He had been born in Beirut of Syrian parents, small traders who had never changed their nationality. Thus he had to do his national service with the Syrian army.

After preliminary training he was sent back to Lebanon and posted to the Syrian garrison at Chteura, a straggling, dusty town, hardly bigger than a village, that lies at the junction of the route to the north of the Beka'a Valley and the main road linking Damascus with Beirut.

I asked him how long he had been in prison.

'Three years.'

Was he expecting to be released shortly?

The touch of derision in his answering smile made me realise my question must have been stupidly insensitive.

Instead of giving a direct answer, he described the events that caused his troubles. Shortly after his arrival at Chteura, he and two other conscripts had been sitting on their beds cleaning their Kalashnikov assault-rifles. Hamoudi had just finished reassembling his weapon when he accidentally pressed the trigger and shot one of his companions in the stomach. Horrified, he and the third soldier did everything they could to get the man to hospital as quickly as possible. The delay was minimal, but the conscript was found to be dead on arrival.

Hamoudi had been immediately arrested, as had the other soldier who had merely done his best to help. After being held on remand for nearly a year, both men were court-martialled. The sentences were hard to credit. Hamoudi was given fifteen years and his totally innocent helper, ten. This in spite of confirmation from responsible witnesses that there had been no disagreement between Hamoudi and the dead man, in fact, the trio hardly knew each other.

Surely, I said, they must have appealed?

They had, and at once, but three years had gone by and they were still waiting. The appeal court had put off their case again and again.

Hamoudi's long-suffering companion and fellow victim of injustice was also in *el Kalaa*. In spite of the appalling way his army had treated him, he always seemed able to show a cheerful face to the world. One of the service staff employed by the guards, he had helped carry my luggage on the evening I arrived.

They both believed – as did many in the Citadel – that these sentences had been imposed because they were Christians, whereas the dead man had been a Muslim, and so had those who presided over the court martial. Neither had entirely given up hope of being set free and both waited, with amazing stoicism, for their appeals to be heard.

Hamoudi, when he was sixteen, had embarked on a career as a karate student in a Beirut gymnasium. The governor had given him permission to organise a judo class for prisoners. These classes became so popular they were suppressed by the next governor who felt they would add to the guards' difficulties in controlling awkward prisoners.

Jean-Pierre, the aspiring black-belt, used to get Hamoudi to give him occasional judo lessons behind the bath-house, the one small area of the yard that could not be seen from the guardroom. As a side line, they were both sufficiently juvenile to enjoy slicing pieces of rock in half with their hands – the edge of the palm being used like an axe-blade. In this ancient fortress, lumps of stone could always be extracted from the walls on which to practise. Hamoudi could split them with ease. Jean-Pierre frequently bruised his hand severely and would complain bitterly, but he never gave up.

I was, of course, much older than anybody in the prison. My only near-contemporary was the Syrian-American, Abou Mustapha, more than fifteen years my junior. During the countless miles we must have sauntered together in the yard, he hardly ever mentioned the multiple killing which had led to his being in jail. When he did, the tone was so casual he might have been referring to events on another planet. He seemed extraordinarily confident the court would take a lenient view and that he would be released within a few years. He chattered happily in his own special *patois* of disc-jockey American about his time with the British army on the outskirts of Alexandria during the Second World War, about his difficulties emigrating to the United States and ultimate triumph as the proud owner of half-a-dozen diners.

At one time we formulated a mischievous plan involving his precious Cadillac which was still privately garaged in Damascus. We agreed I should arrange for it to be taken secretly over the mountains to Ymuni, in the north of the Beka'a Valley, and for 100 kilos of the best hashish to be welded between the back seat and the luggage-boot. It would then be driven back to Damascus. Abou Mustapha would now take over and beg the American consular staff – whose members paid him regular visits – to help him export his beloved car to friends in Spain (who were, in fact, my friends). If they could supply a driver to take the car to Latakia, he would be only too willing to pay all expenses.

If the US Consulate swallowed the story, I was fairly confident the Latakia customs would assume it was being freighted to Barcelona under a quasi-diplomatic umbrella and would not bother to examine it too closely. The Catalonian destination was also my choice. I knew from experience that Barcelona customs officers were a gentlemanly crowd who hated to soil their hands with oily motor cars dropped onto their quays by grubby Levantine cargo ships.

Unhappily, our little plan had to be abandoned. Abou Mustapha's lawyer's fees had become such a heavy item he was forced to sell the car to meet them. Apparently the profit made by the diners was no longer enough to cover such heavy expenses.

As for me, I would have enjoyed watching to see if the Drug Enforcement Agency's staff, attached at that time to the American Embassy, would have twigged what lay behind the request for help in exporting a privately-owned luxury car, its number-plates proclaiming registration in NEW JERSEY – THE GARDEN STATE.

Six years ago, the DEA were not as thick on the ground as they are today, and their meagre success in the Middle East had only been achieved by bribery and entrapment.

This organisation was to grow much larger under the Reagan administration, but their reception in Arab countries has never been cordial, almost anything approved by the American President and his wife being looked upon with hostility. Carter had been regarded as a well-intentioned bungler, who could be credited with making some effort to distance himself from Washington's Jewish lobby, but the Reagans are believed to be lifelong fellow-travellers with the film moguls of Hollywood and therefore unthinking supporters of Israeli propaganda.

It was about this time that Syria's television network began showing a series of early Ronald Reagan films from the 1930s, deliberately repeating those westerns in which he played the baddie. When he did play the good guy they chose films where the good guy was weak and indecisive.

Television sets were not provided, but prisoners were allowed their own. Over-populated *Hofra* was seldom without two or three.

As an alternative to Reagan's films, they began a series starring David Niven, made during the same period. These I could watch with a certain wry amusement as Niven and I had been contemporaries at Stowe from the age of fourteen.

I would squat on my mattress in the smoke-laden air, watching him capering about in those neat, pin-striped, double-breasted suits that I knew had been made by the London tailor we both patronised. His film persona had not altered much from the assertive schoolboy I remembered so well, except for his voice which had always sounded like an asthmatic corn-crake and was now pitched so much lower it hardly seemed to be his.

Although we came from similar backgrounds, being sons of regular soldiers, we were totally unalike. My reaction to parental difficulties, of which we both had our share, was to become more and more aloof and unapproachable, while David's was to put up a mask of frantic bonhomie. Always a superb raconteur, he never allowed undue concern for the truth to spoil a good story. I much enjoyed his two volumes of autobiography but suspected, after his description of his life at Stowe, that they should really have been marketed as fiction.

At school he attracted those with similar characteristics and surrounded himself with a small band of extroverts who communicated with each other in the vernacular of the late P. G. Wodehouse. This little claque always referred to him as 'Binge'. If I ever knew the reason for this soubriquet, I have long ago forgotten it.

All too often, in the opinion of *Hofra*'s inmates, normal television programmes would be cancelled and President Assad would deliver one of his 'State of the Nation and of the Arab World in General' speeches to his people. Even without much Arabic it was easy to recognise that he was a most effective speaker, employing both wit and irony in his barbed references to the United States and the Egyptian government – then still dominated by Sadat. Assad's gestures were few, but they were master strokes of timing by a born orator. His civilised manners on the rostrum – he seemed to prefer being televised in front of a large audience – were in sharp contrast to the rabble-rousing antics of Colonel Gaddafi, whose occasional appearances were greeted with cat-calls and contemptuous laughter. The Colonel's favourite gesture – a frenzied beating of the air with the right forearm – always produced a hilarious reaction.

But Assad, in spite of his urbanity, was a bit too long-winded even for those who could understand every word. His speeches lasted for two to three hours and would be repeated at peak-viewing times during the following three days.

We could laugh at Gaddafi with impunity, but it could be dangerous to express even the mildest criticism of the Syrian government. I well remember the fate of half-a-dozen ex-regular soldiers serving short sentences for possessing small quantities of hashish. They had made mildly contemptuous gestures at the TV set after an announcement that programmes were being suspended for another presidential speech. They were merely annoyed at missing something more entertaining; none of them was in the least politically minded, but tale-bearers reported this little scene to the staff.

Early the following morning the duty-sergeant made an unexpected appearance and ordered the six miscreants to the guardroom where, he said with sadistic relish, members of the secret police were waiting to take them away.

The ex-soldiers' faces were too deep a shade of brown for pallor to be noticeable, but there was fear in their dark eyes that reminded me of Aziz when he was taken from the police cell to be beaten.

Unlike the Aziz episode, these men did not return after a few minutes; they were taken from the Citadel and not seen for five days.

When they did return they were almost unrecognisable; covered from head to toe with purple bruising and open sores, their hands raw and bleeding, their feet swollen and contused. They could only hobble a few steps at a time and they smelt – oh God, how they smelt – of excrement and urine.

They had been shut in a windowless cell without toilet facilities and only taken out, singly, to be interrogated and beaten up. There was only room for one to lie down at a time, so they had to take turns sleeping on the bare stone, damp with piss and shit, while the rest stood upright, tightly pressed together.

Fortunately they returned early in the morning and Anwar was able to give them immediate priority in the showers. Our duty-sergeant that day was the benevolent Abou Talal who allowed them, contrary to regulations, back, at once, into *Hofra* where Fahdi and Fahad seized and washed their filthy clothing.

By early afternoon, most of these young toughs, exhausted by their ordeal, had fallen lifelessly on their mattresses. Their bruised and bleeding bodies looked pathetically vulnerable, their feet just lumps of raw beef. Within a few days their weariness disappeared, but the pain from their injuries took longer, making their sleep fitful and disturbed: they could often be heard groaning at night while only half-conscious. It astonished me that so few prisoners showed any feeling of antagonism against authority for behaving in this way.

From time to time, life in *Hofra* would be enlivened by the arrival of a brazen swaggerer, usually in his late twenties, sometimes a bit older. These types could instantly be distinguished by the amount of expensive luggage (usually Gucci) they brought and by the splendour of their silk pyjamas and dressing-gowns, obviously imported from London's Jermyn Street or Paris or Rome. Nothing could have looked more incongruous in our sordid 'pit'. They all had huge feet and large, muscular hands – an inheritance from forebears who had gained their living from the harsh, rocky Syrian soil. These hands were now weighed down with gold rings and gold medallions, sometimes as big as saucers, dangled in their abundant chest hair.

These fantastic creatures, who seemed to sweat animal magnetism, were invariably uneducated and illiterate but endowed with considerable mother-wit. They were accompanied by a retinue of 'minders', both outside and inside prison. These little gangs were arrested, en bloc, accused of possessing small quantities of hashish. This, of course, was not the real reason for locking them up. The character with the splendid dressing-gowns was usually a brothel-keeper or prosperous pimp, who had unwisely tried to avoid paying the customary bribes to his local police chief.

I was assured it had become an accepted practice to throw those who refused to contribute to what were euphemistically called 'police charities' into a 'cooler' for a brief period. It had also been agreed that their 'minders' could accompany them.

Surprisingly little resentment was shown by any of those involved. They looked upon it as a normal hazard of their profession. Expensive lawyers would arrive for consultations and go off to bargain with the police official who had instigated the arrest. Fahdi and the service staff

165

were delighted to welcome these groups because their tips were lavish. The silk-clad bosses always managed to acquire one of the least unpleasant spots in *Hofra*; in winter, out of a draught; in summer, in one. They did this by offering so much *baksheesh*, the occupant of the space could hardly refuse.

None of the pimps or bordello bosses ever did anything for themselves. They were waited upon by their minders who cooked mouth-watering meals from supplies brought by adoring young women.

Usually, after about a week, a sum acceptable to the police official and the lawyers would be agreed, the gorgeous pyjamas were packed into the expensive luggage and the glamour-boys would be on their way to freedom.

Early one morning, during the second week of July, Kurt and I were surprised to hear our names amongst those called over the *Hofra* loudspeakers (one was immediately above our heads) to be ready to go to court the following morning. As we knew both high courts would be in recess during the last two weeks of the month, and for the same period in August and September, we had not expected anything like this until the autumn.

The next morning Kurt, who normally slept as late as possible, washed and shaved almost simultaneously with myself. In deference to the court we wore clean, well-pressed cotton shirts and trousers, and shoes and socks instead of flip-flops. Jackets, with a midday temperature fluctuating around 95° to 100°F were unthinkable.

The call for those selected to go to court came, as usual, at a few minutes after seven. The guard opened the gate, tapped his keys peremptorily against the bars and we obediently ascended into the glorious morning sunshine.

The guard continued his circuit of the yard, occasionally opening dormitory gates from which one or two prisoners would emerge, most grubby and dishevelled, still rubbing the sleep out of their eyes. Finally, when he was satisfied no one had been overlooked, he returned to the guardroom to drink coffee while we were left to kick our heels for at least an hour. Although we would have appreciated a fortifying drink, in summer these early morning delays were no hardship; in winter they could be very disagreeable.

At last we were summoned for a roll call, and instructed to walk over the ramparts to the tiny courtyard outside the admin offices where we joined a similar group from the *Abraaj*.

We waited another hour before a posse of police sauntered into the little yard, jangling handcuffs in their massive, hairy hands. They lined us up in couples and marched us to a 15cwt Japanese truck. Its canvas roof was held up by a rickety frame and its ground-clearance was rather excessive – getting in was not too easy for an old man with only one unfettered hand. Fortunately, I was handcuffed to Kurt who leapt in like an antelope, lifted me up beside him with his free arm and dragged me along the floor to behind the driver's cab.

There were so many of us on our short journey, we were squashed together so tightly we could hardly breathe. Our driver followed the usual procedure of swinging the nose of the truck on to the pavement opposite the prisoners' entrance and swiftly reversing to within inches of the open door.

We all fell out of the vehicle – in my case, almost literally. Kurt pulled me to my feet and we plunged at speed down the circular stone steps leading to that basement of dreaded memory.

Our escort hustled us past the guardroom, past the cage of heavily made-up women, past the cage for juveniles, with half-a-dozen tear-stained boys on a broken bench, and halted us in front of the big cage. The smell of stale sweat and urine seemed stronger than ever. Our handcuffs were removed and we were pushed inside.

There was a noticeable contrast between the general appearance of our party from the Citadel and the twenty or so who had spent the night – probably several nights – in this squalid basement. They were pathetically grimy and heavy-eyed, many of them sprawling against the scrofulous-looking walls with their dark brown stains under the blackened ceiling, from which I knew large, flat bugs would still be falling like raindrops every night.

Our party spent two hours ambling around the cage, occasionally pausing to rest against the bars. We were always displaced fairly quickly by those who had visitors or wished to talk to their lawyers. Many who had been lying on the floor now began to rouse themselves, intrigued by the spectacle of two Europeans who differed so astonishingly in age. We were questioned exhaustively about our personal lives and the reasons for our presence. Accustomed to the natural curiosity of all Arab peoples, we submitted to this inquisition with as much patience as we could muster. They almost all assumed we must be father and son, a supposition I found most flattering. The fact that Kurt showed no resentment at their mistake made me feel very happy.

Shortly after eleven o'clock I noticed the police were getting ready, with much twirling of handcuffs, to escort most of the crowd up into the courtroom when a young policeman detached himself from the rest, shouting the names of Kurt and myself.

He shooed us, handcuffed, up the staircase. We paused in the ground floor lobby but were urged onwards and upwards. Just as I was beginning to wonder if we should eventually emerge on to the roof, the staircase ended in a wide corridor, extending almost the length of the building. Designed to be impressive, it was now merely tatty: mustard-coloured walls behind a dozen or so fake-marble pillars in mottled sienna-brown, supporting a cornice of peeling plaster.

A door immediately to our right was open and our policeman indicated that this was where we were expected.

It was a large, square office on the corner of the building, with windows on two sides. As the shade temperature must now have been well over 90°, I was relieved they were all wide open, although the noise in the main thoroughfare (Syrian drivers always prefer the horn-button to the brake-pedal) did not make verbal exchange easy.

Kurt and I had been told it was customary for foreign prisoners to be given a preliminary cross-examination in private before being taken into open court, and this would be conducted by the judge who would preside over the trial.

We were therefore surprised to find ourselves confronted not by some legal panjandrum but by six young men behind six large, flat-topped desks piled high with what we later were to recognise as prisoners' case histories.

This sextet were the personal clerks of the six judges of the Damascus High Court: a court which appears to be divided into two halves that function separately, on alternate days, in the same courtroom. Prisoners always referred to them as court number 1 and court number 2. Three judges were semi-permanently assigned to each by the Ministry of Justice; a president, and two of lesser distinction. The judges of number 1 court never operated in number 2, or vice versa; they were not interchangeable.

All six clerks evidently considered Kurt and me an amusing spectacle and made no effort to restrain their sniggers. One of them beckoned to us. We stood obediently in front of his desk while he extracted two fat dossiers with yellow cardboard covers from a pile. Our police escort meanwhile lounged in the doorway.

The young man asked me a question in Arabic to which I did not reply. Kurt and I had agreed, after our unhappy experience in the customs office, that we would never again submit to being cross-questioned in any language but our own. I felt the time had come to make a stand, so when the clerk again asked the question I jerked my chin upwards and said firmly: '*Ana ma bakallinish Arabie!*' (I don't speak Arabic.)

This appeared to stun him. After a moment's pause, he repeated the same question in Arabic to Kurt. He was given exactly the same answer.

'*Turguman min fadluk,*' I said. (Interpreter, please.)

The clerk threw his arms wide in helplessness and launched into a torrent of Arabic, waving his hands. Obviously, the interpreter had been forgotten. His colleagues continued to snigger, but their amusement was now directed towards him, not us.

No one rushed to find a willing amateur linguist. Nor, surprisingly, was any attempt made to telephone for a professional. In fact, the office seemed as devoid of telephones as it was of initiative. Nothing further happened except an exchange of barbed pleasantries between our policeman and the guardian of our dossiers whose face became pink with embarrassment under its tan. He waved the back of his hand to and fro in our direction, indicating the quicker we were removed from his sight, the better.

So we were again locked into the basement cage, now almost empty because the court was in session. I do not remember either of us being particularly surprised that an administrative cock-up had torpedoed the opening of the case against us. We were, however, irritated that neither of our embassies had been told of our possible court appearance. Happily, this was never forgotten in the future. It is often easy for Westerners to criticise Arab bureaucracy, but in the end it usually achieves a successful result.

After the usual waiting we returned to the Citadel about mid-afternoon, at the precise moment when the volley-ball players had finished their game and Anwar was urging them in and out of the showers. As the guards on duty were well-disposed towards the European minority (an attitude that was unfortunately to change as our numbers increased), Kurt and I were allowed to flush the cage

169

smell from our bodies in a swirl of cold water – the players had used all the hot, but in such heat that worried neither of us.

For several weeks we heard no more about our trial. Then, at the beginning of August, the Ministry of Justice made it known that we must be tried by separate courts. The case against Kurt was to be handled by court number 2, mine was to remain the responsibility of number 1. No reason was ever given to us, or to our embassies, for this change.

Yussef, slightly tongue-in-cheek, suggested it was due to the Ministry having at last realised interpreters were going to be essential for both of us, and this would make our cross-examination twice as long as those of an Arabic speaker. To have two foreigners in the dock at the same time would make the judges late for lunch and that would never do!

To me, this was a depressing decision. The judge in number 1 had presided for a number of years and had a reputation for imposing maximum sentences whenever possible, whereas it was universally agreed that the president of number 2 was a genial old duck who had no belief in the value of keeping anybody in jail for long, unless they were dangerous psychopaths.

However, there was nothing to be done but congratulate Kurt on his good luck and brace myself for number 1.

Soon after our abortive court appearance, the month of Ramadan was upon us. For Muslims this means that for twenty-eight days all food, drink or smoking is prohibited between dawn and dusk and there is an absolute ban on sexual activity: some especially devout Muslims believe even the swallowing of one's own spittle to be a sin. This month of abstinence is linked to the lunar calendar and therefore moves back twenty-eight days every year. The prohibitions are particularly difficult to observe when Ramadan occurs in summer; the ban on liquid is excessively hard to bear in the Syrian climate.

Our nights were short because everyone had to be awake at half-past three to cook an enormous meal in the hope of mitigating the wretchedness of the day's starvation and dehydration. As evening approached many would be feverishly listening to the radio or watching television with rapt attention for the moment when the end of the day's abstinence would be announced, usually by the firing of a gun. They could then light up their cigarettes, drink their pints and start to gorge again.

During my first experience of Ramadan in prison, although heavy-eyed from lack of sleep, I found compensation in the privilege accorded us by the humane little man whom chance had made our governor at this time. All dormitory gates were opened an hour before sunset and some of us would take our *barbouas* into the courtyard (another Ramadan concession) and prepare our meal while listening for the cannon that would permit us to begin eating. To sit for a couple of hours in the open air, as the heat of the day slowly evaporated into the dark sky, was indeed pleasant.

Did the European prisoners in *el Kalaa* submit to the discipline of Ramadan? Not entirely, but we conducted our eating and, particularly, our drinking habits with as much tact and discretion as we could manage. The Christian Lebanese amongst us did the same. The only prisoners who seemed to take ostentatious pleasure in ignoring the fast were a handful of *evolué* business men, indicted on fraud charges, who, in spite of their Islamic background, considered the fasting an anachronism.

One bright morning shortly after Ramadan, while meandering up and down the yard, I was suddenly embraced by a radiant Hisham. Six months had passed since our meeting in the police station which, to me, felt like the day before yesterday. The moment had arrived for his release, and happiness seemed to infuse the very air around him. As I kissed his unshaven cheeks I remembered how important his good humour and generosity had been to me during those first days of captivity.

A small group gathered to wish him luck as he disappeared from sight. We urged him to be sensible and to avoid any action that would bring him back. This was a vain hope. Three months later he was with us again.

At this time a trickle of Europeans began to arrive in *Hofra*. In one week two Italians and a German came in on successive days and we wondered if the trickle would turn into a flood; but, apart from two Greeks who arrived the following week, this was the end of the foreign invasion for that summer.

Mario and Carlo were, like so many Italians, lively and good-looking. Surprisingly, they had never met until they were arrested within minutes of each other at Damascus airport while changing flights on their way from India to Italy. They had been staying in Katmandu in different lodgings, dealing with different suppliers. Both spoke French and English fluently and had been highly successful in their legitimate working lives: smuggling for them was merely a profitable and exciting hobby. Carlo, to my great amusement, had an extensive law practice in one of Italy's northern cities. Mario, from the province of Umbria, was a farmer who had used the profits from his buccaneering activities (both had been bringing modest quantities of the drug from India for almost ten years) to enlarge the acreage of his family farm near Perugia. Both normally carried the cannabis in specially made suitcases. Mario, an enthusiastic horseman, would occasionally take a saddle on these trips – several kilos could easily be concealed in its interior. He was careful to complete the disguise by seeing that his jodhpurs and whip were in a prominent position in his luggage.

They had been unlucky to get caught at Damascus, because luggage in transit between intercontinental flights was not usually examined by Syrian customs. However, their connecting flight had been delayed for six hours and both had left the terminal for a bath and a meal at the airport hotel. On their return they found that passengers who had done this were compelled to take their luggage through customs before entering the departure lounge. Disaster had struck.

It was becoming obvious to us in *Hofra* that the airport's customs staff were becoming expert at detecting smugglers. During previous weeks a whole string of young Lebanese 'mules' had arrived; in fact there was hardly a well-known family name in the Beka'a Valley not now represented in our cellar. They had been far too slow to realise that Damascus airport (previously considered 'a piece of cake') had become as dangerous as Beirut had always been.

Carlo had made his position worse by attempting to bribe the Syrians. Caught by the police in India some years ago, he had found an extremely small *douceur* sufficient to secure his immediate release – even the cannabis was handed back to him with apologies. He did not find the Damascus customs so amenable.

They were both a year or two over thirty. Mario was married with a small daughter, a dark-eyed moppet, snap-shots of whom he carried everywhere and whom he obviously adored. Carlo had a permanent relationship with a young Frenchwoman involved in *haute couture* in Milan. She flew to Damascus several times to see him, her elegance and good looks creating a minor sensation among the prison staff, enormously increasing her boyfriend's prestige. Mario would have been equally delighted to see his wife and daughter, but the responsibility for two sets of elderly parents prevented this.

Bruno, the German, was a stolid, heavyweight blond in his early twenties. The son of a small-time shopkeeper in a Hanover suburb, he had been employed as a mule by a powerful German syndicate who had not taken much care of him. He had been sent down to Syria by road, travelling all the way through the Balkans and Turkey by bus. Having been ordered to collect a poorly reconstructed suitcase in Damascus, he had been given sufficient money in traveller's cheques to return by air. His masters, I suspect, hoped customs would mistake him for an innocent, modern type of *Wandervogel* which, in a sense, I suppose he was. It had not been an easy journey for a youth who had never before been outside his own country, and I doubted if there had ever been any hope of his negotiating the airport. The poor lad was desperately homesick for his mother, beer and sausages – we were never quite sure in what order.

Kurt and Bruno were not far apart in age but there was a wide social and educational gulf between them. There is probably less class distinction in Germany than in the rest of Western Europe, but it exists, and Bruno often showed he resented what he felt to be Kurt's condescension and patronage. Kurt's reaction was to murmur occasionally in my ear that Bruno would have been ideal Nazi-fodder. 'Not the SS, just an ordinary, brown-shirted thug!'

The Greeks who arrived the following week were utterly different – young Athenians who had been friends for years and, although not related, astonishingly alike. They were small and slim, with a delicate bone-structure, olive skin, large, mischievous black eyes like good-natured fauns. It was easy, however, to tell them apart because Yanni was clean-shaven (unlike the majority, he shaved every morning and drenched himself with expensive toilet water) while Costa sported a massive black moustache which he constantly brushed upwards. This adornment made him resemble a manikin edition of Kaiser Wilhelm II when young.

Like all the foreigners in *Hofra* except Jean-Pierre, they had been arrested at the airport with suitcases of poorly concealed hash, supplied by my old friendly-enemies, the Benamis.

A girlfriend of Costa's had been with them and had also been charged with smuggling. Her behaviour while she was being questioned by the police had made him almost incandescent with rage. He said she had screamed over and over again that she knew nothing about the hashish in her luggage; it had been put there, she insisted hysterically, without her knowledge and she made a violent public attack on Costa, accusing him of deceiving her.

Costa said fiercely that the girl had been lying. She had been one of the chief planners of their trip and had contributed at least one third of the sum they had paid the Benamis for the hash. Now he was worried because the police seemed to believe her and he thought the court might also. 'She is pretty,' he said in his excellent English. 'She has nice legs and was subtle enough to show enough of them to excite her police audience without incurring their Islamic disapproval and making them feel she was being deliberately shameless.'

Happily, it was not long before he recovered his natural optimism. They could both afford to employ one of the more expensive Damascus lawyers, who knew exactly whom to bribe and assured Costa that his girlfriend's statement would not be taken seriously.

There is often a considerable similarity in appearance and cast of feature between Greeks and Lebanese. When Yanni and Costa first walked into *Hofra* I failed to notice that they were any different to most of my companions. I only realised they were Greek when, after they had wearily put down their wrecked luggage, Costa advanced along the corridor holding out his hand, saying: 'You must be the legendary Tony!'

I admitted to my name but questioned the prefix.

'I'm an old friend of Dinos,' he explained.

Dinos was my Canadian partner who had been brought up in Toronto from the age of four but whose roots were in Greece. When he was thirteen, his parents had interrupted his Canadian education by sending him to school in Athens for more than a year. Here he had met Costa, who exaggerated a bit when describing himself as an old friend. They had met infrequently, and only by accident, since their schooldays.

Like many little men, Yanni and Costa could be arrogant and opinionated and tended to strut about at times like a couple of bantam cocks. Yanni was the quieter and gentler. Costa sometimes felt it necessary to live up to his fierce moustache.

They arrived at a moment when *Hofra* was overfull, and had to doss down in the corridor for many weeks – longer than necessary because they insisted on waiting for a double vacancy on the dais, where they could be side by side. This determination to be together sparked off a row.

The cause was a huge Lebanese, by name Thamir, a bear of a man who described himself as a ship's captain, but who, under the influence of a joint, confessed to me he had never risen higher than second mate on a small Greek coaster. The son of a Sidon fisherman, Thamir was not only exceptionally large, he was also exceptionally hairy with a torso covered by tight black curls like an Astrakhan goat. His biceps were elaborately tattooed and immediately below each nipple was a blue flower like a gentian. He obviously got some sort of 'kick' in our monastic world by encouraging the younger and better-looking prisoners to pull apart the tightly curling fleece to admire the indelible pictures.

This genial giant jokingly suggested the Greeks wished to be together on the dais because they were *poosti* – Hellenic slang for queer. Costa and Yanni erupted with fury like miniature volcanos. They yelled insults and waved their small fists at his bulk as if about to tear him apart.

Poor Thamir, who had never intended his remark to be taken so seriously, was hurt and bewildered. 'Why should they be so upset?' he asked. 'I've often done that sort of thing myself aboard ship – who hasn't?'

I found his unabashed honesty rather touching, but the Greeks would not speak to him for weeks.

Early in September Kurt's name again came over the loudspeakers. He was to attend court number 2 the following morning. This time, I was not mentioned.

He looked lonely and mildly apprehensive as he bowed his head to go through our tunnel-exit just after seven o'clock. I regretted more than ever that we should have been separated and spent most of the morning wondering what was happening to him.

When he returned in the afternoon, he looked tired but cheerful. We had saved some of our meal which he ate with difficulty because of our insistent questions.

Had the German Embassy sent an interpreter?

Yes.

175

Was he a good one?

Not a he, but a she! Yes, she was good. She was also nice to look at.

Did he know who she was?

Only that her father was Syrian and her mother German.

Had he been taken straight into court?

No. There had been a long preliminary cross-examination by the president. He had not seen any of the clerks who had sniggered at us.

Had he any idea how long a sentence he might get?

No.

How had the president acted towards him?

He said the president had been most polite in spite of his own bad behaviour.

Why had he behaved so badly – what had he done?

While sitting in front of the judge he had crossed his legs and waved one of his feet up and down. The pretty interpreter had reproved him sharply, reminding him that such behaviour in Arab countries is looked upon as a deliberate insult.

'*Toujours si mal-élevé,*' sniffed Jean-Pierre, who seemed irritated by Kurt's relaxed state.

How many more times would he have to go to court? we asked.

He shrugged. After being put in the dock nobody had said another word to him, although the others had been questioned at length.

Jean-Pierre reminded us that he had been taken four times to court after his first session, with its preliminary cross-examination by the president. Each time he had just had to sit in silence. It was only on the fifth occasion that his lawyer had been called upon to make a speech for his defence. Two weeks later the judges sent him down for two and a half years – about par for the course, even without a lawyer.

I wondered how much time would elapse before the same ritual began for me.

It was a rule in *el Kalaa* that prisoners must not enter dormitories other than their own. In my case this edict was tacitly ignored by the guards, presumably on account of my age and being a foreigner.

During the long hours in the courtyard I made many friends who would often invite me to a small party. Usually it was two or three friends with conveniently adjoining bunks where a wonderful spread of small cakes and those cornet-like objects called ram's horns (puff pastry filled with thick, sugary cream) would be laid out on a multi-coloured tablecloth. All this *patisserie* would have been brought by visitors and kept in tins for the occasion.

It did not take my hosts very long to spot my lack of enthusiasm for sweet cakes and several provided dishes of chopped, raw liver especially for my benefit. At first, I found this Middle Eastern delicacy more difficult to swallow than the honey-cakes but, gradually, developed a genuine appetite for it.

This glutinous food would, in summer, be washed down with fresh orange or apple juice; in winter, tea or coffee.

One of the most hospitable of these friends had been a member of the notorious PLO Black September unit. Selim was one of many Palestinian prisoners who had had serious difficulties with the Assad government. He had been in *el Kalaa* for more than two years and liked to invite friends at least once a week to share quite a lavish morning meal. He was a marvellous cook, apart from having, for my taste, slightly too heavy a hand with spices, and would serve up a wonderful lunch of several courses. He was an occupant of room 9, which was always open in the morning, and was therefore not compelled to confine his hospitality to his room's bath-house day.

Selim was twenty-six, small but sturdy, with a boyish face, uptilted eyes under bushy eyebrows and dark amber skin. He spoke English quite well and was anxious to improve it.

The contretemps between all the different factions of the PLO and the Syrian government, and also each other, were so many and multifarious, I felt it wiser not to pry into why Selim and his associates were in prison. To me, these young Palestinians were amicable and welcoming and I accepted their friendship in the same spirit.

Selim had travelled a good deal in Europe – doubtless with explosive substances taped to his torso – and had a particular liking for West Germany. He was quick-witted, had wide interests and a great deal of boyish charm. It was a pleasure to discuss almost any subject with him unless it referred, directly or indirectly, to Israel or the United States. If this happened, it was as if his blood had turned to snake venom. This courteous young man who, were I to stumble in the yard, would rush to pick me up, was capable – had I been Israeli or American – of disembowelling me without a flicker of compassion. The bulldozing of his family home by the Israelis, immediately after the '67 war, had aroused a bitterness nothing could appease.

Abou Mustapha also seemed to feel I was in constant need of feeding up. He would invite me occasionally to breakfast with him off pitta bread and boiled eggs.

The fresh eggs were brought by a married sister who lived in Jordan's capital, Amman. Every two weeks the poor woman spent an entire day travelling by bus in an effort to keep up her brother's spirits. She always brought an enormous parcel of groceries. I suspected he appreciated the food far more than the brief presence of his sister, separated from him by fine-mesh wire and unable to stay longer than a quarter of an hour before rushing to catch the bus back. His temper was always shorter than usual on the days of her visits. Yet, apart from the consulate staff at the American Embassy, who spent at least an hour with him every few weeks, she was his only visitor. His grown-up sons and daughters in New Jersey showed a marked reluctance to make the long journey. Other relations, still in Syria, were apparently too shocked to come near him.

He must have felt hurt by their neglect and yet he clung to his hope of a lenient sentence, although I believe his lawyers did their best to caution him. As he served the eggs up in the old-fashioned American way (by breaking them out of their shells into tumblers and stirring them with a long-handled spoon) he would say: 'They're good guys, but kinda nervous!'

He had a lower bunk, heavily screened, tucked in a far corner of room 4. This was one of the smaller dormitories, occupied exclusively by those who had committed murder; many were youths who had killed a sister or another close female relative for bringing dishonour on their families; an action that seldom gets more than a year's imprisonment in Syria.

Another facet of Abou Mustapha's optimism, at this stage, was his belief that some sort of amnesty was 'just around the corner'.

'Tony,' he would say, 'somethin's goin' to happen. Man, I can feel it – and you're goin' to be outa the can, pronto!'

I, having studied the history of amnesties in Syria, would point out they only occurred when there was a change of government or a major victory in war, and neither was at all likely in the foreseeable future.

I felt he harped on this subject to keep up his spirits. When his lawyers told him he would be sentenced on his next court visit, his optimism about his own and everybody else's future seemed to rise to fever pitch. But I could occasionally detect a half-hidden look of panic in his eyes that belied the feverish wisecracking. When the moment came for his final court appearance, many of us held our breath.

As he was not in *Hofra*, we could not question him on his return. Depressing rumours about his fate, however, began to circulate.

On the following morning he was not in the courtyard. When we asked some of the younger fry from his room all we learned was that Abou Mustapha had said nothing to anybody and was now, they thought, *moo-quiess* (unwell).

I decided to investigate, remembering as I walked into room 4 the prison etiquette of asking permission to do so from the chief of the room.

The chief was much older than most of the room's inmates, almost as old as Abou Mustapha. He was a charmless, puffy, overweight creature who had, I was told, strangled his father-in-law with a nylon bootlace.

I found him on his bunk, cutting his horny toenails with massive steel clippers. He looked up sourly and waved me towards Abou Mustapha's corner.

He was on his bunk, his head propped, uncomfortably, on a couple of pillows, wearing the pale blue suit he must have worn in court. Bought, off the peg, at one of New York's more expensive stores, it was his pride and joy; he only put it on for special occasions; now it was rumpled and badly creased. His face and bald head had a yellowish tinge and glistened with sweat. His eyes were open but did not seem to be focussing.

Speaking quietly, I wished him good morning.

There was no answer.

Feeling as if I were intruding into private grief, I asked how he had got on in court.

There was another prolonged silence.

I began to wonder if he was aware of me.

Then, still staring fixedly ahead as if in a trance, he suddenly whispered: 'Jesus!'

I asked if I could do anything for him. He suddenly looked at me with eyes that now appeared to be focussing properly. Still whispering, he said: 'That motherfucker gave me life! Listen, will ya – that scumbag, he gave me life!'

I had already guessed this. Out of my depth, not knowing what to say, I fell back on the suggestion that his lawyers would surely be taking his case to appeal. Later, I was to feel uneasy that in my anxiety to be reassuring I had forgotten the three people he had so capriciously slaughtered.

He turned his head to the wall like an unhappy child. 'Those sons of bitches in the appeal court are worse than yesterday's motherfuckers!' He was now speaking in his normal voice.

I began to mutter platitudes about 'life' not meaning life, and the possibility of those amnesties he had often talked about – perhaps two of them. The first would cut his twenty-five years to fifteen and a second to seven and a half.

He turned his puckish face towards me again, his expression showing he was coming out of the state of shock. 'Tony, you're an even stoopider wiseass than those judges!' he said, impatiently, but the tone was friendly. 'That's the sorta optimism I give other guys – for me, it just don't work!'

I dropped the subject and asked if I could get him breakfast – make tea, perhaps. He declined, saying his immediate need was for a shower and, with an obvious effort, he swung his legs to the floor. He pulled off his jacket and sat upright, still hollow-eyed and very pale. I gave him a bath-towel from the foot of his bed. He pulled an orange-box from under the bunk, taking from it a small, brightly-coloured, plastic sponge-bag. I noticed a large number of aerosol cans of cheap shower-gel in the box. Even after years in North America, Abou Mustapha retained the town Arab's predilection for heavy, cloying scent.

He got up suddenly and almost fell. I grabbed hold of him and he seemed relieved to be able to hang on for support as we covered the short distance to the bath-house. He sank wearily on to Anwar's stool to wait for a vacant shower.

Two hours later I returned from a visit from the Consulate, to hear he had collapsed into unconsciousness while sitting outside the cafeteria. Friendly arms had gathered him up and taken him to the doctor's surgery. Heart trouble had been diagnosed and he had been told to rest.

The surgery was reached through the guardroom, up the long narrow steps to the ramparts. Immediately above the western end of *Hofra*, a sharp turn to the right revealed two adjoining, grubby-looking rooms: the Citadel's medical centre.

The waiting-room was devoid of furniture, so those sick enough to visit the doctor were compelled to lean against the walls or squat on the dusty floor. The surgery was furnished with a desk, a chair and a rickety brown leather couch, its black horsehair stuffing protruding, like fungus, from countless holes. There was also, tucked away in a corner, an antiquated dentist's chair.

Our young police doctor, who wore a uniform with a captain's insignia, was available on Tuesdays, Thursdays and Saturdays. No alternative medical aid was provided except in dire emergency. Arabs being a tough race, dire means recognisably on the point of death. In such cases an ambulance could be summoned on the authority of the governor, or a deputy, to convey the man to a local general hospital with special facilities for keeping prisoners under lock and key. Only three such incidents took place while I was in the Citadel. Two out of the three died shortly after being admitted.

The doctor had only recently qualified. 'Sent to us to get practice on living bodies, instead of corpses!' was the general verdict. He was an ebullient young man, well aware of his good looks. On the mercifully rare visits I made to his surgeries, he insisted I jump the queue. It surprised me that none of the other patients objected to this unnecessary courtesy. With the Syrians and Lebanese, his attitude was that of the good-humoured bully, usually accusing them of malingering. In the majority of cases, this was untrue.

The dentist, whose ministrations I was thankful never to need, was available two mornings a week. Judging by the outrageous suffering he inflicted on some of my friends, his abilities were as primitive as his equipment.

It took a long time for Abou Mustapha's health to improve. Not even the sensational information that the president of the court, immediately after passing sentence on him, had retired to the judges' private sanctum and dropped dead from a coronary, revived his spirits. This news was, however, received with wild acclamation by almost every other prisoner.

For many months he could do little except totter out of his room in a morning clutching his stool and walk, unsteadily, the short distance to the cafeteria where he would hold court until locking up. He lost a good deal of weight and the slightest exertion made him breathless, but to listen to him talking in Arabic was to realise how different a person he was to the character he presented to the European colony.

181

The string of set phrases and wisecracks had gone; he communicated eloquently in the classic version of his own language.

There was much speculation about who would replace the grouchy judge who had dropped dead. Would court number 1 maintain its reputation for tough sentencing, or would it adopt the more liberal attitudes of number 2?

I was amongst the first guinea-pigs. One afternoon at the beginning of October, Fahdi told me he had seen my name on the list of those going to court the following day. This was confirmed that evening when a mangled, Arabic version of my name was broadcast, with about twenty others.

The next morning saw the first of my half-dozen court attendances. The routine never varied. Out into the yard just after seven to wander wretchedly about for more than an hour. In October, the mornings were still delightfully warm, but they gradually cooled until, in December, I wore a tweed jacket against the cold north winds.

After the usual further delays outside the admin office and the short, overcrowded journey in a disintegrating vehicle, I would be found slowly pacing that familiar, sewerage-smelling, basement cage.

On this, my first solo appearance, I was confident I knew precisely what would happen at every stage. At least twenty minutes before the others I would be escorted upstairs to the judge's private office for the cross-examination given to foreigners.

When this failed to occur, I was disconcerted. No special call was made for me. Just before eleven o'clock, a policeman shouted a list of those to go immediately to the courtroom; my name was included.

We lined up in crocodile and were handcuffed to each other. We climbed the stairs quickly, arriving breathless in the long, shabby, brown and yellow corridor. I wondered if I would now be detached from the rest, but no. We remained standing outside heavy mahogany doors, gossiping in nervous whispers. I was handcuffed to a young Syrian with a hairline barely three centimetres above his eyebrows and a livid scar across his chin. These mildly alarming features were mitigated by a beaming smile and the care he took to help me up the stairs.

Suddenly there was an influx of policemen from all directions and much jangling of large keys. The heavy doors were thrown open and we were pushed forward into the lofty courtroom, so large it covered more than three quarters of the whole *palais de justice*.

It was empty, apart from ourselves and the policemen surrounding us. They locked the doors and removed our handcuffs. Each prisoner, as he was released, had to climb four rickety wooden steps into the dock on the left of the door. It was enormous, made of dark, polished wood and resembled a committee-box at any second-rate horse show. More than twenty feet long, it was steeply ramped with three rows of wooden benches extending from end to end. After climbing the steps, you had to push open a small door, no higher than my knees. You were permitted to sit where you wished. Like cinema audiences, some preferred the back row, others rushed headlong to the front.

Being one of the last out of handcuffs, I slipped quietly into a spot on the middle bench, just inside the little door which, I was amused to notice, was immediately locked by a policeman who pocketed the key.

If any of us had been tempted to leap from the dock in a bid for freedom, we could easily have done so. The wooden barrier surrounding us was nowhere higher than four feet. It was the armed policeman that kept us in our seats, not the locking of a knee-high door.

Once more the minutes ticked away and nothing happened. I had plenty of time to look about. The courtroom walls were panelled in dark wood. The high ceiling (there was nothing but the roof above it) had been painted the sort of ivory white that quickly becomes pale custard. From the dock we faced across the court to six immensely tall sash-windows, all wide open; our height above the ground muted, very slightly, the strident horn-blowing of the traffic. In spite of the approach of autumn, the heat was intense. Between each window was a sienna-brown pillar in mottled fake-marble, identical with those in the corridor.

To our right, against the wall dividing the court from the judges' robing-room, was a massive dais with an elaborately moulded and gilded apron-front with a flat top that could be used as a table. Behind it were three elaborately carved, high-backed chairs, upholstered in green plush, in a line, about six feet apart. The chair in the centre was more grandiose than the others and would have made a suitable throne for any Ruritanian monarch.

It surprised me that the main body of the court was filled with rows of small wooden chairs covering its parquet floor. In spite of the catafalque-like object on our right, my immediate impression was of an empty concert hall, not a court of law.

183

The mahogany double-doors on the other side of the dock were flung open. Two policemen took up positions just inside the court to keep an eye on the motley collection of humanity that trooped in. Distinguished lawyers in silk suits; casually dressed young clerks; friends and relations of those in the dock, a few obviously prosperous, others pathetically unsure of themselves.

One of the most nervous was a young woman carrying a baby boy, almost a year old. The apprehension on her gentle face was suddenly transformed by the pleasure of seeing her husband in the front row – the good-humoured young ruffian to whom I had been handcuffed. Affection overcame her shyness; she almost ran up to the dock and handed the baby across the low barrier to her husband who seized the infant, placing it on his knee. The little boy sat up, gurgling contentedly, sucking his thumb and stroking his father's face. The wife made no obvious gesture of affection towards her man – such a display would have been regarded as bad taste, but mutual concern radiated from them as they gazed at the child who had been delighted by his father's kisses and welcomed the touch of his rough hands with cracked nails and blistered palms.

A succession of adult males had approached the dock, greeting those around me with a handshake or a pat on the shoulder, if they could reach.

There was also a frail-looking countrywoman; every movement beneath her threadbare but immaculately clean *kaftan* showed how much she must be suffering from arthritis. She looked old, but was probably barely forty. The object of her interest was a man of about twenty. I was fascinated by his deference to what was obviously his mother. He rose to greet her; taking her hand, he kissed it, then bowed again, touching the back of her hand with his forehead. This courteous act was repeated several times before they exchanged a word.

The police made no attempt to stop these unofficial contacts. I could never imagine such a scene taking place in a British court. I found it a heart-warming spectacle.

It did not last long. The police soon began ordering everyone to their seats. There was a steadily increasing feeling of tension. We all sensed the court was about to go into session.

After a final kiss on his father's unshaven cheek, the tiny boy was gathered into his mother's arms, and as she sped across the courtroom she almost collided with an impressive-looking group from the British

Embassy making their promised appearance to observe justice being done to one of their nationals.

Being decorously British, they made no attempt to pat me, but moved quickly across the court to vacant seats. This dignified little procession was headed by the consul, followed by Richard Lyne and one of the embassy's Syrian staff who had often come to the Citadel and with whom I had established a friendly rapport. To my surprise, there was a fourth man I had not seen before. He was young, fair-haired, with noticeably blue eyes.

They had only just settled in their seats when a robed official bobbed up at the side of the dais and barked an announcement. We stood up. A narrow door to the robing room was pulled open by a policeman and three figures appeared, wearing ankle-length black gowns, heavily trimmed with braid. They clambered on to the rostrum and settled in the throne-like chairs. There was a breathless pause and then the rest of us subsided into our seats.

The judges on each side of the president were as monstrously plump as the majority of Syria's civil servants, but the president was markedly different; gaunt and spindly, with heavy-lidded eyes, he resembled an ageing falcon.

Because of the absence of air-conditioning (the blades of two large fans circled slowly, and uselessly, in the ceiling) the judges were wearing open-necked sports shirts, showing a large expanse of Adam's apple and multi-coloured chest between the folds of their gowns. This added nothing to the dignity of the occasion.

They had been followed into court by a clerk carrying an armful of dossiers, which he placed in front of the president with an obsequious bow.

There was a deferential hush as the president shuffled the dossiers as if they were a collection of paperback thrillers. He finally speared one and held it up like a flag towards the clerk of the court.

I watched the clerk lean forward to squint at the name emblazoned in Arabic script by a heavy felt-pen on the cover. He turned his head towards the dock and shouted one word: 'Anthony!'

I stood up obediently, conscious that every eye in the courtroom was focussing on me. I saw my interpreter leap up and walk quickly to a spot just below the president. A short discussion was ended when the judge said something to the policeman beside the dock. The interpreter turned towards me saying: 'The president wants to ask you some questions but

185

feels, in view of the language problem, the distance between you is too great. He's therefore given instructions for you to stand beside me for a few minutes.'

The policeman was now frantically searching his pockets for the key of the small door. I was strongly tempted to vault over it, but felt such an exhibition of geriatric acrobatics might influence the court unfavourably. I remembered the advice of friends in *el Kalaa*. 'Emphasise your age,' they had insisted. 'Never forget it's your greatest asset in this country. Few Syrians live to be over seventy – make the most of it!'

So I waited until the policeman found the key, stumbled down the steps and clutched at the interpreter's hand, wondering if I were looking sufficiently pathetic.

That handclasp gave me considerable reassurance. The Syrian radiated calm and infectious self-confidence. He appeared to have the same effect on the president, who treated him with greater deference than he sometimes showed towards eminent lawyers. I always felt he put my case in the most convincing way.

The president was flicking through my dossier, licking his forefinger. The judge on his left was nodding and winking, with little smiles and tiny camp gestures at friends among the lawyers. The judge to the right looked incapable of any sort of smile and seemed lost in contemplation of his highly polished fingernails.

The president pushed my dossier away and asked a question. My interpreter said, 'The judge wants to know your age.'

I replied I was seventy-one. This was greeted by involuntary murmurs of surprise.

The president next asked for the full names of my father. I could hardly believe my ears. Surely the ludicrous repetition of basic facts which started seven months ago was not going to begin all over again?

But it was – the next demand was for my mother's maiden name, and so on, through the familiar lengthy catechism. I felt a strong inclination to give different answers this time – just to see what the reaction would be, if any.

When the judge came to the end of the stale questionnaire, he concentrated entirely on the character and whereabouts of the young English runner, Kevin Morton.

What did I know about this Morton?

I said I hardly knew him.

Where was he now?

I assumed a vague expression and shrugged.

Was he not an important operator for the notorious family of Benami?

I agreed this might be possible. Actually, the suggestion was so ridiculous I almost laughed.

The president insisted he must have more information about the activities of this Morton. Investigations must begin at once to discover if he was still in Syria, and any other relevant facts. The police, he inferred, had been sadly remiss in not setting up such an enquiry immediately after my arrest. A date two weeks ahead was fixed for my return to court. By then, he hoped, more would be known about the unscrupulous Morton.

Before returning me to the dock, he asked, as if genuinely concerned for my welfare, if I had not found my luggage dreadfully heavy. This confirmed my impression that he had made up his mind I was the poor, geriatric mule and Kevin the wicked young drug-dealer who had lured me into criminal ways. Well, if he wanted to bark up the wrong tree, I decided to do my best to help him.

'Yes, *sidi*,' I said meekly, 'it was very heavy.'

Later that morning, however, I was impressed by his handling of a frightened youth on trial for murder. The boy had been next to me in the dock and, when it was his turn to be questioned, had trembled so much he could hardly stand. It was difficult to believe he could have killed a fly, let alone a human being. The president gently coaxed the story out of him with tact and patience.

Towards another prisoner, he showed remarkable restraint. The provocation came from a *Hofra* colleague who strongly resembled an Old Testament prophet. This fantastic figure was colossally overweight with shoulder-length, grey-black hair, a beard almost to his knees, his giant frame perpetually swathed in the same black *galabieh*. He smelt like an old dog. Having lost his temper, he roared insults at all three judges as loudly as an Homeric herald. The corpulent ones appeared on the point of apoplexy, but the president remained coolly unconcerned and gradually the overwrought 'prophet' calmed down sufficiently to answer questions.

The British Embassy party did not witness either of these incidents. As soon as I was returned to the dock they had, very sensibly and with a discreet wave in my direction, tiptoed out of court.

When I got back to *Hofra*, while trying to swallow the oily rice of

187

a much-delayed midday meal, I was continuously pounced upon by prisoners wanting to know about the new president of court number 1. Did he resemble his predecessor? Was he the type to inflict swingeing sentences on almost everybody?

I refused to answer, telling them to get their information from the hirsute prophet. After all, he had been trotting in and out of that court for twenty-five years; I was just making my debut!

Within a few days I had an unexpected visit from Richard Lyne who brought the young stranger from the courtroom. Lyne told me his period of service in Syria was over, and this fair-haired Edinburgh Scot, by name Jim Malcolm, would be taking his place.

I was naturally sorry Lyne was leaving. His attitude of sympathetic neutrality had helped me accept the rigours of life in a Syrian dungeon without too much fuss.

My selfish anxiety at his imminent departure proved groundless. His successor maintained what appeared to be an established tradition of the Damascus embassy, showing a helpful concern for any British national who found himself – justifiably or otherwise – in conflict with the laws of Syria.

Jim Malcolm's style was slightly more brusque than Lyne's and at times I was reminded of those sharp winds that can blow the length of Princes Street in his native city. He found it difficult to be ever-patient with several prisoners who arrived later on. These were natives of former British colonies, now fully independent but lacking funds for diplomatic or consular services everywhere in the world. Where they were not represented, the British, for the time being, provided a protective umbrella. The reaction of these men to life in *el Kalaa* was surprising, especially in view of what one hears about prison conditions in their own countries. Although some had African passports, all were of Asian origin. They indulged in tearful bouts of hysterical self-pity and some made repeated threats of suicide. After a few weeks they would gradually pull themselves together, but it could be an exhausting period for many of us.

Jim Malcolm, well-briefed on my tastes in reading, never failed to bring a plentiful supply of English newspapers and magazines. I was also able to keep up to date with French opinion by borrowing Jean-Pierre's *Nouvel-Observateur* which his mother sent every week. Sometimes the supply would be held up for a month or so because the government had taken offence at some Gallic criticism of its policy and imposed an immediate ban on all French newspapers and periodicals.

Mail could be a problem for those unable to claim protection from the British Embassy. The official channels for sending or receiving letters were, to put it mildly, unreliable. One governor tried to insist that incoming mail addressed to foreigners must be censored. As the staff could read nothing except Arabic, everything had to be sent to the Ministry of Justice for vetting. Like government departments in many countries, this ministry often kept letters for weeks and, occasionally, lost them altogether. Universal outcry brought this system to an end after about a month. Even the German Embassy raised its voice in protest.

Being allowed to use the British Consulate as a postbox was a great boon, for only once was an attempt made to interfere with the mail they brought me. This was due to an officious deputy governor who later received a devastating rebuke from an enraged Rachid on one of his periodic visits.

We would all have had similar problems with our outward mail had we not relied on the kindness of our Syrian friends who had long ago pointed out that their weekly food and laundry baskets were never searched when handed back to their owners. All we had to do was stamp our letters – stamps could be bought from the tobacconist's stall – and hand them to a Syrian friend who would place them in a basket with his dirty laundry. The laundress – wife, mother or sister, would understand at once and put our correspondence in the nearest postbox.

My generous friends in England and the Netherlands continued to send books, care of the consulate. In one parcel I discovered Gavin Maxwell's *The Rocks Remain*, included because the dust-jacket mentioned that the author had been at Stowe and, as we were approximately the same age, the sender thought we might have known each other. Actually, Maxwell was six years younger than me and we had not overlapped.

In *The Rocks Remain* he describes a forced landing at Rome airport because of an engine defect while on a flight to Greece. Owing to allegations made against a prominent Sicilian in a previous book – an account of the pursuit and death of the bandit, Salvatore Guilliano – Maxwell had been warned he would be arrested if he set foot on Italian soil. The engine repairs took about an hour and were carried out while the passengers remained in their seats. He gives a vivid description of how, during that hour, he sweated with anxiety at the possibility – if the trouble should prove serious – of being compelled to leave the aeroplane and be taken into custody by the *carabinieri*. This would mean having to endure the unimaginable horror of an Italian prison!

I read these passages aloud to Carlo and Mario who could hardly believe their ears and fell about laughing in derision at Maxwell's alarm; the suggestion that anyone could be frightened of conditions in an Italian prison! Did not this absurd Maxwell know all Italian prisoners were given wine with their meals, and good wine, too! The conditions in *Hofra* would be impossible in *bella Italia*!

I suggested that wine would not, perhaps, be of overwhelming importance to someone who elected to make his home in one of the more remote regions of the Scottish West Highlands. While not sharing all Maxwell's phobias, I doubted at least some of Mario and Carlo's assertions about the home comforts available in Italian jails, and Jean-Pierre was openly derisive; the customary Gallic scorn for Italian institutions rising quickly to the surface, in spite of his Venetian mother.

Kurt was now going to court every two weeks. Occasionally, he would be questioned about his contacts in Lebanon and the identity of those who paid his hotel bills in Damascus; more often he had to sit through a whole session listening to others being cross-examined. He felt the rare questions were tossed at him, like bones to a dog, because of the president's interest in his pretty, blonde interpreter.

In between court visits he had started a campaign for all foreigners to be taken out of *Hofra*. He had the enthusiastic support of the Greeks and of nobody else. These three pleaded with the senior staff that the subterranean life was seriously affecting our physical and mental health. The rest of us could see no sign of these debilitating symptoms and knew the real reason was increasing friction between the trio and Fahdi.

At that time it was unheard of for a prisoner accused or convicted of a drug offence to be housed anywhere except in *Hofra*. The only exception was the immensely competent Yussef, who did much of the administrative work that should have been the responsibility of the deputy governors. In return, he had been allowed to live in room 8, where most had been convicted of major fraud, with a few murderers and rapists thrown in.

The Greeks and Kurt did their best to inveigle me into joining their struggle and were irritated by my refusal. I had always got on well with what Abou Mustapha called the 'bums' of *Hofra*. I had been accepted by them and had no wish to exchange their company for others who might prove less likeable. My feelings were shared by the Italians, Bruno and Jean-Pierre.

In the end, much to everyone's surprise, the triumvirate got what they wanted: berths in the prestigious room 8. The extra comfort they obtained, apart from better ventilation, was minimal, and even this could be misery in winter. None of the ramshackle dormitories had any heating; the roofs leaked and the window-frames did not fit properly. Although frost and snow are comparatively rare in Syria, heavy rain, with temperatures in the low forties, frequently occur between December and March.

Room 8 also had rather more than its share of the fundamentalist type of Muslim who never troubled to conceal their dislike of these 'nasranis' who, although basically a kindly and considerate trio, sometimes showed a lack of respect for Islamic prejudices and accepted good manners.

Kurt, as I have mentioned, was an inveterate lounger, often crossing his legs and making no effort to conceal the soles of his feet. Costa and Yanni seldom bothered to hide their impatience with the more prudish elements of physical modesty. When changing their underwear, they would ignore outraged protests and strip off their brightly coloured underbriefs and stand completely naked while finding a clean pair. This sort of behaviour had caused friction in *Hofra*, and created even more trouble in room 8. But, in spite of the frequent abuse to which they were subjected, the trio vowed they never regretted engineering the transfer; living where the gates were open all morning was ample compensation.

Those of us who had remained faithful to *Hofra* could not help being amused by the initial difficulties suffered by Kurt in room 8. Never an enthusiast for early rising, he was now seldom in the courtyard before midday. To lie in during the morning was forbidden, even in room 8, but the majority of sergeants ignored those who did so, unless there were rumours of an inspection by the governor. Nevertheless, Kurt assured us his belated appearances were due, not to laziness, but to the impossibility of sleep until after four each morning. The bunk beneath him was occupied by a small, simian young man with a dark skin, a misshapen foot – probably the result of clumsy midwifery – and a halo of lustrous black hair, who might be described as room 8's principal – perhaps only – whore.

This monkey-faced lad received a stream of lustful visitors each night, their vigorous frolicking within the heavily curtained space below Kurt causing such vibration, he felt, at times, he might be shaken to the floor.

Knowing he was venturing on very thin ice, Kurt eventually suggested to the young man, as tactfully as he knew how, that he would be grateful if the *culture physique* he obviously enjoyed late at night with some of his more athletic friends could be just a trifle more subdued. To his relief, the youth was in no way offended and promised he would urge restraint on his energetic visitors. With a conspiratorial wink he told Kurt that he himself would be most welcome if he cared to 'drop in' at any time.

The full-scale earthquakes became minor tremors and Kurt's tall figure could be seen in the yard as early as eleven. Two months later, the young man was released and his berth taken over by Yanni, and this particular bunk achieved a quiet respectability for the remainder of their sentences.

This incident may give the impression that the population of *el Kalaa* lived in a continuous state of erotic excitement. This was certainly not true of *Hofra*, although the absence of bunks, and therefore of curtains, may well have been the restraining factor.

The finger of suspicion, however, was occasionally pointed at those who copied the method Jean-Pierre and I evolved to protect ourselves from the rains. We had used transparent fabric, but our imitators substituted an opaque material. The result was like a small tent which could be pulled out from the wall and dropped down to cover a single mattress. Those who did this – never more than a dozen out of more than 120 – insisted they could not sleep except in total darkness. The lights in *Hofra*, although always dim, were never turned out. But there were always whispers, hints and nudges, that several canopies were being used for purposes other than sleep.

Personally, I was usually oblivious of such goings on, possibly because I could sleep under almost any circumstances, even on a few inches of concrete floor with the radios, television and voices all around me. I would usually settle down at about 11 PM and not wake until my internal alarm-clock told me it was getting close to 6 AM – time to brush my teeth and make myself unpopular with the rat population.

However, on a few occasions, long after radio and TV stations had closed down, I would become half-conscious of a faraway voice raised in protest, followed by an angry discussion before I lapsed into deep sleep once again.

In the mornings after these disturbances, it was not unusual for Fahdi to tell me apologetically that he would be temporarily allocating a space in the European section of the dais to a Syrian or Lebanese. I never embarrassed him by asking why; I knew. It would be whoever had protested in the night.

These were rare events, and the youth concerned was invariably about eighteen – just a few months too old to be sent to a boys' reformatory. In every case the youngster would have been arrested with a few grammes of hashish. He would be changing his position because an older man had attempted to masturbate him, and the hand groping under the blankets had been indignantly rejected.

The boy was placed amongst us because it was felt the presence of an elderly foreigner would ensure he would not be molested again. This confidence in me as moral guardian often made it hard for me not to smile; no one in *el Kalaa* ever appeared to suspect the truth about my sexual nature. It had obviously never occurred to them that, from the age of eleven, I had been an unabashed homosexual adventurer.

Belonging to the generation that grew up when homosexuality could only be mentioned in whispers, living in the closest proximity to people unaware of my natural, inborn and compulsive instincts, who would have been shocked and distressed if I had revealed them, was no new experience for me.

In spite of being sexually remarkably precocious, there have been quite long periods of celibacy in my adult life when I have sometimes felt that, had I been granted the gift of faith, I might have found a sort of tranquil happiness within some religious order. A monastery on the shores of the Mediterranean, where I might have been allowed to cultivate a vineyard, was a fantasy that had considerable appeal.

There were other, much longer periods, when I lived a hedonistic, aggressive and disseminatory existence that would have made

193

the much-publicised lifestyles of the late Tom Driberg and Joe Orton seem anaemic and lacking in enterprise.

In recent years I had accepted the fact that an elderly ram is an unattractive creature and, although not yet impotent, I had deliberately reverted to a life of celibacy, finding a surprising contentment in becoming a kind of adopted grandfather to a number of young people of both sexes and different nationalities.

It is, perhaps, something of a paradox that throughout my long life, my real friends – those on whose unfailing kindness and sympathy I could always rely – have, with few exceptions, been women. In spite of a total lack of sexual communication between us, they have provided an important leaven to my life that men never could.

Fahdi, like everyone else in the prison, was unaware of these traits in my character, but his instinctive belief that these youngsters would be safe in my company was, of course, correct. It was shared by the youths themselves, most of whom were likeable and made valiant, if unsuccessful, efforts to improve my Arabic.

Around the middle of October, Kurt was told he would be sentenced on his next court visit. Our little European group waited in intense anticipation for his return. As he was no longer in *Hofra*, and prisoners always returned from court after we had been locked up, we hoped to get the news from the guards or service staff. As it happened, a volley-ball player told us when he came in from practice. Kurt had been sentenced to a year and a half. It seemed court number 2 was running true to form, for this penalty was lenient.

The next morning we found a cheerful Kurt who agreed with us. If he succeeded in getting remission of a quarter, he would be released in seven months' time.

I was still being taken to court number 1 with monotonous regularity. As winter approached, the only change was that the appearance of the judges became more formal. Sports shirts were no longer worn; city suits with plain shirts and sober ties were now discreetly visible.

The president would open by summoning the interpreter to the bench and speaking quietly to him. The interpreter would then whisper in my ear what had become a familiar story: the police had not yet come up with any fresh evidence concerning Kevin Morton and the court was still waiting for this. I, who had known that Kevin had been at home in

West Sussex for several months and could not be extradited, suggested this information should be passed on to the judges, but was told this would be most unwise: delay would probably work in my favour. I was reminded that all sentences in Syria begin from the day of arrest, and when mine was passed I could take comfort from the fact that I would have already completed a substantial part of it.

That autumn, two more Europeans were admitted to the Citadel within a few weeks. Perhaps surprisingly, neither had been involved with hashish.

Pablo was a Spaniard, with a high forehead, a sharply pointed nose, more than a touch of arrogance and a dirge-like Iberian voice. He was twenty-eight, and for some years had been making a splendid income, chiefly in the Third World, exchanging counterfeit American dollars for Swiss francs or German marks.

In spite of draconian financial controls in most of these countries, a judicious bribe almost always enabled him to change his false 'greenbacks' into hard European currency. Unfortunately for him, he was caught exchanging a trivial quantity of *ersatz* dollars at a Damascus bank which had up-to-date methods of detecting forged currency.

Johan could not have been a greater contrast to Pablo; a Norwegian, even taller than Kurt, with a similar cap of pale gold hair and typical Viking good looks. He was a TIR truck driver of just over thirty and lived in an Oslo suburb with his wife and family. Like many big men, he was slow of speech and gentle in character.

Ninety per cent of the space inside his huge diesel truck had been occupied by the legitimate products of the Norwegian company who employed him. The remaining space concealed small arms and ammunition, bought in Scandinavia by expatriate Kurdish tribesmen from south-eastern Turkey. The weapons were intended for their kinsmen who inhabit the frontier area of Iran, Iraq, Turkey and Syria and who consider themselves in a continuous state of war with those countries. A tough, courageous people, their constant efforts to achieve a separate state have been sadly unsuccessful.

Johan, having delivered his normal cargo in Damascus, had driven north towards a pre-arranged rendezvous with a Kurdish reception committee. It had been his intention, after unloading the arms, to drive back into Europe via Ankara and Istanbul.

He was the victim of a random check for contraband by Syrian police just north of Aleppo. The cache was quickly discovered in the otherwise empty truck. He was arrested, brought down to Damascus and thrown into the Citadel.

No one seemed to know what to do with him. No Syrian authority appeared willing to define Johan's offence. The Ministry of Justice insisted a civil court could not deal with his case which was clearly the responsibility of the army. The military courts stubbornly rejected this argument.

The Norwegian Consulate rushed between government departments trying to be helpful, but all they could do was reiterate the truth: the arms had never been intended for dissident Kurds within Syria, but for those on the other side of the Turkish frontier. They were able to provide written evidence from emigré Kurds to confirm this.

But as month succeeded month it became obvious that nobody was prepared to decide whether to send him for trial or to release him. All parties were, apparently, prepared to pass the buck indefinitely.

Pablo and Johan were tucked away in a small overcrowded dormitory in *el Abraaj*. The prison staff normally did not object to them spending their mornings with the European group in *el Kalaa*. Johan, the gentle giant, was welcome wherever he went. Most of us, however, had reservations about Pablo. A violent temper, with a low flashpoint, plus a strong conviction that Arabs were only fit to be a subject race, did not endear him to us. We might have shown more tolerance had we known that he, alone among all Europeans in the Citadel, was to die in custody.

My preconceived impressions about evil heroin dealers received a rude shock when, at the end of November, two middle-aged Lebanese entered *Hofra*. Until now, everyone in our dungeon had been involved only with hashish. The newcomers had been 'busted' while travelling south from Aleppo by bus, each carrying a kilo of heroin.

They were solid, respectable citizens from one of the larger villages in the north of the Beka'a Valley. They were Moslems, with fourteen children between them. Being still in the prime of life, they assured me they were looking forward to having many more. When I suggested that a long sentence for possessing a sizeable quantity of heroin might put, at least, a temporary stop to this population explosion, they smiled patronisingly and assured me their case would never reach the courts – they would be released within two months at the outside.

I found this hard to accept in a community where the statutory punishment for the possession of the smallest amount of soft drug was six months and larger amounts could result in sentences of several years. How could they be so confident?

They explained patiently, as if to an idiot child, that they came from the same village as one of Lebanon's principal political figures. They had attended the same school and could almost be said to have been brought up together. I recognised the name they mentioned. It figured often in the world's press, and does so today. Already, they told me, a plea for help had been sent to this valued friend who had many contacts among Syria's ruling élite, who would easily get them released before serious charges could be brought.

Although their acquaintance with this member of government was obviously genuine, I felt their belief that he would leap to their assistance in helping to quash a charge involving hard drugs was pure fantasy; and, when they were still with us after three months, I was certain of it.

However, I was wrong. On the sixty-seventh day of their remand, orders were given for their release. They were accorded a fond farewell with many hugs and handshakes and waved out into the free air. A week later, we received picture-postcards of the temples of Baalbek and the Corniche of Beirut. They were happily back in their homes.

It was not long before another dealer with a neatly-wrapped kilo of heroin fell victim to a customs inspection while travelling by bus from Aleppo towards Homs and Hama.

The cultivation of the opium poppy, the basis of all heroin, is, in this part of the world, almost a Turkish monopoly. Aleppo, therefore, the most northern of the great cities of Syria, has become the centre for its distribution.

This third dealer, although utterly different from the previous couple, gave even less impression of evil. He was Egyptian, twenty-three, with huge brown eyes, skin the shade of oatmeal, close-cropped, curly black hair, and the look of an attractive urchin. His clothes were similar to his European contemporaries': blue jeans, sweaters, a bomber-jacket.

Abdullah had spent his childhood living by his wits in the area around the *el Azar* mosque in Cairo which had given him a razor-sharp ability to sum up human weaknesses. Yet, possibly because of this rough life, he could be astonishingly kind to those less fortunate.

He told me he had intended to take the heroin back to Cairo and use the profit to buy a small shop. He had worked for a number of carpet-dealers and felt he now knew enough to work on his own. Carpets were what he wanted to sell. The money from the sale of heroin would have set him up for life in the business. He knew a much bigger profit could have been made from the 'smack' if he had taken it safely into Europe, but it was carpets that interested him, nothing else was important.

I never asked how he had managed to accumulate enough cash to buy the heroin which, even in Aleppo, close to its source, is not cheap. He did once volunteer that he had been saving for some years, but those who slave (and it is almost slavery) for the small traders in Cairo's *Khan el Kallili* souks, hardly ever rise above basic subsistence level.

Although completely masculine in character he could, at times, when talking to me, show an unmistakeable trace of coquetry in a sinuous twist of his slim, young body, and I could read from his knowing smile that he was well aware that my feelings towards him, although never given expression, were not entirely confined to my intellect. I could see he tacitly accepted my interest as a compliment, which suggested those traders had sometimes used him for purposes other than stacking piles of carpets and running to fetch coffee. This could have explained his prosperity.

Abdullah had no powerful political friends; he was Egyptian, an appalling disadvantage in a country whose government were in no mood to forgive Sadat for his rapprochement with Israel. He was remanded for longer than any of us and eventually sentenced to five years, plus an impossible fine, making it six.

My sixth visit to court took place early in December. I braced myself to sit silently as usual, while those around me pleaded and disputed. This time, however, there was a slight variation.

After the interpreter had finished his chat with the president, he crossed the court, as always, to tell me I would be brought back in precisely two weeks. I felt like groaning under my breath, when he unexpectedly added a rider. 'It will be for the last time,' he said.

'You mean ... ?' I could hardly believe my ears. 'I'm going to be sentenced at last?'

'Yes.'

'What about the hunt for young Kevin?'

He winked at me. 'They've got tired of getting nowhere!'

He turned to rejoin Jim Malcolm. Both mouthed: 'See you in two weeks!' at me, before leaving.

Those two weeks would bring us almost to Christmas. A jail sentence would be an odd way to celebrate the season of good will; but it would, at least, bring nine months of suspense to an end.

I was still ruminating about my own fate when I suddenly realised there was an unusual tension in the court. The president on his elevated throne was speaking with quiet deliberation to a middle-aged prisoner standing rigidly in front of me. Although I could only see the man's back, I sensed he was terrified. Not even a whisper was heard from the crowded court; the only sound, apart from distant traffic, was the president's voice and the tap of his gold pencil on the bench in front of him as he emphasised each point in a lengthy homily.

The young man next to me was glancing occasionally in my direction. I raised my eyebrows with what I hoped was a questioning look at the taut figure. The young man got the message. With his forefinger, he slowly drew a half-circle around his throat from ear to ear.

I felt suddenly very cold as I realised I had been listening, unknowingly, to the pronouncement of a death sentence. The poor wretch was being told he was to hang.

When the president had finished, the man subsided into his seat without a word. Back in the smelly cage, he was still in a state of shock and would say nothing, even to his friends who were trying hard to reassure him about his chances of appealing, and so forth. As he had been convicted of some action against the government, there was little hope of a higher court reversing this decision – and I could see he knew it.

When the day of my final appearance arrived it was bright and sunny but cold for Damascus. The radio had told us there was heavy snow on the mountains towards Lebanon, but none had so far fallen in the city.

There was the usual delay upstairs in the *palais de justice*; as often happened, the key of the door used for admitting prisoners to the court had been mislaid. There were about fifteen of us. This time I manoeuvred into a seat at the front.

There seemed to be more lawyers and prisoners' relations than usual. I watched Jim Malcolm and my interpreter take up their usual positions.

The doors had been closed and we were fast approaching the moment when the judges would make their dramatic entrance, when a disturbance occurred. The door used by the prisoners was flung open and an embarrassed policeman ushered in a couple of strangers who, looking very self-conscious, crept across to seats next to the British Consulate staff.

The new arrivals were a man of about fifty, dark-haired with a touch of grey at the temples, soberly dressed in a dark suit, and a young woman who looked as if she might be his daughter, wearing a dark blue coat and skirt with bright scarlet shoes whose heels were so high her ankles quivered with every step. Her dark hair was encased, somewhat surprisingly, in a close-fitting hat of the same shade as her shoes. A hatted woman is an unusual sight in Damascus where most women wear headscarves or nothing at all.

I could see bewilderment in a good many faces. As the girl began immediately to chat with Jim Malcolm, I thought they might be friends from one of the other embassies. My speculation about their identity was brought to an end by the judges' entrance.

I was feeling a certain tension in my solar plexus as I sat down. I was sure the moment had arrived for me to be told my fate.

The president glanced at the documents before him and murmured something to the clerk of the court who shouted a name that bore no resemblance at all to 'Anthony'.

To my surprise – and, I think, to everyone else's – the young woman got to her feet. Her companion also got up and stood behind her.

They advanced towards the dais and stood looking up as the president addressed them in Arabic. City-Suit spoke quietly into the girl's ear; he was clearly translating.

It became obvious that she was being told most unwelcome news. She began to scowl furiously and to make incoherent animal noises. When the president ended his short speech you could see City-Suit was urging the young woman to accept what had been said with as much restraint as possible.

This advice she chose to ignore. Suddenly, she threw her head back and emitted a series of piercing screams, waving her fists at the judges and stamping her high heels violently into the parquet floor. With a furious gesture she tore the hat from her head, her hair falling in disorder around her shoulders, and swiped it viciously across the face of her startled companion. She then flung herself to the floor, her screams growing even louder as she beat the parquet with her fists and hammered a frenzied tattoo with her pointed toes. City-Suit stood shaking his head as if totally baffled and waving his arms in despair.

The president snapped crisp instructions at the police guarding the doors. Looking sheepish, they gathered up the hysterical girl, pinioning her flailing arms and legs as best they could. She was half-dragged, half-carried from the courtroom. Her companion, picking up the hat so unkindly used to slap him, gave an embarrassed little bow towards the judges and scuttled out after the noisy cortège. The woman's screams could still be heard through the heavy doors, gradually becoming fainter.

Fascinated by this unexpected scene, I failed for a moment to notice the president had moved on to the next case – and it was mine. In the noise and confusion I had not heard my name, but I now saw my interpreter standing below the bench, listening intently to what became quite a lengthy monologue from the president.

Feeling dry in the mouth, I got to my feet and stood waiting to be told my immediate future. The judge was just out of earshot, and anyway I would only have understood about one word in ten.

The oration came to an end at last. The interpreter bowed to the president and, while walking across towards me, was joined by Jim Malcolm.

When they reached me the interpreter said quietly: 'I'll give you a brief summary of what the president has been saying – all right?'

I could not trust myself to speak, so just nodded.

'Firstly,' he continued, 'Kevin Morton who delivered those suitcases to you in the Meridien Hotel and who has been on trial with you *in absentia* has been sentenced to five years' imprisonment and a fine of three hundred thousand Syrian pounds.'

This amazed me so much I managed to croak I had no idea that Kevin was being tried with me. 'I thought,' I said, 'they were searching for him in the hope of getting more evidence against me.'

'No. He's been on trial. The court obviously considers he was the boss and you were merely one of his mules. You're lucky they formed that impression because you have been sentenced to two and a half years' imprisonment and no fine. It is customary to fine everyone convicted of smuggling hashish, but it has specifically been waived because of your age.'

I felt mildly comforted and wondered if this would include fines imposed by the customs service.

Jim Malcolm made an effort to cheer me by saying: 'Remember you've already completed more than nine months. With the usual remission you'll be out in just over a year.'

Although my sentence was not as light as Kurt's, I knew I had been lucky and said so.

I saw Malcolm look quickly at the judges' dais. I guessed he wanted to see if our voices were disturbing them. They were deep in discussion, seemingly unaware of our existence. He turned back with a glint of amusement, saying: 'I'm glad your reactions have been less dramatic than that young woman's!'

'So that was the trouble – she was being sentenced?'

'She was indeed. She's a Greek who's been in the women's prison some months – caught, like you, at the airport with hashish in a suitcase. Two men, both Greeks, were arrested with her – I expect you know them.'

I realised the flamboyant creature must have been Costa's girlfriend – the one who had tried to shift all the blame on to him.

'That was her lawyer with her,' explained the interpreter. 'He was the cause of all those screams. He had stupidly promised to get her off with one year in jail, and the poor girl believed him.

'And she got more?'

'The same as you – two and a half.'

I mentioned that Costa and Yanni had not yet started their fortnightly court visits. They told me there were so few women waiting for trial they always spent a shorter time on remand.

The president had moved on to question another prisoner. So, brushing aside my inadequate thanks, my friends hurried from the court after reminding me that I would be free in thirteen months.

When I visited Kevin Morton at his Sussex home a year and a half later, I discovered he had never heard anything about the sentence and fine imposed on him by that Damascus court on a bright December morning. The only hint he had had was a cryptic remark by a passport controller at a Channel port when returning from a trip to Paris, six months before our meeting. This official, after taking slightly longer than usual to examine Kevin's passport, had said: 'Keep away from Syria, laddie – they're looking for you there and they're not very friendly!' And, with this casual warning, which he had not fully understood, he had been waved onwards.

HOFRA: PART 3

The prospect of thirteen more months in *Hofra* was not too daunting and I settled down to a quietly monotonous existence. Only those days when something out of the ordinary happened remain in the memory.

Christmas was, of course, ignored in this predominantly Muslim community. For Christians, most of whom were Lebanese with a sprinkling of Syrians – we Europeans hardly mattered – a special service of holy communion took place in the *Abraaj* theatre, a few days before the event.

It was conducted by a young Syrian Catholic priest in a mixture of Arabic and Latin. He spoke neither French nor English, but had brought an elderly, smooth-talking Jesuit who seemed to have most European languages at his command and concentrated on 'chatting up' the Westerners. Of these, only Jean-Pierre and the Italians had not strayed from the 'World's Church'. Pablo had been 'cradled' as a Catholic, but had lapsed a long time ago. The Greeks belonged, in a haphazard way, to the Orthodox Rite.

The Germans and the Swede, being avowed atheists, did not appear. I, being vaguely agnostic, went along partly for a break in the monotony and, possibly, with the faint hope that attendance at an act of worship in the Citadel of St Paul's Damascus, only a few hundred yards from the Street Called Straight, might spark off feelings of belief in my pagan breast. This did not happen, but I was impressed by the unexpected homeliness of the mass, and found the few moments of unintentional comedy before it began strangely moving.

The priest had brought everything he needed to celebrate the holy eucharist in an old cardboard suitcase; his vestments, sadly worn and rather too big for him; a linen cloth to cover the table used as an altar – anxious to conceal several careful darns, he took a great deal of trouble in arranging this cloth. Having no wafers to melt on the tongue, he produced a *baguette* of French bread and chopped it into cubes, as if he were preparing bread and milk. He stuffed the cubes into two large vases of fluted glass, borrowed from a deputy governor. These crusty lumps were to be plucked out on the prongs of a fork and inserted into the mouths of the congregation after they had been consecrated.

Shortly after the mass began, there were moments of spine-chilling horror as a muffled sound of a man in agony could be heard beseeching, as if under torture. These anguished cries came from one of the small cells just inside the theatre entrance, which were the Citadel's death row. It was a prisoner due to be hanged a few days later in this very theatre where we were celebrating the birth of the Prince of Peace.

The priest halted the service and, after genuflecting to the simple wooden cross, spoke to a sergeant standing guard near the main door. After some demur, a cell door was opened, and a pathetic, shabby, unshaven and tear-stained little man emerged, throwing himself on his knees. The mass was resumed and I found myself praying hard to a God in whom I did not believe.

We also, at this time, had a visit from *les religieuses* of the Italian hospital. As always, they brought us good things to eat: fruit, nuts, little cakes and chocolate; but it was not only their gifts we looked forward to, it was more the aura of gentle kindness and laughter that seemed to surround them. They actually seemed to care about us and this was appreciated.

Jim Malcolm and several colleagues, including my interpreter, also paid me a Christmas visit, bringing a most welcome stack of mail and one of those hand-made boxes, elaborately inlaid with mother-of-pearl, that open like a book and combine the functions of a chess set and backgammon board. This was a gift from the staff of the Consulate, and there was a large iced Christmas cake, baked in the kitchen of an embassy family.

The chess-backgammon set gave great pleasure to many in *Hofra*. I left it behind for the small remaining band of Europeans. The cake, on which we stuck tiny coloured candles given us by the nuns, was eaten with great appreciation on the afternoon of Christmas Day.

It was, however, the interpreter who gave me my most valued Christmas present by assuring me that the court's decision not to impose a fine would mean the customs penalty would also be cancelled. Although there was always a scintilla of doubt in my mind about the accuracy of this confident assertion – and my doubts increased as time passed – it did, at that moment, give me a feeling of relief and optimism that lasted quite a long time.

In all the months I had been going to court, the *el Kalaa* dormitories, with the exception of *Hofra*, had been subjected to frequent temporary invasions by bands of bearded prisoners, all wearing white *galabiehs* of the type that button chastely to the neck, have tightly fitting cuffs and extend to the ankles. They were brought in at night by an armed military escort, and none of them ever had luggage. Their arrest had been so swift, they had never been given time to collect personal possessions – even a change of underwear.

No attempt was made to give them a bed. Twenty or thirty would be pushed, roughly, in half-dozens, into the dormitories where, stoically uncomplaining, they went to sleep on the floor.

They were seldom with us for longer than a week. Special Defence Units (an élite corps of the Syrian army to which Rachid belonged) would arrive in the middle of the night, handcuff these men and take them away. A day or two later, those Units would be back with another batch.

These men were members of the Muslim Brotherhood, an Islamic fundamentalist group strongly opposed to the Assad government. The Citadel was clearly being used as a staging post – but to where, and for what purpose? They did not seem to know – and it was some time before we found out.

In all, between three to four hundred must have passed through *el Kalaa*. Their constant arrival and departure continued for over two months.

Without wishing it, I found I was a kind of magnet to many of these fundamentalists. Why an elderly Englishman should have had this effect I never succeeded in finding out. With every temporary invasion a minority would attach themselves to me as soon as I emerged into the courtyard, and remain attached until locking-up.

They looked astonishingly alike. They were almost all between twenty-five and thirty-five; their *galabiehs*, made with the harshest of Egyptian calico, were identical. So were their beards, which were often wispy and untrimmed – could there be some connection between religious fanaticism and a patchy deficiency of hair on a male face? Their eyes, under heavy dark brows, gleamed like watchful tropical fish.

Many of the Brotherhood spoke passably good French and German, and yet showed no inclination to talk with Jean-Pierre and Kurt.

Kurt suggested a simple explanation of why they stuck to me. 'In that white skull-cap you look a bit like Pope John-Paul II – and that makes them feel you must be a pillar of some sort of religion!'

I did my best to keep the Brotherhood at a distance by telling them I was an authority on nothing except the condition of the hashish crop in the Beka'a Valley. I hoped this would make them recoil in pious horror, for fundamentalists believe the penalty for consuming or dealing in alcohol or drugs should be death. Unfortunately, it appeared to make me a more fascinating companion than ever.

When I tried to make them talk about subjects other than Islam, they showed little interest in anything except plans for the destruction of Israel, the restoration of Turkey as an Islamic state and the use of all possible means, including terrorism, to rid the world of the pernicious influence of the Great Satan – the United States. My liberal taste for solving problems by negotiation and compromise only made them more confident of an ultimate victory for their ideas.

All were consumed by a bitter dislike of the Assad government, not because of its methods of arbitrary arrest, beatings and torture, but because these were being used against the wrong people. They hated the Alouite clan, to which the President and many of his closest colleagues belonged, considering them lacking the true spirit of Islam and profanely secular in the way they were running the country.

The Brotherhood had the usual fundamentalist belief that the emancipation of women had been a catastrophe. In this, of course, they were upheld by the Koran, which classifies the female sex with imbeciles, orphans and the feeble-minded.

These opinions did not surprise me. I had met fundamentalists before.

There were moments when, surrounded by these minds closed to everything except Islamic prejudice, I would beg them, rudely, to go away and leave me alone. My exasperation never had much effect, even when I reminded them of the Ayatollah Khomeini's pronouncement: 'Every part of a non-Muslim individual is impure, and this applies to the hair on his head, his body hair and all the secretions of that body.'

I tried hard not to lose my temper because some had already been cruelly treated, and I guessed there would be more cruelty ahead. All were convinced they would be slaughtered by the government unless they publicly disavowed their beliefs. All said they would rather die. In my ignorance, I felt they were over-dramatising.

For nearly two months, the floors of all dormitories except *Hofra* were used as temporary accommodation for these fanatics. Our dungeon had doubtless been made an exception because of the fear of violence between the Brotherhood and a concentration of drug-dealers. It had gradually become known that as many fundamentalists as possible were being crowded into the prison at Tadmor, close to the Roman ruins at Palmyra.

At last, the constant flow of the Muslim Brotherhood began to abate and ceased altogether. My immediate reaction was relief. I could once again walk about the yard without a retinue of zealots. Later, when news of the horrors inflicted on them reached the prison, I was ashamed of being glad to see them go.

In January, rumours of atrocities at Tadmor were transmitted along the 'bush-telegraph' that links prisons in most countries.

The first news was a factual account of the massacre of two hundred supporters of the Brotherhood in Aleppo's principal public square. This had been conducted with no effort at concealment by the SDU. Witnesses soon spread reports of the incident throughout Syria.

Worse was to follow from Tadmor itself. First there were rumours of dozens being shot in the back by the SDU. These stories were no sooner confirmed than they were followed by graphic, eye-witness accounts, from widely different sources, of an even larger number being buried alive. Eventually, none of us doubted that more than three hundred must have been killed at Tadmor by these methods.

When I realised the truth of these atrocity stories, I was ashamed of much of my behaviour towards these over-intense young men; they had had so short a time to live and were to die so horribly.

Not all devout Muslims shared the beliefs of the Brotherhood. Midday prayers every Friday were conducted by imams from the Omayed Mosque – instantly recognisable by their white headcloth, more like an Indian turban than the customary Arab *keffieh*. Most of these imams were mousy little men, but there was one splendid exception who took the session about once a month. Tall, not much more than forty, neatly bearded and obviously something of a dandy, he usually wore an impressive *sillam* (cloak) – gossamer-thin in summer, much heavier in colder weather. But apart from his sartorial magnificence he was clearly a splendid orator.

207

One of the functions of the imams was to provide a short sermon. This was usually ignored by non-participators, but this glorious ham actor had the eloquence to stop those meandering about the yard dead in their tracks. Cafeteria customers, about to raise glass to lip, would be suddenly immobilised, and within a few minutes almost every prisoner in the yard would have gathered behind those at prayer, seemingly to hang on his every word.

I asked my friends if his sermons were similar to the Iranian ayatollahs', and was told he was sharply opposed to the stark fundamentalism of Khomeini and the Brotherhood and emphasized the need for tolerance and understanding. He was, of course, a Sunni Moslem.

In what was obviously a personal effort to demonstrate this tolerance, he adopted the habit, when sweeping grandly into the courtyard, of seeking out all foreigners. He insisted on shaking hands with us in the friendly Syrian fashion that makes the greeting sound like the popping of a paper-bag. In time and, possibly, because I was so much older than the others, I was promoted to a bear-hug as well as a handshake!

Once when summoned to the governor's office to greet embassy visitors I noticed the impressive figure of the imam in an armchair, talking animatedly with the governor and the interpreter. With his usual infectious grin, he promptly enfolded me in his embrace. It was difficult to decide who looked the more startled, the governor or my British visitors.

In the months after my trial I made a lot of friends among the political prisoners. Most of them were young, hardly ever more than twenty-five. Without exception, they had done well at school and completed national service. A number had been to university and several had qualified as teachers. All had learned English, and must have been well taught, because they spoke it surprisingly well.

One, whom I am unlikely ever to forget, I will call Mohammed. He was in many ways typical of them: small and slim with a clear olive skin, enormous dark eyes and looked even younger than his twenty-three years. A teacher in a village school in the north, he had been arrested while distributing pamphlets, handprinted by a democratic, mildly leftist organisation, critical of the authoritarian government.

He had been taken first to a prison staffed by the SDU. Here, the treatment meted out was the sort that has become all too familiar in so many third world countries.

In an attempt to make him implicate his friends, he was confined with a dozen others, similarly accused, in a windowless cell hardly bigger than a cupboard. They were kept for days with just sufficient room on the stone floor for one prisoner to lie down at a time. Since there was no bucket, the floor became coated with urine and excrement. Drinking water was so severely rationed they suffered acute thirst, and the only food was a small quantity of pitta bread, thrown at them twice a day as if they were dogs.

Shut into a small world of evil-smelling darkness, Mohammed lost all sense of time. When he was let out of the black hole, he was surprised to discover he had been there only a week – it had seemed like months.

He was taken into a yard and made to strip to his briefs while a fire hose was turned on him. He was so weak he could hardly stand. After the jet had several times knocked him to the ground, he just lay there and let the water wash over him. His eyes, in the unaccustomed daylight, hurt badly.

He was dragged into a basement and held down while twin coils of electrical flex were unwound and the two terminals, in the shape of crocodile-clips, were fastened to his body: one to bite into his testicles, the other into a nipple. A switch was pulled and Mohammed assured me he had never imagined such pain possible.

This torture, which everyone called 'the crab', continued until the SDU were sure he had told them everything he knew. The current had been repeatedly switched on and off. He said the interval between shocks – waiting for the next spasm of agony – was almost as dreadful as the convulsions.

It was next to impossible to find a political prisoner who had not been subjected to this treatment. All had been in prison several years and none had ever been brought to trial. They assured me there were hundreds more in other jails where conditions were much worse.

From time to time Abou Mustapha and I would receive a joint summons to appear before the governor, and would find him gazing irritably at a letter from Amnesty International. These were sometimes in English from an office in London, occasionally in French from their headquarters in Paris.

None of the staff could read anything except Arabic. Even Abou Mustapha could only decipher a few words of English.

It was therefore my job to read these letters aloud and Abou Mustapha's to translate, sentence by sentence, to the governor. The letters from Paris required a double translation, as I had to provide a version in English.

The subject was always the same – an enquiry about a political prisoner who had been missing for a very long time.

The reaction of the governors varied only in degree of contempt. Some would snatch the missive immediately Abou Mustapha had finished translating, tear it into small pieces and throw them into the nearest wastepaper-basket. Others would sit back, raising their eyes dramatically in the direction of the ceiling, indicating their patience was under severe strain, take the letter gently from me with thumb and forefinger as if it might soil their hands, and place it on the blotter in front of them. They only waited until we had left the office before tearing it up. I was frequently told of their amazement that the West should waste its wealth on a busybody society that concerned itself with traitors.

Even Abou Mustapha, after so many years in God's Great Democracy, was unsympathetic.

'Gee-whizz,' he would say, 'these crazy broads!' (The letters were often signed by women.) 'Do they think anybody cares about these stoopid guys?'

I did my best to memorise the names mentioned in these letters and would conduct my own private investigations. Disappointingly, none were any longer in the Citadel, although I would occasionally find a long-term prisoner who recollected one of the missing. In every case the individual had been transferred and nothing heard of him for years. The assumption that he might still be alive was regarded as Western naivety.

Soon after I had completed my first year in *Hofra*, the European contingent was increased by the arrival of an Irishman. Patrick (not his name) insisted he was forty, though he looked much younger. It was not until he showed us snapshots of two teenage sons and a daughter that we were convinced.

Lithe, dark-haired and blue-eyed, he had been brought up in a County Limerick orphanage where, to judge by his vivid descriptions, Dotheboys Hall conditions still existed.

Like so many of his countrymen, he had made the leap across the Irish Channel before his twentieth birthday. Lucky enough to find a job in a London suburb, he very quickly, because of his intelligence and exceptional dexterity, became a valued employee of light industry.

The pay had been reasonably good and his girlfriend came over to marry him. Within a year or two, he had a family and a house with a garden in one of London's primly respectable northern suburbs.

He had become the epitome of a solid British citizen and was even considering voting Tory; but recently he had been much influenced by friends made during weekend lunch-time sessions at his local pub. These new companions were pleasant enough, if a bit flashy. They could afford expensive clothes and fast cars, describing themselves – tongue in cheek – as freelance, monopoly capitalists. They were successful importers of soft drugs.

Patrick was impressed by their stories of how easy it was – with a suitable vehicle – to make large sums of money transporting hashish from Lebanon or Morocco into the United Kingdom. He already possessed a car and a trailer caravan for taking the family to the coast at weekends, and further afield for holidays.

In spite of his wife's protests, he suddenly decided that the family would have to spend their holidays at the local swimming pool while he took off on a lone expedition. He travelled for the first time in his life through Europe to Greece and took a car ferry across to Latakia.

Upon landing, he was greeted by Lebanese friends of his pub cronies who installed him in the port's best hotel at their expense. They hitched the caravan to their Range Rover and disappeared.

For just over a week Patrick lazed on the beach acquiring a suntan, before his caravan reappeared in the hotel car-park. The keys had been left at the reception desk.

When he looked inside, nothing appeared to have been touched, but close inspection revealed almost everything had been removed and replaced with infinite care. Layers of hashish had been concealed beneath the vinyl-covered floor, similar layers in the roof and behind every article of plywood furniture. Each half-kilo, wrapped in sheets of cellophane and mechanically pressed almost wafer-thin, took up hardly

211

any space. It could only be detected by experts in the art of smuggling – or detecting the smuggler.

Having checked the times of the ferries and made sure his now rather furtive acquaintances had settled his hotel bill, he packed and drove down to the harbour.

Patrick was always convinced the customs were waiting for him – certain that he must have been the victim of an informer. This could have been true. Beka'a Valley hash farmers regularly indulge in savage feuds and their victims are all too often the wretched mules.

As soon as he drove into the embarkation area, the customs staff rushed at the caravan like a pack of wolves. He opened the door for them and stood, watching nervously, as they attacked the vehicle. Each man, hammer in one hand, chisel in the other, busily thrust into every tiny crevice in the veneered plywood.

It was not long before one of them noticed a slight gap between two sheets of plastic, into which he inserted his chisel, widening the hairline space into a gaping cavity. The bevelled edge of the implement, when tapped with a hammer, pierced the wrapping of something hidden behind the plastic. Immediately, the stuffy atmosphere became infused with a faint, but instantly recognisable, aroma.

From just outside the door Patrick watched, with steadily increasing dismay, as the men tore the interior of his beloved old caravan to pieces.

The treatment meted out to Patrick in Latakia was similar to that experienced by those arrested in the Damascus area. He was reasonably well treated by Syrian standards. No one attempted to beat his feet, and none of the other few prisoners had been beaten.

From his description of the Latakia jail – although built in this century, not the seventh – it had much in common with the Citadel, being often just as overcrowded and uncomfortable, but not quite so rat-infested. Water there was cut off in the summer for several hours a day. This made the sanitation, always sparse, even more malodrous.

He quickly discovered that the great disadvantage of arrest in Latakia was being brought to trial in that city, where sentences for drug smuggling were much heavier than in Damascus.

This depressing forecast proved correct in Patrick's case. The only pleasant feature of his many court appearances had been the breath of ozone as he walked, with a small band of well-guarded prisoners, between the jail and the law courts, which are close to each other on the sea front.

He was eventually sentenced to five years and a fine of half a million Syrian pounds – i.e. six years, since he could not pay the fine. With luck, the five years could be reduced by a quarter, but there was no possibility of remission on the final year.

Although he was warned by British Embassy staff about conditions in *Hofra*, he applied to be transferred to Damascus soon after being sentenced, because there were more Europeans in the Citadel, and more English speakers.

Once a prisoner had been sentenced – but never before – it was comparatively easy to obtain a transfer. Written applications had to be submitted to the governor who passed them to the Ministry of Justice who alone could give permission. In spite of these layers of bureaucracy, transfers were granted with surprising speed.

I well remember Patrick's horrified amazement when he straightened up after crouching through the tunnel into *Hofra* for the first time, and gazed at the Hogarthian spectacle of our giant cellar in the evening.

He said afterwards that the shock had been slightly mitigated by the amount of beer he had been allowed to drink on the drive down. They had left Latakia before 5 AM and there had been many halts for refreshments. He, of course, had paid for everything the driver and two policemen had eaten or drunk. No objection to his exceptional capacity for beer was raised, because he wisely provided an equal quantity for his companions.

In spite of the initial shock at our squalid conditions, which he assured us were a good deal worse than in Latakia, he soon settled in.

He seemed to have absorbed all the opinions and prejudices of his north London neighbours. He took pride in travelling on a United Kingdom passport and not one of Eire, and if something was not *de rigueur* in Pinner or Palmer's Green, it could not be civilised. This did not make for an easy life in an Islamic community.

Although basically a kindly man, Patrick had an Irish temper kept in check only by a hair-trigger. This could sometimes lead to trouble with the guards, less often with other prisoners. The staff, who resented being cursed, especially in a language they did not understand, would also lose their tempers and belt him across the face with hands as hard as granite.

During almost two years that I spent in *el Kalaa*, Patrick was the only European I ever saw subjected to physical abuse by the staff. We urged him to be more tactful and not indulge in Celtic rages, but without success.

I was surprised he never lost his temper with me. My general attitude must have irritated him. I did not share his sublime conviction that the United Kingdom was the centre of the civilised world and that English ways of behaving were the only ones to be commended. I enjoyed the companionship of many Syrians, Lebanese and Egyptians whose values shocked Patrick deeply.

Nevertheless, he treated me with an amused tolerance, no doubt attributing my behaviour to my international upbringing and the years I had spent abroad.

I was eternally grateful to him for the hours he put in on the fiddling job of keeping my electric shaver – now becoming unreliable – in working order. If he had not, I would have had to choose between growing a beard or joining the long daily queue for a barber. I had no wish to do either.

The two barbers were long-term prisoners who operated from tiny premises adjoining the bath-house. They were Kurds and, although not related, strongly resembled each other. They were small, light-skinned and dark-haired, with heavy, almost bull-like shoulders. Both were bandy-legged and looked like overweight jockeys. I found it difficult to tell them apart, until one of them grew a moustache.

This was the more notorious, leader of a band of highwaymen who, even today, can be encountered by unlucky travellers on mountain roads at the junction of Turkey, Syria and Iraq. Some make a handsome living and are not averse to cutting a few throats to avoid evidence being given against them.

Our mustachioed barber had admitted to killing more than thirty, pleading he had committed these acts in the heat of the moment and could not recollect the precise number. I would remember this on those, fortunately rare, occasions when Patrick had failed to get my shaver to work and my throat was being caressed by a Kurdish cut-throat razor, as I gazed upwards at expressionless, sloe-black eyes.

Although he shaved me infrequently and trimmed my hair only occasionally, I found it impossible not to like the man. That I should feel friendly towards somebody who could take human life with less concern than I would feel wringing a chicken's neck shook me, anyway at first.

A killer on the grand scale, he had already spent several years in room 1, the smallest dormitory, with only ten double bunks. Its entrance was in the north wall, alongside the steps leading to our cellar.

Another occupant of room 1 was my chubby young friend, Sulieman, who made such valiant efforts to teach me Arabic. On their bath-house mornings, they would often invite me for coffee, which is how I came to know the 'demon barber' and his faun-like boyfriend rather better than I otherwise would.

The bunks, in a room so narrow it was almost a corridor, were in a row against the back wall. The barber and his boyfriend Naif had exclusive use of the two bunks at the eastern end; accommodation intended for four. This no doubt had official approval because they could provide the necessary *douceurs*. They had installed themselves in the lower berths, using the upper tiers for storage. Floral-patterned curtains were draped all round both bunks, making a sort of private apartment.

Everyone assumed that the association, although singularly undemonstrative, must have a strong element of sex in it. Disapproving eyebrows were never raised in the direction of the dominating Kurdish partner, but the same tolerance was not always extended towards the irrepressible Naif.

The boy was only twenty and had an astonishing animal beauty. He was said to accept, from time to time, the advances of other prisoners and at least one guard. The younger son of a rich Syrian industrialist, he had been given a life sentence for raping and strangling a small girl. He insisted it had been a case of mistaken identity. But in view of the eminent lawyers his parents had engaged, without success, his protests of innocence were not entirely convincing.

I could see he was aware, without the subject ever being mentioned, of my susceptibility to his astonishing looks. He would sprawl on Sulieman's bed wearing only skin-tight jeans, stretching himself like a lazy cat and smiling provocatively at me. He made it obvious that any wish for closer intimacy on my part would not be unwelcome, in spite of my age. I did not respond.

Ventilation in *Hofra* was always appalling, and when the single fan broke down – this happened frequently – the atmosphere immediately

215

became so infused with cigarette-smoke and the paraffin-vapour from the *barbouas*, some of us had difficulty in breathing and everyone's eyes became red-rimmed and sore. Suggestions that it might be sensible to cut down the use of the stoves and to smoke less would, however, have been instantly rejected. 'Taking thought for the morrow' is a maxim which had little appeal to most of my companions.

In view of the hours we spent in this smoke-filled cellar – and no prisoner was ever given a physical examination on his arrival at the jail – it was surprising that no more than half-a-dozen deaths took place while I was there. Several had to be taken to a local hospital where they were kept in a heavily chained and padlocked ward – a place that had acquired a frightening reputation. The doctors were accused of being sadists and the nurses, whores.

In an emergency we could not communicate with the guardroom – our only source of help – except by shouting and banging the padlocks against our inner gate. If we were lucky the noise would penetrate up the steps to the courtyard and, eventually, to the guardroom. Often, we had to rely on our cries being relayed by the denizens of room 1. They would lean out of their windows and shout to the guards: 'There's trouble in *Hofra* – you're needed!'

If our sick man was unable to move, Fahad, our giant serviceman with the gap-toothed smile, would pick him up as if he were a small child and carry him into the yard.

There, the guards would decide if the man was sick enough for them to request permission to ring for an ambulance or – much more likely – to give the sufferer a couple of aspirins and have him carried back to his mattress, with an appointment to attend the next morning's sick parade. To be sent to hospital it was usually necessary to be unconscious and starting to turn blue.

Of course death could strike without warning. I remember the case of a small, middle-aged Syrian, the owner of a tiny *bacal* (booth) not far from the Citadel. One of our many Mohammeds, he was a kindly man with a big smile and a brood of young children, serving six months for possessing a small quantity of hashish. He seemed well enough but complained, occasionally, of pains in his chest which he attributed to the smog in *Hofra*. Many of us had similar symptoms and we all tried to ignore them.

It was on an exceptionally hot July afternoon, when the temperature was around 104°F – the sort of weather that makes you drink litres and still be consumed by thirst. I was returning to my mattress after refilling the giant water-jug shared between our European group (we took it in turn). I stumbled over Mohammed's bed, where he appeared to be dozing none too comfortably with his eyes shut. Seeing an empty glass beside him, I decided to fill it but, before doing so, I thought it better to apologise for my clumsiness, so I picked up his hand, saying: 'Sorry if I disturbed— ' The hand fell heavily from my own as I lifted it. His heart had given up the struggle.

This death took place when the Citadel had one of its more humane governors. He gave orders that whenever the fan broke down our gates were to be opened for two hours each evening to allow us into the yard and to make at least a temporary clearance of smog.

During this second summer I made the unexpected discovery that one of the new arrivals in room 8 was a doctor.

Abdul Aziz was about fifty; a tall, ascetic-looking man, pale-skinned with straight black hair, he looked a lot younger than his age. Officially, he had been classified as a political prisoner, although he had never played any part in Syrian politics. He had emigrated to Germany when a very young doctor and qualified in medicine all over again in that country. For seventeen years he had practised as a GP in West Germany. He spoke the language beautifully. Kurt and Bruno were impressed, finding it hard to believe he had not been brought up in their country.

He had decided to return to Syria for two reasons; firstly he felt his children were growing up without roots; secondly, he wished to make a contribution to Syria which, like so much of the Third World, was greatly in need of doctors.

Shortly after bringing his family back to Damascus, disaster had struck. A much younger brother had been arrested, accused of intriguing against the government. A few days later this young man, a junior officer in the Syrian army, escaped and disappeared. This resulted in the time-honoured custom, common to many Arab countries, of all adult men in the family being taken into custody until the absconder gives himself up or is recaptured. The young brother was thought to have fled the country with no intention of returning. The doctor had resigned himself to a long period of captivity.

Dr Abdul Aziz was the first to warn me that a small fissure in my

217

cheek, just below my left eye, was in his opinion an early indication of skin cancer. Having no medical facilities whatever – certainly not those necessary for a biopsy – he could not be certain, but urged me to consult a dermatologist as soon as I got back to Europe.

Apart from this my health in *Hofra* remained remarkably good, in spite of the conditions.

The only bout of real sickness I suffered was a dramatic-looking thrombosis in my right leg. Although uncomfortable rather than painful, the leg swelled to the size of a large bolster, becoming suffused from thigh to ankle with a relief-map outlined in haemorrhaging blood beneath the skin. Its appearance reminded me of photographs of the painter, Gauguin, in the final stages of elephantiasis.

Both Abdul Aziz and the prison doctor withstood the shock of my bloated, hideously-coloured limb being waved under their noses with admirable calm, telling me the only cure was as much rest as possible. The prison doctor gave me a chit permitting me to remain in *Hofra* for three mornings.

At the end of this period, although my leg was as swollen as ever, I made no effort to get another certificate. The mornings in our cellar were altogether too depressing, although Fahdi and the service staff could not have been kinder: in fact, they were too kind, being more concerned about my leg than I was. They kept on looking at it as if it were a primeval monster, with many shakings of the head and clickings of the tongue.

My good friend Anwar found me a spot just outside his bath-house where I could sit comfortably and rest my monstrous limb on a stool. Many weeks were to elapse before it resumed its normal shape.

While enthroned outside the bath-house, I became privy to a secret plot for a mass escape from room 6. This room, housing between thirty and forty, was in the south-eastern corner and was the only accommodation – apart from two classrooms – whose inner wall appeared to abut on to the parade ground that surrounded the southern area of the Citadel.

Amongst those in this room I knew well were two young brothers, Shukry and Majid – both awaiting trial on a murder charge. Sons of a prosperous jeweller, they had been accused of killing one of their father's rivals and of plundering the man's shop. They always insisted it was a case of mistaken identity and I was delighted to hear, some months after I had left, they had been acquitted.

Another friend in room 6 was a frail, grey-haired little man of about fifty, a schoolmaster convicted of sexually assaulting one of his pupils, a fourteen-year-old boy. When younger, this gentle dominie had worked in Algeria and spoke excellent French. He assured me he was virtually innocent of the charges against him. He did not deny there had been a sexual liaison, but confided that the youth was exceptionally well-developed for his age and had been the instigator of their relationship. (As one who was 'making out' with boys when I was eleven and with adult males before I was fifteen, I found this entirely credible.) I tried to console the little man by quoting the late Evelyn Waugh who, in his autobiography, *A Little Learning* had devoted half a chapter to a profile of the flamboyant bachelor headmaster of my own school, saying anyone devoid of homosexual feeling would never take up such a profession. They would find it unbearable.

A somewhat different inhabitant of the same room was a blond young giant who even towered above Johan and Kurt. With china-blue eyes and hair the colour of ripe corn on head and chest, he was thought by everyone to be either Scandinavian, German or Austrian – but bafflingly spoke no language except Arabic. It turned out that his parents were Yugoslav Chetniks whose hostility towards Tito had made them flee their country at the end of the war. After several nomadic years, they settled in Syria where this giant had been born. In every respect, except his startling appearance, he was totally Arab, although dressed in *Lederhosen* and a *loden* jacket he could have strolled through any village in Carinthia without causing a single eyebrow to be raised.

From these characters, and others in room 6, I learned that the younger, tougher inmates were slowly hacking away at the ancient wall they believed separated them from the parade ground. They worked at night, tunnelling with forks and spoons – the largest implements available were a couple of trowels – digging lumps of stone from the mortar that had held them in place for more than a thousand years. They camouflaged the entry to their small tunnel with a screen of orange-box cupboards. If any of the guards noticed that number 6 had more boxes than necessary, they made no comment.

Although most of the work was done at night, the dormitory's chief and his servicemen were usually able to put in short spurts every morning, in between domestic chores.

At last the tunnellers realised they were only a few inches away from possible freedom. There was an air of suppressed excitement among those involved. It surprised me that they had managed to keep their secret for so long; never easy in an Arab community that thrives on gossip and intrigue.

The escapers waited patiently for a night when there would be no moon. When the ideal moment arrived, they whispered their goodbyes to me as we separated at one-thirty locking-up.

The schoolmaster assured me he had no intention of joining the party. Life on the run was not for him – nor, was it, apparently, for more than half the room's population – but none of them had given the escapers away, although they knew heavy reprisals might be inflicted on them for not doing so.

The next morning, the first intimation that something out of the ordinary had happened was excited shouting in the courtyard, which continued intermittently until long after the time when our gates should have been opened. The service staff were standing by, waiting anxiously to dash over to the *Abraaj* to collect the bread.

Suddenly a sound like a herd of elephants was heard rushing down the steps. The gates were unlocked with feverish haste, and a posse of guards, led by a deputy governor and Abou Talal, burst in.

We were rounded up like cattle, some receiving slaps and kicks, and crowded into the western end of our dungeon. First, a roll call; and each man, after answering his name, was told to walk down the corridor and stand to attention at the other end of *Hofra*: a manoeuvre presumably designed to prevent any prisoner from answering on behalf of another.

Having satisfied themselves that nobody had absconded during the night, they went away as swiftly as they arrived and, together with every other room in *el Kalaa*, we were locked up again for the next twenty-four hours; only service staff were allowed out to collect food and empty the dustbins.

The next morning everything reverted to normal. The guards, looking a trifle sheepish, hustled us into the yard at eight o'clock as usual.

We learned from room 6 that only nine in total had taken advantage of the tunnel. Even one or two who had taken a major part in the digging had decided, at the last minute, not to go. Those due to complete their sentences within a few months had always been resolutely opposed to the idea, and many who still had quite long terms of imprisonment ahead had decided, principally for family reasons, that they could not face life permanently on the run.

To my amazement, almost the first person I met was the long-legged Yugoslav. Since he, almost more than anyone, had been responsible for the hard graft, I wanted to know immediately why he had not fled.

In simple Arabic he explained how he had, in fact, escaped with the other nine; they had burst out of the tunnel at 1.30 AM and found themselves not, as they expected, under a night sky in the parade ground, but inside a large army ordnance store, built against the outer wall of the Citadel, containing folded khaki uniforms.

The lock on this single-storey structure was easily broken, and it was then that they split up: having decided in advance each would have a better chance on his own. Only the two jeweller brothers, Shukry and Majid, walked off together; the rest disappeared singly.

He had wandered about the empty *souks* of old Damascus until dawn. He considered going home to his parents in the northern sub-urbs, but decided this would not be wise. He would have liked to see his mother, but thought it probable his father would insist on handing him over immediately to the police.

As morning approached, the booths took down their shutters and the narrow streets became more and more crowded. People stared at him. He was used to this from early childhood, but that morning, the interest shown in his pink and white skin and fair hair began to alarm him. He had no confidence any of his friends would shelter a man convicted of theft, in flight from the police and without money or identity card. Freedom no longer seemed attractive. He had turned on his heel and strode in the direction of the Omayed Mosque and – into the Citadel.

He had been put at first into a 'single cell', but only for a cou-ple of hours before being taken in front of the governor, whose attitude had surprised him. Instead of being given a savage punish-ment, he had been greeted calmly and praised for returning of his own free will. He was told it demonstrated a triumph of common sense over impetuous stupidity and deserved congratulation, not pun-ishment. To his amazement he was dismissed with an injunction to rejoin his more sensible companions and not to make holes in walls again.

The escape had one result that affected all of us. An edict was issued banning the use of orange-boxes. A kind of giant funeral pyre was built whose heat singed our eyelashes.

Jean-Pierre, a great orange-box enthusiast, was deeply upset by this incineration. The fact that we could no longer tidy away our saucepans, plates, forks, etc., disturbed his orderly soul.

I, much to his annoyance, was inclined to welcome the ban. No matter how we tried to keep the boxes clean – and some tried not at all – they became a breeding ground for cockroaches. Every box incubated these russet-brown insects, at first no larger than a man's little finger, but growing quickly, in their hundreds, to the size of bananas. They had claws and long whiskers, and entangled themselves in our bedding. They maintained a certain discretion during what passed for daylight in *Hofra*, but emerged at night to gambol all over us, seeming to take a particular delight in running across our faces as soon as we settled to sleep. I think I disliked them more than the rats.

The only other livestock we ever entertained was a small stray cat, a ginger-coloured female who, on a chilly morning, wandered, hungry and inquisitive, into the courtyard. Jean-Pierre and I – sharing a tendency to become besotted about animals – encouraged her to make her home in *Hofra*. This was before the Great Escape and we were able to provide her with her own box and a soft piece of blanket.

We hoped our puss would do something towards stemming the plague of rats but, as a hunter, she was a big disappointment. The sight of an approaching rat would make her instantly change direction, apparently remembering an urgent appointment elsewhere. She did, however, play a small part in reducing the number of cockroaches. She would play with the larger ones for hours, cruelly tearing their legs off, throwing them high into the air and catching them.

Soon after her arrival a certain *embonpoint* revealed that she was pregnant and, in due time, silently and with no fuss, produced a single kitten; almost an exact replica of herself in a brighter shade of marmalade.

From the moment her eyes opened, the little scrap decided I must be the provider of everything she wanted, apart from her mother's milk. It was I who, with sweetened tinned milk, encouraged her to lap and, gradually, to feed herself. In return, she decided the best place to sleep at night was my pillow, with her tiny head tucked firmly under my chin.

This idyll was short and ended tragically. As the kitten's legs grew stronger, she became more venturesome. One morning when *Hofra* was empty she decided to explore. With a great effort, after several false starts, she managed to climb all the steps to the courtyard.

Having achieved this exhausting feat, she paused in amazement as she looked at the big world for the first time. It could only have been a momentary glimpse of that world, for, almost immediately, she caught the attention of one of those prisoners who should have been in a home for the mentally handicapped; almost every room had a small quota of these unhappy characters. This young man, with a slack, perpetually open mouth and a hairline barely two centimetres above his eyebrows, seized my little marmalade friend by the tail and swung her violently against a nearby wall, smashing her tiny, paper-thin skull to pulp.

I did not see this happen because I was taking a class in English at the time. I wrapped the little corpse in clean paper and kept it at the foot of my bed that night. In the morning, when Fahad took out the over-filled dustbins, I put it on top of one of the piles. If I had put the little body there on the previous evening, I might have had to listen to the crack of its small bones as it was eaten by the rats.

The mother cat was, apparently, not much concerned by the disappearance of her sole offspring, and shortly afterwards found herself more spacious quarters in the *Abraaj*.

For several weeks nothing was heard of the nine escapers. Eventually, news about seven of them filtered through in spasms. Four had got as far as Jordan, and the other three were now, illegally, in Lebanon. Not a whisper, however, reached us about the jeweller brothers until one morning, it became common knowledge they had been caught in a village close to the Syrian/Lebanese frontier. Within a few hours they were back in the Citadel and locked in a special punishment cage in *el Abraaj*, hidden behind high walls at the extreme eastern end of the fortress – a spot no other prisoners were allowed to approach.

We could not find out how they were being treated, consequently rumours of excessive brutality became rife. This 'blackout' of information continued for the four weeks when, suddenly, they were allowed to drag themselves over the ramparts, back to room 6. The tunnel had been filled, long ago, with cement.

Their appearance shocked us all deeply. Skeletally thin, their inadequately-clad bodies were covered with blue and purple bruises. There were running sores on their feet and up their calves. They were filthy and gave off so foul a smell it required a real effort of will to approach them.

Anwar quickly made showers available, and a few of us hung around outside the bath-house, eager to hear their story.

They looked a good deal more human when they emerged, smelling only of typical Syrian soap – home-made from the fibre of crushed olives – wearing jeans and sweaters now far too big for them. Although obviously relieved to be once again with sympathetic friends, drinking coffee, four weeks of semi-starvation had given their eyes a haunted look; their hands, afflicted by uncontrollable tremors, found it difficult to hold the glasses of coffee without spilling them. The story of their escape and recapture was recounted in fits and starts, punctuated by bursts of laughter that seemed close to hysteria.

During the night of the break-out they succeeded in getting beyond the outer, western suburbs. For most of the following week they had been hidden by friends in a house less than twenty kilometres from Damascus. They then set out on foot, travelling as much as possible by night, through the mountains that separate Syria from Lebanon, along rutted tracks that would eventually have led them into the Beka'a Valley. Just before the frontier, they begged a night's lodging from a cousin with a small farm in what was, for their purposes, an ideal position – less than a dozen kilometres from an unfrequented, bridle-path across the border.

Blood was, apparently, not thicker than water in the case of this cousin. (Arabs are somewhat vague about family relationships: almost any kinsman, no matter how distant, is referred to as a cousin, or even a brother.) This 'cousin' obviously feared that Shukry and Majid might be caught by one of the rare frontier patrols, and he would then be in serious trouble. He, therefore, crept silently from the house as soon as they were asleep and hurried through the night to the nearest *poste de gendarmerie*, a few kilometres away. When the brothers woke they found four silent military policemen at their bedside.

They were thrown into a truck and driven back to the Citadel, where a reception committee of guards took turns slapping their faces. With handcuffs on, no defence was possible.

The special punishment cell was really a free-standing cage of iron bars with a rickety tarpaulin roof and a floor of lumpy gravel covered by a layer of dirty rugs.

The only food they had for four weeks was a daily ration of two slices of pitta bread and a litre-jug of water.

Every morning they had been taken out of the cage by half-a-dozen guards and thrown to the ground. Their legs were pulled up through the centre of motor tyres, and their feet and ankles beaten almost to a pulp. They were forced to submit to these assaults until they could no longer walk and had to be dragged in and out of the cage.

They were not even provided with a bucket. When they became unable to stand, they had to pee on their knees through the bars and, to evacuate their bowels, they had to tear a piece from the rugs on which they slept, squat down upon it, fold it and throw the parcel as far away as possible. The accumulation of filth around them was hosed away only once a week, the jet afterwards being directed at them.

I found it impossible to understand how this treatment could be reconciled with Islamic rules for cleanliness. Nor could I fathom the mentality of a governor who, while not punishing the non-escapers for refusing to become stool-pigeons, or the Yugoslav-Arab who returned voluntarily, allowed such revolting savagery to be inflicted on the hapless Shukry and Majid.

Towards the end of the fourth week, the daily beatings were stopped. These few days of grace meant that their feet healed just enough to let them crawl over the battlements to *el Kalaa*. They took weeks to recover.

As time passed, more and more demands were made upon me to help my fellow prisoners improve their English. They were so determined about this that, during my second year, they arranged for me to take over a classroom for an hour every morning except Fridays. With the aid of an old-fashioned blackboard and some chalk, I did my best to help about thirty of them to memorise a few useful (I hoped) phrases and to talk more easily in the language.

My star pupil was a grey-eyed, fair-haired ex-policeman of twenty-three, a native of Aleppo. Brahim had joined the police force when he was eighteen. Four years later, he found himself working with a colleague who seemed to delight in being rancorously abusive towards him. He had been hounded for months by this man, until the attacks ceased to be verbal and became physical. Brahim lost his temper and defended himself with such fury he killed the man. Arrest, trial and conviction for murder had followed inexorably. He had been given a sentence of ten years.

Brahim accepted his fate with astonishing calm, saying his only chance of remaining alive was to stay in prison. The unintentional killing had triggered off a feud.

'When I come out,' he said sadly, 'his brothers will be waiting for me.'

'Need they know when it happens?' I asked.

'They will make it their business to find out.'

'But you didn't mean to kill the man – it was an accident. Man-slaughter – not murder.'

Patiently, Brahim explained the only method of ending the vendetta, as long as he remained alive, would be to give a substantial sum of money to the dead man's next of kin.

'You mean a bribe?' I asked.

'I think it should be described as compensation,' he said primly. 'In my case it will not be possible. I have no money and my father is poor.'

'How much would they want?'

'At least a hundred thousand Syrian pounds.' (At that time approximately £10,000.) 'My father has only a small grocer's shop – even if he sold everything, he couldn't raise that much – and he has to think of my brothers and sisters, all younger than me and most still at school. Nobody in my family has money.'

'So those who want to kill you will get nothing?'

'They will feel honour has been satisfied by my death. But the trouble will not be ended. One of my brothers will consider it necessary to avenge me.' He sighed, wearily. 'It is better I stay in jail.'

In spite of being a target in what might become a chain of vengeance killings, Brahim managed to concentrate so well on his English that, in his *baccalauréat*, he got the second highest marks for English in all Damascus.

When I last heard he was still a prisoner, but also a student at the local university, where he was escorted every day by a pistol-carrying guard. So far, no attempt had been made on his life.

Among the prisoners closest to me in age were a few who spoke passable French. I became friendly with a tiny man in his early fifties, with mild brown eyes set into a face like a russet apple. As a young man he had served with the French army and was, unlike so many of his countrymen, an ardent Francophile.

He was such a gentle, kindly little man, it never ceased to astonish me that he was unashamedly guilty of having strangled his daughter because of her marriage to a Christian Arab.

He showed no other symptoms of fundamentalism, and took an

obvious pleasure in extending my vocabulary of the *argot* of France's former colonial army.

He had been sentenced to a year's imprisonment which, compared with Brahim's ten, shows the Syrian judiciary's attitude towards various types of murder. Any capital crime that could be attributed to Islamic principles was never considered to merit much more than a tap on the wrist.

When the little soldier was released, he stood on tip-toe to give me the conventional bear-hug. I wished him luck. He shrugged his shoulders, saying, 'It will not be long before you see me again.'

I must have looked puzzled, because he added, as casually as if he were referring to tomorrow's lunch: 'I must now search for the Christian dog who defiled my daughter, and when I find him I shall kill him.'

He had still not returned when I left the Citadel. Perhaps the son-in-law had proved difficult to trace. Whatever had happened, I am sure the old soldier would not have had a change of heart.

HOFRA: PART 4

I now had to say goodbye to valued and trusted friends every few weeks as they came to the end of their sentences. One of the first to reach this much looked-forward-to moment was Yussef.

Since his sympathetic welcome on my first day, I had gone to him for advice about many things: regulations, the staff, my frequent failures in understanding the more subtle motives of my Syrian colleagues; and he had given me wise counsel.

As a Christian, he had to tread carefully; yet it was obvious that he was trusted and respected, not only by the prisoners, but by the guards, every one of whom was a Muslim, and by a succession of governors.

We all assumed he would have no difficulty in obtaining the statutory one quarter remission. In theory, this is a reward for good behaviour; in reality, especially if you are Syrian, it depends far more on the number of palms you, or your family, can grease.

Yussef had no trouble in getting the governor's signature on the document recommending remission. This had to be forwarded to the Ministry of Justice who required the additional signature of the judge who had presided at the trial, which ritual usually caused endless delays. We were confident these hold-ups would be minimal in his case. He was sufficiently well-off to employ a successful lawyer to apply pressure.

Nevertheless, the date when Yussef should have been released passed without a sign from the authorities, and this state of affairs continued for weeks. his expensive lawyer paid him frequent visits, but could do nothing except bemoan his inability to understand the delay.

'The old fool knows exactly what is holding it up,' said Yussef, with a shrug of his bony shoulders, 'but it's politically unwise for him to say so. The remission is being denied to me because I'm Lebanese and, *quelle horreur*, a Christian!'

He eventually resigned himself to serving his full sentence; and at this moment the paper authorising his release was discovered amongst the routine bumf delivered daily from the Ministry of Justice.

His wife had been waiting all this time in a Damascus hotel. When told the good news, Yussef pressed a banknote into a guard's palm, asking him to let her know at once. In less than half an hour, she was outside the Citadel in her car.

We exchanged addresses. I asked if he would be returning to his post at the university. He seemed surprised at my question.

'Of course,' he said. 'Why not?'

'No fuss – about your conviction on a drug charge?'

He laughed. 'There is some sand in Lebanon but our university authorities, unlike many in your country, don't bury their heads in it!'

My next friend due for release was Kurt. He had to wait even longer than Yussef for his 'quarter time'. He had been entitled to remission of four and a half months, and was finally allowed to leave when only three weeks of this remained.

The long delay imposed a considerable strain on his natural *joie de vivre* because, like me, he seldom stopped wondering if the long arm of the customs service would not reach out to grab him for a further year's imprisonment for being unable to pay the enormous fine demanded more than a year ago. He remained apprehensive until his flight to Munich was airborne.

He made several appeals to the German embassy for help in obtaining the remission. His pleas were ignored. The embassy only contacted the Ministry of Justice to find out, for their own purposes, the date and number of the flight and the airline that would be conveying him back to Germany at his own expense.

Saying goodbye to Kurt was a saddening moment for me. He had been arrested only twenty-four hours after myself. We had been together in the Kafkaesque world of the police station. We had survived many months living with scarcely a millimetre between us, without exchanging a cross word.

Most of the credit belongs to Kurt. It was much easier for me to accustom myself to these sardine-like conditions with a brightly shining young Siegfried who was always tolerant of my idiosyncrasies, never losing his temper even though I woke him at six every morning.

For a normal, vigorous young man to be compelled to live cheek-by-jowl with an elderly fribble, albeit one comparatively sound in wind and limb, must have been hard to bear. That he showed no sign of the strain was impressive and I shall remain forever indebted to him.

Unfortunately, he never extended the same tolerance towards Jean-Pierre. When this antagonism, plus Fahdi's manic jealousy had driven him out of *Hofra*, I was again lucky to have the young Italian, Carlo, as a neighbour. He showed the same kind of tolerance and was, in addition, an excellent cook, never losing his temper with Jean-Pierre who often accused him of too heavy a hand with the tomato purée and greeting his pizzas with cries of '*quelle aberration gastronomique!*'

As Kurt said goodbye, he promised to write and let me know what happened on his return to Germany and also to report on the procedure for expelling foreign prisoners from Syria. Unpleasant rumours had reached us of such people being kept for days in dark dungeons.

The British Consulate could neither confirm nor deny these stories. The only prisoner for whom they had been responsible in recent years (*Hofra*'s notorious rat-catcher with the plastic bag) had complicated his expulsion by insisting on being deported to the Kingdom of Jordan. This had caused convulsions in diplomatic and government circles. There had been a long delay before my compatriot had his wish, and was taken to the frontier post at Ramptha.

About three weeks after Kurt left, I received the first of a series of letters, all wrily amusing and written in splendid English. I could not help wondering how many Englishmen of twenty-one could write similar letters in German, yet he did not appear to regard this ability as exceptional.

He had little to say about what happened between leaving the Citadel and boarding the aircraft, except to confirm that he had, indeed, been kept for nearly a week in another small prison. He blamed the hold-up on the incompetence of his own embassy. This took up only the first paragraph; the remaining pages were devoted to what had happened on his arrival in Germany.

As he walked from the landing-bay to customs and passport control, he heard his name over the loudspeakers. Would he report immediately, the voice croaked, to the police post in the arrival lounge.

He decided at once to avoid doing so if it were humanly possible.

When he reached passport control he was relieved to see they were short-staffed and only examining with any real interest the documents of Arab nationals; German passport-holders were walking straight through to customs, where the spectacle of an obvious Teuton with a deep suntan (all those mornings in the courtyard!) carrying a few possessions in a carrier-bag and pausing only to pick up a battered suitcase aroused no interest.

He found cheap lodgings and was careful not to be seen near friends' homes or to visit his mother at Tutzing, on the Starnberger See.

His use of public telephones during the next few days revealed that the homes of almost all his friends – most of whom had never smoked a joint in their lives – were being searched by the police, who accused them of complicity in his disappearance; they had also pushed into his mother's home, frightening her to death with threats against her 'evil' son.

Realising he must put an end to this, he telephoned the lawyer who had acted for his mother during his parents' divorce. The man picked him up at his lodgings and they presented themselves at Munich's principal police station.

Kurt said he was out on bail, expecting to be brought in front of an examining magistrate who would decide if the Munich courts could be given the opportunity of imposing a further sentence for an offence committed in Syria, two years ago, and for which he had served one and a half years.

The lawyer had warned he might have to spend at least another year in a German jail and, anyway, the present unsatisfactory situation would be likely to drag on for months. (It did – for more than a year. Finally, he was put on probation for a further twelve months.)

He asked me to warn Bruno – recently sentenced to two and a half years by number 1 court – that he would almost certainly be greeted on his return to the Fatherland by a similar reception. Bruno said, feelingly: 'Ach, we Germans can be such shits!'

Most breaches of the peace in *Hofra* – and there was a minor riot about once a month – had their roots in the sale or distribution of hashish or the enthusiastic gambling over a card game similar to French scat.

The possession of playing cards was, in fact, forbidden, but smuggled packs could be found in every room and gambling was universal. Unfortunately many losers did not pay their debts, which led to physical assaults; friends would join in on either side, and a swirling wave of human violence would flow from one end of our cellar to the other, crushing everything in its path.

As far as hash was concerned, the trouble would begin when someone unwisely continued smoking a joint while one of the guards was present.

Our jailers often dropped in for unofficial reasons: to chat to a relation or friend – several guards were related to prisoners in *Hofra* – or, more often, because they were bored by long hours in the guardroom and wanted a change of scene.

Because these were social visits, and the atmosphere was friendly, it encouraged some to continue puffing, failing to realise that some of the guards (not many) took their duties seriously. If this type detected even a mild whiff of hash in the heavy blanket of far more lethal cigarette smog, they would leap upon the miscreant and propel him swiftly up, into one of the solitary cages.

The duty-sergeant and two or three junior guards would rush into our cellar and scatter the guilty man's bedding, overturning his mattress and scrabbling through his property. If no more hash was found, or only a trivial amount, the man would be kept in the single cell for a couple of days; his head would be shaved by our Kurdish highwayman and he would then be allowed to return to *Hofra*.

If, however, the search revealed a sizable cache, this would be a signal for a general *Blitzkrieg*. The governor would be informed and almost every guard in the Citadel would descend upon us. All mattresses would be tossed into the corridor; while we still used orange boxes, their contents would be tipped out, our luggage torn open and everything would be flung, higgledy-piggledy, into the corridor or on the dais. When they had finished, the place looked as if it had been struck by a tidal wave and took hours to clear up.

On one occasion, the governor summoned a platoon of commando troops from the adjacent barracks to carry out the search. These tough young soldiers were not as ruthless as our guards; one could see their distaste at ransacking other people's paltry possessions.

If what was considered a large quantity of hash was discovered – anything from 250 grams upwards – the guilty party would be taken to the *Abraaj* where, almost ceremoniously, the soles of his feet would be beaten.

I was once an unwilling witness of this punishment while returning along the pathway over the inner wall. I looked down and saw a young man had been laid on the ground outside the governor's office, his feet thrust upwards through a tyre. Surrounding the body were at least a dozen guards, armed with long lathis, each in turn taking a swipe at the wretched man's pitifully bleeding feet. The spectacle, far below me, with its arm-flailing circle around the screaming victim, resembled an obscene, widely-open flower.

The black comedy behind these painful episodes was the eagerness of a small minority of guards to supply certain selected dealers with as much of the drug as they could afford.

They conducted their business in *Hofra* with only three inmates: Fahdi, Abou Khaldoun, our much-loved little Santa Claus, and a well-educated youth from Aleppo with a furtive look and unnaturally long eyelashes. His name was Aissa, which never ceased to astonish me, being the Arabic, and I believe also the Hebrew, translation of Jesus. Somehow, it always seemed out of place to call a young hash dealer by the name the Apostles would have used to the founder of Christianity.

This Aissa, like many wimbly-wambly young men, was not without courage. Unlike the other two dealers who were never caught by these searches — the liaison between them and the 'bent' guards must have been excellent — poor Aissa was one day found to have more than 350 grams in his mattress.

He was beaten, confined half-naked, without bedding, in a single cell for days and compelled to endure the final indignity of having his head shaved. Several guards had good reason to look desperately anxious while this was going on, but Aissa did not give them away, although repeatedly told his punishment would stop at once if he revealed the source of his supply.

The moment when Jean-Pierre could joyfully apply for his release was only a few weeks away, when a bombshell destroyed most of his confidence.

One fine morning the loudspeakers announced, in their distorted mixture of croak and shriek, that he was to go immediately to the admin office. Assuming he had been called to sort out some minor difficulty with the French language, he went off cheerfully.

To our surprise he had not returned by locking-up time. Not until half-past three in the afternoon did *Hofra*'s gates clang open, admitting a distinctly anxious-looking Jean-Pierre.

I handed him a plate on which a portion of our midday meal was congealing. He pushed it away with an expression of nausea. The Italians and I looked at him anxiously.

'What's happened?' I asked. 'Where have you been for the last four hours?'

'With the customs,' he said miserably.

'You mean they took you to their big office near the Sheraton?'

He nodded.

'And they propose to fine you for importing the hash?' said Mario.

He nodded again.

'How much do they want?' I asked.

'*Cinq cents mille.*' It was almost like a sob.

'French francs or Syrian pounds?'

'Either will do. At the moment they have approximately the same value.'

'Did they threaten you with another year if you cannot pay?' asked Carlo.

'Of course.'

I did my best to sound reassuring: 'Remember they made the same threat to Kurt and me, more than a year ago, and neither of us has heard anything since. Kurt's troubles in Germany have nothing to do with the Syrian customs.'

'How about a lawyer?' suggested Mario.

We all knew his mother had provided him, at his trial, with one of the major stars in the firmament of Damascus barristers, and guessed she probably would again.

A faint thread of light began to show in his heavy depression. 'They allowed me to telephone my lawyer from that disgusting office. He was busy, but we spoke. He also spoke to the customs and arranged for my case to be heard again in two weeks' time.' He looked up at us pathetically. 'D'you think there is anything he can do?'

None of us could answer. In Latakia, the customs had got their hooks into Patrick as soon as he came up for trial. In Damascus, the behaviour of their headquarters was very much a hit or miss affair:

only the Greeks, Kurt and myself, had aroused their interest.

Yanni and Costa had the good luck to be called to the customs HQ when their lawyer was at the Citadel. He accompanied them, and when the usual enormous demand was made, offered a tenth of the amount. Much to his clients' surprise, the offer was immediately accepted. They, alone amongst us, could now be sure of not having to serve an additional year. Like the Italians, they had been sentenced to one and a half years by the always lenient court number 2.

Bruno had shared the bad luck of being sent to the other court and getting two and a half years. The customs had, so far, ignored him completely.

For the next two weeks Jean-Pierre's anxiety made him more hyper-critical of the rest of us than usual. He was not sleeping well either. Normally, he would never wake when I slipped out of bed but now the first object I would see would be my French neighbour sitting with his arms around his knees, staring into space. When the time came for his next visit to the customs, he went as though facing execution.

He returned in a brighter mood, although still not convinced he would escape the net. His lawyer had merely had the case postponed on a technicality for a further two weeks and whispered in Jean-Pierre's ear that he would continue to get deferments until he was out of the country.

Never entirely confident these tactics would enable him to leave Syria without alarm bells being rung by the customs, Jean-Pierre still spent long hours awake every night.

He was therefore able to tell me on my waking one morning that some kind of disturbance had taken place in the yard during the night. There had been a lot of shouting, a strong smell of burning paraffin had wafted through the tunnel.

Sure enough, the wooden frames of two windows in room 5 had been blackened and scorched by what must have been a serious fire. The risk of fire was, of course, appalling in every dormitory and one that was totally ignored.

Room 5 was the second largest in *el Kalaa*, having a normal complement of about eighty prisoners. One of its inmates, a frail Egyptian by name Cremoni, was a friend of mine. He told me something of what had happened over coffee that morning.

Cremoni had been given a life sentence for spying and had already spent more than twenty years in the Citadel. His large, dark eyes had sunk deep into a skull-like head and his skin had the texture of grey, crinkled tissue-paper. His name suggested Italian origins, but he assured me he had none. A small town in the Nile Delta has this name which had been adopted long ago by his family. He was, he told me, forty-six years old. He looked sixty.

He was eager to tell me about the fire and, at the same time, demonstrate how well he spoke French. Did I know, he asked, that one man had burned to death?

I said the courtyard was agog with rumours of a suicide. Was the man who had killed himself a friend?

'He was a man without friends,' said Cremoni. 'None of us knew much about him. He was, mentally, in a sad condition and sometimes accused of failing to keep himself clean ... but to kill himself in such a way, to put us all in danger ... to soak his bedding in *petrole* and then to lie down and strike a match ... *a quoi ça sert, de faire cela*? It was fortunate our shouting woke the guards. It was that unpleasant Kurd who really saved us – the one who is always hitting people – while the rest were fumbling, he seized the keys, got the gates open and threw us all into the yard. Of our two chemical fire-extinguishers, one did not work – but they brought another from the guardroom.'

'But they couldn't save the man who'd done this?'

'No, he had poured the *petrole* over his head, his chest, his whole body, as well as his bedding. He was no longer recognisable as a human being.'

Self-incineration was not uncommon in the Citadel, as I had learned so horrifically on my first morning, but in every case it took place in the courtyard. There would be a flash, an explosion, followed by a pillar of fire. None of these unhappy, disturbed men had ever put anyone else at risk; this prisoner had been different.

I think many of us were surprised no attempt was made to investigate the reasons behind this strangely tragic death. The corpse was quietly shovelled out of sight and, within a week, the only reminder of the incident was the lingering smell of paraffin.

Jean-Pierre, after a third visit to customs, returned with the news that a further hearing had been fixed for three weeks ahead. This, if all went well, would be twelve days after he had left Syria.

Months ago, he had stuck a large calendar on the wall behind his head. It formed a centrepiece within the circle of medallions given to him by the Italian nuns.

Every evening he would cross off the day just ending. As the dates remaining were reduced to half a dozen, he became more and more jittery.

The day he was finally due for his 'quarter time' arrived. He moved as if in a trance, listening to nothing we said, his ears cocked only to the loudspeaker system. The anticipated call for him to pick up his luggage (it had been packed for several days) and present himself to the sergeant by the main gate who would send him on his way to freedom – this time with no excuse for groping his genitals – just did not happen.

For forty-eight hours there was no mention of his release. A guard was bribed to take a letter to his lawyer. Still no result.

However, early in the third evening, when he was lying beside me with his eyes closed and his thin, mobile mouth twisted in misery, a guard stumbled noisily down our steps and halted barely a yard from Jean-Pierre's head. He looked down with amusement at the Frenchman's expression and rattled a huge bunch of keys against the bars, before opening the gate.

Jean-Pierre's eyes opened with a look of concentrated loathing. He began to protest: '*Mais voyons, quel*— ?'

The guard interrupted. 'Pick up your luggage,' he said, 'and come with me. A truck is waiting for you at the main gate!'

From the moment he understood deliverance was at hand, Jean-Pierre's departure resembled a scene from a Keystone Cops film where all the characters move at the double.

In a flash, he was on his feet, his right hand barely touching – just for a second – those of the Europeans with whom he had lived for over a year. With his left, he clutched his suitcase and anorak and, before we had time to murmur '*bon voyage*,' he had vanished. More than a dozen Syrians and Lebanese, who had hurried to say goodbye, were astonished to be denied even a farewell wave.

We should not have been surprised at the speed of his departure; he had often shown he had little interest in or patience with those unlikely to be of use to him, and yet I was sorry to see him go. It must have been because he belonged to a country which, from my earliest childhood, has been a second home. Throughout my life, with few exceptions, the people who really mattered to me have been French. I would not claim Jean-Pierre fell exactly into this category, but there were to be moments when I missed his caustically Gallic approach to life.

His *religieuses* were able to tell us of his success in evading the customs, in spite of ten days in a small Damascus prison – a strike of Air France personnel had cancelled all flights to Paris.

My last contact with him was a picture-postcard of the Canbiere in Marseille, received after an interval of many weeks. He wrote that he was happily settled in that great port, employed by a highly respectable import/export agency who found his knowledge of Arabic most useful.

I took over the space in *Hofra* Jean-Pierre had occupied on the foreigners' dais. This meant a move of precisely twenty-two inches. Immediately to my left there was now a gap of almost six feet to the next prisoner on the other long dais that extended to the western end of the cellar. Between us were the gates.

In warm weather I much appreciated the modest amount of fresh air that filtered through the tunnel and helped to dispel the paraffin vapour and cigarette smoke. However, when autumn gave way to winter, the draughts that blew into our unheated, rain-splashed vault made my privileged position a lot less enviable.

Jean-Pierre's departure meant that the foreign section moved a few inches to the left, which allowed Bruno, until then at the far end of *Hofra*, to join us. My neighbour was still the infinitely kind and handsome Carlo, the Milanese lawyer. We were, on the whole, a surprisingly contented little crowd.

I had recently been inveigled into a new part-time occupation. The prison library had been allocated more extensive accommodation in *el Abraaj* and Abou Mustapha had been appointed librarian. He began a programme of stock-taking and renovation, dragging me along between English lessons to help.

His predecessor had been a fresh-faced ex-army sergeant whose life sentence for the murder of a child had suddenly been quashed because of new evidence coming to light when he had already served nine years. I shall always remember the unalloyed happiness that illuminated this young man's face when he was told his conviction had been set aside and he was free to go.

He left immediately but returned the next day to collect his things, still generating a kind of internal joy that raised the spirits of all who saw him.

Confident there would always be a minority of Westerners in the Citadel – or in the new civil prison rumour suggested was being built outside Damascus – I decided, with Abou Mustapha's enthusiastic approval, to donate all the English and French books my friends had sent me as the nucleus of a foreign section. Mario and Carlo added a sizable number in Italian.

We had doubts, however, about how long these books would be allowed to remain part of the library. The present governor had given his approval, but several predecessors had insisted on bonfires being made of previous such collections. Unable to read anything but Arabic – and some of them could barely do that – they had succumbed to the all-pervading fear that the works of Western writers contained much that was inimical to Islam. We took a chance this would not happen again.

Although busy in the library, I had time to notice that my chubby little Teddy bear friend, Sulieman, was now going regularly to court. He was always bubbling over with such good humour, it never occurred to my smug western mind that these visits to the *palais de justice* could be the prelude to a nightmare.

This was brought home to me on a sunny November morning when we were walking in the yard. His usual string of questions and cheerful comments about my answers in Arabic were not forthcoming. His round face wore an unusually serious expression as he glanced at me from time to time with big, luminous eyes.

I asked why he was so silent. I knew he had been to court the previous day. Was it, perhaps, something to do with his trial?

He looked up at the sky for a moment before replying. Yes, he said, it had. He had been sentenced yesterday. With unforgivable brashness, I asked how long he had been given.

He said nothing, but silently made a sawing motion against his throat with the edge of his hand.

The implication of this gesture was so awful I hoped I had misinterpreted it. I remember standing, suddenly, quite still, saying repeatedly: 'No ... No ... ' as if the parrot-like repetition could banish my anguish.

He ignored my effort to avoid reality. Yes, he said, he had been sentenced to death by hanging. The verdict had not been unexpected.

Surely, I said feverishly, he would appeal?

Oh yes, and it would be heard within a few weeks, but he had no confidence the result would be different.

None of us ever knew the details of the case against him, except that he had been accused of helping the enemies of Syria. He said to me, cryptically, several times: 'It was only a small matter, but I knew too much.'

The forecast that his appeal would be heard quickly and rejected proved, unhappily, to be true.

We were appalled by the arrival, one wet December night, of a special type of gallows designed to hang four simultaneously. Three others were to be hanged with Sulieman, men whose appeals had been turned down some time ago and who had been waiting, without hope, ever since.

One of them was the tall, taciturn Nasir from room 9, one of Fahdi's little group with whom I had shared meals on my arrival. Even then, Nasir had spent most of his time gazing wistfully at snapshots of his children, as if he knew he would never see them grow up. The other two were Palestinians whose only crimes had been to get involved with factions of the PLO now out of favour with the government.

On the morning after the arrival of the gallows we were forbidden to enter the theatre, from which a great deal of hammering could be heard. The guards were short-tempered and on edge, apt to shout hysterically at any minor infringement of regulations. The general atmosphere was one of acute apprehension.

Sulieman came into the courtyard quite late and spent the time talking quietly to close friends. Only when the guards began their roll calls did he approach me. Silently, he enfolded me in a bear hug, kissed me on both cheeks, and broke away to enter room 1. I crawled down into *Hofra* so blinded by tears I was thankful my bed was just inside the tunnel.

None of us could eat much lunch. I ate nothing. I tried to read, but found it impossible to concentrate.

Late that afternoon, when *Hofra* was unnaturally quiet, I heard the guards open the gates of room 1, overhead, and call for Sulieman. They had come to take him to one of those narrow, cupboard-like death cells with solid steel doors just inside the theatre.

Prisoners were not kept for long in these places. They were usually hanged just after midnight.

Although there was a stillness in *Hofra* that night I had never previously experienced, I did not sleep at all. Most of us kept on making tea and talking in voices hardly louder than a whisper about everything under the sun, apart from the one subject that occupied our minds: the gentle, good-tempered, generously kind little Teddy bear from whom life was now being taken.

With the first sign of light in the sky – a patch could be seen through the skylight – I got up to wash, then returned to my bed, shaved, folded my blankets and sat in silence, waiting for the guards. There was none of the usual early morning bustle and chatter. Even the guards, when they finally arrived, talked in whispers.

Two of the younger ones sat down on my bed. Knowing of my long friendship with Sulieman, they patted my shoulder in sympathy. Both were obviously suffering from having had to witness the executions and to take a particularly dreadful part in the final stages.

The hangman, they told me, had miscalculated Sulieman's weight. On the gallows, the necks of the other three had been broken immediately by the 'drop', but Sulieman's had not. These two guards had been ordered to hang on to his legs and pull downwards as hard as possible, strangling him slowly to death over a period of at least fifteen minutes.

Several years have elapsed since those guards, still quivering from the shock of what they had been compelled to do, sat on my bed to tell me their story. The memory of Sulieman's terrible fifteen minutes of slow strangulation still haunts me.

It was the same two guards, on duty together about a week later, who told me they had just given a meal to Sulieman's father.

The old man had travelled by bus from his native village. Frail and pathetic in his grief, they had been surprised at his age. Sulieman had been his youngest and most favoured son. He had made the journey to find out where the boy had been buried and to collect his possessions.

Neither wish could be gratified. In Syria, the corpse of a man hanged as a traitor is buried anonymously and all his property – even the most trivial objects – confiscated by the state. The guards had been saddened by the spectacle of the poor old man being sent away empty-handed and in tears.

The deaths by hanging cast a shadow over Christmas. None of us felt like celebrating anything, and the kindly nuns with their happy platitudes about immortality and the love of Jesus were no help whatever.

At the beginning of January, Jim Malcolm brought me belated Christmas mail, mostly from friends in California and South America.

I could not resist mentioning I would be due for my quarter time at the end of the month, but the reminder was unnecessary, he had already noted the date. He promised the embassy would do its best to expedite my release but warned me not to expect miracles and to be careful to fill in all the right forms.

These, of course, had to be in sextuplicate and, naturally, in Arabic. I got our dear white-bearded Abou Khaldoun – who, when not trading in hash acted as scribe for our many illiterates – to fill them in. He did so meticulously.

On the morning of the twenty-ninth, I went in search of the two Citadel signatures needed before they could be forwarded to the Ministry of Justice.

The first to sign had to be the senior sergeant of guards; Abou Talal of the Zapata moustache and the kind eyes presented no difficulty.

Next, the governor; I took the precaution of taking Abou Mustapha with me as interpreter. He found it necessary to be facetious, saying: 'Gee-whizz, Tony, you leavin' already!'

I placed my six copies in front of the governor, while my companion explained in his most flowery Arabic – so different from his disc-jockey patter – how grateful I would be if *sidi* could see fit, out of the goodness of his heart, to append his signature to the six applications for my remission.

The governor was obviously not over-burdened with work, for he silently persisted in reading every paragraph as if he had never seen such an object. He then looked up with a grin and said something to Abou Mustapha which was translated as: 'The governor – he surprised you wanna leave his holiday camp! He don't wanna lose you – he thinks you're a nice guy!'

I said: 'Tell him I think he's a nice governor but, please, I'd like to have my quarter time!'

Much to my relief, the governor, still grinning, signed with a splendid flourish. He then placed the forms carefully in what I knew to be his out-tray. When, in halting Arabic, I did my best to thank him, he waved us away.

The forms would, I knew, be taken that afternoon by despatch-rider to the Ministry, and from there forwarded to the judge who had presided over the court that sentenced me. His would be the most important signature. Without it, there would be no hope of remission.

Although it was officially due to me on the following morning, I expected nothing to happen for at least a week. So, during the next few days when there was no change in routine, I was not at all depressed, although I must admit to a steadily increasing tension that seemed to localise itself behind my breastbone.

However, only four days after the governor had signed, while I was listening to an Israeli symphony orchestra on the radio, I suddenly saw one of the guards – a likable type with a perpetual five o'clock shadow – less than a yard away. He must have tiptoed down our steps in his great heavy boots and now stood looking at me through the gate with a smile as wide as a Cheshire cat's.

'I have good news,' he said.

I said nothing, fearing the good news might turn out to be trivial.

He pulled open the gate. 'Come with me, Monsieur Tony, your time in prison is over.' He was now speaking seriously. 'We have orders to release you at once into the custody of the Damascus police.'

When I saw two servicemen emerge from the tunnel behind him ready to carry my luggage, I realised the long looked-forward-to moment had arrived, and I could hardly believe it.

Unlike Jean-Pierre, I had not packed in anticipation, but it did not take long. After two years of prison wear and tear, my chattels were not numerous.

The servicemen disappeared with the shoulder-bag and my battered suitcase, so cleverly repaired by Patrick's expert fingers it looked almost new.

I exchanged formal handshakes with my European companions while making an inadequate attempt to thank them for the kindness they had always shown me.

I was embraced by at least a dozen of my Arab friends, who swept me into their arms, kissing me repeatedly on both cheeks. The last to do so was our little Santa Claus, followed by Fahdi and Fahad: Fahdi who, from my first evening, had looked after me with an affectionate concern few sons are capable of showing their fathers, and had tactfully guided my clumsy footsteps through the minefield of Syrian prison etiquette; and Fahad, so incredibly tough and yet always eager to help me. Saying goodbye to these two was deeply saddening and I was close to tears.

In the yard I was astonished to see clusters of prisoners gathered in the dormitory entrances, thrusting their arms through the bars to say goodbye. The news of my release must have travelled at exceptional speed.

I made a final circuit from gate to gate, shaking every hand I could reach. I lingered for a moment with old friends and with all pupils of my classes.

The delay began to irritate the duty-sergeant who had come out with his staff to watch. I was urged to 'get a move on', so I said goodbye to the guards, who were less effusive than the prisoners, but wished me good luck.

My luggage having gone ahead, I made my final journey over the inner wall of the Citadel alone, carrying my prison-issued blankets and half-a-dozen English books: my last gift to the library.

When I reached *el Abraaj* I dumped my blankets in the admin office and arrived at the library as Abou Mustapha was about to close it for the day. He opened up again to accept the books, and decided to walk with me to the main gate before saying farewell. I was glad of his company on this sunny January afternoon, and touched that he should be capable of sharing my pleasure at the fairly immediate prospect of my freedom, when his own fate was so different. It was good to be able to tell him I had left instructions with Fahdi for my interior-sprung mattress to be sent up to him in room 4. Almost everybody wanted that mattress, so I decided to bequeath it to the oldest 'lifer': a decision which, given the Arab attitude to age, I knew would stifle argument.

Back at the admin office I was told a car would collect me in a few minutes, and I must report at once to the main gate with my luggage.

I prompted Abou Mustapha to ask where I would be taken. The guard shrugged his shoulders.

'They don't know nuttin about what happens to foreign guys when they leave here,' said my companion. 'I guess they'll put ya in some calaboose with small-time pimps and bag-snatchers until it's fixed for ya to leave the country!'

This did not sound too good and I made a silent prayer that the embassy would get me out of Syria as quickly as possible.

The servicemen who had carried my luggage had gone back to *el Kalaa*, their pockets filled with as much *baksheesh* as I could spare. I picked up my suitcase, Abou Mustapha insisted on carrying the shoulder-bag, and we made our way to the giant stockade before the main gate.

This was as near to the external world that even a privileged librarian was allowed without handcuffs. So, when the sergeant pulled open the small door in the stockade, I stood still talking to Abou Mustapha.

I soon sensed that the sergeant was on the point of ordering me to move forward and wait alone, beside his blue-painted hut, when the governor suddenly appeared. He had finished work and was on his way home.

Wearing a uniform greatcoat that extended almost to his heels, he resembled certain colonels of the Red Army whom I had met on the banks of the River Elbe in April, 1945.

He shook hands, gave me a reassuring pat on the shoulder and walked out through the door in the gate, hastily opened by a frantically saluting sergeant.

As I watched the governor haul up the skirt of his greatcoat to slip into his car, I spied a much-battered, elderly Peugeot 504, bumping along the rough track towards our ancient pile.

Abou Jaouar signalled impatiently for me to come forward and emitted a yelp of 'Mohammed!' The call was answered by a pale young guard who bounced out of the hut with a handcuff swinging from one hand while the other hurriedly buttoned his jacket.

I had now to say goodbye to Abou Mustapha, and there was nothing transatlantic about it. I was given a bear-hug to end all bear-hugs: for what seemed as long as half-a-minute, he clung tightly to me like a frightened child. Then, as if ashamed of having shown his feelings, he slapped me on the back, saying: 'Now don't do nothin' I wouldn't do. Remember to keep ya nose clean!' He turned and almost broke into a run as he hurried out of sight.

When I reached Abou Jaouar he was still standing in the gateway, shouting at the police-driver. He held out his hand with not so much a smile as a display of gold teeth. As I shook his clammy paw, I suspected this courtesy was due to his fear of Rachid, rather than any liking for myself.

The young guard clipped his handcuff around my wrist and tugged me (luggage and all) like a dog on a leash out of the Citadel and into the car.

I felt no inclination to look over my shoulder as I was driven through the *souk* into the traffic-congested streets. I wondered if this could have been Jean-Pierre's Peugeot, and if there were still hashish welded between me and the luggage-boot.

As we drove westwards through the city centre I began again to speculate on our destination. My companions appeared to be deaf-mutes on this subject. Our route could lead us to the Sheraton Hotel – unlikely – or the anti-narcotics squad's police station, or to customs headquarters.

For several minutes I wondered, seriously, if the customs house was the objective: had nemesis finally caught up with me? I breathed a sigh of relief as we stopped outside a large office block that I knew housed the drug squad whose prisoner I had been for the first few days.

I was hauled out of the car and humped my luggage into the building – my guard apparently feeling he would lose face with the police if seen to give me any help.

To my surprise, instead of descending into the basement, I was led upstairs into a part of the building I had not seen two years ago. My escort, after a polite knock, dragged me into a room.

I had been hoping to find myself once again before the colonel who had been very much in command two years ago. Instead, there was a young captain with a slack, sensual mouth, and eyes so heavily lidded they looked like inverted spoons. He was lounging in an armchair, watching a badly adjusted television set that was flickering away in a corner. He switched his gaze towards us with weary distaste. We were clearly neither expected nor welcome. Without moving a muscle below his neck, he enquired our reason for bursting in upon him.

When my escort explained, he put a lackadaisical finger on an electric bell-push in the desk and with another tired gesture, indicated I was to put my luggage down and sit on a wooden bench against the wall. I was glad to obey, but the guard was less pleased. Linked by the wretched handcuff, he was compelled to sit with me.

The bell was answered by an elderly, curly-haired sergeant who showed obvious bewilderment at the sight of me. It was clear, from his answers to the captain's questions, that no one in the station had been forewarned of my arrival.

My knowledge of Arabic was just sufficient for me to realise their cross-talk had become a debate about whether to accept me, in the hope that the necessary documentation would arrive later, or to send me immediately back to the Citadel.

The captain was clearly one of those officers without much confidence in their own judgement who prefer to rely on the advice of their NCOs. The thought of taking a decision in my case appeared to alarm him so much, he actually made an effort to sit upright.

I leaned my head against the wall, feeling miserable. I had prepared myself for days of discomfort, but the possibility of being taken back to the Citadel, when I had said my goodbyes less than half-an-hour ago, seemed too awful to contemplate.

When my spirits had sunk to zero, a policeman burst in without knocking, waving a sheaf of documents which he placed, almost reverently, in front of the captain. Everybody looked relieved. It was obvious these papers referred to my remission and had either been overlooked or had just arrived.

At a weary command from the captain, who was once again sprawling untidily, the prison guard removed my steel bracelet, shook my hand and left.

Keeping one eye on the television, the captain now revealed he had some basic English. He explained I would normally have only been kept for one night in this police station but tomorrow was, of course, a Friday, and I would therefore be staying until Saturday morning.

I asked what would happen then.

I would be taken to the central police station – to the section responsible for issuing exit visas.

I knew better than to ask why I should have been brought here in the first place. (It is seldom wise to question the workings of Arab bureaucracy.) I did, however, ask how long it would be before I could leave the country.

'You have a good lawyer?' he asked, his attention now more on the flickering television than on me.

I said I had no lawyer.

'Then it may take some time.'

'How long?'

The Egyptian soap opera was proving irresistible. 'Maybe one week – maybe more … ' He waved an impatient arm at the sergeant and the soldier, indicating he wished to be rid of me.

A few minutes later I was locked into the cell where I had spent the first few days after my arrest, almost two years before.

It was more or less in the same condition. The low dais was still there. Unsuccessful attempts had been made to repair it. The shower continued to leak its trickle of cold water; the privy beneath it was still encrusted with dried excrement, emitting the same appalling larynx-inflaming stench.

The jailer in charge was a good-tempered looking young man, wearing jeans and a sweater. It seemed that the sour-puss of two years ago had been sacked or transferred. There was no longer any meanness with blankets – I was given three without question.

Almost immediately, a youth from the sandwich-bar appeared. I ordered a cream-cheese and honey sandwich and asked what had happened to his predecessor. Now doing military service, I was told.

I lay down and began reading a novel by James Baldwin. I soon heard the clanking of the steel gate, followed by approaching voices, and guessed other prisoners were arriving who were all too likely to be pushed into my cell. This would be regarded as a favour to all of us.

A moment later I was on my feet, shaking hands and muttering '*Aliekum salaam*' to three bulky, moustachioed men in their mid-thirties with traces of gold in their teeth. All were limping, holding their shoes and socks, their feet showing unmistakeable signs of a recent beating: a sight that seemed strangely incongruous with their dark suits, now dusty and badly creased, their cream shirts and sober ties.

Remembering how the sound of a beating used to penetrate every corner of the basement, I wondered why I had heard nothing. Had they changed the location for such punishments, or had additional soundproofing been built into the floor above?

Our jailer returned with more blankets and tea. He mentioned he would soon be going off-duty and we should not be seeing him until Saturday morning.

He asked if anyone would be bringing me something to eat, as the sandwich-bar would be closed.

I held up my long sandwich, still in its greaseproof paper. It would have to last me, I said, until Saturday.

My new companions overheard my reply and, in the true spirit of Arab hospitality towards the stranger, insisted I must share everything their wives would bring. Their generosity was embarrassing but I was grateful, and glad I remembered some of the more mellifluent Arabic phrases of thanks.

I had realised almost at once, from their arguments with each other, that they were in trouble because of hashish. It seemed that a car-load had been caught by the police. The vehicle was registered in the name of the eldest but, somehow, all three had become implicated. They were members of the same family and directors of a company legitimately involved in importing heavy machinery. They had now got into serious trouble by importing a load that was, probably, far more profitable.

Not wishing to become involved in their problems, I said nothing.

Folding my jacket as a pillow, I tried to sleep, without much success. The strip-lighting in the low ceiling was much brighter than the dim bulbs of *Hofra*, and the trio never ceased for a moment, while massaging each other's wounded feet, to conduct an endless post mortem on their arrest. This continued until dawn.

Remembering how cold I had felt in this cell on those snowy March nights two years before, I was thankful the weather, although it was now the beginning of February, was much warmer. The silence above us on this Friday morning continued until about ten o'clock, when minor thumps and bumps, plus constant shouting, indicated the station was waking up.

About half an hour later a sound like a platoon of soldiers could be heard descending the stairs; it proved to be a mere half-dozen policemen. Two were in uniform, two in sweaters and jeans, and two – obviously of higher rank – wore cheap suits, creased at the crutch.

I looked to see if I recognised any faces from my interrogation by the colonel. I did not. They were larger and more thuggish than those I remembered. With their hair slicked back with highly scented pomade and hands like pigs' trotters, they were an unpleasant bunch.

I was not surprised at the tight lips and the fear in the eyes of my fellow prisoners as they were marched away, surrounded by this posse of minders.

As the more reasonable-looking of the uniformed men was locking the door, I asked if the colonel would be on duty today. His answer depressed me. The colonel was on leave for two weeks.

Alone again, I listened with apprehension for the sound of blows or screams from above, but there was silence. Even the routine noises had ceased.

I began to concentrate on my book, becoming so absorbed I hardly noticed the passage of time. It was only when I began to feel thirsty and got up to fill a Pepsicola tin from the dripping shower, that I noticed it was after two o'clock. Nearly three hours had elapsed since my companions had been taken away. What had happened?

Another hour passed in silence. My attention was no longer so riveted to my book. I kept on looking at my watch, and listening. At last the tramp of heavy feet could be heard, this time much slower, and no one appeared to have a word to say. The little party resembled a funeral cortège.

Three policemen were carrying the elder of the Dark Suits, who seemed to be unconscious. His companions, limping at the rear, were again pathetically carrying their shoes and socks; this time their feet were making imprints of blood on the floor.

The whole party entered the cell and what I had assumed to be an unconscious body was lowered on to the dais beside me. As this happened I saw, from the agony in the man's eyes, that he was conscious and in excruciating pain. They put him gently down, but he could not restrain a nerve-shattering scream as they did so.

We all urged that he be taken to hospital or, at least, to a doctor, immediately. The police, now smelling far more strongly of sweat than haircream, looked embarrassed and kept on thrusting their chins upwards, endlessly reiterating the word '*boukra*' (tomorrow): a word all too often used in the same way Spaniards say '*manana*'.

With a sudden explosion of rage, the most senior of the policemen, whose trousers were more creased than the others' – shouted that if the Dark Suits expected favours, they would have to supply a hell of a lot more information. After more threats in a similar vein, he swept the party away.

The two who were still able to hobble on their bleeding stumps, tried to explain to me how it had happened. Unfortunately, my vocabulary was not extensive enough for me to understand the details, except that a heavy blow with a stick had been combined with a fall.

I asked if it had been an accident or deliberate? They admitted it could have been an accident, but were understandably outraged by the neglect being shown by the police. The injured man kept moaning under his breath, and running his hand lightly up and down his right thigh. Something was seriously wrong above the knee. I was sure if the man's thigh were not fractured his hip must be.

It was clear these beatings had been an attempt to make them disclose the source of their hashish. Surely, I asked them, the stuff must have come from Lebanon?

They admitted this was so.

Then why not say so? The Lebanese were safe from prosecution under Syrian law. Why submit to this torture?

They looked uneasily around as if to reassure themselves there were no microphones hidden in the walls, and whispered they had not been dealing directly with the Lebanese grower – there had been an intermediary – a go-between who was a member of their own family.

And was this relation, I said wickedly, perhaps a junior officer in Syria's army of occupation in the northern area of the Beka'a Valley? They gaped at me as if I must be psychic. There was, of course, nothing paranormal in my accurate guess. They had been dabbling in a world I knew better than they did.

Having only the clothes they stood up in, they were glad to use my soap and towel to remove some of the congealed blood.

Towards evening, the more amiable uniformed policeman returned with shower-gel, disposable razors, after-shave and quantities of fluffy towels for all three of them. There was also a large meal: two cold, roast chickens, a salad, *homus*, many layers of pitta bread and a lot of fruit. Although this was our first meal that day, none of us were hungry and much was left uneaten.

That night sleep was impossible. The wounded man's kidneys had clearly been affected and he had to pee at half-hourly intervals. Because any movement was so acutely painful, we had to use our only Pepsi tin as a piss-pot.

Then, to add to his misery, at about 3 AM he began to suffer from bouts of diarrhoea. Getting him across to the privy and lowering his trousers was exhausting for us and almost unbearable agony for him. In spite of the after effects of thrombosis, my old legs proved more capable of supporting his weight than the recently lacerated limbs of his companions.

With each attack of the 'runs' we did our best to manoeuvre him gently, moving an inch at a time, each step punctuated by half-suppressed groans of anguish. In between cries, he urged us bravely to keep pushing him forward and to ignore his pain. It was a nightmare, and the sun must have been well up before I fell into an exhausted sleep.

It was a relief to wake up to the cheerful face of the young jailer whom we had not seen since Thursday evening. I was glad to be told I must be ready to leave immediately. He brought tea, and listened with sympathy as we insisted something must be done for the injured man.

He promised he would explain the situation to the senior officer as soon as possible: but I was never to know what happened, for at that moment a shout from above announced I was wanted.

Although urged to hurry, I said a lingering goodbye to my companions of thirty-six hours. The two who could stand up enveloped

251

me in hugs – unusual after so short an acquaintance, especially with a *nasrani*, but we had shared some traumatic moments.

To this day I have no idea what quirk of Syrian bureaucracy made it necessary for me to be taken back to this police station, even for five minutes, let alone almost two days of misery.

The jailer had my luggage waiting. At the top of the stairs I was met by a dwarfish policeman with hard, black eyes and a flattened nose, who clipped on a handcuff and dragged me out to an elderly Renault 16.

After circling the enormous roundabout at the foot of the hill leading up to Malki – the city's equivalent of Belgravia – we turned eastwards along a straight, tree-lined avenue with the sluggish, weed-choked Barada River on our right, passing the Meridien Hotel and on to the centre of Damascus, weaving through heavy traffic to the lights at the crossroads opposite the offices of Air France, then straight ahead for another three hundred yards, slowing in front of the central police station.

A painful jerk on my handcuff pulled me out of the car. I draped my shoulder-bag around my neck and seized the suitcase with my unfettered hand.

Our destination was on the fourth floor of this mausoleum-like building, devoid of lifts, but with an immense, open staircase that zig-zagged sharply in an enormous central hall, from the ground to the roof.

The dwarf towed me mercilessly to the top floor without a moment's pause to catch my breath. I was pulled into a small office where a young warrant officer sat behind a large desk, talking animatedly to a visitor with his back to me.

The WO broke off his conversation to say in perfect English: 'Do sit down, Mr Aspinall – you look exhausted.' He then told my escort to remove the handcuff and to put my luggage in a corner. When this had been done, the tough mannikin was dismissed.

Meanwhile, the visitor had risen and turned to greet me. To my surprise it was one of the Syrian staff of the embassy who had, in recent months, often accompanied Jim Malcolm to the Citadel.

As soon as I was settled in a comfortable chair with coffee, they explained they were doing their best to get me out of the country quickly.

'Unfortunately,' said the WO, there's only one government official in Damascus who has the authority to sign your exit permit. Yesterday, Friday, he was of course not available. He is still on leave, but his staff assure me he will be in his office tomorrow. Everything has been prepared for his signature and I hope to have it in my hands within twenty-four hours.'

My friend from the embassy quickly interjected – in English, out of courtesy to me – 'You'll give us a ring as soon as you've got it?'

'Immediately.'

'If it's early enough in the day, we might get him away tomorrow.' He turned towards me. 'We're keeping all our options open on flights to London.'

'In the meantime, what happens to me?' I asked.

The WO answered. 'You'll be taken to a small prison in a south-eastern suburb, where I'm afraid you'll have to remain until we get clearance to put you on a flight out.'

'If I were Syrian,' I protested, 'I should have been free from the moment I left the Citadel. Why can't I be treated in the same way?'

He raised both hands in a mixture of regret and apology. 'I know – I know – but our regulations for foreigners are different.'

'And racist!'

'Not so. Ex-prisoners from other Arab countries often have more problems than you British. And their embassies don't always show the same concern for them.'

My friend from the embassy soon got up to go, saying he would return early the following morning.

'You see,' he said, as we shook hands, 'we're not going to forget you! You'll be on the first-flight as soon as your permit is signed.' He was gone before I had time to thank him properly.

I was told to sit down again and my coffee cup was refilled. 'I have work to do,' said the WO, 'and an appointment in half an hour. If you don't mind being ignored, you're welcome to stay until I leave.' He was obviously providing me with a short respite before I was locked up again.

I thanked him and sat quietly while he wrote what appeared to be a lengthy report in longhand. After about twenty-five minutes, he threw down his pen and grabbed the telephone, asking for an extension (the telephone system was almost as old as the building); when he got through, he ordered a car to the front entrance.

A shout summoned a clerk in police uniform, who had been darting in and out with coffee. He was given several buff-coloured forms and precise instructions about where to take me.

The WO stood up and held out his hand, politely indicating my dismissal. He had been remarkably courteous since I had been dragged, breathless, sweat-stained and unshaven, into his office, due, I felt, not to pressure from the embassy, but to his essentially nice character. I can only hope he realised how much it had been appreciated.

I was just turning to my luggage when he said quickly: 'Leave your case here – it will be safe enough. I'll see it's put into the vehicle that will take you to the airport.' As I reached for my shoulder-bag, he added: 'Give that to my clerk. He will be your escort and you won't be handcuffed.'

With feelings of elation mixed with qualms about my immediate future, I followed the young man downstairs. A car was waiting with an elderly driver, far from the most skilful I have known. As he jolted and jerked us through the narrow streets of Old Damascus, every gear change produced horrible sounds of grinding metal.

We arrived, at last, in a suburb of recently built shops and shoddy apartment blocks, most looking as if they would collapse into rubble within twenty-four hours; the ground between each edifice was strewn with the usual litter of builder's debris, old cans and orange peel.

With a scream of brakes we drew up in front of a completely circular block of flats. I noticed that several first-floor windows had been recently bricked up, like sightless eyes.

The policeman picked up my bag as he leaped out of the car and I trailed after into a large entrance hall and up a wide staircase of greyish marble. The whole place looked as if it had never seen a broom or a duster since it was built.

On the first floor we walked along a crescent-shaped corridor, lined by numbered front doors. My escort stopped in front of one and rang the bell.

After a pause, heavy bolts were drawn back and a key turned. The door was pulled open with difficulty, scraping the floor. It revealed a large man of about forty, with pouchy cheeks and a pendulous belly; he was wearing a suit that appeared to be made of grey sacking and a very off-white shirt with dark brown stains down the front.

He waved us inside, closing the badly warped door behind us.

We were in a small lobby lined with cupboards and drawers from floor to ceiling. The only extraneous objects were two rickety arm-chairs, a camp bed and a table with a couple of *barbouas* on a tin tray.

I saw that the door separating the lobby from what, in a normal studio-flat (for that was what it was) would have been a large bedsitting room, had been removed and a steel gate installed. A small crowd of prisoners stood with their noses pressed through the bars, curious to see the new arrival.

Grey-Suit accepted the documentation, signing one of the forms and handing it back; presumably, a receipt for my delivery. The door was again hauled open. The clerk shook my hand, wished me luck and was gone.

Once more the door was shut with difficulty, Grey-Suit having to lean his protuberant belly against it: the bolts were pulled across and a heavy key turned in a mortice lock.

My shoulder-bag was dumped on the table and its contents laid out for inspection. I was allowed to keep pyjamas, shaver, toothbrush, soap and towel (the latter somewhat bloodstained); also, after some demur, my shaving-mirror and several paperbacks. Everything else was put back into the bag which was immediately thrown with my sheepskin jacket, into a cupboard.

Grey-Suit produced two rough blankets, draping them around my shoulders. Next, he unlocked the steel barrier and I staggered with my armful of clobber into a room about twenty feet long and twelve wide. Its three windows had been bricked up (it was these I had noticed as we arrived) and the only light – bright enough almost to hurt my eyes – was provided by neon strips.

I was at once surrounded by friendly young men showing Levantine curiosity. As they bombarded me with questions that would be considered outrageous in northern Europe, they laid my blankets lengthways on the cement floor, folded in half, choosing a spot where they said I would be well protected from the draughts from the lobby. Mattresses were an unknown luxury in this prison. After my last two nights, the prospect of sleeping on a rock-hard surface did not worry me unduly.

I was shown the bathroom, which was small, the walls lined with cheap white tiles, many of them badly cracked; the plaster above was peeling in strips. The shower provided only a trickle of cold water; there was a raspberry-pink wc without a seat, and a bidet and basin to match, all made of glossy plastic. I doubt if a lavatory brush had ever been used, so the wc certainly made its presence felt throughout the little jail.

When I lay down on my blankets after the conducted tour, I found the only neighbour on my left was a handsome, long-legged Somali with a hawk-like profile, superb teeth and a skin that was almost blue-black. On my right were three Iranians who all had light brown hair and blue eyes.

Across the room were two Algerians, a Saudi and three Kuwaitis. One of the Algerians was a Kabyle who was astonished to hear I had known his native city when it was called Constantine, long before he was born. The other Algerian's mother came from Alsace and he clearly took after her, being almost Teutonically blond and blue-eyed.

Most of my companions had been charged with having no legal right to be in Syria, their temporary visas having lapsed months before.

The Iranians were fervent supporters of the Ayatollah and prayed five times a day. They each carried a photograph of the bearded Khomeini in plastic wallets close to their hearts. After prayers, they would often take out these photos and kiss them. In spite of their fanaticism, I found them a lovable trio and it saddens me to think they will, by now, almost certainly have been killed or badly maimed in the war with Iraq.

The Kabyle, who had allowed his visa to lapse for more than a year, had lived the life of a petty criminal in many countries since leaving Algeria for France at the age of twelve. He was now twenty-eight. He had not had much success in his chosen way of life, but it had provided him with an encyclopaedic knowledge of prisons. It was hardly possible to mention any city in Europe or South America that did not immediately trigger off recollections – usually scabrous – of its jails and reformatories.

We all got on very well; the only friction was between the Saudi and the Iranians. The Saudi was a lusty, coarse-fibred young man who, some time ago, had been a truck-driver and delighted in teasing the somewhat prim Iranians with accounts of his sexual adventures while driving round the Middle East; giving us vivid descriptions of his behaviour with European and American girls and boys. These travelogues did not surprise me as several heterosexual young Englishmen hitch-hiking in the Levant had told me they always avoided, if possible, accepting lifts from Saudi-Arabian lorries, because the drivers and their 'mates', would park in some remote spot and try to insist that payment for the trip should be made, as the French say, *en nature*. Our disciples of the Ayatollah who had made sodomy a capital offence, professed to be deeply shocked, although I noticed one of them was unable to restrain his giggles at the Saudi's more outrageous recollections.

In this friendly, if ribald, atmosphere time did not drag too heavily. The midday meal was brought in pails from the Citadel kitchens and reheated on the *barbouas* in the lobby. This made the food taste even worse than it had done in *Hofra*.

It was the old story: those with sufficient cash could send out for sandwiches. The runner, a bovine youth with a cast in one eye, was Grey-Suit's assistant. Always in jeans and denim shirt, he kept himself a good deal cleaner than his master. He never had much to say but would flush with an embarrassed sort of pleasure every time the Saudi made loud personal remarks commending the shape of his bottom.

Sunday passed without incident. Every time the doorbell rang, I hoped it would be a messenger with good news for me; but it never was.

On Monday, I got up and dressed before anyone else. The majority usually spent every day in pyjamas as no one was ever allowed outside for exercise, although several prisoners had been there for weeks.

Before I could shave, I had to search for my shaving-mirror. This was an object of great fascination; made in Germany, it was small, compact, with exceptionally powerful magnification, making every follicle look like the crater of a volcano. They enjoyed gazing at their own reflections with obvious pleasure for minutes at a time. It had not been returned to me on the previous evening. I guessed it must be under somebody's makeshift pillow and it was – under the Saudi denim blouson.

Throughout the day I hardly allowed ten consecutive minutes to elapse without looking at my watch. By three in the afternoon, still having heard nothing from the central police station, I gave up in despair and got back into pyjamas, having decided I must face yet another night in prison. I had no sooner done so than a shout from Grey-Suit told me I was wanted: two policemen had arrived to collect me.

Enthusiastic shouts greeted the speed with which I threw off the pyjamas and threw on my old flannel suit. I said a hasty goodbye, picked up my few possessions and hurried into the lobby where the bovine youth had my bag ready. As I zipped it, I saw the younger policeman holding out handcuffs. I made a sharp protest, but it was ignored.

The older policemen seized my bag, Grey Suit yanked open the front door, the handcuffs were clipped on and a moment later I was being hustled across to a small Japanese truck.

They pushed me in between them on the bench–type front seat; the elder drove. I was bewildered. Why the handcuffs? Had something gone wrong with the plans to put me on a flight? As we took off at speed, the younger policeman kept repeating the word '*matar*' to all my queries about where they were taking me. I could only remember this word meant 'rain' in Arabic; a fatuous response to my anxious questions on a sunny afternoon.

Suddenly, with enormous relief, I saw we were approaching the only stretch of dual-track motorway in the neighbourhood of Damascus and, as we accelerated onto the concrete highway, turning south and away from the city, I remembered the Arabic for airport is also '*matar*'. To my imperfect ear it has almost the same sound as the word for rain – there is a difference of inflection, too subtle for me to catch.

I glanced over my shoulder; to my inexpressible relief, my suitcase was bouncing about in the back. The splendid WO had kept his word. I was now sure my journey back to Europe had begun.

Responding to my newly-found optimism, the younger policeman grinned and unlocked my handcuffs.

Never had those eighteen miles between city and airport taken so long. As we got closer I noticed the new terminal buildings looked as incomplete and deserted as they had done two years ago.

There was the usual congestion in front of the departure terminal but, to my surprise, we ignored it and drove a further fifty yards, parking in front of the 'arrivals' exit.

I grabbed my luggage and the two policemen, having deliberately by-passed the usual departure route through customs, led me directly to the long row of airline desks. There, they disappeared without a word, leaving me amongst a crowd of passengers whose suitcases were being weighed, labelled and despatched on the grunting, squeaking luggage-belt.

For a moment I felt almost afraid of being alone in a crowd of strangers. It was a great comfort when I spied the youthful pink face of Jim Malcolm pushing towards me. He was waving a brightly-coloured airline ticket. This, together with my passport, he thrust into my hand.

When my suitcase had been labelled and had disappeared, I rifled through my passport while Malcolm looked over my shoulder. We both assumed there would be something in writing that indicated I was a convicted criminal, to be refused re-entry into the Socialist Republic of Syria for five years. It was not until the last page that I noticed something I could not recollect seeing before – six lines in mauve ink. Neither of us could read Arabic and we assumed this must be the ban.

We were mistaken. Six months later my passport was examined in the Netherlands by an Arabic scholar who assured me it bore no mention of my record or veto on re-entry at any time. The violet ink referred to a car I had imported into Lebanon five years previously. So much for an old man's memory.

My flight was almost due to take off. It was time to join the passengers in the departure lounge, and I had to say goodbye.

I was concious of how much I owed Jim Malcolm and other members of the embassy staff – British and Syrian, past and present – for their kindness, humour and unfailing support. They were busy men and I must at times have been an appalling nuisance, but they never showed it. When I tried to express some of these feelings, he cut me short and pointed towards the soundproof glass wall between the departing passengers and those who had come to wish them god-speed. Behind the glass was a small crowd and, in the very front row, semaphoring as excitedly as any, were the Syrian interpreters who had done so much; one at my trial, the other, to get my remission so speedily.

Malcolm explained that their lack of diplomatic status kept them behind the barrier. 'They just wanted to wish you good luck for the future,' he added.

I went up to the glass and mouthed my thanks, hoping they appreciated how grateful I was. Now feeling somewhat overwrought, I gave Jim Malcolm a quick final handshake and fled from their sight to the departure lounge.

Queues were already moving slowly through the two exits on to the tarmac, where a large single-decker bus was waiting. They were still using the system common to most third world countries of parking aeroplanes on some remote corner of an airfield and ferrying passengers to them.

Two exits were necessary because everyone had to be frisked from head to toe before being allowed on the bus, so the sexes had to be separated. The customs officers worked in pairs. One concentrated on hand luggage, while the other probed the chest, belly, crutch and legs of the luggage's owner, who was then turned round and prodded again from neck to ankles.

In the queue, I remembered a pixie-like young Lebanese friend in *Hofra*, who had been frisked at this exit by a customs officer who lacked experience. Detecting an oblong package taped to the small of the pixie's back, he had asked, in apparent amazement, what it was. 'Just a packet of henna,' said my friend, calmly. He swore the young official would have let him go, if the man's partner had not snarled: 'Don't be a bloody fool! Body-packs are always guns or drugs!'

The aeroplane was a jumbo-jet. My ticket was a Saudia Airways one, which depressed me slightly. It was a 'dry' airline and I would have to wait until London for a whisky and soda. It was just my bad luck that this should be the first available flight to England.

It had taken off from Delhi some hours previously, had stopped briefly at Riyadh before landing at Damascus and was now en route for Munich and Heathrow. There were not more than 150 passengers aboard and the cavernous cabin was half-empty. The majority were young Germans who had embarked at Delhi. Their appearance suggested they had spent a long time commuting between Katmandu and the beaches of Goa. Boys and girls had superb suntans, shoulder-length hair and were wearing clothes that reminded me of the hippy era.

I had barely time to settle in a window seat before we were airborne. It was just after five o'clock and the giant aircraft seemed to lumber into a pale blue, early evening sky.

Peering at the tawny Syrian landscape below, I wondered how long it would be before I saw it again. Should I ever do so? After all, I was now seventy-two and could hardly expect to go on much longer. Apparently I was not allowed to return for five years, and this might well be outside the span of life the fates had allotted me.

It would perhaps surprise some of my friends that I should want to return, for the last two years had hardly been the most congenial of my life. But I felt no resentment towards the Syrians, amongst whom I had many friends. I had offended against their laws and, according to their lights, they had treated me fairly, and it must be admitted, leniently. Unlike the penal system in England, it is not imbued at all levels, from high court judges to prison warders, with the sickly determination to strike moral attitudes so dear to the hearts of British bourgeoisie.

During the previous year, a scheme for the repatriation of British prisoners held in foreign jails had received a good deal of publicity.

I remember Richard Lyne asking me whether, if such a project were agreed between Britain and Syria (unlikely, he thought), I would wish to take advantage of it. I shall always remember his astonishment when I answered: 'No! Never!'

Darkness had fallen a long time before we landed at Munich. It had been snowing heavily and the Germans, most dressed in thin, white Indian cotton clothes, were shivering as they disembarked into an icy draught blowing through the cabin's open door.

I was thankful when we took off again from a Christmas-card landscape into impenetrable darkness.

I was now almost alone in the aeroplane, amid row after row of empty seats. After living for so long in a space no larger than a coffin, it made me slightly uneasy. I began to wonder if I had contracted a mild form of agoraphobia.

At Heathrow it was cold but there was no snow. My progress through customs and passport control aroused no flicker of interest from half-asleep officials. At the desk for hotel reservations I booked into an impeccably respectable South Kensington establishment where a much-loved spinster great-aunt had spent her declining years in genteel comfort.

After walking Heathrow's endless corridors and, at one point, through a tunnel, I hopped on an airport-bus that trundled me through the unlovely, semi-detached villadom of West Middlesex towards central London. It was nearly midnight and I was the only passenger. I was relieved that my incipient agoraphobia had disappeared. I got off at the junction of the Cromwell Road with Queen's Gate and finished my journey on foot.

The night porter at the hotel received me politely but, of course, the bar was shut.

After a few days in London and a week with old friends on the Kentish-Sussex border, I flew back to my home in Amsterdam.

While in England, I had written to Carlo describing, briefly, my experiences between leaving the Citadel and my exit from Syria.

Not long after my return to the Netherlands I received his letter of thanks, from which I quote the following paragraph: 'I know you will not have forgotten our little Syrian-American friend, Abou Mustapha. Two days ago he got up as usual at half-past six in the morning. He took a shower and put on his best white *galabieh*. He then went off to his *biblioteca* in the *Abraaj*. We know now he must have locked himself inside, taken the two-litre can of *paraffina* and poured the contents all over his body. He then struck a match. I need not describe the result ... you will know what happened.'

There was a postscript. 'Pablo (our counterfeit dollar expert) is also dead. Three days after you left us he was taken to hospital with hepatitis. Yesterday he die.'

THE NETHERLANDS: COCAINE

ARRIVAL IN AMSTERDAM FROM PERU
Hoofdbureau van Politie
Penitentaire Inrichting

Six months later, at about seven-thirty on a Saturday morning towards the end of July, I staggered out of an Air France jumbo-jet into the tubular glass and concrete monstrosity that is Charles de Gaulle Airport.

I was feeling decidedly jaded. Although I enjoy flying, I seem to be constitutionally incapable of sleeping in an aircraft. Twenty-six hours had elapsed since we had taken off from Lima and, apart from two brief stops in the humid, Amazonian heat of Manaus and the swamps and jungle of Cayenne, I had been airborne the whole time.

I hoped I was giving an impression of elderly English respectability: a dark grey, lightweight suit, a cream silk shirt, a sober tie.

I feared I looked like the cartoon character that has advertised Michelin tyres for decades. I found it surprising my fellow passengers did not notice I was bulging in places a man does not normally bulge, for I was, once again, involved in the smuggling of drugs. This time it was almost three kilos of pure, uncut cocaine in the form of a body-pack.

To be accurate, I had a number of packs fastened to my body with adhesive tape. Long, flat packages were wrapped round my calves; larger, heavier packages were strapped to the inside of my thighs, and from groin to waistline I was encased in an object resembling a medieval chastity-belt, made especially to fit me out of tough white cotton, liberally stuffed with at least a kilo of cocaine. It was a hot, uncomfortable garment but, fortunately, easily detachable.

Shortly after leaving Lima, while the aeroplane was still climbing towards the starkly inhospitable Andean peaks towards Brazil, I sauntered into the lavatory, taking my shoulder-bag, as if I were going to wash. Inside, I took off my trousers and the *cache-sexe*, slipping the latter, thankfully, inside my bag – glad to be still sufficiently agile to cope in the aircraft toilet.

The chastity-belt remained in my bag almost as far as Paris. I experienced, however, a somewhat uneasy half-hour when, after skimming over the wide, opalescent Amazon to land at Manaus, we were invaded by a squad of Brazilian Mrs Mops with vacuum-cleaners and all passengers in transit were ordered into the airport's lounge with their hand luggage while the plane was tidied. I guessed it was possible for an over-eager customs officer to want to inspect the contents of my bag as I returned on board, so I wandered nervously about, hoping my trousers were successfully camouflaging my legs. Beneath the pin-striped flannel, I felt as if I were suffering from elephantiasis. Happily, nobody seemed to notice anything odd and there was no customs inspection when we re-embarked.

Flying against the sun, it was already evening as we approached Cayenne at tree-top level – necessary because the island's runway is only just long enough for jumbo-jets. The low altitude approach means the aircraft has to drop, almost instantly, onto the narrow ribbon of tarmac as soon as it appears under its landing-gear.

Cayenne Airport is small and friendly. The staff are black, handsome and speak softly in a French *patois*. Each time I have flown in for a brief stopover I have felt instantly at home and wished I could stay longer – not my usual reaction to any airport.

Having taken an enormous quantity of fuel on board, we took off into the warm, moist darkness on the long flight across the Atlantic. Nothing but the ocean beneath us until, at about seven in the morning – it had been daylight for some hours – our captain's voice told us we were crossing the west coast of France and La Rochelle was just below. This announcement, forecasting it would only be a few minutes before we arrived in Paris, produced the usual Gadarene rush to the lavatories; queues formed outside each one, while I sat quietly watching them – doubtless wearing a rather smug expression. Unable to sleep, I had alleviated my boredom by replacing my chastity-belt as soon as the first flush of dawn appeared.

We made so perfect a landing at Charles de Gaulle that the pilot received a spontaneous round of applause from his passengers, mostly well-heeled young French couples returning from package tours to Cuzco and Lake Titicaca.

Anxious not to miss my connecting flight to Amsterdam, I was already moving towards the exit before the engines were switched off, earning me a rebuke from a stewardess.

I broke away from the passengers crowding on to a half-mile moving walkway to passport control and customs, and followed signs to a bus-stop on the road that links the terminals with a shuttle service of buses. My only luggage, at this moment, was my leather shoulder-bag. My suitcase, would, I hoped, be switched by baggage staff from one terminal to the other.

In less than a minute a white bus approached and, at this moment, two smart young business men with expensive briefcases hurried out of the building behind me. The bus stopped. We all got in and the driver moved off without a word. Within a very few minutes I realised we were being driven away from the KLM terminal. I was on the wrong bus, as a question to the driver confirmed. He let me out, telling me to take the next to come in the opposite direction.

The business men had obviously made the same mistake and stood waiting with me. After my long flight I was not in need of bright chit-chat and hoped they would ignore me. It was a relief when they appeared to have nothing to say, even to each other.

At Charles de Gaulle, a bus is seldom out of sight before another appears, and this time I made no mistake. Within half an hour I was at the KLM desk, and swiftly aboard one of the smaller jet aircraft regularly used by this airline on their inter-city services in Western Europe.

I was glad to accept strong Dutch coffee and apple-cake from the stewardess. The plane was only half-full and I noticed with surprise the two yuppie-looking business men, were now just across the aisle, still, apparently, with nothing to say to each other.

In just over forty minutes the roar of our engines changed to a purr as we rapidly lost height over the estuaries of the Netherlands' two great rivers, and ceased altogether as we swooped down to Schiphol Airport.

Realising I was looking more weary and dishevelled than the average passenger from Paris, which might provoke unwelcome interest in customs, I decided not to hurry out of the only civilised airport in Europe but to use its excellent toilet facilities (super cleanliness and masses of hot water) to wash and shave before making (I hoped) a discreet exit into Amsterdam.

I had flown in and out of Schiphol half-a-dozen times since returning from Syria. During those six months I had visited several European cities, some more than once. My passport number had been fed – together with everyone else's – into a computer at the beginning and end of every flight. The only result had been a bright smile and a casual wave from the operator, indicating there was nothing in his machine that might throw doubt on the legitimacy of my journey. Rumour suggested that Syria never co-operated with Interpol and the names of those convicted of drug offences in her courts were never communicated to Western Europe.

My reception this morning at passport control was as cordial as ever. The smiling official's computer had, apparently, no unkind information about me and I entered the enormous baggage hall. A plate-glass wall acts as a barrier between those who have flown in and friends waiting to greet them.

The luggage was already circulating on a baggage-loop, and I was delighted to see a large crowd flocking around a heavily-loaded belt nearby, like pigeons in search of corn (so many, they could only have been in a jumbo) and the indicator showed the flight had come from Bangkok. I congratulated myself on having arrived at a singularly opportune moment. I was sure the customs staff would concentrate on the possibility of nabbing a heroin smuggler from Thailand; few, I suspected, would bother with an aged Englishman in from Paris.

I picked up my case and made for the exit. The customs staff at Schiphol seem to focus mainly on this steel-framed glass doorway that operates electronically and is the only way out from the baggage hall. Most of them are young, many are women, and all give the impression of having X-ray vision as they gaze at each passenger, regardless of whether they may be carrying one small parcel or pushing a trolley under a mountain of luggage. There were often rumours of customs staff milling around, in plain clothes, amongst those waiting beside the luggage-belts, but this was never confirmed.

As I walked out with my suitcase and shoulder-bag – their combined weight did not necessitate a trolley – there were fewer staff than usual at the exit, and none even glanced in my direction. I felt this must be due to excitement over the arrival of the Bangkok flight.

As I emerged, my Greek-Canadian partner, Dinos, took my suitcase saying: 'The car isn't far away – I was lucky to find a parking place so close.' He looked me up and down. 'You're looking pretty good, but you've lost some weight,' he said. Then, in a faintly anxious tone: 'You *have* brought the coke, haven't you?'

'D'you need to ask? Look at the width of my hips!' I replied, dodging airport buses and taxis. 'I feel like a peg-top!'

'You're crazy if you believe that! I watched you as you came into the baggage hall. I couldn't believe you were wearing a body-pack. Nobody could have guessed.'

I admitted the chastity-belt had been well-designed, but could not resist telling him he was lucky to have a working partner who had nothing wrong with his waterworks. 'Most old fribbles my age,' I insisted, 'have prostate trouble and have been piddling in their knickers for years!'

'Tony, you'll never piddle in your knickers – it's unthinkable. You'll remain healthy and active until you're ninety-five and then be gathered up to heaven like that guy in the Bible, who was it – Elisha?'

I thought it more likely that I would be hurled below into the other place.

The car was my own little nondescript Citroen 2cv and not Dinos's flamboyant Pontiac coupé, imported from the USA. He threw my luggage on the back seat and, at my request, settled behind the steering-wheel. It was a fine, sunny morning and the fabric roof had been rolled back.

I was just about to get in, when I noticed the silhouette of a policeman against the sun – so far away I could not see if he were looking at us, but near enough to be certain he was talking into a walkie-talkie. Somehow, the sight gave me a faint twinge of anxiety: the first I had felt since my flight had landed.

I said as much to Dinos as I leaned back in my seat. He was not impressed. 'It'll be a traffic-cop,' he said. 'Probably asking for help to move a car that's parked illegally.'

As we joined the motorway towards Amsterdam, Dinos said sympathetically: 'I guess you must be real tired?'

I admitted I was and we agreed to go straight to his flat in a modern block close to the Sloterpark, one of Amsterdam's green open spaces, not far off the motorway. There, I would remove the cocaine from my body – after my thrombosis I wanted to be rid of the constrictions around my legs as soon as possible. I would then drive to my home near the city centre – a two-room flat at the top of an eighteenth-century house in a district called Jordaan – an area that was settled by Huguenots and is now somewhat bohemian – where I could have a much-needed shower and drop into bed.

As we got nearer to the Sloterpark, Dinos seemed to be looking more often than usual in his rearview mirror. I asked if he thought we were being followed. He shook his head saying, as if to an anxious child, that what I needed was a good night's sleep.

When we reached his flat we left my luggage in the locked car. There was no lift to his eyrie, just a great many flights of pleasantly carpeted, but steep, stairs to what was, after all, only the fourth floor.

This small, red-brick block had been built about twenty years before, when Dutch architects were more enthusiastic than British ones about designing houses and flats in 'open plan'. There was no hall, one walked straight into a large sitting-room divided from the kitchen only by a half-moon breakfast-bar, flanked by high stools. The small bedroom was through an archway, with no door. The bathroom did have a door, prominently placed in the centre of one of the sitting-room walls – the Dutch are less coy than the English about their natural functions.

I declined Dinos' invitation to use his bedroom and stripped off standing next to the breakfast-bar. It was only a yard or so from his refrigerator and, as coke is apt to deteriorate quickly in warmth, I guessed that was where he would want to put it.

Removal of the giant *cache-sexe* was easy, I just unfastened it and chucked it at him. The packets around my calves and thighs were a different matter. I had to sit down to take off the layers of broad adhesive tape; previous experience had taught me that if this is done too quickly one's skin is apt to come off with the tape, and the wounds, at my age, can take a long time to heal.

The job finished, I was able to put on my clothes, feeling almost youthfully agile without those bandages.

Dinos, who had been kneeling in front of his 'fridge carefully arranging the packets on the shelves, stood up with a happy smile. At this moment, with a noise like a small explosion, the door burst open and half-a-dozen young men wearing jeans and white shirts rushed at us. They had come up the stairs as softly as foxes.

It took me several seconds to realise who they were. My immediate reaction to their violent entry – the door had almost been broken off its hinges – was that Dinos must have acquired enemies who were about to hijack the coke. It was only when the shouts of '*Politie! Politie!*', emitted by the enormous young man at the head of the squad, penetrated my bemusement that I knew them to be policemen. Dinos and I were plainly the victims of what is known in our vernacular as a bust.

Two seized me and, holding my arms tightly, pushed me down the stairs out to a car. I saw it was an elderly Volvo, not a police car, and guessed we had been caught by an undercover operation.

A small crowd had collected in this normally quiet street. My captors shouted at one of their number standing outside the entrance to the block. He jumped into the driving-seat while they thrust me, between them, into the back. We took off at a surprising speed for so sedate an old banger and followed a straight line towards the city centre, along Postjesweg and Kinkerstraat, reaching the police headquarters on the corner of Marnixstraat in less than five minutes.

The wide gates opened electronically into the courtyard and shut with a menacing 'clonk' behind us. We all got out. The tension built up by the raid seemed to be dispersing. Now my captors felt there was no danger of my escaping (there never had been any) they no longer held on to me.

Amsterdam's *Hoofdbureau van Politie* had been built very recently out of the materials so popular today – glass and concrete. In my brief time there I found it a rabbit-warren. I was constantly being led up and down short staircases and across innumerable small courtyards.

I was taken first of all to a well-equipped photographic studio and waited about twenty minutes for the police photographer, during which time I was told to strip and stand with my back to a white screen. When I had done so and was dawdling in front of it, the younger of the two policemen who had grabbed hold of me in Dinos' flat asked how old I was.

The answer – seventy-two – produced a gasp of astonishment from everyone in the studio.

'You are serious?' The young man sounded genuinely surprised.

'Of course.'

'What an extraordinary old man you must be – you are much older than my father-in-law and he, for years, has been sitting in an armchair watching television and waiting for death!'

A possible discussion on geriatric smugglers of cocaine was stymied by the arrival of the photographer: a tall young man with a bearded chin and a shaven upper lip. Like almost everyone in police headquarters, he wore a white shirt and pale blue jeans. I had occasionally glimpsed a uniform in the background, but they seemed to be of a lesser breed.

Using a highly desirable Hasselblad camera with a wide-angle lens, he took a tremendous number of close-ups, from every possible angle, of my wretched body, concentrating unblushingly on the area between my waist and ankles. Under the glare of floodlights, I had to twist and turn while an elaborate photographic record was made of the crimson welts all over this part of me. Ageing skin is, unfortunately, not very resilient and the imprints of those packets of coke and the outline of my chastity-belt had not had time to fade. The lower half of my body looked like some obscene relief-map.

All the time the photographer was snapping away, the policemen who had arrested me kept up a barrage of questions.

'Do tell us – how did you get those marks on your legs?'

'Yes, and those strange blemishes around your waist and down to your crutch? Do tell us how you got them – please, we are most interested!'

When they realised I was not going to answer, I was allowed to put my clothes on. While doing so I chatted to the photographer, asking his opinion about various types of zoom and macro lenses. Realising I was an ignorant but enthusiastic amateur, he gave me a lot of information and some amusing advice on how to get the best out of my own photographic equipment.

I was taken to a large, general office, filled with young men in shirtsleeves. Most of them were sitting on, rather than at, their desks. There was a good deal of laughter and waving of official-looking papers at each other – a general atmosphere of bustling good-humour. I realised this must be the nerve-centre of the anti-narcotics brigade.

I was guided into a small room adjoining the big office. The scene reminded me of newspaper offices in American films. I felt as if I had been ushered into the editor's sanctum.

Sitting behind the desk was the leader of the raiding posse, the one who had clipped handcuffs around Dinos' wrists, thrown open the refrigerator door and shouted to his henchmen to take me away.

He was searching through typescript. He looked up for a second, pointed silently to an empty chair beside him and dismissed my escort with a wave. The inspector, for such he was, returned to his search and ignored me.

I watched him sift deftly through the sheets of paper. I guessed he was probably in his late thirties, although he looked younger. He was tall, even for a Dutchman, whose height is often phenomenal compared with the male population of Great Britain. His head was square, his face pink, with a short, straight nose and a wide, generous mouth with a jaw-line like a strip-cartoon hero's; his light brown hair curled closely to his head; he had the heavy shoulders of a prize-fighter and there could be no doubt about his toughness. I could sense he was tough inside, as well.

He found what he was looking for, putting it to one side with a grunt of satisfaction. He then sat staring at me for what seemed like an age. I stared back and was relieved to see the square face break, at last, into a smile of genuine amusement. He had exceptionally good teeth.

'You are a most extraordinary old man, aren't you?' he said. It did not surprise me that his English was as good as mine, with only the faintest of accents.

'One of your staff,' I said, 'used that word about me less than half-an-hour ago. What is it you find so extraordinary? After all, this is Amsterdam where drug smugglers are two a penny.'

'Of course,' he interrupted, 'and we flatter ourselves we can detect them at a distance of a thousand metres in bad visibility!'

'Well then?'

'You don't exactly conform to the accepted pattern, and that confuses us.'

'I feel you expect me to apologise?'

'Not for a moment.' He took a blue-backed British passport from his desk drawer. Holding it up he said: 'This was in the shoulder-bag in your car – all your luggage is safe, by the way. We know you have been travelling under the name of Anthony Aspinall. Is it your own name?'

'It is.'

'I'm sure you know that genuine British passports, in any name you fancy, can be bought without difficulty in Amsterdam and elsewhere for around two thousand guilders?'

I nodded. The average price for an authentic British passport on the black market of almost any Western European city was about the equivalent of £500. Mine, however, had been issued legitimately by the British Consulate in Amsterdam.

He slipped the document back into the drawer, saying: 'I'm afraid

273

you'll have to be locked up for the rest of the day. I expect you're tired after your long flight and won't object too much. Tomorrow morning I shall have a lot of questions for you.'

I guessed he would be spending the day interrogating Dinos, whom he probably suspected of being the boss of a large syndicate, whereas I could be put into the category of just a poor deluded old mule.

'Before I take you down to the cells, have you any questions?'

'Yes,' I said. 'As a foreigner, am I entitled to legal aid?'

'Of course.' He seemed surprised by the question.

'Could I see a lawyer as soon as possible?'

'You may. I'll have one sent to you this afternoon.'

He got up and motioned me ahead of him downstairs to a large central hall. About a dozen police, men and women, wearing the hot-weather uniform of blue shirts or blouses, were sitting at desks behind a long counter. A woman sergeant came forward and placed two felt-lined boxes on this counter in front of me.

I had to empty my pockets of everything but my handkerchief. I also had to take off my tie, braces and shoes. A final demand for my wristwatch caused my sole protest. Somehow, being compelled to hold up my trousers with my hands could be endured more calmly than being unable to tell the time. My plea was refused. Watches were against the rules.

The inspector took me down some stairs, through electronically-controlled gates to a corridor lined on one side by a dozen steel doors set into a concrete wall. It required no special intuition to guess these were cell doors.

The inspector ushered me to number 5, giving me a grin not entirely devoid of sympathy.

'I can see you're used to more luxurious accommodation but you won't be too uncomfortable. A mattress, a pillow and some bedding will be delivered this evening. Until then, I'm afraid you'll have to make do with cold concrete. In about an hour, you'll get a hot meal and another, smaller one – cold – at the end of the day, with a hot drink. Any further requests before I leave you?'

'Am I allowed something to read?'

'Of course. I'll see what I can find.'

The cell was aggressively stark. High up in the wall opposite the door, across its full width was a strip of frosted glass about twelve inches deep through which the diffused rays of the sun were shining.

I now knew exactly where I was in this great building, for I had often noticed these oddly-shaped windows while walking or driving beside the Nassau Canal at the rear of this headquarters. I wished they could admit air as well as daylight. Unfortunately, all ventilation was by air-conditioning.

Below the frosted glass was a concrete bench, built out from a wall of the same material. Opposite, to the left of the door, a stainless-steel washbasin had been welded into the wall. Hot and cold water was available as long as considerable muscular strength was used to depress the taps. The basin had no plug. Below, and slightly to one side, was a metal wc that flushed with considerable exuberance at the press of a button. Above the basin was a metal drinking-water fountain. All these appliances were so firmly built into the wall, it would have required a pneumatic drill to displace them.

The inspector returned with a bunch of magazines.

'These are the best I can do,' he said. 'Can you read Dutch?'

'After a fashion.'

'You ought to do better than that after all the years you've spent in the Netherlands! I'll see you tomorrow.' He must have been investigating my background.

I riffled through the magazines, amused to see a popular illustrated Dutch weekly that specialises in the sort of soft porn that makes *Playboy* and *Penthouse* seem tame. I wondered if I would have been offered something similar in an English prison and decided it was unlikely.

In the centre of my door was a hinged metal flap, about eighteen inches long by six deep; immediately below it was a small oval shelf, resembling a miniature table with a rim. The flap suddenly shot up to reveal blue eyes under heavy brows looking straight at me.

'You eat ordinary food or you want vegetarian diet?'

Mildly surprised, I said ordinary food would be fine.

'Do you take heroin?' So casually, he might have been asking if I took sugar.

I said I did not take heroin. The eyes disappeared and the flap dropped.

I had had no sleep for nearly thirty-six hours. The shock of my arrest had temporarily boosted the adrenalin in my system but the effect was beginning to wear off. I sat back on the bench and dozed fitfully. This was interrupted when the flap was flung up again, and a plastic tray was pushed onto the shelf. I thanked the donor, whom I never saw.

On a large, cardboard plate was a generous helping of a sort of tarted-up cottage-pie – I suspect the cook would have described it as *moussaka*. On a smaller plate was a slice of Dutch apple-cake under a blob of synthetic cream. I had been given two cardboard dessert spoons. Obviously few opportunities to commit suicide were given.

The *moussaka* was well-cooked but I was too tired to eat much, and I could not face the apple-cake although, as a rule, I was happy to eat quantities of the stuff.

I made my jacket into a sausage-shaped pillow and stretched out on the unsympathetic bench, feeling that my ability to sleep on rock-hard surfaces had been tested rather too frequently in the last few years.

It seemed as if I had only just closed my eyes when I was suddenly awake again. Someone was standing over me; a smiling, fair-haired young man in a blue open-neck shirt, white cardigan, blue jeans and white 'trainers'.

As I took his proferred hand, he said: 'My name is Cor – Cornelius van Akker. I've been told you're in need of a lawyer and I've come to offer my services.'

He quietly explained the Dutch legal aid system; if I were to put my case into the hands of his firm, all expenses incurred would be paid by the state. If I became dissatisfied with the way my case was being handled, I could throw them out and appoint others.

He pulled a leather notecase from his hip-pocket and extracted his card.

'If you decide to let us represent you,' he said, 'your case will be mainly handled by one of my partners, Jan Drukker. He's a young lawyer with a great future. He also has a splendid asset from your point of view – he speaks English exceptionally well and is a frequent visitor to your country.'

Although I had friends in many of the professions in Amsterdam, I knew no lawyers. Instinctively, I liked and trusted this young man and told him I would be glad if his firm would take my case.

He asked a number of personal questions. How long had I been a resident of the Netherlands?

'Almost ten years.'

'All that time involved with drugs?'

'No. Only the last four years. Prior to that I was working for a publishing house.'

'What brought you here in the first place?'

'Two reasons. The offer of a job when I needed one badly. The second – because I'm homosexual and Amsterdam, to somebody like myself, is one of the least oppressive cities in the world, apart from San Francisco.'

He showed no surprise; I might have been expressing a preference for brown bread rather than white. He asked why I had left the publishers.

'Principally because I wanted to acquire sufficient capital to settle in some remote hill village in Provence and live out my last few years in a part of the world where I spent a happy childhood and which has always seemed more like home to me than anywhere on earth.'

'Were you not happy in Amsterdam?'

'Yes, and I enjoyed my work. But I was already beyond retirement age and I knew I couldn't keep it up indefinitely. This is an expensive city and I wasn't able to save anything from my salary.'

'And have you now acquired the capital you need?'

I shook my head. 'No,' I said wearily. 'From the moment I became involved in the drugs scene something always seemed to go wrong. Couriers would disappear into the wide blue yonder. Bribes necessary to operate an illegal racket can run away with nine-tenths of the profit. Every cent I possessed was invested in the coke that was taken from us this morning. Now, I'm totally broke – I've nothing left.'

'D'you use cocaine, yourself?'

'Occasionally – ever since I lived in new York in the 1930s.'

'Would you describe yourself as an addict?'

'No. I've never found it addictive.'

'How about cannabis – hashish?'

'An occasional joint. But I haven't smoked tobacco for thirty years and my consumption of alcohol is minimal.'

'Heroin?' he asked.

'No. I'm not that stupid.'

He seemed mildly amused. 'We'll do our best for you,' he said as he stood up. 'The inspector will be questioning you tomorrow morning. You'll have to cope with that on your own. When he's completed his report you'll be taken in front of the public prosecutor who will make formal charges against you. The charges will be investigated by an examining magistrate, and from that moment you'll have the support of either Drukker or myself.'

'How long will I be kept here?' I asked.

'Tomorrow being a Sunday, I expect until the day after. As soon as the prosecutor has made formal charges, you'll be transferred to what we call a "house of detention", where you'll be far more comfortable.'

'There's no such thing as bail under Dutch law, is there?'

He shook his head.

'I'd like your advice about what to say to the inspector tomorrow. You know the details of my arrest?'

He nodded.

'Would you agree I've no choice except to admit my guilt. I've more or less done so already.'

'Of course. Any attempt to deny responsibility would irritate everybody and land you in worse trouble.' He pulled open the door – I noticed he had left the keys in the lock. 'I'm sure you need rest, so I'll leave you now. It won't be long before we meet again.'

I got up and thanked him for coming. As we shook hands he said: 'Don't get too depressed – it's not the end of the world.'

'It's probably the end of my world,' I said, and immediately regretted this unprovoked whine of self-pity.

He gave me an apologetic smile, saying: 'I regret the discourtesy of having to lock you in, but all hell will break out if I don't!'

After he had gone I dozed until the evening meal: wholemeal bread and margarine of the sort that is supposed not to fur up your arteries, and an apple. I can only remember munching the apple. There was also a carton of good hot coffee which I much appreciated.

Not long after, my door flew open to reveal an elderly policeman resting his stout belly against a trolley piled high with bedding.

He beckoned to me, and I stood in the doorway, clutching the waistband of my trousers to prevent them from telescoping around my ankles.

Obviously accustomed to prisoners in my predicament, he draped a thin, kapok-filled mattress across my shoulders, followed by two blankets and a large double sheet made from white paper. With a dexterity clearly the result of long practice, he flung a pillow of a similar type to the mattress straight onto the bench. He then waved me back into the cell and locked the door. I could hear the muffled sound as he followed the same procedure with my neighbours.

I made my bed on the bench, and slipped naked between the layers of paper. It felt surprisingly clean and comfortable. The pillow, too was encased in paper.

Just as I was about to fall asleep, I was startled by a single, loud, metallic 'clonk' from the lock on the cell door. This noise became very familiar; it signalled the simultaneous electronic locking of all cell doors with a single switch – a precaution only taken at night.

In the morning I was awakened by an identical 'clonk' as the mechanism was switched off. I was surprised how well I had slept; no doubt exhaustion was a contributory factor. I did my best to clean up with the plentiful hot water, but wished I had my shaver and a toothbrush.

When breakfast arrived (hot coffee and as much wholemeal or white bread as I wanted) I asked the policeman who delivered it for the time. He told me it was eight o'clock, later than usual because it was Sunday. He also said I might keep my mattress and bedding throughout the day. On weekdays it would already have been taken away until nightfall, when it would be returned with a clean paper sheet and pillow-case.

I lolled restlessly about for what seemed like an hour. I was then taken to the big office where the inspector was waiting. My shoes and braces were handed back. I spied my watch in one of the felt-lined boxes on the counter and pleaded for it once again.

'Give it to him,' said the inspector.

We walked across an inner, open courtyard and up stairs to a room that looked like some sort of laboratory.

Here he took my fingerprints. The equipment being vastly more up-to-date than that employed by the Syrian police, the job was completed with astonishing speed. Nevertheless, in spite of the inspector's kindness and tact, it was the only occasion while I was in police custody (both here and in Syria) that I felt like a trapped animal.

When it was over he led me to a row of washbasins and gave me a special detergent that removed every trace of ink. While I was rinsing my hands, he said almost nonchalantly: 'You were not the only Englishman arrested in Amsterdam yesterday.'

'Oh?' I wondered if it might be somebody I knew.

'He gave us a lot more trouble than you did.'

'How was that?'

'He shot one of my colleagues dead – and seriously wounded another.'

It seemed incredible. 'Are you serious?'

'Never more so.'

'Someone involved with drugs?'

'No. Someone who escaped from an English prison for psychopaths and has been living with his English girlfriend in Amsterdam for quite a while. We knew where they were. Yesterday, two uniformed policemen were sent to enquire something quite trivial – there was no question of deporting him, anyway not at present – but he shot them both, killing one and injuring the other.'

'But who is he – this Englishman?'

'His name is Alan Reeve. Your British police say he was convicted about twenty years ago for the murder of a girlfriend. The court decided he had serious psychological problems and sent him to this place you have in England for prisoners who are considered dangerous ... '

'You mean Broadmoor?'

'That's the name. And while he was there he was accused of killing a prisoner – a young man with whom he was said to have had a close friendship.'

'I remember the case – it was given a great deal of publicity in our tabloid newspapers. Is he here, in this police station?'

'No – in another, on the other side of the city. But I expect you'll meet him before long. You may even find yourself in the same *paviljoen.*' Seeing I looked puzzled, he said: 'In English, I think you say "landing"?'

After two years in the Citadel I had become accustomed to living with killers, psychopathic or otherwise, but as we went back downstairs I began to wonder how the Dutch police would react towards me. I belonged to the same race as the man who had wantonly, in cold blood, killed one of their number and severely wounded another. They had every reason to be deeply angry and I could hardly blame them if this should become noticeable in their attitude towards me. It did not. The treatment meted out to me by all the staff of Amsterdam's central police station was a model of civilised behaviour.

We mounted yet another flight of stairs, eventually reaching the inspector's office, where his first question was: 'I think we both deserve coffee, don't you?'

I suspected the 'softening up' treatment was coming, but saw no reason to deny my ability to drink coffee at all hours of the day or night. I assumed he would shout to an underling, but no, he fetched it himself, leaving me alone for a few minutes.

I looked around in the hope of finding something exciting to look at, but there was nothing except filing cabinets and an old-fashioned manual typewriter. The only window, wide open, admitted a shaft of hot, end-of-July sun and overlooked an inner courtyard.

The inspector returned with two disposable beakers of black coffee. From a drawer he extracted a handful of packets of sugar and coffee-milk which I hastily rejected.

As he emptied one paper sack of sugar after another into his coffee, he said: 'I'm going to be unusually frank. Before asking you any questions I'm going to tell you what we already know.'

Relaxing slightly, I sat back waiting for him to continue.

'I'm sure,' he said, 'you know you have enemies in Amsterdam – enemies amongst your own kind. Do you realise you're sitting at this moment in that chair because you and your partner have been the victims of an informer?'

He was silent for a moment, stirring his over-sweetened coffee. I was too surprised to say anything.

'The informer gave us your partner's name and address. We were told he was keeping a low profile, having made a much-publicised escape from a Swiss prison six months ago. We were also told an elderly Englishman was working with him who was at that moment in Peru and would be shortly returning with a quantity of cocaine. Our informer didn't know your surname but said your friends always called you Tony.'

He paused to sip coffee. I remained silent.

'We therefore,' he continued, 'installed ourselves in an apartment immediately opposite Dinos' and started checking the passenger lists of every international flight out of Lima. It wasn't long before we noticed a Mr Anthony Aspinall, British subject, booked on an Air France flight to Paris.'

'The names Tony or Anthony are ten for a penny in England nowadays – you could have been making a mistake.'

'But not all of them have been convicted of attempting to smuggle hashish through Syria!'

'So you already knew that?'

'Only after we'd discovered your name on the international list of those guilty of drugs offences. From that moment we were confident we'd found our man. The only thing we couldn't be sure about was your destination. Were you on your way back to Amsterdam, or were you going somewhere else – staying in Paris, perhaps?' He took another sip. 'We decided you were too big a fish to be allowed to escape, so we got special permission to send two of our staff to Paris.

'Might that not have provoked the anger of the Sureté?'

'It might – if it hadn't been arranged at the highest level, and this wasn't easy because we had very little time. Your flight had already left Peru before we got the information about your previous conviction. We got our men there just in time. You were under observation from the moment you disembarked at Charles de Gaulle. It had been agreed if you attempted to leave the airport you would be immediately identified to the French police. We hoped – but couldn't be sure – you would merely pick up a connecting flight to Amsterdam. Did you realise you were being watched?'

I shook my head.

He turned towards the open door and called 'Henk!'

A slim, dark-moustached young man answered his call. He stared straight at me with a friendly grin on his thin, bony face. 'You recognise me, yes?' he said.

I was about to say I had never seen him before when his jeans and shirt seemed, for a few seconds, to be magically transformed into a dark suit. 'Good God!' I said. 'It's one of the French business men! You were sitting across the aisle from me … '

'And I was behind you when you got on the wrong bus at Charles de Gaulle.'

'There were two of you, with briefcases – I was sure you were French business men.'

'That's what we hoped you would think!'

The inspector dismissed him.

'Weren't you surprised the customs at Schiphol showed no interest in you?' he asked me.

'With passengers from Bangkok picking up their luggage close to mine?' I said impatiently. 'No, I wasn't surprised.'

'Nevertheless, instructions were given not to stop you, yet you were under surveillance all the time.'

'How about the uniformed policeman in the car park who was chatting furiously into his walkie-talkie?'

'So you noticed him? Did he arouse your suspicions?'

'I admit to a momentary feeling of uneasiness.'

'But not enough to stop you from driving with Dinos to his apartment?'

'I remember asking him to see if we were being followed.'

'You weren't followed, we were already there! Some of us in the apartment opposite, the rest in two cars, parked on the corner of the next street. You drove past us!'

'I guessed that's where you'd been hiding as soon as you burst through the door.'

'You'd no suspicion you were being watched until you noticed the policeman in the carpark?'

'Even then I didn't take it seriously. Policemen are always using their walkie-talkies. Having been so long without sleep, I thought I must be getting over-imaginative – and Dinos agreed.'

The inspector leaned forward, saying, very deliberately: 'You are not attempting to deny that you entered this country yesterday with a body-pack of almost three kilos of cocaine?'

'No,' I said, equally deliberately, 'I can see no point in wasting time with useless denials.'

My reply clearly pleased him. 'And you were acting as a mule for your friend Dinos?'

I shook my head. 'Only to a limited degree. He had supplied a small amount of the capital necessary to buy the coke. My contribution was slightly less but I paid my own travelling expenses – no small item on a trip to South America and back.'

'And who put up the rest of the capital?'

'Our Peruvian contact for whom Dinos and I were acting as joint agents.'

'A frequent visitor to Amsterdam whose first names are Eduardo Luis?'

I nodded. Although both names were false, I guessed from whom he had got them. 'So Dinos has told you?' I said, blandly.

'Had you met him before Dinos introduced him to you?'

'No. The Peruvian was looking for someone trustworthy to make the run between Lima and Amsterdam. Dinos suggested I might be available and asked us to dinner at a restaurant near the Museumplein.'

'What can you tell me about him?'

'Very little. I make a point of never being inquisitive about fellow drugs operators – no addresses, no telephone numbers. It saves embarrassment if I'm asked the sort of question you've just put to me.'

'What *can* you tell me?'

'He met me at Lima Airport and drove me to the affluent seaside suburb of Miraflores. He'd booked a room for me in a pleasant, small, ultra-respectable hotel. He occasionally turned up without warning to take me to one of Lima's more expensive restaurants. Sometimes alone, sometimes with a girlfriend, occasionally with his brother.'

'Did all your business discussions take place across restaurant tables?' he asked.

'No. We would drive to a small flat in a down-at-heel area, taking a different route each time. In spite of a good sense of direction I doubt if I could find it again. Luis obviously didn't live there because there was not a stick of furniture in the place. When he and his brother were not busy trying out various shapes of body-pack on every part of my anatomy, we sat on the floor.'

'So he has a brother?'

'He has three brothers – all policemen, except himself. Their father is one of the most senior police officials in Peru. So take note of what you're up against!'

'It's a familiar situation in more than one South American country.' He pulled open a drawer and took out some paper. He put a couple of sheets, with copying film between them, into the old typewriter and began typing an account of what I had told him.

He warned me the job would take some time. If I wished, I could return to my cell and come back later: 'It's a Sunday, so they'll have left you something soft to sit on.' Alternatively, I could remain and be entertained by the spectacle of a hard-working Dutchman who, thanks to my inconsiderate return to Amsterdam on a Saturday, was being deprived of his much-overdue weekend leave! I elected to stay.

The telephone gave a single short ring. He listened in silence for a moment. 'Yes,' he said at last, 'how much did the boy have on him? Two hundred grams?' After a slight pause, he said impatiently: 'Confiscate the cannabis and put him back across the frontier, but not too obviously – there's no need to get him arrested by his own people. Yes, that's all. No charges – no further action!' He slammed down the receiver. 'One of our frontier posts. Wants to arrest a nineteen-year-old German with two hundred grams of cannabis in his pocket. Some of these fools should be put back into traffic policing!'

I asked why the Dutch had not taken a lead in legalising the importation of soft drugs.

'Many are openly in favour of doing so – in the last public opinion poll around forty per cent supported legalisation. But we are surrounded by countries – your own included – who insist on treating pot-smoking as a serious crime. If we amended our laws there would be shrieks of outrage from the other EEC countries. So we just keep quiet and go our own sweet way. Cannabis importers have little to fear from us as long as they don't start bringing it in by the ton.'

'And you permit certain discos and coffee-shops to sell small quantities over the counter ... '

'We do – yet if customers take it out on the street, they're offending against the law. Hypocritical, I grant you – but I don't make the laws of this country, I just do my best to enforce them.'

'How about alcohol?' I asked. 'Doesn't that give you more trouble than drugs?'

'About a hundred per cent more. But if you say so publicly, the powerful drinks lobby, operating in every country, will kick your teeth in. And every politician knows that.'

At this moment an unshaven Dinos appeared in the doorway. He looked at me with amusement, saying: 'How are you doing? Don't tell him all our secrets, will you!'

He advanced into the office. The protests of a detective who was with him were cut short by the inspector: 'It doesn't matter any longer about keeping them apart. They both tell, more or less, the same story.' He enquired from Dinos, now boldly seated on the windowledge, if he had signed the English version of the statement he had made yesterday.

'Sure,' said Dinos.

'You agreed it was accurate?'

'I did.' Looking at me he said: 'Not having seen you since these gorillas burst so impolitely into my apartment, I haven't had a chance to say I'm sorry.'

'For what?' I asked.

'Well – for dropping you in the shit.'

'But you're in it as well.'

'Sure I am – even more so than you. But I was crazy not to see what was going on right under my nose.'

'How?'

'For days, half the staff of that bloody office out there have been holed up in an apartment across the street from mine. Most of the time you've been in South America they've been watching me through field-glasses – playing peek-a-boo behind those goddam Dutch lace curtains!'

I could hardly restrain my laughter. 'And you never noticed?'

'Didn't see a thing! But I was brought up like any good Canadian boy – not to be nosy about my neighbours.'

'Who's this informer,' I asked him, 'who hates us enough to chatter to the police?'

With an arrogant lift of his chin, Dinos said: 'Maybe the inspector won't like my saying this, but I don't believe there was an informer.'

'Then how d'you think we got our information?' asked the inspector calmly.

'You just tapped my phone.'

The inspector shook his head.

'You tapped my phone,' Dinos repeated, firmly. 'You heard me talking to my girlfriend. That's for sure how you found out I was waiting for someone called Tony. You've admitted that was all the information you had about him, at first.'

'If your story is correct, how d'you explain we knew which number to tap?'

'Because you got your basic information from one of the old ladies who live below me. I guess I wasn't as careful as I ought to have been – another apology to you, Tony. As I've told you in my statement, I've been working on commission – packaging other people's hash, brought here from Lebanon and Morocco, and fitting it into other people's luggage. I had a lot of visitors who would walk up to my apartment with a suitcase of one colour and leave, after a while, with a suitcase of another colour. I'd stupidly convinced myself the elderly widows would be too busy entertaining their grandchildren to notice anything.'

'It was probably those knowledgeable grandchildren,' I said, 'who explained the origin of the funny smell on the landing.'

'Smoke from joints?' asked the inspector.

'No – just the fumes hashish gives off when heated to soften up for pressing into packets. Sometimes the smell was so strong it would penetrate down to the entrance-hall. When calling on Dinos, I would often be almost stoned before I'd climbed the stairs!'

Dinos looked like a small boy caught scrumping apples. 'I know – I know,' he said, 'I was taking chances I shouldn't have taken, but I never mentioned your name to anybody except Sigi and I'm convinced the only way these guys could have heard it was by phone-tapping.'

The inspector said quietly: 'Let me assure you we never listened to a word said on your telephone ... ' Seeing Dinos was about to become argumentative, he held up his hand to silence him. 'To get permission to tap anybody's phone in this country requires authority, in writing, from the highest level. This takes time and means, when we finally get clearance, it's often too late for the tap to be of much use. In your case, it was never asked for.'

'Maybe not,' said Dinos, quickly, 'but maybe you went ahead without permission and now can't admit it.'

'Why won't you accept the truth?' said the inspector, as calm as ever. 'Because that's what I've been telling you. Choose your friends more carefully in the future and stop being suspicious about your telephone!' He turned to the detective. 'Take them back to their cells, or they may miss their meal – and tell the office I shall want Mr Aspinall back here at two o'clock, so there's no need to take away his watch or braces. He'll be too busy eating lunch to swallow the one or hang himself with the other.'

I cannot remember what I was given for lunch, or if I ate it. My general recollection of headquarters meals is of good food, well cooked and more than sufficient. That I ate very little was due to anxiety about my own future and Dinos' who, after his jail-break in Switzerland, was almost at the top of an international list of wanted escapers.

Neither of us ever knew if the 'informer' existed. I was inclined to believe that no phone-tapping had taken place, which made Dinos almost explode with impatience at what he considered my naivety. A long time afterwards, however, friends told me the drugs coterie of Amsterdam had been alive with unaccountable rumours while I was in South America. It had been whispered all over the city that somebody was determined to bust Dinos and myself. Some of his friends were so convinced of the truth behind this tittle-tattle, they begged him not to meet me at the airport, saying if he failed to turn up I would obviously take a taxi to my flat, where I would ring him. They urged him not to arrange any get-together for at least twenty-four hours. If the police took no action against me during the interval it would show the rumours about a 'grass' to be false.

It was typical of Dinos to reject this advice contemptuously, saying he would never consider using his old mule as a decoy duck!

After lunch I was taken back to the inspector's office where I found him putting the finishing touches to my statement.

After more coffee, we were joined by a small woman of about forty, whose dark hair was swept straight back from a high forehead. She was, I gathered, the official Dutch/English interpreter for the Amsterdam police. She surprised me by saying, as we shook hands: 'Why, we've met before!'

I gaped at her in silence.

'I don't think you saw me at the time. Two years ago, I peeked through the door while you were being interrogated by the colonel in charge of Syria's anti-narcotics brigade.' She sat down opposite me, smoothing her skirt. 'Nice man, wasn't he?'

'Yes . . . yes, he was . . . ,' I agreed, still open-mouthed with surprise.

'He liked you, too,' she said with a smile.

'I can't think why.'

'Because you have good manners.' She turned to the inspector. 'Wouldn't you agree?'

'Good manners, but no morals,' was the reply.

'Well, that's better than neither.' With a wink at me, she picked up the typescript and translated it into English, sentence by sentence.

I felt it would not be good manners to ask what on earth she had been doing in a Damascus police station. To my certain knowledge there had been no Dutch prisoners in Syria at that time. News of the arrest of any Westerner travels swiftly along the bush-telegraph between jails in Middle Eastern countries. Even today, I am ignorant of what her real terms of reference could have been within the upper strata of the Netherlands police.

When she had finished her translation I had no hesitation in signing the typescript. It was a meticulously accurate account of everything I had said – adding nothing, subtracting nothing. When I handed it back to the inspector, he opened a drawer and took out my passport. The sight of it made me ask the lady if she spoke Arabic.

She said she did, fluently.

'Can you also read it?' I asked.

'Yes.' It was a confident answer.

It was she I asked about the ban in my passport. I could hardly believe her answer.

'Are you sure?'

'Positive.'

'But I was kept waiting for days in a small, lousy jail for a special exit stamp – '

'Yes, that's here.' She held up another page. 'It's an ordinary extension of the visa that expired while you were in prison. It indicates nothing criminal.'

'So I can return to Syria if I get the opportunity?'

My question produced a snort of laughter from the inspector: 'I wouldn't recommend you to make any immediate plans. Tomorrow you'll be taking a much shorter journey to the law courts, where you'll be taken in front of the public prosecutor.'

'What will he do with me?'

'Almost certainly send you to the big detention centre out at Spaklerweg.'

'Those white skyscrapers beside the metro station, on the line to the Bijlmermeer?'

'That's the place.'

'I lived for some years in the Bijlmer when I first came to Amsterdam. I still have friends there. I've watched those buildings rise from the ground.'

'Now you'll be able to find out what they're like, inside.'

The interpreter stood up, amusement in her eyes. 'They say it's very comfortable – I've been told there are prisoners who never want to leave!' Shaking hands, she said: 'I can't promise to be around on the next occasion you're arrested, Mr Aspinall, but it's been nice to see you again.'

When she had gone, the inspector said: 'Perhaps I should have told you before – we've searched your flat in the Jordaan.'

'I suppose you could hardly fail to do so – and found nothing of interest, I trust?'

'No drugs, certainly. But many interesting books about exploration in Arabia and Africa from the nineteenth century to the present day. It's obviously a subject that interests you?'

'My chief reason for being a smuggler. It has taken me to interesting places I couldn't otherwise afford to visit.'

'Some of your books must be valuable?'

'One or two in years to come, perhaps – but not now.'

'Any more questions before I take you down to the cells?'

I shook my head.

The next morning, when I was taken up to the general office, my luggage was waiting. 'Please, can I have my shaver for five minutes?' I touched my unshaven chin. 'This awful stubble – it makes me feel so dirty.'

'Go ahead,' said the inspector, and asked if I needed a mirror.

'I can do without.' I must have sounded doubtful because he said immediately: 'Come with me.'

He took me into what I presume was a staff washroom; white-tiled and antiseptically clean, six basins with a splendid mirror behind each. As I set to work on the white fuzz, the inspector seated himself on a heavy, tubular towel-rail looking like a healthy farmer on a five-barred gate.

We chatted about life in Amsterdam, discovering we both had an appreciation of serious music and had frequently been part of the same audience at the Concert Gebouw. I found it impossible not to like him, although always on my guard; never forgetting that even the most normal of men, deprived of their liberty, are apt to feel a kind of warmth, almost affection, for any jailer who treats them well.

When we got back to the general office all the objects taken from my pockets on arrival were returned, including small change, most of it Peruvian. My notecase was empty, which did not surprise me. I was given an official receipt for the dollar bills it had contained.

I was now no longer the responsibility of the inspector. We said goodbye and I felt very much alone in a world that might become more hostile.

Two young Dutchmen were brought up from the cells, and the three of us were taken into the central courtyard where a Dutch version of the British black maria was waiting.

Vehicles used for transporting prisoners in Holland are white, not black. They are square and boxy, somewhat like giant Range Rovers but built on the chassis of medium-sized Mercedes trucks. They have large windows of toughened glass, from the vehicle's waistline almost up to its roof. One has the impression of sitting in a goldfish bowl – but this is not so. The glass is of a special type, enabling passengers to see out but allowing the populace only a shadowy glimpse of those inside, unless the interior is illuminated.

The distance between the *Hoofdbureau van Politie* and the *Paleis van Justitie* on the Prinsengracht can be covered on foot in five minutes. Our white maria probably took the same time, via a roundabout route to the rear of the courts, where there was just room to back into a small internal garage.

In contrast to the majority of Amsterdam policemen, most of those at the law courts appear to be around fifty. Two took me along narrow, cavernous passages and put me in a cell on my own. It had whitewashed walls covered with grafitti in many languages, most of it obscene. The only ventilation was provided by a tiny window behind steel crossbars just under the ceiling. Wooden benches, bolted firmly to the base of each wall, encircled the area.

When the courts are in session these cells often have to hold more than a dozen; some waiting for their cases to be heard, others for transport back to detention.

It was still early; the courts were not yet in session, so I was alone.

After about an hour of absolute silence the door was unlocked and a policeman beckoned to me to follow him. As we meandered along a maze of corridors, the background changed subtly. Although still gloomy, the stone floors were left behind and there was now a carpet; the doors were no longer made of deal, coated with peeling grey paint, but of polished mahogany. Standing outside one was another policeman. We halted.

The sentry rapped on the door. The wood was far too thick for any sound to penetrate, so he peered inside, and indicated I was to walk in.

I was to appear in front of Amsterdam's public prosecutor. The grand title led me to expect someone almost as old as myself, but infinitely more impressive; probably bewhiskered and arrogant. I found myself facing a round-faced young man who looked about the age of my youngest godson.

The prosecutor was sitting behind a beautiful eighteenth-century writing-table. In front of it was a lone chair. He waved me towards it.

There was a long silence while he studied the dossier – obviously a police report on my recent adventures. He looked up, saying: 'I see you were released by the Syrian authorities less than six months ago. You certainly didn't waste any time before returning to your criminal pursuits.'

'If you're suggesting my behaviour demonstrates the utter uselessness of prison as a means of reforming anybody's character,' I said coolly, 'I'm happy to agree with you.'

He had the grace to smile for a second at my arrogance and made no further comment about my checkered past, going on to explain what I had already heard from the inspector: that I should now be taken to the big detention centre on the outskirts of the city and all decisions about my immediate future would be in the hands of a judge of instruction.

Escorted back to the same cell, I was left in isolation for another hour. Then, to my surprise, a policeman appeared with coffee. It was another half-hour before I was told transport was waiting to take me to the *penitentaire inrichting*.

The two young Dutch prisoners travelled with me again, chattering like sparrows. They had also been before the public prosecutor and did not seem to have relished the occasion. We had a brief glimpse of the Leidsestraat, one of Amsterdam's more expensive shopping streets; after passing the faintly baroque exterior of the Stads Schouwburg Theatre on our right and turning left in front of the barrack-like Marriot Hotel, we sped east along the Stathouderskade. In a few minutes we were circling the giant roundabout close to the Amstel railway station: in early spring, its centre is a dazzling carpet of crocuses, but the summer sun had faded the grass to light brown.

We crossed the canal that links the Amstel River to the Ijessel Meer and saw the six white tower blocks of the detention centre. To reach the only entrance to this most modern of prisons we drove the whole length of the immense complex, across a wide moat and through two electronically-controlled steel gates like giant, slow-moving roller-blinds, high and wide enough to admit the largest vehicles. We then crossed a small open courtyard and entered an underground garage, through a third huge gate. Each of these great barriers descended slowly behind us before the one in front rose, equally slowly.

From the garage the Dutch boys and I were taken up narrow stairs to the administrative centre. Here, we found ourselves in a bewildering maze of offices, most of whose doors were open and everywhere guards – mostly young and in shirtsleeve-order – were dashing to and fro, seeming genuinely busy. Bright sunshine was streaming through the big, permanently sealed windows; the entire prison was air-conditioned and, with its glossy white walls and doors panelled in light-coloured wood veneer, it seemed more like the power base of an up-to-date commercial company than a jail.

I was taken into an office like a small bank, where my identity, date of birth, etc., were checked. Small change and credit cards were taken away for another receipt. I was then told to stand with my back to the wall while a photograph was taken – just one, full face, with a Polaroid camera. I was then led to a wide corridor lined with lock-up cells whose shining, white-painted doors made them look more like a hairdresser's cubicles than jail pens.

A young guard motioned me inside one of the cells. He smiled sympathetically, saying: 'Today we are most busy. I fear, before the judge of instruction can see you, there will be much waiting!'

The 'cubicle' was about eight feet long and six wide, empty but for a wooden bench, its steel base welded to the back wall. The walls were concrete and almost obliterated by a multi-coloured rash of grafitti. (I sometimes wonder if the inventors of the felt pen realised how much vandalism would be perpetrated by their inspiration!) Most of what I could read described an outrageous diversity of sexual experience and claimed to be autobiographical. If they had written the truth, my future companions would clearly make good Christians take to the hills with shrill cries of alarm.

I sat on the bench and waited ... and went on waiting. Occasionally, I could hear murmurs and cell doors being opened and shut. I leant my head against the wall but found its rough surface too unsympathetic to doze for long in that position. I still had my watch. I had been locked up just after midday and when I saw it was four o'clock, I banged on the door.

It was opened by the guard who had warned me I should have to wait.

After a moment's hesitation, I said: 'I wondered if I'd been forgotten?'

Obviously tired but showing no irritation, he patted me on the shoulder. 'We never forget anybody! The waiting is almost finished. To piss – you want?'

I said it was not urgent.

'Good! I take you to toilet before you go to judge.'

Half an hour later he led me to a white-tiled lavatory at the end of the rows of cells. I saw that the offices across the hallway were now deserted. My guard was, apparently, alone.

'Much work today for the judge,' he said. 'For keeping you waiting, we are sorry.'

I wondered if warders in England apologised to their prisoners.

When I emerged from the lavatory he had disappeared. Waiting in his place was a tall young man (I subsequently learned he stood 6ft 8ins in his socks) with a closely-trimmed light brown beard below serious grey eyes. He was wearing a vivid blue shirt, open at the neck, and almost white corduroy trousers; from his shoulder hung a large brown leather bag that looked made for carrying maps rather than briefs.

'Good evening, Mr Aspinall,' said he. 'The judge of instruction – examining magistrate – has allowed me to come and fetch you. This is an unusual privilege, granted because of your age, because you're a foreigner and, above all, because you've been kept waiting so long.'

He guided me to a wide, carpeted corridor with large windows overlooking the city. 'Allow me,' he continued, 'to introduce myself. I'm Jan Drukker – your lawyer. I believe Mr van Akker spoke about me.'

I murmured something about it being kind of him to come and make himself known to me, while thinking how young he looked, in spite of his beard. Was he old enough, experienced enough, to make any sort of impression on the judges?

The walk to the small courtroom, where the magistrate was waiting, took a couple of minutes. I noticed internal television cameras at strategic points along our route. Our destination looked more like a City boardroom than a court of law.

There was a long, polished table, surrounded by high-backed chairs, of which only two were occupied, one by an elegantly dressed woman at the foot of the table with her back to the door. She turned towards me, holding out her hand in welcome and saying in impeccably accented English: 'Come in, Mr Aspinall – do come in and sit down!' Like a gracious hostess in her drawing-room, she indicated I was to sit beside her. 'I'm sure you must be tired. It's been a hot day and you've been kept waiting an outrageously long time. We're all very sorry, it just couldn't be helped.'

Surprised by this reception, I obediently took the seat next to her while Jan Drukker sat opposite. For a moment I wondered if this was the judge. There were, I knew, many women among the Dutch judiciary.

She cut short my silent speculation by indicating the male figure, some distance from us at the head of the table, saying: 'The judge wants you to know we shan't be keeping you for long this evening. You'll be back here at two o'clock tomorrow for the evidence against you to be investigated.'

I was no longer baffled. The woman was my interpreter. Her voice had a touch of what the late Joyce Grenfell used to call 'Pont Street'. This convinced me that she was English, married to a Dutchman. I assumed – rightly or wrongly – that it must be necessary to have Dutch nationality to be an official interpreter in a Netherlands court. Later I discovered she was Dutch, married to a Scandinavian ship-owner. I shall refer to her as Mrs Johannsen, but that was not her name.

She was a perfect example of the way so many Dutch speak not only English, but also German and often French, with a fluency that should shame most Britons, who are seldom able to utter a word in any language but their own. Admittedly, most Dutch have a slight accent or use an occasional turn of phrase that reveals their nationality. Not so this interpreter.

Elegance is not a noticeable characteristic of Dutchwomen, but there are exceptions and this woman was certainly one. To my old eyes she looked comparatively young, though she had worked with the British army during the last war; there had been times during the Allied advance into Germany in the spring of 1945 when she and I had been only a few miles apart. Like so many who lead busy and useful lives, she looked considerably younger than her age.

We all gazed expectantly at the judge, who looked no older than the public prosecutor. He was lean with prominent cheekbones, a ruddy skin and eyes as blue as cornflowers. He had discarded his jacket and rolled up his shirtsleeves. In front of him, apart from what I presumed to be my dossier, were two enormous ashtrays and a tobacco-pouch. His hands – bony, with long fingers – played constantly with an unlighted, straight-stemmed briar pipe. He looked more like a young officer who has recently achieved field rank in a good regiment than a lawyer.

'Mr Aspinall,' he began, 'I see you've lived in the Netherlands for some years, so you won't be surprised that all of us around this table can speak a certain amount of English.' His own was as flawless as the interpreter's. 'But I must tell you,' he continued, scraping the bowl of his pipe with a matchstick, 'that this is a Dutch court and its business has to be conducted in our own language. When I question you officially, I have to do so in Dutch. Your interpreter, Mrs Johannsen, will give you an immediate translation. You, of course, will reply in English, which again has to be translated for our tape recorders, if not for me. It's a slow process, but it can't be avoided – you understand?'

He glanced at his watch. 'Don't worry, I'm not going to start this evening – it's already after six. It only remains for me to apologise for having kept you locked up for so long today. We had an unexpected flood of work and we still haven't finished.' He spoke in Dutch to Drukker, asking him to tell the guard outside I was ready.

As I got up, Mrs Johannsen asked why I was wearing a jacket.

'Don't you appreciate Amsterdam has a heatwave at this moment? You must be far too hot!'

'I thought the court might consider it disrespectful if I didn't.'

'How typically English!' she laughed. 'We Dutch are terribly casual about such matters.' Then, after a moment's pause, she said: 'D'you read much?'

'Voraciously.'

'Every block in this centre has a library – most of the books, I suspect, are cheap thrillers.' (She was wrong – the libraries were run in conjunction with Amsterdam's central library and provided an astonishingly wide choice in several languages.) 'I've just finished the new Salman Rushdie. Have you read it?'

'No.'

'Would you like to?'

'Very much.'

'I'll see it reaches you tomorrow.'

I thanked her and, as I turned to go, heard Jan Drukker say he would be coming to see me in the morning.

'Do I have to do anything about it – from my end?' I asked.

'No. Leave it all to me.'

As I walked back to the administrative offices I felt a mixture of bewilderment and reassurance. The last quarter of an hour had been so informal and friendly I could hardly believe it had happened.

I was glad not to be put into a cell but taken to a room where two of the staff, wearing jeans and T-shirts, were sorting out piles of newly-washed cotton underwear. I was left in their charge.

The elder stopped counting vests, dived below the wooden counter between us and reappeared with my case and shoulder-bag which he slapped down in front of me. Both were unlocked and had been searched, but their contents had not been too seriously ruffled.

He chucked a couple of towels in my direction. Pointing at a door behind me, he said: 'That's a bathroom. Take what you need from your luggage and have a shower!'

I seized the towels, grabbed clean underwear and spongebag, and bounded into a white-tiled bathroom which had three curtained shower stalls separated by frosted glass.

The Dutch are pro-shower and anti the British bathtub habit of soaking in their own dirt. The showers were good; the water gloriously hot. I luxuriated for at least ten minutes, until the elder guard peered at me through the steam; I had not bothered to draw the curtain.

'I'm sorry,' he said, 'but I have to make sure you have no obvious skin trouble. D'you mind turning around?'

Obligingly, I twirled on my axis like a slow-moving top. 'Do I get a clean bill of health?' I asked.

'Sure,' he said. 'I don't like to embarrass you like this but we have to check everybody.'

'I'm not embarrassed,' I assured him. 'But is this the only health check we get?'

My question shocked him. 'Certainly not. Within twenty-four hours of arriving at the *Demersluis* you'll be sent for an interview with the doctor.'

'What's the *Demersluis*?'

'The tower-block where all prisoners are sent for the first week or ten days.'

'What happens after that?' I switched the shower to tepid.

'You're transferred to another tower. The *Demersluis* staff have to assess how you're likely to behave. If they think you're going to be difficult, you'll be sent where there's more discipline and less freedom. You, for sure, will be sent to one of the easier towers.'

I turned the water to cold. 'Are many prisoners here serving long sentences?' I asked.

'Nobody at all. This is not a prison, it's what we call a *huis van bewaring* – a house of detention. A prisoner is kept here until his trial. This usually means three to four months – if it's a difficult case, perhaps six months. When it's all over there's a further delay of at least a month, to give both sides time to decide whether to appeal against the verdict.'

'Both sides?' I asked, turning off the shower and seizing a towel.

'Yes – a prisoner can appeal against his sentence and so can the public prosecutor if he considers the judges have been too lenient.'

'Does that often happen – an appeal from the prosecutor?'

'No, very seldom – not more than once or twice over a period of years.'

'Where are prisoners sent when they leave here?'

'It depends on a number of factors – age – previous record – length of sentence – general character. The majority go to one of the two new prisons up in the north, close to the German frontier.

'Are they like this place?'

297

'Similar, but not so big. Others go to the older prisons in places like the Hague and Alkmaar. Not so comfortable, but easier for visitors.' He looked at his watch. 'It's getting late. I should have been off duty more than an hour ago.' He left me, saying, 'Don't be too long, will you.'

As I was dressing, he said: 'Would you mind if I sent you to the *Demersluis* with just the things you need for tonight? I'll have you back in the morning and we'll sort out your stuff together … ' It astonished me to be asked if I minded. It was not a phrase I expected to hear from a prison guard. 'There'll be no hurry tomorrow. I can explain how much you can take with you, and what must be locked away until you're released.'

'Can I take my shoulder-bag with me tonight? Everything I'll need is in it.'

He shook his head. 'No luggage is allowed in the cells. He seized a black bin-liner from under the counter and dropped into it two sheets, two pillow-cases and three blankets, all ready for me on the counter. He now added three towels – two rough, one smooth – and a striped mattress-cover. 'Now,' he said, holding the bag open, 'just put in the stuff you can't do without.'

I slipped pyjamas, shaver and spongebag inside. It was now so full it was difficult to grip, so I nursed it like a baby.

The guard held a green card like a credit card under my nose. In one corner was a tiny photo of myself – the polaroid taken earlier in the day. 'This,' he said, as he tucked it into my breast-pocket, 'is your identity card. Don't lose it.'

'Do I have to keep it with me all the time?'

'It will be kept in the control-room at the entrance to your tower. You'll surrender it when you reach the *Demersluis* this evening. When you leave the tower, for any reason, you'll pick it up. You won't be able to move anywhere in the centre without it.'

This guard was the third person I had met that day who spoke colloquial English like a native. Half an hour earlier, however, I had heard him talking fluent Amsterdam-accented Dutch. Curiosity overcame discretion. 'Are you Dutch or English?' I asked.

The question amused him. 'I'm Dutch all right,' he said, 'but I spent twelve years in Australia.'

'Without picking up the accent – how did you manage it?'

'Probably because I was working most of the time with Englishmen who had recently emigrated.'

'Whingeing poms?'

He laughed. 'I think I whinged more than they did!' He led me the short distance to the centre's glass-walled, central control-room, where two guards in shirtsleeves sat before a panel of push-buttons, overlooking an enormous space, like the interior of a Zeppelin-hangar, that seemed to stretch into infinity, with tall windows on either side.

'You're looking at the internal walkway that provides access to every tower-block and links them with the administrative offices, the courtroom and the reception area for visitors, all at this end of the complex.' As he spoke he took the ID card from my pocket and dropped it into a metal tray at the base of one of the windows. The guard inside, like a railway booking-clerk, pulled the tray towards him, examined the card, pressed buttons on his computer and glanced at a galaxy of television screens. What he saw seemed satisfactory, for he put the card back on the tray and pushed it out to me.

A steel-framed glass door clicked open and, as I walked into the walkway that extended ahead for at least a quarter of a mile, I heard my friendly 'Australian' guard call out that the entrance to the *Demersluis* was about a hundred metres ahead on the left. Just before his voice was cut off by the closing of the door, I heard him say: 'See you in the morning!'

Apart from two cups of coffee and a thirst-quenching draught of cold water swallowed under the shower, I had had nothing all day. Somehow, entering this enormous empty space made me feel suddenly exhausted. The floor was on a lower level than the control-room and, to reach it, one could descend a wide, central, sloping ramp or shallow steps on either side.

I chose the steps. Still clutching the over-full bin-liner, I had almost reached the bottom step when my shaver fell with a crash that reverberated for several seconds. I stood still, hoping it had not broken and feeling slightly sick, when a figure detached itself from the wall ahead and strode towards me. It was a lean, agile young guard with a curly mop of fair hair and a sympathetic grin.

To my surprise, he stooped and picked up the shaver, saying in heavily accented English: 'You have trouble with the many things you carry?' He gave the shaver a shake, as if he had guessed my anxiety. 'The case is strong. I think you will find it is OK.'

'How did you know I was English?' I asked.

'Because you say "Oh God!" when you drop the shaver!'

'I didn't realise I'd said anything.'

'You said it very softly. I think you are tired, yes?'

'Yes, I'm tired.'

'You are new prisoner for the *Demersluis*?'

I nodded.

Still holding my shaver, he said: 'Come with me, I will show you the way.'

As we walked, I saw big, steel-framed, glass doors on either side at intervals of about seventy-five yards. Each door had an illuminated sign above it indicating the tower to which it gave access. When we had covered about 150 yards, the guard halted. We had reached the doorway marked *Demersluis*.

There was no door-handle, no visible lock – nothing but a bell-push. Through the glass panels I could see a covered passage, about fifty yards long, leading into the base of the tower.

The guard put his thumb on the bell: the door sprang open a few inches. He put his foot in the space, to prevent it from shutting again.

'Your *persoonsbewijs*, you have?' he asked.

Clutching my bundle with one arm, I took the card out of my pocket and waved it at him.

Still keeping his foot in the door, he carefully rearranged the contents of the bin-liner, making it easier to carry. He replaced the shaver where it was unlikely to fall out again, and pushed the door wide open, saying: 'Straight on for the control-room – they will tell you where to go.'

I thanked him, which seemed to surprise him. 'This evening I patrol the walkway,' he said. 'It is for me to be helpful to those like yourself. But, please, when this door is shut, do not drop anything more – it will not be possible for me to reach you!'

HET DEMERSLUIS

When I reached the tower's entrance-hall, I saw two large lifts. There was actually a third, which I failed to notice because its doors were shut: this was for the staff. The control-room was in front of them – a scaled-down version of the one at the head of the walkway. It was occupied by a man and a woman in uniform. They sat facing a console of computer and television screens. Between us was a glass wall. The young woman was nearer, so I waved my identity-card at her. She gave me a friendly smile and pointed to the metal tray in front of her.

After checking the card, she startled me by switching on a loudspeaker above my head and telling me to take the right-hand lift up to '*paviljoen drie*'.

Inside the lift I looked around for some sort of handle or button for setting the thing in motion. Before I had time to realise such objects are not built into prison lifts, its gates sprang together with a hiss like angry serpents and we began our ascent. In the ceiling were two television cameras, focussing a basilisk stare directly upon me. It seemed to take a long time to reach pavilion 3. I had not yet appreciated that the floor immediately above the entrance incorporated a surgery, library, shop and conference room; each pavilion, although isolated from its neighbours above and below, consisted of two landings. I was therefore on my way up, not to the third floor, but to the sixth.

Standing waiting for me was a slight figure of medium height with neatly-brushed grey hair, wearing a pale blue shirt with a navy tie, and dark grey trousers. His grey eyes, behind horn-rimmed spectacles, were kind. He spoke quietly, in good English. 'I expect you've had a tiring day,' he said, like a courteous host. 'Let me take you to your room.' I followed him into surroundings amazingly different from what I expected.

My immediate impression was of dazzling white walls above a great deal of veneered panelling in pale-coloured wood, extending across the entire width of the tower. At each end of this spacious hallway (the lower landing) were two enormous windows. In between, on each side, were closed doors of light oak.

The guard led me towards a wide central staircase that provided access to the balcony-type upper landing. I caught a glimpse of a recreation room divided from the lower landing by glass panels. It was furnished with small tables, armchairs with dark green plastic seats and, in one corner, a television. The room had large windows overlooking the metro line between the central station and the south-eastern suburbs.

I noticed, as we climbed the stairs, a table for billiards on the upper landing and another, for table-tennis, in the hall below.

The only sign of life were two younger members of staff sitting in a space screened off by yet another glass barrier, at right-angles to the entrance lobby. This was obviously a watchroom-cum-restroom for guards on duty. It was furnished with a large desk surmounted by a microphone and a console of push-buttons, several telephones, a large refrigerator, several cupboards and a couple of green plastic armchairs.

At the top of the stairs, the guard turned left, and opened one of a row of eight doors, all panelled in the same light oak veneer. Although officially designated as a cell, it was almost as large as many bedrooms I have occupied in expensive modern hotels.

I put my bundle on the bed. Its head was against the outer wall, alongside the single large window. A slim mattress and two pillows lay on it.

The guard asked if I were hungry.

I shook my head; all I wanted was sleep.

'You may feel hungry later,' he said. 'I will bring you something in a few minutes. Have you any special requirements?'

I must have looked puzzled for he went on quickly: 'You can have any sort of diet you prefer. Vegetarian, vegan, macrobiotic, kosher, Muslim.' He smiled. 'You name it, we can supply it!'

I assured him I was not what my parents would have described as a 'fussy feeder', apart from an excessive dislike of white bread, dating back to my time in an English preparatory school.

This seemed to amuse him. 'In twenty minutes there will be a free association period for this landing. It will last for one hour and a half. Would you like to come out and meet your neighbours?'

'If it's allowed, I would rather stay here until tomorrow.'

'Of course you may. I'll leave you now while you make your bed.'

I took a close look at my new temporary home. In addition to the bed there was a metal table with a plastic top, faked to resemble grained, dark wood; two chairs, one a length of green canvas attached to a metal frame in which it was possible to sprawl comfortably; the other upright, steel and plastic, and useful for sitting at the table to eat or write letters. Apart from a multi-coloured bedside rug in a man-made fabric, these were the only free-standing objects: everything else was built-in.

Opposite the bed, the wall was lined with shelved cupboards; there was also a sizeable hanging wardrobe; all were painted white.

Next to the wardrobe was a door which I promptly pushed open. The interior was pitch dark. I felt for a light switch; a bar of strip-lighting revealed what the French call a *cabinet de toilette*. White tiles from floor to ceiling; a wc; a washbasin with a large mirror, brilliantly illuminated by a second fluorescent tube; close by was a socket for shavers or hairdryers – to my surprise, the latter far outnumbered the former amongst my fellow prisoners. The tubular towel-rail was hot: the hot water flowed through it before reaching the tap.

As I made the bed I noticed a spotlight with a dark red shade protruding from the wall above the head of the bed: its swan-neck could be adjusted to throw a beam of light in any direction. The principal means of lighting was a fluorescent strip of such eye-assaulting brilliance that many of us seldom used it, preferring our bedside light for all purposes.

The guard returned with cheese and tomato sandwiches and a glass of milk.

'I'm afraid this is the best we can do,' he said.

I thanked him, which brought the reply: 'It's all part of the service!'

He told me he would wait until morning before explaining the rules about visitors, letters, telephone calls, the timetable for each day and the general routine. He ended by saying: 'We are here to help.' As he wished me good night, he said: 'I hope you will sleep well.'

I was so tired I only managed to eat one sandwich. Looking out of the unbreakable window, I slowly sipped the milk – a drink I normally detest. Set into the wall, between the ceiling and the top of the window frame, was a grating through which a continuous blast of air was pouring. This was the inlet of the air-conditioning system. The outlet, I discovered later, was above the wc in the *cabinet*.

It was dusk. The window faced north-east and I could see three other tower-blocks in the same complex where the lights, in windows identical to mine, were being switched on, one after the other. I wondered if the centre's electricity would be switched off automatically later on. (It was not.) I was too tired to care. I brushed my teeth, threw off my clothes and fell into bed – a bed which I found, somewhat to my surprise, to be remarkably comfortable.

For some time I listened to the prisoners having their free association time. The door was thick and muffled most of the sound, but the rhythmic plop of table-tennis filtered through. The murmur of voices increased briefly as they returned to their cells. This was followed by the guards' final circuit, double-locking each door after a quick look through the spy-hole. Then silence, followed some time afterwards by the clunk of the central electronic locking switch: a precaution that always seemed absurd to me.

I slept well and, because I dislike sleeping with drawn curtains, awoke early. The sun was shining from an oblique angle through my window.

I soon heard the faint hum of the lifts ascending. The guards were presumably returning on duty. By the time I had finished dressing, the rattle of teacups could be heard. Eventually my door was opened, and there were two guards with a trolley bearing metal urns of tea and coffee, bottles of milk and a bowl of sugar.

Smiling genially, they wished me good morning, and offered tea, coffee or milk. I said coffee. The brew was pleasantly strong, almost boiling.

Now hungry, I ate the remaining sandwiches. They were getting curly at the edges, but still tasted reasonably pleasant.

While making my bed I heard doors being opened all round and a steadily increasing buzz of voices. Most seemed to be talking in Dutch, but I heard an occasional exclamation in German and Spanish.

The spy-hole in my door was rectangular and protected on the outside by the usual hinged metal screen. Unlike those at the police headquarters, there was no opening below.

When the hubbub was at its peak, my screen was suddenly lifted and knuckles could be seen tapping on the glass, about ten inches long, five deep.

The knuckles belonged to a fresh-faced youth, who put his mouth close to the glass and shouted: 'They tell me you're a Brit – is that so?'

I nodded.

'Me and my mate are leavin' today for another tower. We've been here ten days, you see.'

I said I did see and was sorry they were moving on.

'Maybe you'll be sent to the same tower as us,' he shouted.

I said I hoped so.

'Got anything to read?'

'Not at the moment,' I shouted.

He waved a bunch of newspapers in front of the spy-hole. 'Three copies of the *Guardian* any good to you?'

'Yes, please.'

'I'll tuck them under the flap of your spy-hole. You'll get 'em when they open your door.'

I thanked him.

'What are you in for?' he asked. 'Coke is it?'

I nodded again. 'Why are *you* here?'

'Oh, we've robbed a few banks!'

A distant shout made him look over his shoulder. 'I've got to go now – see you soon, I hope.'

The voices grew fainter, the lifts hummed in descent, then silence.

The grey-haired guard of the previous evening unlocked my door, dropped the *Guardian*s on the table and sat on my bed. Had I slept well? he asked.

'Surprisingly well,' I admitted.

'Good,' he said. 'The pavilion is peaceful at the moment because this landing has gone to work.'

'Is work compulsory?'

'No, voluntary – but you get paid if you do it. Twenty-five guilders for a five-day week of three hours each day.'

'Always mornings?'

'No. This week the upper landings will be working from nine until twelve. Next week, their hours will be two until five. The lower landings will then work the morning shift.'

'What sort of work is it?'

'In this tower it's not very interesting. Just packaging up stationery – writing paper, loose-leaf notebooks, paper-bags ... '

'And you get twenty-five guilders a week for doing it?' (At this time twenty-five guilders was worth approximately £6.00.)

'You do. If your money has been confiscated it's useful for the shop.'

305

'Shop?' I enquired.

'Every tower has a general store on its first floor. They're open one morning a week – our turn is on Fridays.'

'What do they sell?'

'Breakfast cereals, tinned food, jam, detergents, crisps, salads, fruit, chocolates, writing-paper, postcards, many things . . . '

He was interrupted by a disembodied voice, speaking from a microphone I had not noticed just above the door. Two short sentences in Dutch that began with my name.

'Your lawyer is here,' explained the guard, 'and wants to see you.'

'How do I get to him?'

'Collect your identity card and take it to the central control-room – they'll direct you.'

He led me to the lower landing and put me in a lift. Raising his head towards a concealed microphone, he shouted: '*Mijnheer* Aspinall *voor zyn advocaat!*'

When I reached the bottom I found my ID card waiting with a scrap of paper on which my lawyer's name had been scrawled.

Hurrying along the walkway I passed two guards meandering in the opposite direction. They smiled cheerfully and gave me the usual Dutch greeting of '*Dag!*' – an abbreviation of *goedendag*. I returned the salutation, slightly bemused by these courtesies.

The control-room checked my name and that of my visitor on a computer. I was directed through two electronic doors to a room where security guards were sprawling on the leather-covered benches round the walls. One, who looked the most important, was at a desk in the middle. Security guards were more like ordinary policemen and did not work inside the tower-blocks. Apart from being general watch-dogs, their principal duty was the supervision of official visits with lawyers, probation officers, etc.

As I handed my card and the lawyer's name to the guard at the desk, I heard a sharp intake of breath amongst those lounging on the *banquettes*. One sat up suddenly, saying: 'It's him!'

I failed to realise he was referring to me until another seized a copy of that morning's *Die Telegraaf*, and got up to show it to me. 'You see,' he said, pointing to banner headlines, 'we know all about you!'

With steadily increasing dismay I saw it was an account of my arrest supplied to a press agency by the police. The report, headed

SIR — ACCUSED OF IMPORTING COCAINE!, filled two columns and, after giving every detail of the expedition to Charles de Gaulle Airport to tail me back to Amsterdam, the report concentrated on my appearance and manners, which they considered those of the perfect English gentleman. They ended by confessing surprise that I was not at least a knight bachelor!

Reading paragraph after paragraph in this vein I began to sweat with embarrassment: my only consolation being that nowhere was there any mention of my name. Under Dutch law, the media is forbidden to disclose the surname of any offender, even after conviction. The press, however, may give the initials of the prisoner's Christian names. Not for the first time in my life did I regret I was provided with more than the customary number at baptism, for they were given here – and given correctly, several times. I guessed the telephone lines between my many Amsterdam friends would, that morning, have become red hot.

Meanwhile, my ID card had been filed by the guard at the desk who handed the slip of paper to a uniformed, tall young black, whose forebears had obviously immigrated from the former colony of Surinam. I was taken into an anteroom, a door was unlocked and I was led into a long, fluorescent-lighted corridor with rows of cubicles on either side.

Each cubicle was solidly constructed and soundproofed; all furnished with wall-to-wall carpeting in a beige, flecked pattern, a small writing-table with a green-shaded table-lamp in addition to a strip of lighting in the ceiling, and four chairs of unvarnished deal with beige cloth seats.

Jan Drukker's lanky silhouette appeared in the distance, clutching the enormous leather shoulder-bag with both hands. He wished us a breathless good morning, swept me into the cubicle ahead of him and threw his bag on the table, almost knocking the lamp over. The door was closed quietly behind us. After telling me to sit in what looked the most comfortable chair, he seated himself at the table, his jean-clad legs extending well beyond it.

He asked what my first reactions had been to this detention centre.

After thinking for a moment, I said: 'Bewilderment ... astonishment ... '

'Why astonishment?'

'Because so many people have gone out of their way to be helpful.'

'That astonishes you?'

'Of course. I've never visualised a prison where guards pick up the things I drop. My only grumble is the length of time I was left, yesterday, without food or drink.'

'Due, so I understand, to what you call an administrative balls-up. One of the reasons being the unexpected length of time taken to cross-examine your partner.'

This worried me. 'Oh God – that sounds ominous.'

'Not necessarily,' he said confidently, extracting official-looking documents from his bag. Holding up a piece of paper, he said: 'I've just received this. It's confirmation that you're to appear in front of the judge of instruction – at two this afternoon. I shall, of course, be there.'

'Will it be the judge I saw yesterday?'

'Yes, and as you've made no attempt to deny responsibility, I don't think you've much to worry about.'

'I suppose I shall be sent for trial?'

'No doubt at all. You and your partner are bound to be tried together in the Amsterdam High Court.'

'After how long?'

'At a guess, I should say three months.'

'Are you defending Dinos as well?'

'No, he has another lawyer.'

'What sort of sentences d'you think we'll get?'

He leaned backwards, his chair creaking in protest as he gave me a look of mock despair. 'That's the first question I'm asked by every client – and it's impossible to forecast accurately.'

'Can't you give me an approximate idea?'

'Difficult, because so many factors are involved.'

'Such as?'

'The character of the three judges on the bench. We shan't know until about ten days beforehand who they will be. Judges are human – they have their idiosyncrasies. How you react to cross-examination will also influence their decision.'

'But you're unwilling even to hazard a guess?' I persisted.

With obvious reluctance, he said: 'Well, don't hold it against me if I'm wrong but, taking your age into account and the frankness you've shown up to now, I would say you're unlikely to get more than two and a half years. You might, if you're exceptionally lucky, get less, but not much.'

'And Dinos?'

'I would think at least a year more than you. He has all that hashish in his apartment to account for.'

'Do we get one third remission for good behaviour?'

'You do.'

'And will our sentences begin from the date of arrest?'

'They will.' He now asked if I had any particular problems, and could he help?

I was chiefly concerned about what to do with my possessions, now in a rented flat.

'Furniture?' he asked.

'No, just books, clothes, radio, typewriter. It's a furnished flat.'

'D'you intend to give it up?'

'Yes, I simply can't afford to keep it on. Fortunately, although it's officially rented on a monthly contract, I've always paid quarterly, in advance. The rent won't be due for two months – so, if I give notice immediately, I shall be well within the time limit. It's just my stuff I'm worried about – clothes are expensive to replace nowadays, and my books – I'm a compulsive buyer of books, English and French – and I should hate to lose them.'

'No television or videos?'

'No, I've never wanted them.'

'What happened when you were in Syria?'

'The owner stored everything in a spare room in his own house, and sub-let the flat. Almost miraculously it became vacant again two weeks after I returned.'

'He won't be willing to do that again?'

'I feel enough is enough. I can't expect him to give a repeat performance.'

He tapped his excellent teeth with a pencil. 'Our offices in the Prinsengracht,' he said, 'have extensive attic space we seldom use. You're welcome to store your stuff there.'

He waved away my inadequate attempt to thank him. 'I must warn you,' he said, 'none of my colleagues or I can spare the time to pack your things and transport them across Amsterdam.'

'I have friends who would, I know, do it for me. But they're at work all day ... '

'And our offices are locked at night! But don't worry, this won't be insoluble. I was, anyway, going to ask the probationary service to

309

take up your case. I'm sure whoever they appoint to look after you will be able to fix everything. He looked at his watch and made a face. 'I'll have to throw you out in a moment – I've two more clients waiting.' There was a bell-push in the wall, which he pressed. 'But before I do so,' he continued, 'I want to ask you to do something for me. I want you to write an account of your life.'

Astonished, I said: 'What? From cradle to grave?'

He smiled, saying: 'Not quite so far back and certainly not as far ahead! Just a dozen or so pages, giving brief details of your family background and the sort of work you were doing prior to your involvement in the drug scene – not forgetting to mention your reasons for getting into that scene.'

'But I haven't a typewriter, and I always write, even personal letters, on my portable. Will I be allowed to have it in here?'

'Of course, but don't wait for it. Just get going with pen or pencil.'

'My handwriting's awful.'

'That doesn't matter. I'll get my secretary to type it.'

'Your poor secretary – she'll go crazy! But why d'you need it?'

'I want to attach it to your dossier when it goes to the high court. The judges will then know something about you before presiding over your case.'

He accompanied me politely to the door where we almost collided with the black guard ushering in Jan Drukker's next client, a sad, pale young man, wearing gold-framed spectacles.

The same guard took me back to the security office. As we entered, he grinned at his colleagues, saying: 'I bring Sir Anthony for his *bewijs*!'

I told him he should be ashamed to make fun of a poor defenceless old man. As my tongue was obviously in my cheek, this produced a burst of good-humoured laughter. In a languid, upper-class voice I accused them of showing insufficient respect for my age and infirmities which made them laugh all the more as I began the long trek back to the *Demersluis*.

When I got out of the lift the place appeared deserted. Then, through the glass wall of the recreation room, I spied the chief guard at a table filling in forms. He heard me approaching and looked up, saying: 'There's still tea and coffee on the trolley by the office door. Help yourself.'

While I was pouring coffee, he called out: 'Bring it in here! There's nobody else in the pavilion. Your crowd, upstairs, are at work and this landing's gone out for exercise. My two colleagues have gone with them.'

I obeyed, and while he continued to fill in forms I stood sipping the coffee and looking out of the wide windows. I watched a metro train, like a scarlet caterpillar, pulling out of Spaklerweg Station. It appeared to do so in absolute silence, due to the sealed windows and the all-pervading hiss from the air-conditioning.

I watched the little train until it disappeared, knowing that in about ten minutes it would pass close to a high-rise block of flats where I had made my first home in Amsterdam nearly ten years before.

The guard finished his forms. 'You had no difficulty in finding your lawyer?' he asked.

'None at all.'

'It was a good interview? You like your lawyer?'

'Yes,' I said confidently, 'I like him very much. When I first met him, I was a bit worried because he looked so young. But now I feel he's exactly what I need.'

'I ask because you are permitted to change lawyers if you wish.'

'I'm sure I shan't want to change.' I was later to learn that many prisoners did so, repeatedly – often to their detriment. 'He tells me I must provide the court with a potted autobiography. Can I be allowed writing paper?'

'Of course – as much as you need. It's all A4, so you can use it for letters. You do know such letters must be left open?'

'I guessed as much.'

'Only those to your lawyer may be sealed.'

This concession surprised me, and I said so.

'We have to take precautions,' he said, 'but we do our best to be civilised.'

'To someone whose only experience of prison was in the Middle East, you've certainly succeeded! How long have you been a guard?'

He smiled gently. 'Perhaps too long,' he said. 'I'm the second oldest in this centre.'

'To me, you don't look old.'

'I'm fifty-two. Most of us are between thirty and forty. A few in their late twenties, not many over forty-five.'

'Have you worked in the *Demersluis* ever since this place was built?'

'No, at first I was in another tower. But soon there was a vacancy for a head guard in this pavilion. I applied.'

'You like it?'

'I find it interesting. There are many who don't like to work in the *Demersluis* because the people are always changing. They prefer the towers where prisoners remain for three to six months, or longer. We're a kind of staging post where a man remains only long enough for us to decide which tower would be most suitable for him.'

'Do they vary so much – the other towers? Don't they all follow the same routine?'

'Every tower has its own director – in England he would be called a governor. Each has complete autonomy over his own tower. Of course they consult frequently, but there is no supreme authority over them all. Each director is linked separately to the Ministry of Justice in the Hague.'

'And every tower has a different atmosphere?' I asked.

'There are differences and similarities. Every tower absorbs something of the personality of its director. It's rather like a school. They may follow the same educational programme, but every headmaster has a different way of interpreting it.'

'How do they vary?'

'Well, one tower is occupied exclusively by those we feel to be mentally unstable and who would benefit from psychiatric help. The others are more or less evenly divided between those where discipline is fairly strict and the remainder where it is more casually imposed. In some towers the cell doors are only closed at night. In others, as in the *Demersluis*, a prisoner is only allowed out during free association. And there is of course another tower, just to the east' – he pointed over his shoulder – 'the women's tower.'

'Staffed by women?'

He shook his head. 'No, mixed – like everywhere else. But there are more women guards there.'

I said I hadn't seen many in the *Demersluis*, except in the control-room.

'We haven't any in this pavilion, but others have several.'

'How do they cope with violent prisoners?'

'Usually very well. Often better than the men – they have more tact. But we get surprisingly few tearaway types.'

'D'you get many escapes?'

He gave a wry smile. 'A few – but not from the *Demersluis*.'

'It beats me how it's done – when every door is locked electronically.'

'You want me to give you a special plan of how to do it?' He sounded amused.

'A blueprint might help!' I said, in the same tone.

'One thing I will tell you – every successful escape so far has taken place in the open air.'

'While taking exercise?'

He nodded. 'If, at your age, you can climb walls seven metres high and cross a wide, deep moat, then you may be able to imitate them, but you'll need outside help.'

'Let me relieve your mind by saying I know my limitations! But how often is one allowed out into the fresh air – just for exercise?'

'At least once a day for sixty minutes. If you wish to come back in after half-an-hour, you may. If the temperature is above 27° Celsius, you're allowed a second hour – usually in the evening.'

The telephone rang in the office and he went to answer it. When he returned he dumped a packet of A4 paper and half-a-dozen long envelopes on the table. Then he asked if I would like to make any telephone calls.

Pleasant surprises seemed to be piling up. 'You mean,' I said, 'I can ring up anybody?'

'There are some restrictions. Phone calls within the Netherlands are free, but if you make too many we cut down your quota.'

'What d'you call too many?'

'Well, more than two a week – unless it's an emergency. When you arrive here you're allowed one international call for nothing; after that they have to be paid for.'

I asked if local calls could be made at any time.

'Normally only during free association, on weekday evenings and Sunday afternoons. Just go to the office earlier in the day and ask to put your name on the list. You may be told the evening is already booked and have to reserve your call for the following night.'

'Do the same rules apply to international calls?' My eagerness must have been reflected in my face, because he said: 'If you want to make that free call right away, you can.'

I followed him to the office where he picked up a portable instrument, then up to the top landing, into a narrow room where sports equipment was stored. In a corner near the window were two chairs with a small table between. He plugged the telephone into a socket and put the instrument on the table, telling me to sit down, taking the other chair himself.

'I ought to have warned you,' he said, 'all calls have to be monitored by a member of staff. I must have scowled at this, because he added: 'As soon as we can be sure you're not plotting something illegal, we don't listen too closely – so you mustn't be embarrassed.'

He asked for the number I wanted to ring, and jotted it down. He then lifted the receiver which I now noticed had a single earphone attached on a short length of cable. He spelt my name to the operator and gave the number of the pavilion and my cell, then the number I had asked for. After a brief interval he handed me the receiver, saying: 'The number is ringing.' He picked up the earphone and listened with me to the instantly recognisable double-grunt of the British ringing tone, ending in a sort of suppressed squawk. I heard a woman's voice say: 'Hullo … ?'

It was the voice I was hoping for – that of a dear friend for more than forty years. What we said to each other is of no concern to anybody except ourselves, now only to me, for she was to die within the next two years. That this was a very private conversation quickly became obvious to the guard who put his earpiece gently down and got up to stare intently out of the window.

In my impatience to get to the telephone I had left the writing paper on the floor below. When I came upstairs again, somewhat chastened, the guard was waiting. As he opened my door, he pointed to an alcove close to the lift-shafts: 'That's the shower-room and there's another below it on the lower landing. There are four showers in each and they can be used at any time during free association.'

I hardly had time to settle in front of a blank sheet of paper before the chief guard was telling me there was a call from the admin block: would I go and sort out my clothing at once.

So, a few minutes later, I was again hurrying along the walkway, flourishing my ID card and passing the time of day with patrolling guards. After being quizzed through loudspeakers by the control-room and negotiating my way through just one electronic door I was back again with the kindly 'Australian'.

My clothes had been stacked neatly on a counter, my case and shoulder-bag on the floor. I exchanged the suit I was wearing for a pair of slacks and a sweater, and put to one side the clothing I felt I would need during my incarceration. The only forbidden items were my nail-scissors (nail-clippers were permitted) and my rolled-up 'housewife', containing needles (banned) and reels of thread.

'How am I to sew buttons on?' I enquired plaintively.

'You ask for a needle and thread – and hand them back immediately you've finished with them.'

I staggered back to the *Demersluis* clutching three bin-liners bursting at the seams.

A young guard greeted me in pavilion 3. With a golden skin and almond eyes, he was obviously of Indonesian origin. He looked no more than sixteen but was probably in his late twenties. The majority of far eastern races seem to retain an air of perpetual youthfulness until they reach about forty, when they become recognisably middle-aged without warning.

'You look,' he said mischievously, 'as if you could do with some help!' He took two of the bags and put an expertly wrapped, small parcel into my free hand. 'This,' he explained, 'has been sent over from the small court – it feels like a book.'

We mounted the stairs. Putting the bin-liners on my bed, he warned that lunch would arrive in the next few minutes.

'Where do we eat?' I asked.

'Here, in your cell.' He grinned engagingly. 'It is room service for everybody!'

'Always in our cells?'

'Always – except perhaps Christmas Day – and Easter!' Amusement at my questions had made his almond eyes almost disappear into his skull as he shut me in.

I tore open the package. It was indeed a book: Salman Rushdie's *Midnight's Children*. So Mrs Johanssen had kept her promise.

I had just finished putting my clothes away when lunch arrived in a large box-like truck of shining metal on wheels; its stainless steel sides could be pulled up in the manner of a roll-top desk to show twelve compartments on each side designed to hold hermetically-sealed containers in which was a two-course meal – a main dish and pudding, as well as some fresh fruit. Within the containers the food was always on china plates or in unbreakable glass dishes. It was not *haute cuisine*, but sensible bourgeois Dutch cooking of a surprisingly high standard. I cannot remember ever being given a bad meal in the detention centre, still less ever feeling hungry.

On every container was a card with the name of the prisoner for whom it was intended. Having to cater for a wide variety of diets, the kitchens prepared every meal individually, arranging them in the trucks in numerical order making delivery straightforward. (Cells 1 to 12 were on the lower landing, 13 to 24 on the upper.) Only rarely was a mistake made and the horror of a macrobiotic or vegan meal presented to a staunch carnivore.

Just before mealtimes it was sometimes necessary to take quick, evasive action to avoid being run down by a long crocodile of these trucks in the walkway. Twenty or more, linked together, were pulled along at surprising speed by a small, battery-operated, tractor-like vehicle. A truck for each pavilion would be shed automatically at the entrance to every tower. The tower's staff were responsible for pushing them into the lifts and accompanying them aloft.

About half-an-hour was allowed for eating one's meal in solitary state, before the truck was again wheeled around, like a giant perambulator, to pick up the empties.

Immediately after lunch I was summoned before the judge of instruction. It was about a quarter of a mile from the *Demersluis* to the small court; at least ten minutes' walk.

I was greeted by the same guard as before who gave me a friendly pat on the shoulder as he locked me up, saying: 'Today it will not be for long – I promise!'

He spoke the truth. Before I had had time to read all the graffiti I was escorted to an anteroom and ushered into the boardroom-type court where I had been the day before.

The charming interpreter gave me a welcoming smile. The judge was standing filling his pipe. He waved his pouch, indicating I was to sit at the foot of the table. The room (I could not think of it as a court) was empty, apart from the three of us.

Mrs Johanssen asked how I was coping with life in a Dutch penal establishment. She seemed sympathetically interested.

I said I had often stayed in hotels where the rooms were smaller and less comfortable and where the service lacked the personal touch it had in the *Demersluis*!

Their reaction was a mixture of surprise and amusement. 'We've occasionally heard that sort of comment before,' said the judge, as he settled himself at the head of the table, 'and it always seems to be made by an English prisoner.'

'Possibly because of the contrast between conditions here and in England,' I suggested.

'You have no experience of those conditions, I gather?'

316

'None.'

'But you know what it's like to be a prisoner of the Syrians?'

'I do indeed.'

'Was it quite dreadful?' asked Mrs Johanssen.

'At times it could be tough for an elderly, self-indulgent European but, to someone of my anarchic temperament, I'm sure it was easier to bear than being shut up, three to a cell, in an insanitary, red-brick, Victorian monstrosity.'

'Not all our prisons are like this centre,' said the judge, who had been lighting his pipe with a series of waxed matches. 'We still have a number that are old and not unlike those in your country.'

'But not so overcrowded,' insisted Mrs Johanssen. 'I think every prisoner in the Netherlands has a cell to himself.'

'Perhaps not for much longer,' said the judge. 'We too are getting very overcrowded.' He looked at his watch and opened the substantial-looking dossier in front of him. Clearly, he was bringing to an end what had seemed, up to now, almost a social occasion. 'Your lawyer's a bit late,' he said, 'I think we'll have to begin without him.'

He had hardly got beyond asking me to confirm my name and date of birth before Jan Drukker arrived, out of breath. Apologising to all three of us, he subsided onto a chair to my left. It was a hot afternoon and he was still wearing jeans, an open-neck shirt and trainers. In spite of living for years in the Netherlands, I never quite got used to the astonishing informality of the Dutch; they seldom dress up for any event and only diplomats ever seem to wear a tie.

The next two and a half hours passed quickly and without any feeling of strain on my part. The judge began by saying the case against me would be confined to the charge of having brought two-and-three-quarter kilos of cocaine illegally into the country. Similar actions, in which I might or might not have been involved in the past, would not be investigated.

With all the information I had given in the dossier, he took me through the whole story once again; the only difference being that he required me to describe certain episodes in much greater detail.

He showed what I found, at first, to be a totally baffling interest in my original meeting with Eduardo Luis. Had this taken place in a restaurant in Amsterdam, he asked, and, if so, was it one I frequented? Who had made the introductions? How many had been in the party? What had been the seating arrangements when we left the bar to go and eat?

This last question showed me he was checking my story against whatever Dinos had told him. I said that the restaurant had been full. We had been a party of six and, after sitting for longer than any of us wanted at the bar the only tables to become vacant were, respectively, for four and for two people. They were widely separated and could not be joined together, the place was much too crowded. I had therefore suggested to Eduardo Luis that we dine *à deux*. This would give him a better chance of getting to know me, and for both of us to decide if we had sufficient confidence in each other to work together.

I realised Dinos must have given him a similar account and my confirmation of seizing the initiative to dine alone with the Peruvian was one of several small incidents that showed us to be, more or less, equal partners.

He asked how the expedition to Lima had been funded. I replied, truthfully, that it had been a tripartite venture. Dinos had added a small sum of his own to a larger amount subscribed by several anonymous friends. Eduardo Luis had contributed a similar sum, while I had supplied a smaller amount chiefly culled from the interest accumulated from a small bequest left me by a great-aunt. I also paid for my return flight, so my contribution had been almost equal to the others'.

I felt it only fair to emphasize this had been a co-operative venture. The police seemed anxious to persuade themselves that Dinos was the bold, bad drugs baron and I just his geriatric stooge, and I wanted to correct this impression. Unfortunately, the discovery of a good many kilos of hashish in his flat was not much help in my efforts to lighten the load of suspicion against him.

The judge asked why we had not chosen to employ a runner.

I told him that runners were all too often unreliable. I could think of at least half a dozen who, having been sent halfway across the world to collect a special suitcase, had picked up the luggage and disappeared without trace.

He asked why Dinos had not made the trip instead of me.

Because, I said, he had been convicted of importing cannabis into Canada several years ago and the Canadian police circulate the names of drugs offenders to almost every other country.

'But you also have a previous conviction?'

'Yes, but the Syrians don't bother to tell anybody unless specifically requested to do so. During the six months following my release I

318

travelled a good deal in northern Europe, and not a single passport controller's eyebrow was raised in my direction.'

He asked suddenly if I enjoyed taking risks.

The question surprised me. 'Did Dinos tell you that?' I asked.

'Never mind what your friend told me. Do you?'

'You're asking if I enjoy fooling the customs service? Yes, I do! I believe I enjoy fooling any kind of state institution.'

He showed considerable interest in the methods used by Eduardo Luis and his associates in handing over the cocaine and equipping me with the special underclothing. I was encouraged to describe how Eduardo Luis and I, accompanied by one of his policeman brothers in plain clothes, had toured the more expensive gents' outfitters in Lima and Miraflores. Eventually we discovered exactly what was needed in nearby Santo Isidro. A vast department store was having a sale of underbriefs made from the strongest white calico. Two pairs, neatly machine-sewn together and stuffed with cocaine, were just what we wanted – even if they did make me look as if I was wearing a giant baby's nappy! They also had the merit of being easily detachable.

The judge continued to probe into every detail of my trip, with occasional pauses to relight his pipe. Jan Drukker, listening intently, occasionally objected to the way a question was phrased. Mrs Johanssen quietly translated with remarkable ease and fluency.

When the lengthy period of question and answer was nearly over, the judge told me, almost casually, that he would be sending me to stand trial in the high court of Amsterdam. As there was no system for bail I should be remaining 'on remand' until the trial. He went on to explain that the authority to keep me in custody until then would have to be renewed at regular intervals by the 'small' court.

While the judge was explaining, the guard from the anteroom entered to ask if he could escort me back to the admin offices.

'Is it time you went off duty?' enquired the judge.

The guard admitted this was so.

'Then off you go,' was the answer. 'I'll escort the Englishman myself.'

Jan Drukker now got ready to leave, promising to keep in constant touch and saying he had already asked the probation service to take an interest in my case.

Turning to the judge I asked if I might be paroled for half a day in order to arrange for the storage and disposal of my property.

'Outside my competence, I'm afraid. That's a matter for the public prosecutor.'

Drukker said quickly he would raise this question at my first appearance in the small court, within the next few days. 'I'll ask the prosecutor on your behalf – he will, of course be present.'

'D'you think he'll agree?' I asked.

'I doubt it – but we'll have a go.'

It had been, for me, an afternoon of surprises. Instead of encountering self-righteous hostility, I had been treated courteously by someone I instinctively liked and trusted. I knew I had been far too indiscreet for my own good, but did not really care.

The charmingly mondaine Mrs Johanssen now left us. Nearly three hours of instant translation seemed in no way to have exhausted her.

The judge and I walked along the carpeted corridors, exchanging reminiscences of previous summers in Amsterdam, as if a polite host were escorting a departing visitor to his door. This impression ended, however, when, after shaking hands, the electronic barrier between the court area and the detention centre snapped shut between us.

On my return to the *Demersluis*, the chief guard told me the shade temperature in the early afternoon had just touched 27°, so we would be allowed a second exercise period in the evening. My landing would be taking the first hour, beginning at half-past six.

This was the first opportunity I had had to meet my fellow prisoners. Until now, I had hardly been aware of their existence. My first impression was surprise at the multiplicity of races. Every shade of skin was represented, with only a minority of what appeared to be ethnic, white Dutchmen; and some of these, I discovered later, were German. The only common element was youth. Few were more than thirty, many much younger.

It was a warm August evening and none of us wore jackets. The South American contingent (every one a professional pickpocket!) made a particularly dazzling spectacle, vying with those from North Africa and the Middle East in who could wear the most vividly coloured shirt.

Although I must have stuck out like a sore thumb, being so much older, they seemed to accept me without question. I felt an immediate, welcoming camaraderie.

We crowded into one lift. At ground level we were joined by

a similar colourful party from the pavilion above, in breezy good-humour. Our custodians unlocked the small door to what, for want of a better description, we called the exercise yard.

These wide spaces where prisoners were allowed to breathe fresh air and move about as they wished, were certainly dwarfed by the surrounding walls; but each one covered more than half an acre and had been quite attractively landscaped with small trees and flowering shrubs, chosen either for their exceptional foliage or because they flowered at different times of the year. The yard was ringed by a path of flagstones that zig-zagged amongst the trees and bushes, just wide enough for two to walk abreast. Obviously the path had been designed to avoid giving an impression of walking monotonously in a circle and, provided one refrained from looking upwards, it could be almost like sauntering around a private garden.

Of course there were always those who wanted to jog, causing the more sedate to leap constantly into the bushes. There were also a few who regarded all exercise with loathing, preferring to laze on a smooth patch of lawn close to the tower entrance. There, if the sun was shining, they would strip to their mini-briefs in an effort to lose what they imagined to be their prison pallor.

Close by was a sort of elongated bus-shelter. With the first drops of rain, we would rush for its long, dark green, metal roof. If the shower became a downpour, those who wished would be allowed to return to their pavilion.

On this first experience of the yard, I found my companions friendly but not intrusive. The first to fall into step beside me, when I began what was to become my usual brisk walk, was a tall young Dutchman with light red hair and a profusion of freckles. He spoke excellent English, as did almost everyone bar the Spanish and South Americans. Those from the Iberian Peninsular seem to suffer from an almost British incapacity for learning a foreign language.

My companion told me everyone on the landing had known who I was the moment I walked out of my cell. Copies of *Die Telegraaf* had been circulating since early that morning. Had I seen what the police had said about me?

Wincing with embarrassment I admitted it had been pushed under my nose. He asked if I would like to keep his copy when he had finished with it. I thanked him, but said no.

'You do not like what the police say about you?' he asked.

'I find it difficult to believe they weren't pulling my leg,' I said, and asked what an upright young man like him was doing in jail.

He was, he said, a fully qualified nurse who had specialised in cardiac cases. He had applied for a job with a famous hospital on the eastern seaboard of the United States who had asked him to fly over for an interview. Somewhere in mid-Atlantic a passenger had collapsed with a heart attack. The purser had hastily enquired if there was a doctor on board. When this enquiry was repeated, my companion explained that he was not a doctor but an SRN with special qualifications for dealing with cardiac cases, and asked if he could help. He was welcomed enthusiastically by a desperate cabin crew and encouraged to do everything possible for the now semi-conscious passenger with the drugs available in the first-aid equipment.

The man happily recovered but all hell broke loose over the nurse's head. After a successful interview, he returned to Amsterdam to arrange for the disposal of his flat. On landing at Schiphol, he found himself accused of having injected a special drug for the prevention of cardiac arrest whose use was expressly forbidden unless authorised by a doctor. He insisted he had acted independently out of concern for the patient and because no doctor would be available until they reached the airport, more than three hours away. Nevertheless, he was arrested, and was now waiting for his case to be heard.

The decision to prosecute this man who, presumably, had saved a life by his admittedly unauthorised action, seemed a triumph of bureaucracy over common sense, unusual in the Netherlands. These were certainly the victim's feelings. He admitted he felt bitter. The one bright spot had been the reaction of the American hospital. They confirmed that, if he was acquitted, the job would still be open to him. 'If that happens,' he said sadly, 'I think I shall never come back to this country. I'll settle permanently in the United States.'

I have always regretted I never discovered the outcome of this case. All of us in the *Demersluis* were transferred after a week or so. We did not meet again and I never saw any reference to his case in the newspapers. Possibly it was never mentioned; the Netherlands' press has never shown the obsessive interest in court cases that British tabloids do.

Later on this sunny evening, I was accosted by a handsome young black who had a mischievous look in his eyes and an infectious smile. I assumed he must be a Dutch-Surinamer until he suddenly spoke French, asking if, *'par hasard,'* I understood him. When I replied in the same language that I certainly did, the floodgates opened. He was an *emigré* from Guadeloupe and it had been a long time since he had been able to speak French and be understood. Although the Dutch are remarkably fluent in English and German, they are often surprisingly ignorant of even the simplest French.

Jeannot had got a job on a freighter when he was fourteen and had jumped ship two years later in a French port. Since then he had lived by his wits in France and Belgium. Recently he had arrived in the Netherlands and found work in a pub in Amsterdam's *Zeedijk* (red light) area. He had been happy in the job and astonished, after constant insults from the Fleming population of Antwerp, at the lack of racial prejudice amongst the Dutch. *'Ils n'ont pas m'insulté une seule fois!'* he said in amazement. He had managed to pick up a good deal of the language and was doing his best to lose every trace of Flemish accent. The language is basically identical but the accent of Flanders is apt to produce looks of amused condescension from the Dutch.

I asked him if he did not sometimes regret having run away from an island many Europeans consider paradise. He had no wish to return to the Caribbean. 'If I go back I shall be hungry again, and I had enough of hunger as a boy.'

He was anxious to tell me what he had done to get arrested and came close to tears as he explained it was through lack of a visa and work permit. He was sure his *patron* would speak up for him. Did I think that would help him?

I could not honestly give him much reassurance. His *patron* would almost certainly be in trouble for employing someone with no legal right to be in the country. I guessed the small court would expel the lad from the Netherlands. As a French citizen, he would be escorted to the Franco-Belgian frontier and handed over to the French police who would release him immediately, unless he was wanted for some previous offence in that country. But I had little doubt that, like so many of his type, he would be back in Amsterdam within twenty-four hours, looking for a similar, illegal job.

He was a bright, enterprising youth, if a bit young for his twenty years. I tried to persuade him to get the promise of legitimate work from a Dutch employer and supply written evidence of this to the authorities. I could see my advice did not impress him. Like so many youngsters from the Third World who float nowadays around Europe, from capital to capital, snatching a meagre living from the black economy, he was convinced all authority was against him.

For some time we had been followed along the path by a big, brawny Arab who smiled a good deal and whose teeth seemed to be made whiter by his heavy black moustache. He now broke into our conversation and did so in French, supporting, to my surprise, the argument I had been putting forward: that it was occasionally possible for a poor foreigner to find work in the Netherlands and, at the same time, receive a blessing from the underlings of the Ministry of the Interior.

Jeannot was not impressed, but he introduced the Arab with Gallic formality, then added: 'Larbi does not understand my difficulties because he is married to a Dutch girl and is no longer considered a foreigner.

'You could do the same!' said Larbi. 'You've said yourself there is no colour-bar in this country. But please remember I was already working when I met my wife.'

I asked what his work was.

'*Je suis mécanicien dans un garage.*' He had been working in Amsterdam for seven years. He had been married for five and had a son and a daughter.

After such success, what was he doing here? I asked.

He gave me a good-natured grin; it was all because he had got very drunk. '*Vous savez bien, monsieur, que les arabes ne sont pas habitués à boire beaucoup.*' He had beaten somebody up in a bar – the victim had been taken to hospital. The man had insulted him and Larbi had broken his jaw. 'I am strong!' he said. This statement was hardly necessary, he was built like a gorilla.

'Will your victim recover?' I asked.

'*Bien sûr.*'

'Larbi is dangerous,' said Jeannot.

'Not true – only to people who are shit! I could never be dangerous to *ce vieux monsieur anglais, ici!*' He gave me a friendly slap on the back that knocked most of the air out of my lungs.

I asked what Arab country he came from. I had already guessed it must be North Africa.

Algeria. Did I know it?

I had spent a holiday there in the thirties, long before he was born. I had landed at Algiers and driven south to friends in Biskra.

It was now time to return to the tower. As we entered there was a sudden rush to a small window onto an internal courtyard; it was quite a small space compared with the great exercise yard, but open to the sky. The nurse was close to me and I asked him the reason for this sudden excitement.

'It's your compatriot,' he said with a smile. 'The Englishman who kills people. He shot one of our policemen dead a few days ago, and the papers say he has killed before, in England.'

'You mean Alan Reeve?' I asked.

'We don't know his name – only what he is supposed to have done. He's not at present allowed to associate with other prisoners. He even has to take exercise alone.'

I asked where they were keeping him. The question provoked another smile. 'He's in our pavilion – and, what's more, his cell is number 17, next to you! But you're unlikely to see him.'

I found I shared the general anxiety to take a look at this notorious figure. As the guards marshalled us towards the lifts, I managed to catch a glimpse of a tall, skeletal young man with a cap of light brown hair brushed straight back from a high forehead. He was walking alone, his hands in his pockets. I had seldom seen anyone look less dangerous and more lonely.

A tidal wave of prisoners from the lower landing streamed into the lift as we vacated it. It was their turn for fresh air, ours for free association.

My cell was open, so I grabbed towel and spongebag and dashed into the shower-room; the next quarter of an hour was sheer hedonism.

Afterwards, I joined a group lolling in the recreation room in front of a blank television screen. In the weeks to come I realised the pattern adopted by *Demersluis* prisoners during free association was more or less universal throughout the centre. We had our table-tennis enthusiasts and billiards players: snooker seemed to be virtually unknown in the Netherlands. From time to time, couples would play endless games of chess, but the majority only wanted to lounge with their feet up on the low tables in front of the television, with the sound switched off, unless the programme was pop music or *Dynasty*. *Dallas* was almost always ignored.

Everybody was friendly and welcoming. They all knew who I was: such are the advantages of newspaper publicity.

The landing's only Chinese put down the *Telegraaf* and came to sit next to me. He was, I think, anxious to show off his English. He looked hardly more than a boy, with a pale ivory skin, several shades lighter than the Indonesian guards', close-cut hair like blue-black silk. He spoke English with the faintly nasal accent of his native Kowloon. He told me he still travelled on a British passport adding, with a touch of bitterness: 'One of those you issue to subject peoples – to confirm to the world we are second-class citizens!'

Wong (a pseudonym) had a wife and two children and had lived for some years in Amsterdam, ostensibly in the catering trade (Chinese take-away is universal throughout northern Europe). He had hoped to become a Dutch citizen but had blotted his copybook by getting arrested on a charge of importing heroin. Dutch leniency towards drugs offenders does not extend to heroin dealers unless they are also addicts. He had no illusions about his future.

We were later sent to the same tower and, although in different pavilions, we often met in the exercise yard. He was sentenced to twelve years, an exceptional penalty by Dutch standards. Cute and engaging as a Chinese doll, he could be, I was sure, utterly ruthless if anybody got in his way. Like so many of his race, he delighted in any form of gambling and was disappointed to learn I was no relation of the founder of the Clermont Club in London's Berkeley Square.

I spent the next morning writing an account of some of the more creditable episodes in my life. In the afternoon I went out for exercise, spending much of the hour with the Algerian, Larbi, zig-zagging around the shrubs and sitting on the grass while he sprawled in the sun like a giant, lazy cat.

Lying on his back, he pulled open his shirt to disentangle a small medallion on a thin gold chain from the cruciform of black chest hair. He took it off to show me. It was a St Christopher, and a good one: many look as if they had been found in a Christmas cracker: this was obviously the work of a master craftsman in 18-carat gold.

I asked him why a good Muslim wore an effigy of a Christian saint.

He gave me a wide grin of splendid animal teeth. 'I tell you yesterday I like Englishmen, yes? That I have good English friend?'

'I believe you did mention it.' I felt it would be tactless to add that my years in North Africa had taught me to treat those who spoke my language, even hesitantly, with a certain caution.

'*C'était un cadeau*, a present from my English friend. He has been good to me and I wear it for his sake. After all, it can't do me any harm!'

I agreed it was unlikely to hurt him and handed it back saying, truthfully, it was one of the best I had ever seen. I asked if he had met his English friend in Algeria.

'Ah no,' he said, 'here in Amsterdam.' They had met in a bar whose name I knew well. It was on the edge of the red light district and had a reputation as a rendezvous for Arab hustlers – most of whom had legitimate jobs but were not unwilling to add to their incomes by getting picked up by the passive homosexuals who frequented the bar. 'We met seven years ago and he has come back regularly to see me ever since.'

'*C'est un pédale?*' I asked.

'*Bien sûr, mais il est gentil quand même,*' he said defensively. 'He has done a great deal for me. He helped me with money to get married. He comes with his car. It is a Renault and I work for a Renault agency. He always has it serviced while he is here and recently he bought a new one through my *patron*. This does my reputation much good. Because of him my job will still be waiting for me when I get out.'

'Is he a young man?'

'*Ah non! Plus jeune que toi, mais pas beaucoup.*'

Larbi's relationship with an elderly Englishman did not surprise me. I have known of many similar liaisons, some lasting more than thirty years. Few North African Arabs are wholly homosexual but many have a streak of bisexuality which the Muslim attitude towards women tends to activate from puberty. Being highly sexed they will then take on anybody – even anything – as a sexual partner. Arabs are not romantic about sex; all they want is a straightforward screw in which they are the active partner; if this can earn them money, or other material advantage, so much the better.

During free association that evening I noticed my name, among others, on the big noticeboard outside the recreation room. I was to attend the small court at ten o'clock the following morning. This would be a formality to extend the time I could be kept on remand.

At the appointed hour I was ushered into the courtroom next to, and almost identical to, that of the judge of instruction – except that the long central table had been arranged across the room instead of lengthways.

All the chairs around it were occupied except for two, close to the door. Mrs Johanssen, sitting next to these spaces, held out her hand to me. There was a general hush as I sat down.

Directly across the table was a distinguished-looking man of about forty-five who patronised a good tailor and shirtmaker and was actually wearing a tie. He was flanked by casually-dressed individuals of both sexes whose significance I never found out.

Mrs Johanssen did her best to set the scene for me. 'In front of you,' she explained, 'is the presiding judge. On your left, at the end of the table, you will recognise the public prosecutor ... '

I had already discerned his chubby face. In fact, my immediate impression was of a band of pleasant-looking juveniles, all at least thirty years younger than me.

My interpreter's whispered guide was interrupted by the arrival of Jan Drukker who apologised to the judge for being late and slipped into the chair beside me. He launched into an appeal that the court should allow me parole for twelve hours to arrange storage of my possessions.

I was sure I could detect a look of sympathy from everybody around the table. Surely none could doubt that, given a few hours' freedom, I would return at the appointed time? Being old and penniless, I was hardly likely to begin a life on the run.

Unfortunately, the authority to grant parole was, in this court, vested solely in the public prosecutor. When the request was finally put to him, the answer was a flat negative.

This brought a *sotto voce* expression of regret from my interpreter and a look of suppressed fury from my lawyer.

The urbane judge returned to the subject of remand and authorised that I should continue to be held for (I think) another fourteen days. The session was over.

Jan Drukker and I withdrew, after I had murmured thanks to Mrs Johanssen who was remaining to translate for other prisoners. English was only one of her languages.

Drukker told me probation had promised to send somebody to take up my case either that afternoon or the following morning. 'Tell whoever turns up to telephone me,' he said, 'and we'll solve the problem of that stuff in your flat.'

I was at work on my autobiography the following morning when the chief guard came in and, with a suspiciously deadpan expression, told me I was wanted by the *reclasseringsambtenaaur*.

Stunned, I said faintly: 'By whom?'

His serious expression dissolved into a smile. 'In English you say probation service. Here, I admit we usually shorten that big word and say, simply, *reclassering*.'

I arrived at the security guards' office to be greeted with cries of '*Ah, reclassering voor* Sir Anthony!'

There was a good deal of good-humoured banter before I was led to that now familiar corridor lined with cubicles.

My probation officer was a diminutive lady with light brown hair piled, somewhat casually, on top of her head in a cottage loaf; a delicately tanned face devoid of make-up; large grey-blue eyes and a smile that showed a genuine sense of fun as well as kindness. She was wearing a loosely-fitting frock of printed Provençal cotton with beautifully polished, low-heeled leather shoes.

She swept me into a cubicle, pushed me into a chair and said in impeccable English: 'I'm sure you're dying for coffee, I know I am. Stay there while I get it.' She shot away along the corridor to what I now learned was a canteen for visitors.

We sipped as we talked. For me to do this without making a face was a test of my acting ability, for the coffee had been heavily laced with sugar and synthetic milk. I had not the heart to tell her I loathe both.

She told me to call her Françoise and handed me her card. It was an official one, with the name and address of the organisation to which she belonged. It showed she was a *mevrouw* with no fewer than six initials and a surname among the most distinguished in the Netherlands. It added that she was a specialist in alcohol and drugs abuse.

She snatched the card from me and wrote something on the back, saying: 'I've added my private address and number. If you find yourself in an emergency, don't hesitate to ring. If you tell the guards it's a call to your *reclassering* there will be no opposition.' She sat back and looked at me. Her smiling face reminded me of a russet apple, she looked so wholesome and healthy. 'I've told you to call me Françoise,' she said, 'I'm going to call you Tony – after all, I'm not a great deal younger than you are.'

'Give or take about forty years,' I said.

She shook her head with a laugh. 'It would be nice for me if that were true.' Then, more seriously, she asked if I had any serious problems.

While admitting it could not be described as serious, I explained I was now almost obsessively concerned about the contents of my flat. 'If only I could be paroled for a few hours, I could pack everything I want to keep. The rest could be given to charity and the rubbish thrown out. But the public prosecutor refused parole.'

'A pity I wasn't appointed to your case a few days ago. I could have asked for you to be paroled into my charge. The prosecutor might have agreed – he's done so before.'

'What makes you so sure I wouldn't run away?'

'The police report – and my own instincts.'

Briskly taking a sheet of paper from her bag, she put it in front of me with her pen. 'Make me a list, right now, of everything in your flat you wish to keep. Then make another column of things to be given away, or thrown away.'

The lists seemed shorter than I expected. I wondered how many things I had forgotten and said so.

'Then you'll have to let me decide what to do with the unexpected. Let's hope I won't make too many mistakes. What I'm really concerned about is where to take your luggage.'

'My lawyer says there's room in his firm's attic in the Prinsengracht.'

'Splendid! All I have to do is to take it there and dump it?'

'I'm afraid it's a dreadful job ... '

'Nonsense, it's what I'm here for – that and your spiritual and physical welfare. How is your welfare, by the way?'

'All the better for seeing you!'

'Stop talking nonsense and write down the lawyer's phone number. It's a Mr Drukker, isn't it?'

I nodded as I wrote down the number.

'I don't know him, but I know the senior partner, Mr van Akker – a nice man, and a good lawyer, too. I think you're in good hands.'

'I'm sure I am.'

'Is there anything in your flat you want me to bring here?'

'Oh God – I'd forgotten. My radio – it's a smallish one – and my portable typewriter which is abominably heavy. Get somebody to carry it for you.'

'That won't be necessary. I'm stronger than I look.'

She asked many questions about myself and my background; the sort of life I had lived and the opinions I had formed. As we talked I remembered several more items, tucked away in cupboards or drawers, that I wanted to keep or to have thrown away.

Our chat was interrupted by a security guard asking if Françoise wanted to see the other prisoner on her list. It was getting late. Should they send for him or cancel?

She gave a squawk of amazement that the time had gone so quickly. Of course she wanted to see the other prisoner. 'It's your friend Dinos!' she said. Both of you are now my responsibility.' Half seriously, she added: 'Has he also a flat I must empty?'

'He has a flat, but I'm sure his girlfriend will cope.' She looked relieved.

As I left she asked me to arrange with the admin office for her to borrow my flat key, and promised to return within a few days with my radio and typewriter. I felt greatly relieved.

On my way back to the *Demersluis*, I spied Dinos sauntering in the opposite direction. It was the first time we had run into each other since the police station. Having a romantic turn of mind, he asked if I did not consider the walkways to be exactly like a spaceship. Not being a devotee of science fiction, this had not occurred to me, but forever afterwards he and I referred to the 'spaceship'.

He also wanted to hear about Françoise. I saw his macho Greek emotions rising to the surface, infecting the co-educated, clean-cut Canadian with a feeling that, in some intangible way, his masculinity was being impugned.

'Probation people are for kids, or the sick,' he said. 'Not for guys like you and me.'

I disagreed, saying how much I had appreciated her help.

'My girlfriend would have done it all for you,' he insisted. He then asked if I would agree to us being on the same landing when we were moved.

I said I would be delighted – but would the authorities allow it?

'I've already asked the welfare guy,' he said. 'He's checked and says there'll be no objection. We've both admitted joint responsibility for importing the coke, so there's no reason to keep us apart. I guess he'll ask for your reaction before it's finally agreed.'

'I'll tell him it's OK by me.'

'Great! I suppose the police haven't sent for you again, have they?'

'No, why should they?'

'They had me down at headquarters yesterday afternoon, for about an hour with the inspector.'

'What did he want?'

'He was very civilised – very laid back. He wanted names and addresses of anybody I knew who was engaged in importing hard drugs into this prosperous little piece of waterlogged real estate. In other words, would I grass on my friends.'

'What did he offer in exchange?'

'Just a few hints that the public prosecutor would take a lenient view of my criminal behaviour. Naturally, I refused.'

'You think they'll try the same tactics with me?'

'I doubt it. They've convinced themselves you're the perfect English gentleman – and perfect gents aren't good material for converting into police narks! I must go to meet this broad who's waiting for me. Is she beautiful?'

'She's nice,' I said firmly.

'Nice?' he echoed. 'That means a dirndl with bare legs and sandals, I suppose?'

'Go and meet her. You'll be pleasantly surprised.'

'I hope so. You're in pavilion 3, aren't you? I'm in 5.'

'Right at the top?'

Two patrolling guards, deep in conversation, walked past.

'Sure,' said Dinos. As he moved off, he gave me a provocative grin and called loudly over his shoulder: 'It's going to be a long drop when I finally get the cell window out of its frame!'

If the guards, who were still within earshot, heard him, they gave no sign.

The next morning I did indeed receive a visit from a chubby, pink-faced welfare officer who was part of the centre's establishment. He was anxious to point out the disadvantages of being even in the same tower as Dinos and did his best to persuade me to accept a transfer to another block. The routine in at least two of them, he assured me, was far more liberal than in the one picked out for my friend.

I asked why Dinos should be barred from this much-vaunted easygoing atmosphere.

Because of his previous record, was the not unexpected reply.

Surely I knew he had escaped from a Swiss jail less than a year ago? Did I not know the guards at this Geneva prison had shot dead another prisoner attempting to escape less than a week before Dinos had made his successful bid? (I did.) Surely I must realise this showed him to be a high security risk and a dangerous man?

I could not agree that Dinos should be described as dangerous. We had been friends for over seven years and I knew how much he disliked physical violence. 'It may surprise you to learn,' I snapped, 'that we've a number of mutual friends with young children who have often said, if they were to die suddenly they hoped Dinos would adopt their beloved infants – because they were always so happy with him.'

Chubby-Face, embarrassed by my vehemence, said: 'But a man who has already made one escape – and who has two more years of his sentence to serve – he must be treated with a certain caution. Surely you understand?'

'I know he walked out of that prison without laying a finger on anybody. He did it by chipping away, night after night, the cement round his window frame. It took him three months before he was able to lift out the window. He knotted his sheets into a rope and dropped to the ground where, in spite of the floodlighting, none of the guards noticed his departure. I believe they only discovered he'd gone when the governor received a letter from across the French frontier, apologising for the damage and suggesting that if a bill for the repair were sent to his bankers in Athens, the amount would be met in full. And you call that man dangerous?'

'All you've said tells me he's very good at escaping.' Chubby-Face was almost pleading. 'When he is moved it will be to a tower with a similar routine to the *Demersluis*, where the cell doors are only open during free association. Are you quite sure you wish to be with your friend?'

Without hesitation, I said: 'Yes, I'm quite sure.'

I doubt if that worthy young man knew my decision was not entirely unselfish. Having been sandwiched for almost two years with well over a hundred others in the notorious 'pit' of the Damascus Citadel, to me, being alone was a luxury, even behind a locked door. Those blocks where the cells were open all day were not the magnet they were to many others. When Chubby-Face left me, still shaking his head in disapproval, I put the finishing touches to my brief autobiography.

I had begun the story of my life by explaining I was the descendant of a prosperous family of Liverpool merchants who had been sailmakers and shipbuilders on the banks of the Mersey in the sixteenth and seventeenth centuries. In the eighteenth century they had enormously increased the family's fortune out of the slave trade. I was a direct descendant of the William Aspinall, subsequently known as 'the old devil', who found it more profitable to allow his ships' captains to throw overboard any black who became sick during the Atlantic crossing, because a larger sum could be obtained from marine insurance for 'cargo' lost at sea than from the sale of an ailing slave. By such tough trading methods the wealth of Imperial England was built up.

In the early years of the nineteenth century, my immediate forbears had acquired breweries in Lancashire and North Wales at a time when the newly urbanised working classes liked to wash down a pennyworth of gin with a draught of ale, a habit that played hell with their health and domestic life. None of this impeded my great-grandfathers from becoming justices of the peace, masters of hounds and churchwardens. By the time I was born, in the first decade of this century, the number of breweries had been reduced to two and the bonanza of the previous 150 years was declining rapidly, although ships built by other members of my family had only just ceased to transport opium by the ton (quite legally) from Calcutta to Shanghai.

After a brief mention of school and a year of pleasurable idleness in the cafés of St Germain des Prés while ostensibly a foreign student at the University of Paris, I pointed out that for much of my life I had been employed by international organisations working on behalf of the less fortunate of the human race: a perhaps surprising activity for someone with my ancestry. This began in the final stages of the Second World War, when I assisted in the evacuation of the infamous Belsen concentration camp. From that moment onwards, until I was approaching sixty, I was involved with the resettlement of refugees and in trying to improve the quality of their lives.

Eventually, I had to give this up to look after my mother, who was approaching ninety. I did the job that in Victorian England was usually performed by the youngest daughter. My mother, an autocratic old lady, suffering from the steadily increasing ravages of arteriosclerosis, had no daughter and I was her only son. All my efforts to find someone she would consider suitable to look after her ended in failure. So, with a daily visit from a district nurse, I combined the functions of housekeeper and cook-general for the last few years of her life.

After her death I went abroad again, this time to Morocco. I had decided, perhaps selfishly, to live out whatever time was left in doing something for myself.

I chose Tangier, which I had known since I was a boy in the days when the smaller liners, plying between the United Kingdom and India or East Africa, via the Suez Canal, would anchor in its crescent-shaped bay and passengers had to land or embark in rowing boats.

I had always felt if I were to settle somewhere permanently in old age, it would be on the outskirts of this small but ancient city, built on seven hills at the junction of the Atlantic and the Mediterranean; a place that is no longer Europe and yet not quite North Africa, in spite of the narrow streets of its Medina with their pungent smells of kif, coffee spiced with cardomom, mint-tea and donkey shit.

Tangier has always had a substantial colony of European and American residents. Many of the British expatriates were retired members of the armed forces or the foreign service; the majority being bachelors, one was spared the presence of those bridge-playing, blue-rinsed wives that make the Algarve, the Spanish *costas* and the French Riviera so intolerable. In addition there was, in those days, a small group of young adventurers – mostly Scots or Australians – busy smuggling cigarettes into Italy and kif into Spain in fast, but not always seaworthy, motor boats. I much enjoyed the company of these youthful buccaneers, although it never occurred to me, at that stage of my life, to join them in their illegal enterprises.

I was, however, unwise enough to invest my small capital in a bar which had been expressly designed to resemble the interior of a Russian *dacha* by its original owner, a glamorous Slav lady whose father had been Roumanian, her mother Russian, and who had been born in Bulgaria. In appearance, Natasha was very much a *femme fatale*; she was rumoured to be the dear friend of a successful industrialist whose business interests were largely concentrated in Casablanca – a noisy city she detested. So she had made her home in Tangier, preferring its gentler, hybrid atmosphere to the raucous Casa.

She operated the bar herself with a devoted staff of four Moroccans. Opening hours tended to be elastic – depending on whether she was in the mood to be a gracious hostess. If the customers bored her she would turn them out, shut the place, dismiss the staff for the night and go home to bed. If she was in a happy frame of mind she could be enchanting, especially if she could be persuaded to sing some of the sad folksongs of Eastern Europe to her own guitar accompaniment. Although the bar was always well-stocked with every kind of drink, she was a past mistress at making customers feel that to order anything but the best champagne would be a grave social gaffe.

By the time I took over the little *dacha*, it had ceased to be quite so idiosyncratically up-market and I was happy to offer my customers a much wider selection of wines, spirits and even two brands of Moroccan beer. I ran it with a staff of four, two of whom had been employed by the gorgeous Natasha and still worshipped her. In winter, I worked behind the bar from 9.30 in the evening until 2.30 in the morning. From May until October, when Tangier was invaded by legions of homosexuals from Northern Europe and the United States who spent money like there was no tomorrow, I would often not put up the shutters until 7 AM. I would then drive to my home outside the city, take a shower, have three hours' sleep and return to check the bar stock before midday. Perhaps surprisingly, as I was already over sixty, I thrived on this life, enjoying it enormously.

It was gratifying to be told by some of Tangier's older residents that my bar was the best thing that had happened since the demise of the famous Dean, who had been a legend in his own lifetime. Dean's bar, a lot smaller than my own, had been for years a popular rendezvous for the resident international colony and for a great many visitors. There is an affectionate portrait of Dean in one of Ann Bridge's novels and venomous caricatures in the works of Rupert Croft-Cooke and Robin Maugham. He liked people to believe he was the son of a titled Englishwoman and an Egyptian *dragoman*; a harmless form of vanity that could have been true or just romantic fiction. Like all good barmen, he knew most of the secret vices of his clientele – some of them hair-raising – and kept this knowledge to himself, although much of the information he was able to give British intelligence during the last war was said to be extremely useful.

My interlude as a bar-owner was brought to an end by an unexpected fit of fundamentalist morality on the part of the Moroccan authorities. Without warning, they took away my licence. It was the summer invasion of so many screaming queens from Europe and America (North and South) that provided the excuse. Tangier, as far back as the Roman occupation of North Africa, has always been a rallying point for homosexuals and my bar and two others were accused of being the magnets that continued to attract them.

I received better treatment than the other two owners, a Frenchman and a Belgian. Their bars were raided, staff and customers being taken away in *panniers à salade* to the evil-smelling cells of the local *sûreté*. The customers were released after a few days without charges; the Belgian was kept in custody for a week and then left the country so quickly it was said he had been deported; serious charges were brought against the Frenchman who was later condemned to a long prison sentence. The only action taken against me was the cancellation of my licence.

I was told, off the record, by a good friend in the local *sûreté*, that the scheme to shut down every so-called gay bar in the city had been plotted for some time at a high government level in Rabat, and the excuse to put it into action had been an article in a quality British Sunday newspaper. I knew immediately this must have been the *Observer* and the author had been Katherine Whitehorn. She had been staying with friends in Tangier and her facts were, as always, strictly accurate; but the tone of her article had been gently mocking and had been printed under the, to us, unfortunate heading: 'Queersville on Sea'.

My friend warned me that, even with a change of owner, the bar was unlikely ever to be licensed again. Consequently, I had to dispose of the lease for a fraction of what I had paid for the 'good will'. I then discovered my accountant had for a long time been lining his pockets with the sums given him to pay the bar's taxes and had now done a moonlight flit to another country. It was no comfort that I was not his only victim; several of my friends had also been defrauded.

I settled my tax-debts by selling all my old furniture, silver and glass, returning to Europe at the age of sixty-five, devoid of possessions, capital or income, to hawk myself around an unsympathetic employment market with steadily increasing despair.

At this moment I happened to pick up a well-known travel guide. One that, a few years later, received a flattering review in the *Observer*, where it was described (but not by Miss Whitehorn) as the homosexual *Baedeker*. It is published annually in English, German, French and Spanish from offices in Amsterdam. This edition had a section devoted to tourism in Morocco so out of date it almost induced physical pain. I could not resist writing to the editor with a long list of corrections and amendments. To my surprise, he rang me the morning he received the letter. After talking for an hour and forty-five minutes (I was to learn that this was his usual practice, not only with associates in Europe but also those in the Far East, New Zealand, Australia and America – simultaneously complaining bitterly of the high cost of his company's telephone bills!) he ended this marathon by saying: 'Come over and join us. As you're not too flush financially, take the day boat via Hook. I'll meet your train the day after tomorrow. It gets in around a quarter to eight in the evening. Be there!'

I was, and remained with the publishing house for several years.

I was still working for them when a Greek friend lent me his cottage on the island of Samos for a late autumn holiday. Here, I ran into two young American acquaintances from Amsterdam who I knew were involved in the drugs scene.

When the time came to close up the cottage, I accepted an invitation from the Americans to drive with them (they had a large Mercedes) through southern Turkey and the north of Syria into the Lebanon – a journey that ended for me in the Beka'a Valley, as a guest of one of the great hashish-growing dynasties of that beautiful country.

In their large white villa not far from Baalbek, I met a steady stream of those involved in the world-wide distribution of marijuana. My hosts were lavishly hospitable to their guests from the four corners of the earth, as well as from every country in Europe on both sides of the Iron Curtain.

I relished the international atmosphere, even in the cold, damp houses, where ostentatious luxury contrasted sharply with the more primitive world of the Middle East. The marble bathrooms were magnificent, but the water would often be cut off for days, and the bidets and wcs would, frequently, have been blocked for weeks, and smelt like it. It was late November and the mountains were snow-capped. The days were like a perfect English summer, but the nights were cold and even rich Lebanese only use small charcoal-burning stoves in winter. They believe all other forms of heating to be unhealthy and suffer more from summer heat than winter cold.

I liked most of the visitors enormously. Like almost all whose chosen way of life is under attack from a venial and ignorant officialdom, they were thoughtful, quick-witted, generous and tolerant of human frailty.

Having worked for most of my life in countries where it is freely permitted to buy medication and not have to sit in a doctor's malodorous waiting-room to beg for a prescription, I have long been convinced that all free men and women should have the right to take whatever illusion-providing drug they fancy – as long as they know what they are doing.

Certainly all soft drugs should be made available and for sale at cost price. This would effectively put the skids under the pushers and the Drug Enforcement Agency, who both have a vested interest in maintaining the status quo. Label each drug with a health warning similar to that now compulsory for cigarettes. But do not lie about it – do not suggest hashish, cannabis or marijuana are as dangerous or addictive as nicotine or alcohol, for there are millions who know this to be untrue. I have a suspicion these methods would have been adopted long ago if it were not for a political ramp, activated by powerful drink and tobacco lobbies, who dread the increasing popularity of mind-bending substances other than the ones from which they can profit.

Instead of behaving sensibly, governments have allowed themselves to be influenced by the paranoia of the United States who, during the First World War, thought it had a divine mission to stamp out the evils of drink and, in doing so, unleashed the greatest crime wave in the history of that country, and is now stupidly repeating the mistake.

It would be salutary if customs and excise were called to heel and reminded that many of today's great fortunes were founded on wealth gained by the 'pushing' of 'black ivory' into the West Indies and opium into China by British merchant families such as my own. I feel it ill becomes those stuffed to the gills with alcohol and tobacco to harass people who prefer drugs less injurious to health and well-being.

When I handed this screed to Jan Drukker, I told him he was free to blue-pencil any part of it. I learned later he attached it to my dossier without deleting a word.

Having finished this somewhat incautious account, I told the chief guard I wanted to start work as soon as possible. Doubtless due to his good influence I began the following day.

This so-called work – it hardly merited the name – took place in large workshops on the ground floor of each tower. Each director made his own arrangements with commercial firms willing to subcontract various simple tasks to be carried out by prisoners.

The work in the *Demersluis* was provided by a supplier of office equipment and stationery. Two, three or four of us sat at small tables putting typing paper into cardboard boxes or brightly coloured plastic envelopes.

The job quickly became so automatic I could almost have done it in my sleep. The *werkmeester*, a tough-looking but agreeable Dutchman with fair curly hair, who looked like a grown-up version of Millais's 'Bubbles', raised his eyebrows in amusement at the end of my first afternoon's employment, saying I had completed a week's work and would I, please, slow down a bit! I did my best to oblige.

We were all paid the flat rate of 25 guilders for a five-day week: a sum worth, at that time, about £5.60. I was able to live quite comfortably on this. None of us ever saw a single coin or banknote. We would get a weekly statement from the finance department, showing how much we were in credit, or the reverse.

On our weekly shopping spree, I would buy fresh fruit (they even stocked avocados), butter and honey and, because I have always been something of a health freak, quantities of muesli and yoghurt; also an occasional carton of washing powder. I began by wearing (and washing) my own underwear, but quickly switched to the prison issue of good quality white cotton. Each week we were issued with two T-shirt type vests and two pairs of briefs, as well as a clean sheet and pillow-slip. Everything was washed in the laundry operated by the prisoners from the women's tower. This, I believe, was the only employment available to women prisoners and seemed a surprisingly chauvinistic arrangement for the Netherlands, where women's lib has a powerful voice.

At the end of my first week's work I was surprised to see a bonus of ten guilders credited to my account. Although the *werkmeester* had frequently patted my head, saying: 'Too much speed – too much speed!' he must have decided I deserved a reward, and I was grateful for the additional 'capital'.

I soon received a note from the indefatigable Françoise, telling me she had delivered my radio and typewriter to the admin offices. They would shortly find their way to me through the usual channels.

She also told me that the owner of my flat had been waiting to greet her and had already packed my possessions. It had only been necessary for her to drive my half-dozen suitcases to the lawyers' office – any sorting out would have to be done when I was released. I was only later to learn that Françoise had locked herself out of her car outside my flat, and had had to take a taxi to fetch her spare keys. In future, she declared, she would keep them on a chain around her neck!

340

The typewriter and radio arrived only an hour or so after her note. Although Hilversum 1 and 2 were piped into our cells – with dials to switch from one to the other and control the volume – it was a boon to listen to the BBC's Radio 4 which, on long wave, can be heard as distinctly in the Netherlands as in England.

Midway through my second week, I was told I was to be transferred within a couple of hours to a tower called *het Schouw*. I heard the news with mild regret; although almost all the prisoners had changed since my arrival, I had grown to feel comfortable with the staff.

The more knowledgeable prisoners were astonished to hear I was going to the *Schouw*, which had a fairly tough reputation. Besides, I was destined for pavilion 5, right at the top and normally reserved for the more dangerous type. Why was I being put in among the heavies, they wanted to know. I shrugged my shoulders and let them make inaccurate guesses.

After lunch I was given bin-liners into which I emptied my drawers and cupboards. Now, having to cope also with typewriter and radio, I loaded everything on to a supermarket-type trolley – every pavilion had a small stock.

I said what I believed to be *au revoir* to the guards on duty; but in fact, although I was moving only a few hundred yards, I was never to see them again.

The quiet, gentle chief guard, who had met me when I first stag- gered out of the lift, conducted me back to it, saying that if I found life in the *Schouw* too restrictive – that was his term – I could always put in an application for transfer. Such a request, he was sure, would get a sympathetic response.

HET SCHOUW

The corridor into my new tower was identical with that of the *Demersluis*. I surrendered my green identity-card, and was later issued with an orange one.

As I wheeled my trolley into a lift, a young prisoner leapt in beside me, carrying beakers of coffee on a tray. He raised his head in the direction of the lift's microphone and shouted, to my surprise, in English: 'Coffee for the guards' meeting in pavilion 4.'

As the lift ascended, he looked at me with obvious curiosity.

In reply to his unspoken question, I said: 'Yes, I'm English.'

'Christ! For months I've been the only Englishman in this tower and now I'm going, two of you come in!'

'Are you being released?' I asked.

'Wish I was. No, I've got a four-year stretch ahead of me. They don't keep you here for long once you've been sentenced – I'm going to this new prison, somewhere up north.' He asked which pavilion I was going to, and told me the other Englishman was in 5 too.

I thought he must be referring to Dinos. 'Don't you mean a Canadian?' I queried.

'No, English – been up there several weeks, a Londoner – comes from Hackney.'

The lift jerked to a halt. We had reached pavilion 4.

'Sorry I can't offer you any coffee. The guards in this pavilion are having their weekly get-together to discuss problems. They'll need all of it to give them strength! I expect we'll see each other quite often before I'm sent to the frozen north! I'm a sort of general dogsbody for the director and staff – within the tower I can go where I want. It's a good job,' he called over his shoulder, 'you should try for it when I leave.'

I did indeed see quite a lot of this young Englishman during my first weeks in the *Schouw*. We always met at the weekly film shows for the whole tower and he would often join pavilion 5 for daily exercise.

The landing I arrived at was identical to the one in the *Demersluis*: the same shining white paint, the same light oak panelling.

The chief guard gave me a friendly welcome. He was considerably larger and tougher in appearance than my good friend in the other tower. He was also much younger and heavily moustached.

The pavilion was almost oppressively silent. I guessed one landing must be at work, the other at exercise.

The guard showed me to my cell and helped unload my trolley, saying I could rearrange the movable furniture however I wanted. After telling me the evening meal would be at five-thirty and free association from six-thirty until eight, he took away the trolley and locked the door.

The cell was identical to the one I had just left, except that it had a wonderful view over the north-eastern suburbs of Amsterdam.

Immediately below was a wide expanse of grass; I was too high up to glimpse the moat round the whole prison. A hundred yards away was a minor road lined, intermittently, by small semi-detached houses of pink and yellow brick. I recognised a shortcut I sometimes took to visit friends in the outlying district of Duivendrecht. Beyond the road was a greenish-blue ribbon of water – the Weespertrekvaart – a barge canal that links the River Amstel with the open water of the Ijsel Meer, about seven miles away – on which motor cruisers were travelling sedately. Having enjoyed messing about in boats since early childhood, the spectacle delighted me.

On the far side of the canal, the tall trees in two of Amsterdam's largest parks, that interconnect – the Prins Bernard and the Juliana Parks – seemed to stretch into infinity. It was a panorama that never failed to please me, and I immediately pushed the bed under the window where I could lie and watch the constant traffic along the canal. In winter, there were no yachts but always plenty of commercial craft, the enormous, black, diesel-engined barges that carry cargo along the rivers and canals of northern Europe.

The evening meal appeared punctually, delivered by two blond, blue-eyed guards who were cheerful and friendly. They left me a lengthy form for ordering newspapers and magazines; you had to tick those you wished credited to your account. Although most of the publications listed were Dutch, it was possible to have any European daily delivered to your cell door. Having a good wireless set, I decided, in my present state of penury, to do without an English newspaper.

In fact, a Moroccan on my landing would generously insist on sharing his copy of *Le Monde* with me. He belonged to one of the rich and princely families of Fez and was a graduate of Montpellier University. Accused of dealing in heroin, the case against him had later to be dropped for lack of evidence.

A kind friend in England also provided me with a subscription to the *Spectator*; alas, no longer the exhilarating weekly it had been when owned by Sir John Gilmour and edited by Brian Inglis, when its regular contributors included the youthfully provocative Katherine Whitehorn and Bernard Levin. It had not yet, however, sunk to its present level of High Anglican/Holy Roman priggishness.

But it was the magazine section that provided the greatest amusement. As well as the many titles concerned with politics, motor cars, sailing, photography, computers and so on, there was a substantial group of hard-core pornographic monthlies. I laughed to myself when I noticed the number of illustrated homosexual porno-mags was almost as great as those portraying heterosexuality.

At half-past six our free association period began. I found Dinos, grinning broadly, waiting to greet me. We had a lot to discuss.

He had already been in pavilion 5 for several days and introduced me to other prisoners as they watched billiards and table-tennis or went to take a shower.

'Some of these guys are pretty tough,' he murmured. 'Quite a few have a history of violence.'

He sounded so surprised I could not resist asking if the welfare officer had not muttered a few words of warning about his own reputation. Nothing, apparently, had been said and he found it difficult to believe I was not pulling his leg.

Looking around, I found it hard to credit anyone in this international crowd of boyish-looking men treating each other with ribald but good-tempered courtesy could ever have deliberately injured anybody.

It was the other Briton on the landing who first interrupted our mobile tête-à-tête. Ian's appearance was as Scottish as his name, but he had been born and brought up in north-east London and firmly discouraged any reference to his ancestry. 'My great-grandfather,' he would say in his London accent, 'took the high road south from Paisley, but it was all a fucking long time ago.' He was in trouble because of an affray in which he had threatened a couple of policemen with a sawn-off shotgun. Just over thirty, he had shining black hair, a ruddy skin and eyes like chips of blue-grey ice. Since early adolescence he had experimented with a succession of hard drugs and subsequently kicked the habit. He had begun a life outside the law while still a schoolboy and had spent long periods in various Borstals before graduating to more prestigious 'nicks' in the British Isles. Contemptuous of those who rob individuals, it was obvious that banks and post offices had good reason for apprehension if he were in their neighbourhood.

He was the product of a broken home and his own marriage had suffered a similar fate. He had two small daughters for whom he obviously cared very deeply. I never asked why he had come to Amsterdam, which he knew as intimately as I did. He was also very much at home in certain areas of the Mediterranean, from the Greek islands to the Spanish *costas*. His temper could be violent but the spasms of fury were always short-lived and he was capable of extraordinary kindness and generosity.

I shall not forget how he asked immediately if there was anything I needed; how he dragged me into his cell and invited me to choose whatever I wanted. Did I need extra food? Would I like jam, honey, marmalade, cornflakes, biscuits? How about something to read – would I care to borrow any books? He had catholic tastes; his shelves were loaded with a wide selection of biographies and a good deal of Gavin Maxwell, Thesiger, Graham Greene, le Carré and Ambler in paperback. He had a portable typewriter – lighter, more up-to-date than my own – would I care to borrow it? I told him I would be very happy just to accept the loan of Patrick Leigh Fermor's *A Time of Gifts*, a book which I re-read every few years, on each occasion with increased pleasure. My own copy, bought immediately after first publication in the early 1970s, was stolen by some anonymous thief whom I have never felt inclined to forgive.

In spite of his rages and a tendency to be surly early in the day (if you wished him a cheerful good morning, he might well snarl, 'What's fucking good about it?') I enjoyed Ian's company enormously.

Another who made a considerable impression on me that first evening was Bob – a Dutchman, despite his name. He resembled a pale, languid, but endearing polecat; and was always draping himself over furniture as if devoid of bones. He spoke English so well he could almost have passed for an Englishman; he had even picked up that vile habit of interposing 'you know' after practically every sentence.

In the late 1970s, Bob had served a two-year sentence in Lebanon for attempting to export hashish through Beirut, having failed to appreciate the necessity of establishing a close connection with at least one of the authorities dominating that airport. He had been shut up with a dozen Europeans and Americans – no contact was permitted with Lebanese prisoners, and no access to the open air or any physical exercise was allowed, even in summer. Every prisoner when released, he assured me, looked like a wilting hot-house plant.

He was now awaiting trial in the Hague, because substantial quantities of hash had been discovered in some premises he owned near Rotterdam's docks. I did not learn until sometime later that he was also accused of threatening to kill a runner who was attempting to blackmail him. The blackmailer had panicked, leapt out of a window and rushed to the nearest police station where he 'sang' loudly.

Living in close proximity to Bob for many months, I found him a gentle creature. It was hard to believe anybody could take his threat to kill seriously. The Arabs in the pavilion (we had three, two Moroccans and one Tunisian) had convinced themselves that Bob, because of his languid manner, must be *un pédé*. They were wrong, of course. The first time he had been in trouble with the law was for getting an under-age girl pregnant when he was fifteen.

And then there was Wim, who looked like every mother's *beau idéal* of a son. He had red-gold hair, cornflower blue eyes, the pink skin of a baby and the epicene looks of a Michelangelo angel. Seldom has physical appearance been more deceptive as I learned, when he asked Dinos and myself, with genuine concern, if it was true we had been victims of an informer. Would we be satisfied, he wanted to know, if the man's knees were capped with a shotgun, or would we prefer something more lethal? He could not have been more casual had he been asking if we preferred Indian tea to China.

Dinos and I were open-mouthed. Our silence obviously made him think we were calculating the expense of such a revenge, because he said quickly it would all be done by his staff and cost us nothing. Just a friendly gesture. He was deadly serious.

We hastily assured him we were by no means sure anyone had informed against us and anyway, we were not vengeful types. Wim seemed disappointed and, I suspect, looked on us from then on as sentimental amateurs in the criminal world.

Neither Dinos nor I made any effort to probe into Wim's background. We felt it wiser not to ask questions. We knew him to be the leader of a mafia-type organisation involved in smuggling hard drugs into the Netherlands and Pakistani emigrants into Britain and Canada. Just how much he continued to dominate his henchmen outside, and to plan their activities, we never knew. His manner indicated he was still confident of being the boss. He was also very much a family man. His attractive wife was a constant visitor, bringing a trio of golden-haired infants whose appearance was as angelic as their father's.

The staff regarded him with considerable suspicion. He was the only one of us regularly put in a punishment cell for a few hours; just time for the guards to search his cell. They would take every single object carefully apart and, equally carefully, reassemble it. They were convinced Wim was getting a small but regular supply of heroin and were anxious to discover both the source and the hiding-place. Although, like every other prisoner, he was strip-searched after every visit, nothing was ever found on him. Sniffer-dogs were brought in to his cell and drew a blank. He maintained an air of bland indifference, insisting he had kicked smack a long time ago. But we who lived alongside him knew, in spite of his appearance of radiant health, this was not so – although we were never privileged to know how he got it or where he kept it.

The punishment cells were in the summit of each tower. I never had any personal experience of them but was told the top landing was similar to those beneath, with one important difference; the cells were furnished only with a single mattress. A flat roof in the centre of the landing could be opened electronically in fine weather. Prisoners confined for more than twenty-four hours (this never happened to Wim) took their daily exercise underneath it.

We were a mixture of nationalities in pavilion 5. The Dutch were the most numerous only if the blacks of Surinam origin were included in their total. I never met a Dutch prisoner of Indonesian origin – their crime rating must be exceptionally low. A number worked as guards in every tower. Although most of them looked hardly older than schoolboys, their smiling good humour and scrupulous fairness could usually disarm the most purposely difficult of prisoners.

Dinos provided me with a sort of potted vade-mecum on the criminal patterns of the races surrounding us.

'You'll soon find out,' he said, 'almost all the Spanish-speaking,

South or Central Americans are thieves or pickpockets. You once lost a suitcase in the Central Station, you'll probably run up against the guy who took it. It's the only work they've had any training for and, oh boy, are they good at it!'

'How about the Surinamers?' I asked. 'They're South American, surely?'

'They're the exception. They don't pick pockets – they push smack.'

'All of them?'

'The majority are small-time pushers of hard drugs.'

'Who are the big-time pushers?'

'The Chinese, mostly. There's only one in this pavilion and he's quite sure he'll get twelve years.'

This Chinaman, like Wong in the *Demersluis*, told me at once he was a second-class British citizen with a second-class British passport. I began to wonder if every Chinaman in Hong Kong felt equally aggrieved. This one was good-looking, almost six feet tall, with a skin like parchment and eyes like black olives that peeped narrowly from their deep settings. In spite of my first-class passport we became good friends and, months later, he asked me for a written translation of a long screed in French, sent to his Amsterdam lawyers by Parisian attorneys. It was a detailed account of an attempt by the Paris police to entrap another Chinaman whom they suspected of delivering heroin to dealers who waited for him in the *Denfert-Rocherau* metro station. The exercise ended in failure. The Chinaman was carrying nothing but small parcels of cheap aftershave. What this episode had to do with my Chinaman's case, I never discovered – I was not told and it was not my habit to ask questions. As a reward for my translation he insisted on filling the larder in my cell (we also had access to a large refrigerator) to overflowing with bamboo shoots and tins of noodles. I did my best to thwart this generosity, not being over-fond of Chinese food, but in vain.

Dinos continued to assign various categories of crime to a variety of nationalities. Although there were no Turks in pavilion 5 at that moment, he said there were plenty in the tower and I would certainly meet them at work. To a man, he insisted, they were killers, but very likable killers. I found this hard to believe, but discovered he had not exaggerated. Most Dutch and German prisoners, he said, had been involved in bank robbery, car theft or drugs. The majority of Arabs were guilty of repeated attempts to enter the

348

Netherlands illegally or for beating the daylights out of each other when drunk.

Amongst those who were to become good friends was a middle-aged, rapidly-balding Dutchman who had beautiful manners and a different, expensive cashmere sweater for every day of the month and a selection of gorgeous silk dressing-gowns in which to go from his cell to the shower-room. He was, I was told, one of the most expert safe-breakers in the north of Europe. He was much too modest to tell me so himself. He took as much care of his hands as a concert violinist, rubbing pots and pots of cold cream into them. His fingers were long and slender, but the tips were exceptionally blunt and well-padded with soft flesh.

Marcel was a *hotelier* in his mid-forties, cherubic, red-faced, red-haired, short and obese, he looked like Tweedledee. He had stashed away the profits (several million guilders) from his flourishing hotel business into a numbered Swiss bank account. Unfortunately, he owed every cent in taxes. He told me the authorities had whispered that if he would agree to the transfer of the bulk of his millions from his Zürich account to the Netherlands' tax office, he would be treated very leniently. He was not impressed. Knowing they could not give him more than five years, he decided the benefits of hanging on to his money far outweighed the inconvenience of a few years in prison.

He was, in fact, released after about two and a half years, but his passport was not returned. The Ministry of Justice apparently hoped this would prevent him spending his ill-gotten gains in some tax-free haven. Incredibly, they failed to realise that in jail he had been surrounded by people who knew how to obtain an authentic passport of practically any country in Europe, including Great Britain, for not more than £500. To Marcel, such a sum was chicken-feed, and he probably bought them by the dozen.

The majority of my companions were young. Pieter, in the cell next door, had celebrated his twentieth birthday the day before my arrival. He was waiting to be convicted (for the second time) of stealing high-powered motor cycles in one Dutch province and selling them in another. He was an engaging youngster with abundant energy; never walking if he could run, hogging the table-tennis table until dragged away. He took an enthusiastic part in the twice-weekly, voluntary sessions with the sports instructor, who alternated PT with football in the open air and volley-ball in an enormous gymnasium.

Pieter radiated irrepressible cheerfulness. True, he was noisy, but to me it was pleasant noise. He enjoyed wearing a minimum of clothing. An extremely brief pair of denim shorts was the only concession he was prepared to make to convention. This was not to flaunt his body, for, in spite of several years on Amsterdam's juvenile criminal fringe, he was, in many ways, remarkably innocent. He was genuinely unaware that his semi-naked, almost hairless young body, with its pearly translucent skin could be disturbingly attractive, even to heterosexuals, given this enforced monastic existence.

For some reason I never quite understood, Pieter attached himself to me like a rumbustious puppy. After my first night in the *Schouw*, he asked me, rather nervously, if I had been kept awake by his radio. I had only been aware of a faint rhythmic drum-beat, which had not disturbed me at all. Relief and incredulity lit up his face. He told me the previous inmate of my cell, a middle-aged German, had never stopped complaining about the pop music Pieter listened to until around midnight. He had also complained to the staff who had instructed the boy to keep the volume down. Personally, I found the cells so excellently soundproofed, Pieter could have been host to a twenty-piece brass band without disturbing my sleep.

The cell on his other side was occupied by the young Moroccan from Fez who, like myself, could not have cared less if the sound had been twenty times as loud.

So Pieter was now really happy. 'As soon as the staff have gone off for the night,' he said, 'I turn up the volume and have my own private disco! You may think I'm crazy, but I dance and dance for the next hour, then switch off and fall asleep at once.' I told him when I was his age I did very much the same, but in my day it was called the Charleston!

During the free association periods he would challenge everybody in the pavilion to beat him at table tennis. They seldom succeeded. On Saturdays and Sundays the number of his possible opponents was increased, both landings having free association from six-thirty until nine o'clock. In the rare intervals when he was not playing, he would sit on the arm of my chair, extending his slim thighs and taught muscled calves. Slipping an arm around my shoulders, he would peer down at my book or newspaper, saying: 'And what is the Big Criminal reading tonight?' It amused him to refer to me as the Big Criminal; in return I used to call him the Little Criminal. Unconsciously, I provided him with a good deal of friendly amusement which I did my best to encourage.

I discovered he had never been on good terms with his father; perhaps he was subconsciously seeking a substitute – an old grandfatherly figure whose leg he could pull with impunity. I cared very deeply about him, but managed to conceal my feelings, from him and from the others, under a mask of casual, silly jokes. At the same time I did my best to build up his self-confidence, hoping to convince him that the possessor of so bright and enquiring a mind would do much better operating within the law than outside it.

He received a year's imprisonment and was transferred, a few weeks later, to a new prison in north Holland for the eighteen to twenty-four age-group. For a time I felt utterly bereft, and was not cheered by a succession of postcards of powerful motor cycles addressed to Dear Big Criminal – Dear Sir Tony – Dear Muppet Man – saying he was not happy and wished very much he was back in the *Schouw*. However, the tone got more cheerful over the weeks, as he settled down and began to enjoy the athletic facilities. There was a final postcard, telling me how much he was looking forward to being released in a few days – and nothing more. It is unlikely our paths will ever cross again which, for me, will be a lasting sadness.

He called me Muppet Man because he insisted I resembled one of the grandfatherly puppets in the television series, who sit in a theatre box criticising the performance. I pretended to be deeply offended. The Sir Tony referred of course to the police report made to the press, and also to the nameplate that appeared on my cell door in the *Schouw*. Every cell had to have its occupant's name on the door in large, black lettering on a white background. On my first morning I was appalled to find a strip of pasteboard under my spy-hole which read: Sir Anthony Aspinall.

I hurried to the guards' office saying: 'For God's sake – how much longer is this stupid joke to go on?'

To my surprise, when the guards realised what had annoyed me, they looked embarrassed. 'You do not like to be called Sir?' one of them said.

'Of course I don't. If it wasn't gummed to the bloody door, I'd have pulled it off myself!'

'It was Henk,' said another. 'He does all the nameplates. He won't be on again until tomorrow.'

'Have I got to wait until then before anything can be done?'

'Henk will regret very much you do not like. A compliment he meant it to be.'

'You can't be serious?' At this moment I was joined by Dinos and Ian. To my astonishment, they said they were sure the nameplate *was* intended as a genuine commendation and not a joke.

As if speaking to an idiot child, Ian said: 'In England you'd know at once they were taking the piss out of you – but it's not England, it's Holland – you should know that better than anybody – and here it's meant as a compliment. If the screws like you, don't complain – just be glad. Anyway, why shouldn't they like you – you're not such a bad old sod!'

So I shut up, but found it difficult not to wince every time I saw the thing. Then Ian and Dinos extracted a page from a glossy magazine and fixed it below the nameplate. It was a vividly coloured illustration of the largest Samsonite suitcase, captioned: THIS IS HOW YOU SHOULD TRAVEL! I was delighted. I felt the notices provided a correct perspective of my recent activities and kept them on the door.

Some time later, another youngster apparently in need of a grand-father-figure latched on to me. This was a twenty-one-year-old German, very much the blond Aryan; big and brawny, but lacking Pieter's tendency to throw his clothes off. In fact one hardly ever saw him without his black leather blouson. Franz had been arrested for dealing in small quantities of drugs and was released after a few months.

Sexually very experienced, he was a complete contrast to Pieter and took pride in declaring he was capable of fucking anything that moved. Son of a Duisburg woman, who was the mother of several children by different men, he had no idea who his father had been. He had been working in one of Amsterdam's most fashionable brothels, changing the sheets between customers. He assured me he frequently slept with the proprietress, who was over sixty, and always enjoyed the experience. He had enormous violet eyes and a deceptively innocent smile. He had considerable charm and, I suspect, a touch of gerontophilia towards both sexes, because he plainly preferred my company to those closer to his own age.

I quickly became accustomed to life in the *Schouw*, where regulations were almost identical to the *Demersluis*.

Monday was the day for a change of laundry.

On Thursdays the shop was open. Each pavilion would descend, half-a-dozen at a time, to the first floor. I am improvident by nature, and on these weekly expeditions, for the first time in my life, I was careful not to spend more than I was earning. My salary was sufficient and I never felt in any way deprived.

Friday we visited the library, housed in two large rooms close to the shop. Also on the first floor were the doctor's surgery and a conference room, used for meetings between prisoners and representatives of voluntary agencies, some Muslim or Christian, others humanist, which I found infinitely preferable.

Every tower had a library, staffed and administered by Amsterdam's central library. They did their best to cater for a multilingual readership and, in my view, succeeded remarkably well.

Most books were, of course, in Dutch, but the stock in English, French, German and Spanish was surprisingly extensive; that in Arabic and Asian languages, less so. This caused some criticism from the North Africans and Pakistanis.

We were allowed to borrow four books at a time and, reading French as easily as English, I had a wide choice of thrillers, detective stories, serious novels, biographies and travel. The stock was circulated through the towers and, eventually, back to the central library, who kept up a continuous flow of replacements. If you particularly wanted a book not in stock in the centre, a written request would usually secure it for you on the following Friday. The central library were rarely stumped by any request for English, French or German books.

A cursory glance at the shelves showed that the prison library service did not suffer from censorship. Most European language sections contained a certain amount of literate pornography. On the English shelves there was always a selection of fiction by the younger and more outrageous gay Americans. In French, I was delighted to make the acquaintance of three distinguished exponents of autobiographical travel writing: Renaud Camus, Juan Pineiro and Georges Lapassade, whose frankness about their homosexual lifestyle in Paris, the French provinces and North Africa would probably induce apoplexy among the British moral majority.

I put in an immediate application to work, which was swiftly accepted. Work in the *Schouw* consisted of assembling electrical equipment – chiefly the sort of multi-plug adaptors that encourage householders to run too many appliances from one socket. Hours were the same as in the *Demersluis*: three hours a day, with a quarter of an hour's tea break which usually extended to twenty-five minutes.

When empty, the workshop looked like a large, cheap restaurant, with metal tables with shining white tops, capable of seating four; so many, they were often shared by only two. The table-tops would be covered with screwdrivers of every conceivable size. These were carefully checked when we finished.

I joined Dinos' table, where he had already established the beginnings of a sort of Mediterranean clique; he had become friendly with the two enormous Turks on our table and a couple of Algerians close by.

When the Turks, on that first morning, went off to collect bits and pieces from the storeroom, I hissed 'Do they know you're Greek, or have you been deceiving them with that Canadian accent?'

Dinos looked hurt. 'They know my name,' he said defensively, 'and it could hardly be more Greek if it was Ulysses.'

True, his long surname had far too many 'ous' in it to be anything but Hellenic.

'They're nice guys,' he insisted. 'They're not interested in politics.'

'I've never met a Turk who wasn't politically minded where the Greeks were concerned.'

'You'll soon see how wrong you are.'

Remembering what he had told me, I hissed: 'Are they both killers?'

'Sure,' he said casually. 'But not to worry – they keep that sort of thing amongst themselves, you know.'

The Turks returned with cardboard boxes from which we could select bits of plastic adaptor to be screwed together, then chucked into another box.

The Turks were heavily built, in their late twenties, with pale skin, dark hair and jet-black eyes; much addicted to short-sleeved T-shirts in brilliant colours, even in cold weather, presumably because they enjoyed showing off their muscular biceps, elaborately tattooed with exotic blue and red flower-patterns. Both came from small towns in Anatolia and looked so alike they might have been brothers. They were not, in fact, related, but had met while working in Germany.

We got on very well and established a particularly cheerful liaison with the Algerians at the next table. Having lived in North Africa, I had acquired a few expressions in Mograbi Arabic that are sometimes used to relieve stressful feelings – phrases not normally in the vocabulary

354

of an outwardly respectable elderly foreigner. I am unlikely to forget the incredulity on their faces when I, jokingly, used one of these expressions to admonish Dinos – deliberately raising my voice. They gaped in disbelief, gazed at me as if I had developed an extra head, and burst into roars of delighted laughter.

It was an accepted practice that we should take turns fetching the components from the storeroom, but the Turks refused to allow me to do so. My protests had no effect. Apparently it was *de rigueur* in their part of Anatolia for old fribbles like me to sit back with folded hands and watch the young do the work. They even tried to insist on assembling my share of the wretched adaptors, but I firmly put a stop to that. I told them how I had driven through Turkey several times in recent years and, while always treated courteously, had not found quite the same attitude. 'Ah!' they said, 'all you know of our country is Istanbul, Ankara and the coastline from Canakalee to the Syrian frontier – all of it corrupted by Western tourism – beaches crowded with your shameless women showing their naked breasts to the world – that's not the real Turkey.'

They were plainly conservative, but in a strictly Turkish fashion. I once asked one of them if he were married. His reply, in simple German, was: 'No. Women, no good. Prefer young boys – they give you less trouble.'

Visits were barred during working hours, but interruptions from lawyers, the *reclasseering*, or calls from the doctor's or dentist's surgeries, were allowed. Our Turks were defended by the same lawyer and would be absent together. Dinos was also frequently closeted with counsel, sometimes for hours. I gathered they spent most of the time disagreeing, for Dinos had very definite ideas about how his case should be conducted.

I received visits from Jan Drukker and from Françoise, to reassure me I had not been forgotten. Drukker was immensely kind and I always felt I could not be in better hands. Françoise made her visits seem like social occasions. Voluble and exuberant in clear, incisive English, with Gallic gestures that often caused havoc to her always insecure cottage-loaf of cinnamon-brown hair, I enjoyed her company and we laughed a great deal.

Unfortunately, Dinos did not share my appreciation of Françoise. Being a macho man (not tall, but dark and handsome) he had been accustomed to women falling at his feet (or into his bed) from early adolescence. Françoise remained impervious to his charm – even made it plain she rather disliked him. Poor Dinos was incredulous. 'I just don't understand that woman's attitude,' he would say grumpily.

Unlike the *Demersluis*, which had a *werkmeester* permanently in charge of its workshop, the guards in the *Schouw* supervised us in turn. When they were bored, they would take a vacant chair and work alongside us. This would often happen when Dinos or the Turks (or all three) had been summoned away to meetings. The guards seemed glad to practise their English, which most spoke well. Only one had ever been to England – he had spent his honeymoon in London – the rest had achieved their remarkable fluency at school, which suggests that the British have a lot to learn from the Dutch about the teaching of languages.

One guard I am unlikely to forget was a quiet young man with protuberant grey eyes and curly fair hair who asked where I lived in Amsterdam. I told him the Jordaan district, and before that the Bijlmermeer: a dark-grey, concrete collection of high-rise flats, built on marshland. Although many of the blocks have been given an unwise coating of psychedelic paint, the district remains a monument to the mistaken theories of so many European architects in the years following the last war. So many cities have a Bijlmermeer. I told the guard that if I squinted out of my cell window I could just see my old block of flats.

To my surprise, he said: 'I expect you can see mine as well – I live in the Bijlmermeer.'

I asked which block, and was startled when he mentioned one that I presumed to be occupied exclusively by black Surinamer families. I said as much and he agreed. At first, he confirmed, the residents had been multi-racial but, as more black tenants arrived the whites had steadily gone elsewhere to be replaced by more Surinamers.

'We are the only white family left in the block,' he said. 'But they are such kind people. My wife has taken the children to visit her parents in Friesland and while she's away, the mothers of the families on either side of us insist on cleaning my home while I'm at work and have a hot meal waiting when I come off duty.'

'That's kind of them.'

'Isn't it? And when I protest that I'm not one of those helpless men incapable of looking after himself, they say: "You did not run away from us like all the other white people. We want to show you we are grateful for your confidence and that we can be good neighbours." '

I remembered English and Dutch friends who had been among the first to move into this block, only to flee soon afterwards from what they described as the Surinamer Invasion. How could they be expected to live, they asked querulously, alongside those whom everyone knew to be dishonest, dirty and noisy?

As one who, in the *Schouw*, was compelled to live in close proximity to a number of Surinamers (most of them born in the Netherlands) I can refute almost all the slanders made against them. Possibly some may have been thieves – the light-fingered can be found in every race – but none of my fellow prisoners had been accused of theft. As for being dirty, they spent most of their free association time under the showers.

They seemed more family-orientated than the rest of us, decorating their cells with photographs of their progeny in rows on cupboards, window-sills and shelves, and pinned to the wall. (Every cell had about six square feet of white, rubbery material inserted into one wall, where almost anything could be pinned up; this discouraged the vandalising of wall space.)

Surinamers are, however, definitely noisy people. When they talked and laughed together, the decibel count climbed astonishingly. Their friendly discussions caused painful reverberations in every white eardrum in the pavilion. But their kindliness and sense of fun were so much more important than the noise they made. I loved every one of them.

Few whites decorated their cells with family photographs. Most preferred something much more basic, such as the centrefolds of magazines like *Playboy*, *Penthouse* and even more explicit colour photographs of female genitalia from German and American hard-porn magazines.

One of my neighbours, a handsome young Israeli, a diamond cutter accused of pushing drugs, not only filled his pin-up board with photos of women's crutches, but covered every inch of the surrounding walls with similar close-ups and enlargements. To enter his cell was to walk into a collage of pubic hair. He was, however, an extreme example of a general trend. The few homosexuals amongst us were very restrained by comparison, confining themselves to a few small snapshots of a fully clothed boyfriend.

One day when my guard friend from the Bijlmermeer was supervising the workshop, he told me his six-year-old daughter had been raped.

Shyly at first, and then with increasing confidence, he told me the story. The child had been returning from a nearby shopping centre with groceries for her mother when she had been dragged into bushes surrounding the block and sexually assaulted.

I asked immediately if the rapist had been black. The answer was no – white and middle-aged. The police had not been successful in tracing the man.

It was difficult to know how to express sympathy to a young father confronted by something so appalling. Apparently I did not make too bad a job of it because, as the weeks went by and we met from time to time in the corridors, he would give me the latest news about his child; how she was making a splendid recovery, mentally and physically. He was full of praise for their doctor and social workers. They all insisted the rape must be discussed by the little family as an unpleasant but perfectly ordinary occurrence. They were cautioned not to speak about it in horrified whispers, still less to treat it as too dreadful to mention. The best way to help the child was to show great sympathy while avoiding unnecessary drama.

His wife, who came from Friesland, had never shown much enthusiasm for life in the Bijlmermeer. After the attack she found it impossible not to feel uneasy in Amsterdam. I was, therefore, not surprised when the father asked for a transfer and was quickly given a posting to the north. I saw him a day or two before he left and asked after the child. He told me she was fine but added: 'I shall never stop worrying how she'll react to her first boyfriend.' I wished I could have said something reassuring, but I could not.

The trees in the Juliana Park, beyond the Weesp Canal, were showing signs of approaching autumn, making Dinos and me more and more conscious that our joint appearance in the high court was getting closer. We had been making fortnightly appearances in the small court, to extend our custody.

Dinos had been given special duties and no longer worked with the rest of us. Always a fine athlete, he had attracted the approving eye of the physical training instructor and had gratefully accepted the job of assistant athletics coach. He could now spend the whole day, apart from mealtimes, out of his cell.

These privileges made him absurdly anxious to find his old courier a job with the same sort of freedom. The Englishman I had met in the lift was to be transferred and the staff were looking for a replacement runner for their canteen. Dinos threw out constant hints to those guards he considered most influential, that I would be an admirable choice. He was, I am afraid, disappointed and hurt when I begged him to stop lobbying, and incredulous when the job was offered and I turned it down.

Most prisoners very much desired work that allowed them to spend time outside their cells. I did not. My experiences in Syria had made me only too happy to be alone. My cell was as pleasant as many hotel rooms. I could read; listen to Radio 4; write letters; and, as long as I was let out occasionally to take some gentle exercise in the fresh air, to chat with other prisoners and to work at some simple task for my 25 guilders a week, I did not mind how often I was locked up or, within reason, for how long.

Early in October, Dinos and I received official notification of our trial, two weeks ahead. These important-looking documents arrived with the mail. They were identical, brief and to the point, stating the charges against us and naming the three judges who would preside, and the public prosecutor.

The names meant nothing to us, but that of the judge designated president meant a good deal to my lawyer.

'You're lucky,' he said. 'This man is humane and never bullies. His cross-examinations can be deadly for those with something to conceal – his courtesy lulls them into a false sense of security and they give themselves away. That can't affect you, because you've already been exceptionally frank. Another advantage will be his knowledge of English. He'll have to wait, of course, for your interpreter, but he'll know your answers before he gets the translation.'

'I suppose it's all going to be rather alarming,' I said.

'I don't think you'll find it so.' He drummed nervously with his fingers on his shoulder-bag. Then he said: 'What I'm going to say now, you may consider alarming.'

I looked at him, waiting for him to continue.

'You have admitted in the story of your life to being homosexual?'

'Yes.'

'You will not suddenly deny that in court?'

'I don't expect to have to affirm or deny it. Surely it's totally irrelevant?'

'I want to be sure about your attitude because I intend to make it part of my defence.'

Surprised, I said: 'But is that really necessary?'

'I think so.'

'But what connection is there between my sexual nature and the carrying of drugs – and even if I'm not what the younger generation calls a "closet gay" I believe, at my age, in maintaining a certain discretion – a certain reticence – about my sex-life which, after all, now lies almost entirely in the past.'

'I feel it to be something that must be taken into account if you're to be properly defended.'

'You want to strip me naked in a public courtroom?'

'I hope you will trust me to be discreet – and please remember you're not in England now; we have a different approach to such matters.'

'I know – and yet I would rather you didn't bring it up.'

'The state is employing me to give you the best possible defence. Won't you trust me?'

There was a long pause while we looked at each other. Then I said: 'All right. I suppose I'd better leave it to you.'

The great day arrived. As usual, a notice showing the departure times of the shuttle-service of squat white marias between the detention centre and the *Palais van Justitie* had been pinned to our board the previous evening. Dinos and I were amused to see some wretched bureaucrat had decided to split us up on our journey to court. As we had been in the same pavilion for nearly three months and would be sitting side by side in the dock, this seemed ridiculous. I was more irritated by it than Dinos, because I was to be ready to leave at 11.30, whereas Dinos would not be required until an hour later. I would have an hour to wait in the gloomy depths of the law courts.

Prisoners are permitted to wear any sort of garb when appearing in court in the Netherlands. You are told almost anything will do, as long as it covers your nakedness. Nevertheless, Dinos and I decided it would be common courtesy to put on jackets and ties. This resulted in a certain amount of leg-pulling from the other prisoners.

Soon after eleven o'clock I was told to make my own way to the internal garage. I waved to Dinos as the staff put me into the lift, wishing me luck. I made the long trek along the 'spaceship', surrendering my ID card in the admin office – this time in exchange for a packet of sandwiches. I descended the narrow, twisting staircase into the garage where I was ushered to a seat in the inevitable Mercedes prison-van. My companions were a trio of black-haired, pale-faced, South American *meztizos* who assured me, in voluble Latin-American Spanish, that they had been wrongly accused of pickpocketing.

The garage doors opened upwards without a sound. The driver, a security guard by his side, drove us gently into the open courtyard between us and the twin tunnels, with their traffic lights and steel gates at each end. The lights flashed to green and we moved quickly through the underpass, away towards the city.

It was a bright autumn morning and Amsterdam was looking its best as we drove north up the Amsteldijk and west along the Stadhouderskade. The river and canal were the colour of green apples and sparkled in the sunshine.

We arrived at the law court, not by its impressively pillared main entrance in the Prinsengracht but by the small entry at the rear that had been used for my visit to the public prosecutor.

As soon as the garage doors were shut – by hand, of course, in this nineteenth-century building – we were escorted along dark corridors by two policemen whose age suggested these jobs must be kept for those close to retirement.

Our little party was suddenly halted, while one of the policemen unlocked a door with a giant key. A cloud of tobacco smoke blew into our faces. I had a fleeting impression of a dozen men on benches in dim, artificial light. The three *meztizos* were gently pushed inside. I was taken a further twenty yards to another door. This time it was me who had to enter an atmosphere of cigarette smoke and the reek of damp plaster. I sat on a wooden bench with my back to a wall with three prisoners exchanging laconic reminiscences in Turkish, and four talking animatedly in German with strong Bavarian accents. They all broke off to give me a friendly murmur of 'Hi!' – this American monosyllable having become an almost universal greeting among the young.

The large cell was illuminated by a single bulb in the mottled grey and white ceiling. The only other source of light (and ventilation) was a rectangular opening no bigger than a man's hand high up in one wall, through which a faint trace of daylight was visible.

The presence of so many others puzzled me. It was just after midday and I wondered if the courts would be sitting throughout the lunch-hour. It seemed incredible. I realised my mistake when the three Turks were told that transport was now waiting, and would they please hurry. I had been put amongst those whose cases had already been heard; a similar call was made for the Germans about half-an-hour later.

After I had been alone for a little while, a policeman appeared with coffee. I had now learned to accept milky, sweetened coffee in the same way I had learned to accept milky, sweetened tea during the war. I drank it gratefully after eating my cheese and ham sandwiches, and the bar of chocolate I found inside the wrapping.

The next hour passed so slowly I regretted not having taken Ian's advice to slip a book into my pocket. I kept looking at my watch, hardly believing it had not stopped. I doubt if anyone could look forward to appearing in the dock of a criminal court, but I cannot deny feeling almost pleasurable anticipation when muffled sounds began to be audible in the corridor: the *Palais van Justitie* was slowly awakening from its lunchtime somnolence. I pressed a bell-push. There was no sound but it must have rung somewhere, because a policeman arrived. I told him I wanted to pee. He pointed down the passage to a door which, he assured me, was the toilet: the word is the same in Dutch, but without the bourgeois connotation it has in English.

It was indeed a remarkable toilet. The enormous wooden thunderbox was a perfect example of the Dutch equivalent of early Victoriana. If auctioned in London it would probably fetch a small fortune.

When I returned, the waiting policeman warned me I should be going into court within ten minutes.

He was back in less than five, gesturing that I was to walk ahead of him along the corridor – in the opposite direction to the toilets. I saw Dinos being towed out of another cell, some distance ahead. He was attached to an elderly policeman by a special handcuff with long, twin chains, a type I had never seen before.

Our little party mounted a narrow mahogany staircase that curved gracefully up to a first-floor landing. Dinos' policeman led the way, hauling his prisoner along. My confederate was not in the least put out by this treatment and turned, several times, to wink at me as, still unfettered, I followed at his heels.

We were led through a heavy oak door into the impressively spacious high court of Amsterdam which, to me, bore a strong resemblance to a theatre; an impression largely created by the stage-like judges' dais, with its three splendid high-backed chairs, at present unoccupied, facing the main body of the court with its seats in neat rows. Accommodation for visitors and the press was provided in a steeply ramped gallery.

As we entered, Dinos was released from his handcuff and a small group chatting quietly below the dais came to greet us. It was our lawyers, plus our interpreter.

The lawyers looked as if they had stepped out of a seventeenth-century painting; enclosed from neck to ankles in tubular, black robes, relieved only by the frill of a white collar with long, starched streamers extending below the knees. Mrs Johanssen was wearing the sort of trouser suit instantly recognisable as *haute couture*. Lively as always, she was able to give us just the right amount of reassurance.

While the police faded into the background, she took us to a bench-seat, upholstered in champagne-coloured leather, raised above the body of the court, to the left of the dais. To my surprise, this was the dock.

We took our places, I on Dinos' right with Mrs Johanssen on my right. Everyone seemed confident the judges would question me before turning to Dinos. In front of us was an object like a heated towel-rail. It supported two microphones.

I looked quickly around for faces I could recognise. Apart from Françoise, sitting with a small knot of people below the dais, who smiled and gave us a cautious wave, there was no one I knew on the floor of the courtroom. In the public gallery, there were fewer than a dozen people, all strangers. Neither Dinos nor I realised that one of the young women in the front row had been sent by his girlfriend to give her a verbatim report, because she felt too emotionally involved to attend.

Our lawyers were sitting above the dock behind two objects like church lecterns. A microphone had been installed over the top of each.

Everybody in court tensed as the public prosecutor entered with two underlings. The trio, wearing black robes with starched white trimmings, took their seats on the other side of the dais, facing Dinos and me. The prosecutor, between his colleagues, looked as boyishly pink and white as ever.

Everyone had stopped talking before the judges made their entrance through a door at the back of the dais, and we all rose. They were an impressive sight; apart from the absence of wigs, they were robed not unlike their counterparts in an English high court. One almost expected a fanfare of trumpets, but there was only the faint rustle of material as they sat.

My first impression was of their astonishing youth. The judge nearest us, thin, pale and fair-haired, looked hardly more than thirty and was apparently so shy, or nervous, he found it next to impossible to raise his head to look at anybody – even the prisoners for whose immediate fate he was presumably to be partly responsible.

His colleague was a complete contrast. Slightly older – he might have been forty – tubby, dark-haired and ruddy-skinned, he was wearing 'granny specs' and looked remarkably like Mr Pickwick. This judge had no difficulty in keeping his head up, never ceasing to quiz Dinos and myself with what seemed intense but not unfriendly interest.

Between them sat the impressive figure of the president of the court. Like a hero of romantic fiction, his hair was touched with grey at the temples; I would have guessed him to be a year or two under fifty; a manner that combined urbanity with charm, lit by flashes of gentle irony. I was to be occasionally reminded during the afternoon of the legendary headmaster of Stowe in its early days, the late J. F. Roxburgh.

The silence continued while the president arranged large files bound in sober colours on the table. He then held a long, obviously friendly, conversation with my interpreter. She turned laughingly to explain. 'The president's been pointing out,' she said, 'that much of what takes place in court this afternoon will have to be conducted in English. And because, in previous cases involving foreigners, he's noticed that defendants always reply looking at the interpreter and not at him, he wants to try a little experiment.' She moved behind me to another pale brown, leather-covered bench, sat down and leaned forward, saying: 'I shall be sitting here, instead of beside you. You must look straight at the president when you answer. You understand?'

I nodded.

The president was looking at us with some amusement. 'I think, perhaps, you deserve an apology, Mr Aspinall, he said, in what could have been the English of a native. 'I'm sure you'd much rather talk directly to Mrs Johanssen than to me.'

He took a typescript from a slim folder and waved it at me, speaking quietly in Dutch. Behind my right ear Mevrouw Johanssen began to translate. The case against me had started.

'Mr Aspinall,' (I wondered if English judges addressed the dock in this manner) 'this is the *aide-memoire* in which you've described your background and working life. My colleagues and I would like to thank you for it – we've read it with great interest. We would like to give you our personal assurance that, no matter what happens in court this afternoon, we shall none of us forget the candour you have shown about yourself.'

Taken aback by this unexpected courtesy, I could only mumble thanks and admit I had not found it easy to write a suitably concise account of my nonconformist manner of living. I feared there had been regrettable *longueurs* for which I apologised.

'We didn't notice them,' was his answer. 'Is there anything you would like to add? If so, we're prepared to listen.'

I said there was nothing more I felt would be relevant.

'In that case will you now give us a full and accurate description of your recent expedition to Peru.'

Taking a deep breath, I said: 'Where d'you want me to begin?'

'At the very beginning. From the moment your plan to fly out to Lima was conceived, and by whom.'

So once again I launched into a description of my visit to South America, beginning with my meeting with Eduardo Luis. I had repeated the tale so often it sounded, to my ears, tediously mechanical – especially now, when I had to chop everything into short sentences for translation. To vary the monotony I included half-forgotten incidents I had never previously mentioned – one of them actually causing laughter in court. This was my brief account of a reception at the United States Embassy for the organisers of a Miss Universe competition, taking place under the sponsorship of an American television company. Most of the visitors connected with this glamorous event spent their time at the reception enquiring loudly where it was possible to obtain 'the best Peruvian coke'! They even persisted in asking those I knew to be undercover members of the Drug Enforcement Agency.

At moments like this I would become aware I was talking too quickly, taxing Mrs Johanssen's abilities, and slowed down, although she never complained.

Helped by occasional promptings from the president, I gave as accurate a summary of my journey as possible, up to the moment of my arrest.

As I was finishing, the president, who had been glancing at photographs on the table, looked up saying: 'This – this undergarment in which you carried most of the cocaine – did your friends help you to put it on when you left Lima?'

I shook my head. 'No. I'd taken everything back to the hotel with me the previous evening. I got up early, had a shower, then attached all those packets to my calves and thighs with tape. The padded chastity-belt (a woman in the public gallery tittered) was the last item I put on before getting into my clothes. I then finished packing and went down to breakfast. None of the staff appeared to notice anything unusual about my hips, so I asked them to ring for a taxi, settled my bill and left for the airport.'

'Wasn't this – this garment, very uncomfortable?' His tone indicated genuine sympathy with my discomfort which surprised me.

'Hideously so,' I agreed. 'I was thankful to take it off during the long flight to Paris.

'The hotel where you stayed – what sort of hotel was it?'

'It was in Lima's fashionable seaside suburb of Miraflores. A small hotel of impeccable respectability – my friends had chosen it for that reason. A place where an elderly English visitor would be most unlikely to bump into the criminal classes.'

I detected a hint of amusement in the corners of the president's mouth. When it had faded, he looked at me for a moment before saying: 'Would it surprise you, Mr Aspinall, to be told we find you a somewhat puzzling character?'

'In what way, sir?' I asked. (Jan Drukker's advice on how to address a president of a high court when talking in English – interpolate an occasional 'sir' and never use 'm'lud' or 'your honour'.)

'The lighthearted manner in which you admit having imported nearly three kilos of cocaine into this country.'

'Surely it would be pointless of me to deny the charge? I was caught redhanded.'

'It is the fact of there being a need to catch you that surprises us. How could this happen to someone who has spent many years working for the betterment of the human race? We know you took part in the evacuation of the notorious concentration camp at Bergen-Belsen in 1945. Much in your life demonstrates that you have never forgotten that experience. You spent a number of years after the last war with an organisation that still speaks enthusiastically of your work among the deprived of this world. Can you wonder we are disconcerted by your presence in this court?'

'It is true,' I said, 'that much of my life has been spent as a professional do-gooder – to use the derogatory term so often employed by the English tabloid newspapers – and, frankly, I'm hopeful you may take those years into consideration when you decide my fate. But if I'm to be honest, I have to admit my life might have taken quite a different course if I hadn't, until I was sixty-five, been cushioned by a private income. Not much of one, but enough to keep me out of the gutter if I should ever get fed up with my employers and tell them to take their work and go to hell.'

'What sort of life would you have led without that income?'

'Judging by my recent activities, I might have been just as unscrupulous as my forbears who built up the Great British Empire with slavery in the West and Opium in the East.

'Does anything frighten you?'

'Yes – a poverty-stricken old age. Now staring me in the face with greater certainty than ever.'

'You have written that you believe cannabis, hashish, marijuana, to be less harmful than alcohol. Are you convinced cocaine is also harmless?'

'I now have reservations about cocaine – most of them acquired during the last three months in your detention centre. Until then I was totally unaware of the habit of mixing cocaine and heroin into what is described as a cocktail and shooting it into a vein. Previously I only knew the method of snorting it through a tube from a polished surface. I have many friends, particularly in the United States, who, like me, have been using their shaving-mirrors for this purpose, off and on, for more than thirty years, without doing ourselves any noticeable harm. But I now realise if coke is abused and adulterated it can reduce a healthy human being to a zombie.'

'You don't consider yourself to be an addict?'

'Certainly not.'

'For whom were these kilos of cocaine intended?'

'My trip had been commissioned by one of the more important drug rings in this part of Europe – for their own personal use. None of it would have found its way on to the street.'

'If you'd not been caught, would you have returned to Peru for another run?'

I was silent for a moment, wondering what was the truth. 'I might have done,' I said at last. 'Although the profit from my last jaunt, if successful, would have provided me with enough cash to live quietly for the rest of my short life, I could perhaps have been tempted to do it again.'

While Mevrouw Johanssen was translating, the president was slowly turning the pages of my dossier. 'I see,' he said when she had finished, 'you had twelve hundred American dollars on you when arrested. Where did this money come from?'

'As the police searched my flat, they presumably have my bank statements. These will show you the dollars were the residue of a sum drawn from my London bank after my return from Syria. I exchanged the sterling into dollars here just before I left for South America – there are statements to prove this.'

'Why change sterling into dollars?'

'Since the Falklands episode, the English visitor and the English pound are not particularly welcome in South America. On my second evening in Lima I was asked to leave a restaurant where I'd intended to dine alone, because of my nationality.'

'The money in your English account – where does it come from?'

'It's credited with the interest, twice yearly, from a small trust fund left to me by a great-aunt. I use it only in an emergency and had drawn nothing out of it during my life in Amsterdam or the Middle East. No profits from the drug scene have ever been paid into it.'

'Then what have you done with the money you must have made? After all, you've been involved in this highly profitable business for some time.'

'There never has been much profit for either of us – and when there was any, it would be ploughed back into the next run. The number of accidents and blatant rip-offs my partner and I have had to suffer since we joined forces has been almost beyond belief. I, personally, would have been far better off if I'd remained in that publishing house, here in Amsterdam.'

'You regret not having done so?'

For a moment, I hesitated. 'I'm not sure,' I said at last. 'Surprisingly, perhaps, I don't think I do. In spite of a succession of disasters, I've been able to live a life filled with travel and excitement unusual for my age. It would be hypocritical to deny having enjoyed most of it. But, naturally, I regret finding myself indicted on a serious charge, particularly in a Dutch court.'

The president said quickly: 'Why should a Dutch court make any difference?'

'Because I've always had a great admiration and affection for this country, ever since I sailed into Flushing when I was eleven years old. I'd crossed the North Sea with my father in an old gaff-rigged cutter. It saddens me to be branded a criminal in the Netherlands.'

'You feel we're being unfair to you?'

'Not for a moment. In homely, downright English I would describe it as a fair cop.'

'Is there anybody in court today who wishes to give evidence on your behalf?'

I indicated Françoise, sitting with her small chin resting on her clasped hands. 'My probation officer may, perhaps, wish to say something ... '

Françoise moved forward. I watched her take the oath, raising two fingers – not in the Churchill fashion but with the fingers pressed together in the manner of a brownie salute. (In continental courts the oath is administered only to witnesses, never to the accused.) As she had no microphone and spoke softly in Dutch, I heard little of what she said. Whatever it was made the president smile a good deal. I saw her hand over two sheets of a familiar blue writing paper. I guessed this was a letter written by a beloved woman friend who had first got to know me in post-war Germany. We had been trying to help those who had survived Hitler's concentration and forced-labour camps and could no longer, for political reasons, return to their own countries. I knew she had written that she would always have a high regard for me and that she and her graduate son looked forward to welcoming me into their home as soon as I could return to England. I knew this confidence in me was undeserved, but was none the less grateful.

The letter was read by all three judges. The president then slipped it between the pages of my dossier. After a final exchange of courtesies, Françoise resumed her seat.

I was asked again if there was anything else I wished to tell the court. Feeling I had already been too garrulous, I declined.

Attention switched to Dinos who had been sending out, I was sure, waves of disapproval at my unwise loquaciousness.

For the first time since the judges' entrance, I looked at my watch and was startled to see my cross-examination (if it could be called that) had lasted more than two hours.

Before the trial, I had asked Jan Drukker how long the case would be likely to last. Would it go on all afternoon – would it, perhaps, be resumed the following day?

He had laughed: 'Remember you're pleading guilty – the court will have little to do except decide how dangerous you might be to the world at large. Drugs cases are ten a penny in the Amsterdam courts. Even when contested, they don't usually last longer than an hour and a half. Your presence, of course, may make a difference.'

'In what way?'

'They'll probably question you for longer than usual.'

'Why me – and not Dinos?'

'Greek smugglers, or even Greek-Canadians, are no novelty to our judges, but an Englishman of your type will be. Remember the police report to the newspapers?'

Now that I was no longer the focus of attention I was able to turn slightly and look up at Drukker who grinned reassuringly. Apparently he felt I had not done too badly.

I sat in silence, hardly moving a muscle, while Dinos was interrogated. The questions were politely phrased, but I detected an undercurrent of asperity that had not been noticeable when I had been the object of their interest.

Dinos, like me, had written a short autobiographical account, emphasising his achievements at school and university, both in Greece and Canada – these had mostly been athletics and were impressive. He had also summarised the legitimate work he had undertaken since leaving the parental roof in Edmonton, spotlighting his travel agency in the West Indies, a janitor service in his native city and part-ownership of a bar on Mykonos. Every word was true, and yet, somehow, it gave the general impression of a smokescreen. He also pleaded, in the final paragraphs, not to be sent to prison but to be allowed to become a sports instructor in a centre for young offenders. He had shown it to Ian, Dutch Bob and myself, and was deeply hurt when we all three begged him to scrap the final pages. None of us could make him understand the utter impossibility of such an idea being accepted, even in the liberal-minded Netherlands.

Dinos ignored our opposition and his lawyer, unwisely we felt, allowed the document to go forward. When the president opened the case against him, he made no mention of it; an omission which, to me, looked ominous.

He was questioned for just over half an hour. This time, the auxiliary judges also took part. They said nothing while I was being interrogated, but now, both the weak-stemmed daffodil and Mr Pickwick, who was plainly not as benign as he looked, seemed determined to prove Dinos was of much greater importance in the drug business than was the case. Although he rebutted these accusations quietly and truthfully, he, nevertheless, gave an impression of being uneasy and on the defensive.

After the cross-examination, the president looked across at the public prosecutor who rose and stood in silence for a moment, pushing back a lock of corn-coloured hair from his forehead. By the simple action of standing up, this comparatively young man had the power to evoke an immediate atmosphere of tension. I remember thinking that thunderbolts were going to be launched and they would be aimed at me. This feeling was reinforced by Mevrouw Johanssen moving to a position equidistant between Dinos and myself.

I certainly had not expected the prosecutor's polite question. 'Mr Aspinall,' he said calmly, looking directly at me, 'I understand you've recently been suffering from a form of skin cancer. Is that so?'

'Yes.'

'A small area, just below your left eye, I believe?'

I acknowledged this was correct.

'Have you had treatment for it?'

'Yes – from a skin specialist in England, in May and June of this year.'

'Are you cured?'

I could sense Dinos urging me to pull out every *vox humana* stop of which I was capable, his Mediterranean temperament exhorting me to play on the sympathies of the court. It was probably the genes inherited from my hard-headed Lancashire forebears that made me reject any idea of seeking clemency by indulging in a false emotional appeal.

'Treatment over many weeks with a drug called Efudix seems to have cleared up the trouble,' I said, 'but I've been warned the cure may only be temporary.'

'You've been examined by doctors in the detention centre?'

'Yes. First in the *Demersluis* and again in the *Schouw*.'

'What have they said?'

'That I must report any suspected recurrence immediately. An appointment will then be made for me to see a dermatologist.'

'Are you satisfied with the care you are receiving?'

'Entirely.' Dinos told me later he felt like cleaving my skull with an axe.

The prosecutor then quietly outlined the case against us. Both of us, he said, had shown ourselves in words and action to be totally unrepentant; true, we had co-operated with the police, but only up to a point. We had been reasonably frank about our own activities but had refused to say anything about the major drug rings operating throughout Northern Europe, although it was obvious we were part of the same mafia-type organisation. He ended by accusing Dinos of failing to recognise the serious nature of his actions and myself of treating the whole affair with unforgivable levity. We must be taught a lesson. He would therefore ask that Dinos be sentenced to a term of five years, and myself, to two and a half.

Dinos' instant reaction was to say loudly: 'Five years – Jesus!' In his misery he seemed to crumple.

He had shown unreasoning optimism for days before the trial, insisting that the prosecutor would not ask for more than two years for him and one for me. When I suggested that even the progressively-minded Dutch felt law-breakers should expiate their debt to society, I was dismissed as 'stuffily British!'

The court suddenly quietened as my defending counsel, looking more than ever like an eighteenth-century portrait by a Dutch master, stood in his elevated pulpit. His manner in court, I was to discover, was just a shade more flamboyant than is customary today among English barristers.

He began by saying he was well aware that those presiding – he bowed courteously to the judges and gave a curt nod to the public prosecutor – he was very much aware of how lively an interest was taken by them all in the work of English writers. He had no doubt they would have read, and appreciated, an outstanding work of fiction published within the last year. There was a slight pause and then, raising his voice he said: 'The book to which I refer is *Earthly Powers* by Anthony Burgess. I feel it will hardly be necessary for me to point out we have in this court the living embodiment of the novel's central character – ' From his position on the rostrum I sensed rather than saw that his arm, like a bat's wing in its black gown, had been extended towards me. 'It is, of course, my client!'

I felt a stab of agonising embarrassment. I had once skimmed through this much-praised book on an aeroplane, and had noticed, with some amusement, that four other passengers in club class were reading the same novel. I was late for an appointment with a skin specialist in London, I was tired and my concentration was not at its best. Almost all I could remember was the opening sentence which read something like: 'It was the afternoon of my eighty-first birthday in Tangier and I was in bed with my catamite when Ali announced the archbishop had come to see me ... '

I fought a strong inclination to bury my face in my hands as Drukker continued eloquently to develop a thesis that, to me, had little connection with the Maugham-like character in *Earthly Powers* who finds so much difficulty in reconciling his homosexual nature with his Catholic faith. In my case, he insisted, the conflict had been between my inborn sexuality and the anachronistic laws of England.

'How can we expect this old Englishman,' he said forcefully, 'to take seriously the laws of any nation when his own country has, from his earliest infancy, because of his natural instincts, arbitrarily placed him in the category of a criminal until he was almost sixty. Which even now has only accorded him, and those like him, a kind of second-class citizenship.' He continued to extend this proposition, insisting it was crucial to an understanding of my obvious alienation from the respectable and the law-abiding.

The judges, even the shy one, kept their eyes on him, showing no trace of surprise or disapproval. When at last he finished, the president thanked him gravely.

It was now the turn of Dinos' lawyer. As Mevrouw Johanssen had moved, once again, to immediately behind my partner, I only heard an occasional phrase of the translation, and what I heard I found unimpressive. His client's excursions outside the law could, it seemed, be ascribed to youthful high spirits. I caught at least one side-swipe at myself, when counsel suggested Dinos had possibly been too much influenced by this elderly, amoral, upper-class Englishman. I was relieved to see his client turn slightly to wink at me. He was clearly recovering from the shock of the prosecutor's demand for five years.

The case was over. The president announced the court would give its verdict in two weeks. We stood up as the judges and the prosecutor disappeared. It was a quarter past five. The hearing had lasted just over three hours.

Before rejoining our police escort, Dinos and I thanked Mevrouw

Johanssen, whose afternoon must have been more exhausting than anyone else's. Scarcely a word had been spoken that she did not have to translate, and yet she appeared to thrive on it, looking as well-groomed and relaxed as she had before starting. She told us it would not be possible for her to be in court in two weeks' time, as she was taking a holiday on board one of her husband's ships in the Mediterranean – a break that had been arranged some time ago. She promised her first action on returning to Amsterdam would be to find out what our fate had been. She had been wonderfully supportive and kind, making us feel she genuinely cared about our future and wished us well. We were grateful for such generosity of spirit.

Jan Drukker fell in beside me as I walked towards the door. I thanked him for his brave attempt at my defence. I did not, at this moment, tell him how shaken I had been by the arguments he had used.

Although I was left free, Dinos was again handcuffed as we were taken down to the cells. This time we were locked in together. There was silence everywhere. All the other prisoners had gone and most of the policemen as well.

Dinos' outrage at the prosecutor's demand re-surfaced. 'That guy must have something personal against me,' he insisted. 'What's it going to do to me – locking me up for all that time? If I'm a bad guy now, I'll be a worse guy when I come out! When I think of how long it took me to draw up my scheme for the rehabilitation of young criminals and get it down on paper – and just nobody in court this afternoon was polite enough to even mention it— ' He broke off resentfully, shaking his head in disbelief.

'They probably thought it savoured of the drunkard lecturing on temperance,' I said. 'Let us count our blessings – in a British court we should almost certainly have been given ten years apiece.'

'You can't be serious?'

'I'm deadly serious – the British are paranoid about cocaine.'

'What a stupid, ignorant, bloody race!'

I told him to stop worrying about the five years. 'It's a habit among prosecutors to ask for more than they expect to be given – judges nearly always lop something off.'

Soon we were in the white maria, in the gathering October dusk. The city lights were being switched on. We were too busy looking enviously at the passing scene to continue wrangling.

The next day I carefully examined the newspapers to see if our trial had been reported. There was nothing.

During the next two weeks I received short visits from Jan Drukker and Françoise. Both considered it likely that the court would cut the prosecutor's demands, but not by much.

I was, at that moment, more or less indifferent to the future. I was virtually penniless and the only alternative to prison would require me live on national assistance or the charity of friends.

I was more concerned about Dinos than myself. An ardent supporter of CND, he was nevertheless quite sure the third world war would break out within the next few years – and be a war to destroy mankind, including himself. As so short a time was left, freedom to make the most of it was all important; hence his acute frustration.

Kind friends in Amsterdam continued to visit me. The reception for visits was just beyond the corridor reserved for interviews with officials. Each tower had its own spacious hotel-lounge type of sitting-room, with half-a-dozen large coffee tables surrounded by sofas and easychairs. A guard sat at a desk just inside the doorway, to whom you gave your identity card on entering, and who would walk across and hand it back, with a regretful smile, when the time had come for your visitors to leave. This was usually after an hour; but if your friends had travelled a long distance or had not seen you for some time this could be lengthened to two hours.

Prisoners were strip-searched after visits. You were taken into a narrow room, lined on one side by six cubicles with glass-panelled doors; large steel boxes containing nothing but a metal seat. Locked inside, you stripped down to underbriefs and handed your clothes through a trapdoor to be thoroughly searched. Before they were handed back, you had to drop your briefs around your ankles, under observation through the glass panel, and turn slowly round to demonstrate that nothing had been concealed in your crutch. I was always impressed by the tact and discretion shown by the guards. They could so easily have made me feel like a trapped animal, but they never did. When you were dressed again, they pressed a button and the back of the cubicle swung open into the corridor leading to the central control-room.

On the frosty morning of Guy Fawkes Day, Dinos and I were once again driven to the law courts. This time we were allowed to make the journey together, but put into separate basement cells.

About twenty minutes later I was escorted upstairs. Drukker was waiting just inside the courtroom door. He held a finger to his lips, so we shook hands in silence. He led me towards the well of the court. I realised the judges were already in their places and the president was speaking to a prisoner. With a slight shock, I saw that the prisoner was Dinos.

'You present yourself, individually, to be sentenced,' Drukker whispered. 'Be ready to take his place as soon as he gets up.'

The president was speaking in Dutch and a young woman was translating. Her voice was inaudible from where I was sitting.

Drukker was again whispering: 'Your friend has just been sentenced to three years … '

I thought immediately: three years – one third remission – a total of two …

Drukker interrupted my thoughts: 'To begin from the date of his arrest … to be served under conditions of maximum security … '

I wondered what that meant. Would we now be separated? I hoped not.

The president's homily came to an end. Dinos got up, gave a curt little bow to the judges and turned to say a few words to the interpreter. She was pretty and I wondered if he was asking her for a date when he was released. I knew he was capable of it – but he assured me afterwards he was merely thanking her. He moved towards the exit, accompanied by two policemen. His expression was one of quiet determination which I suspected masked dismay.

It was my turn. Although I am sure every word the president spoke was accurately translated, only certain sentences were to remain in my mind. 'The court,' said the interpreter with more than a hint of nervousness, 'the court sentences you to a term of one and half years' imprisonment to begin from the date of your arrest … '

With remission, I thought to myself, that's only one year. Oh bless them!

'The court has also decided that the United States dollars and the Dutch currency you were carrying when arrested, and which were confiscated by the police, must be returned to you.'

When the president had finished, I felt great relief and could almost have blown him a kiss, but decided it would be wiser to behave decorously. So, like Dinos, I stood up, bowed, thanked my interpreter and shook hands with Jan Drukker, who told me to expect a visit shortly. I made my way out of court feeling as if I were walking on air.

In the damp basement, I was locked into a cell with Dinos who was contemplating his highly-polished shoes.

He looked up enquiringly.

'One and a half,' I said, sitting beside him.

'That means one year,' he said quickly, 'and I guess you know they gave me three and that means two.'

'A lot better than five.'

'Yeah,' he said, as if he were not too sure. 'Don't forget the Swiss want me back to complete a four-year stretch when the Dutch have finished with me.'

I reminded him of what the inspector at the central police station had told us: the Swiss might forget to ask for him, and the Dutch would not consider it their business to jog their memories.

'It would be great if they did forget,' he said, 'but I've got to be prepared for the worst. The judge said something about serving my sentence under conditions of maximum security. What d'you think he meant?'

'Basically, I suppose he doesn't want you to give a repeat performance of your Swiss escapade.'

'Do they have maximum security prisons in this country?'

'I don't know. You'd better ask your lawyer.'

'I don't think he's much good.'

'That makes two of us – but at least he should know something about his country's prisons.'

'I'm thinking of sacking him. I've heard of a woman lawyer who they say is really smart. Maybe I'll get her to take my case to the court of appeal.'

'Surely you're not thinking of doing that?'

'I sure am.'

'Don't forget the appeal court can lengthen sentences as well as shorten them – and often does.'

'That's a risk I'll have to take. How about you?'

'I'm supremely thankful to have got off so lightly.'

There were no changes in routine during the following two weeks in the *Schouw*. Dinos continued to assist the sports instructor and I went to the workshops to assemble adaptors, which was known as 'brain damage' to the British, Dutch and German prisoners. Once or twice

I asked Dinos if he had made any definite plans about an appeal. His reply was: 'I'm thinking about it.'

Françoise did her best to dissuade him. When I told my lawyer of his probable intentions, he was incredulous. 'Do your best to stop him,' was his advice. 'He won't get his sentence reduced, and he may well find the prosecutor's demand for five years is reimposed.'

Jan Drukker's visit had taken about half-an-hour out of my morning's work. When I returned, I spent the rest of the time mentally rehearsing the verbal assault I intended to make on Dinos' appeal intentions. The persuasive arguments I planned, however, had to be discarded.

Soon after twelve o'clock we returned to our landing and were greeted by the astonishing news that Dinos had been locked in his cell and none of us were to communicate with him. We were not even permitted to shout questions through the tiny window in the cell door. (These spy-holes were made of toughened glass and, to make yourself heard, it was essential to bang the flap, before yelling with all the power of your lungs.)

None of the staff would tell us why Dinos had become incommunicado. I bided my time for a moment when I could question the chief guard. He was middle-aged, with a dark, well-trimmed beard and kind eyes; always quiet and good-tempered, never having any trouble getting the most recalcitrant prisoner to do what he wanted. I got my chance when – just before the working party were locked up – he seized the morning's mail from the office desk to distribute it. As he handed me two letters, I said: 'You know young Dinos has been my partner for some years? Please, can't I be told why he's been locked away?'

He looked at me for a moment, then said in his precise English that was sometimes distorted by Dutch syntax: 'An exception in your case I think can be made. A rumour has reached the *direction*, downstairs, that your friend is planning to escape. Are you surprised?'

I knew Dinos was continually plotting escapes, but had nothing serious in mind at the moment, so said I was surprised. Had these rumours, I enquired, anything to do with the judge's remarks when he was sentenced?

Looking me in the eye, the guard said: 'Perhaps you also know this friend of Dinos who is planning to fire an arrow from a crossbow over the wall into the exercise yard – an arrow with a long rope attached?'

'That was just a joke,' I protested. 'Everybody knows Dinos escaped from a Swiss jail. Even some of the staff pull his leg about it. He's always being asked how long he proposes to stay and what methods he will use to get out. Just to keep us all amused he invents one way after another – like this crossbow nonsense. Surely nobody's taking it seriously?'

'I'm afraid they are – very seriously. The director and his deputies believe him to be a most dangerous man.'

'Can't you change their minds? Can't you explain he's a pacifist, a vegetarian, a teetotaller, a devout member of the Greek Orthodox Church – don't they notice he goes to church every Sunday? He may look like a cut-down edition of Robert Redford, but he's basically a flower child of the 1960s who's never quite grown up.'

He laughed: 'My colleagues and I have told the *direction* that no trouble we have had with him since to this pavilion he came more than three months ago. The welfare people and the sports instructor all say he should remain until it is possible for him to go to the new prison in the Groningen area.' He shrugged. 'But, downstairs, to us they do not listen.'

'What are they going to do with him?'

'He is to be transferred, probably this evening, to the prison at the Hague.'

I knew this to be one of the few nineteenth-century penitentiaries left in the Netherlands. Friends in the *Schouw*, who had personal experience of the place, assured me it had resisted all attempts at modernisation – it was still grim, dark and cheerless and used mainly for prisoners regarded as a danger to others. 'Can nothing be done to stop this move?' I asked, feeling helpless and wretched.

'Dinos has asked for interview with the director. It has been granted and will take place this afternoon. But much hope for a change of heart I would not hold out.'

When our landing returned to the pavilion at four o'clock, after an hour's exercise, I was told his meeting with the director had taken place. It had lasted a quarter of an hour and, as the guard had forecast, there was no change of plan. The transfer would take place that evening.

During the interval between supper – I had not felt hungry and had sent most of it away – and the first period of free association, my door was flung open. The chief guard gave me a conspirato-rial wink. 'Your friend,' he said, 'is about to leave us. For you to say goodbye is not officially permitted – but if your door has, accidentally, been left open, we cannot stop you from saying an unofficial goodbye, can we?' He disappeared in the direction of Dinos' cell.

I could see my partner stacking his possessions on to a trolley with grim resignation. Within a few minutes he had thrown the final item from his wardrobe on top of the pile. The guard began pushing it towards the lifts.

Dinos followed, then, seeing me, swerved across the landing to stand outside my door. For a moment neither of us said a word: we were tongue-tied in mutual gloom. I made a feeble joke, accusing him of having moved heaven and earth to get us into the same pavilion, only to walk out on me.

He grinned sheepishly, saying: 'I guess I should have kept my big mouth shut.'

I said we had all been guilty of encouraging him to talk about escaping, and now there seemed to be nothing we could do to repudiate it.

'Don't worry,' he said, 'we'll get together again before long — and I'll tell Sigi to come and see you regularly.'

This did nothing to raise my spirits. Sigi was the latest in a long succession of girlfriends and the only one I had never managed to like. She never appeared.

The chief guard shouted from the lift. He must hurry — they were waiting. As Dinos obeyed, he called over his shoulder: 'Look after yourself! Say goodbye to the others for me. Keep in touch — I'll write ... ' I listened to the hum of the lift, then shut the door of my cell.

After my release eight months later, I discovered that Dinos might never have been implicated in my trip if he had been selfish enough to distance himself from me on my return.

The Hague prison had sent three staff to collect him. The two guards who had taken him to the internal garage had been grabbed by the visitors and asked, in nervous whispers, just how dangerous was this maniacal Canadian-Greek. I was told the relief on the Hague faces when they were told he had never given any trouble was almost comic.

Dinos did indeed keep in touch, and I was always glad to receive his letters. The Hague prison lacked many of the advantages of Amsterdam's detention centre. The whole place, he wrote, was permeated with a damp, fusty smell common to old institutions. He had, like every prisoner, a cell to himself with a comfortable bed, a table, chairs and cupboards: a basin with hot and cold running water but no *cabinet de toilette*. 'When I want to pee,' he wrote, 'I have to ring a bell for a guard to let me out for a run down the passage. Sometimes they're busy and take their time, while I try to curb my impatience by doing a tap-dance routine!' What he most hated, he said, was the absence of a window; the only source of daylight being an object hardly bigger than a ventilator, high up in the outer wall.

His letters were not all grumbles, however. He praised the food, saying the Hague cooks provided a more varied macrobiotic vegetarian diet than those in our centre. He also found the staff exceptionally pleasant and even established a cordial rapport with the director. This surprised several of the *Schouw*'s inmates who had been in the Hague, and considered the director a distinctly unsympathetic character.

We also got news of each other from Françoise, who visited him regularly. She was annoyed by his increasing determination to appeal. He had also changed his lawyer for someone of whom she strongly disapproved. She never hid the fact that her visits to Dinos were more of a duty than a pleasure, remaining impervious to his undoubted personal charm. She even asked me several times if I knew of any mental illness among Dinos' relations or forbears. I assured her he came from exceptionally healthy stock. His father had made a fortune out of legitimate business interests in Canada. Dinos was anxious to excel in the same way but was too impatient to wait for success by conventional routes. He found it difficult to resist the back door approach.

The list of cases waiting to be heard by the appeal court was always long, and Dinos had been told he would have to wait until spring, possibly summer, before getting a hearing. Meanwhile, Christmas was only a few weeks away and there would be no possibility of a transfer to a more modern prison until his appeal had been won or lost. This did not deter him for a moment. His appeal, nine months later, failed, but his sentence was not increased.

The small crack in the skin of my left cheek, which had disappeared after treatment with a chemical paste on my return from Syria, suddenly reappeared. This time it was wider, resembling a diminutive open mouth. It was as painful as a wasp's sting and haemorrhaged slightly at night: I would wake to find my pillow bespattered with thin streaks of blood.

Suspecting this would get worse, I put in a request to see the doctor.

He was a pleasant young man who took a quick look and said: 'We must get you an appointment with the skin specialist on his next visit.'

A week later, I was summoned from work to go to the tower reserved mainly for prisoners suffering from psychotic disorders. Judging from the paucity of lights visible through its windows at night, the block was usually two-thirds empty. The first floor, however, was occupied by consulting rooms for visiting medical specialists and by the centre's two dentists.

The dermatologist was in his late forties; small, pale and quiet, wearing a dark blue pin-stripe suit with highly polished black shoes. This surprised me, having become accustomed to Dutchmen of all ages, and in almost every profession, wearing sweaters, jeans and trainers. Even more of a surprise was the woman with him. He extended a casual arm towards her, saying: 'My wife – who is also a nurse and my assistant.' She was dressed more for comfort than elegance in russet homespun tweed. But she had a kind, motherly smile and my heart warmed to her.

After a careful examination, the doctor insisted on carrying out a biopsy. I tried to protest this was unnecessary. Documentary evidence of the one performed less than six months before at an East Sussex hospital was lying, with the rest of my medical history, on the table in front of him.

Insisting he must make his own tests, he made me lie on one of those glossy, ultra-hygienic couches, while he punctured my cheek with a hypodermic needle. His wife handed him an object like a miniature cut-throat razor. I felt nothing as a sliver of skin was sliced from the affected spot and sealed into a small container, or when the wound was closed with a single stitch.

I was told I would learn the pathologist's verdict on their next visit, in the second week of January. It was three days before Christmas; not an ideal moment for speedy action. I suppose a touch of self-pity must have been noticeable in my expression, for the doctor said: 'Don't be anxious. Your cancer – if that's what it is – is the sort that develops very slowly. It will be no worse in three weeks' time.'

As I left, they wished me a happy Christmas. They were a charming couple who seemed to epitomise a kind of cosy, Dutch warm-heartedness I had not expected from a visiting specialist in a penal establishment.

During the next two evenings, both landings in pavilion 5 joined forces for a double period of free association. We were busy putting up decorations: paper streamers, tinsel, spun-glass ornaments, fake snow and real holly had been provided in vast quantities. By Christmas Eve, I doubt if any department store in Europe could rival the garish splendour of our surroundings. Each pavilion was given a Christmas tree, illuminated in the Dutch and German fashion with *white* frosted lights.

Various Amsterdam charities had donated quantities of fruit and nuts, including pawpaws, avocados, pineapples and melons, as well as the more prosaic tangerines, apples and walnuts.

After supper on Christmas Eve there was a knock on my door, which opened to reveal two guards – Frans, who resembled an amalgam of a contented baby and a youthful Winston Churchill, and Khan, whose grandparents had emigrated from Lahore to what was then Dutch Guiana at the beginning of this century. Both were trying not to laugh when, to my astonishment, they burst into song. It was a Dutch carol. They were somewhat under-rehearsed, noticeably off-key and found it difficult to restrain their giggles. They quickly reduced me to the same state. Khan picked a gift-wrapped package out of a sack at his feet, pushing it into my hands as they chortled: 'To wish you a most happy Christmas from the guards of pavilion 5!' Still spluttering with laughter, they said something about: 'Free association in half an hour!' and closed my door. A moment later I heard the same scene outside my neighbour's cell.

I unwrapped their present. With it was a card – a reproduction of a Dutch winter scene by Andreas Schelfhout wishing me a *prettige Kerstdagen en gelukkig nieuwjaar*. Inside the Christmas wrapping was a box of chocolates, almonds and raisins. I was astonished and touched by this unexpected gift.

The next morning all the Christians went to church; the Muslims, Hindus, the agnostics and the atheists did not. Our cells were left open most of the day.

About eleven o'clock, a large cardboard box arrived for me, con- taining a quantity of books and a great many good things to eat, gifts from generous friends in Amsterdam who could not be persuaded that life in a Dutch remand centre did not consist of picking oakum on a diet of thin gruel. However, even if their concern was unjustified, it was heart-warming. I distributed a lot of the edibles amongst my fellow prisoners.

I had booked a telephone call to England and, a few minutes before lunch (on this occasion all of us together in the recreation room – we pushed the small tables into one long row) I was allowed to ring up the friend whose letter had been produced at my trial. For a brief moment I was once again, as I have been throughout my life, an outsider looking in upon that, to me, curious institution, the heterosexual family – so often hiding its miseries and emotional violence behind a cosy wall of dissembling. Today being Christmas, my friend had nailed the mask of good cheer firmly in place, although my antennae could detect the stress beneath her words of cheerful reassurance, a stress that was to culminate within a short time in coronary and death.

Almost as soon as Christmas was over, I was unexpectedly summoned to be interviewed by a buxom blonde whose enthusiasm for apparently wrought-iron bangles and necklaces seemed to have got out of control. She positively rattled with every movement. I had already been told she was an emissary of the Ministry of Justice in the Hague and responsible for allocating prison places to those convicted.

She welcomed me with a nervous smile, indicating a comfortable armchair, facing her. Her barbaric-looking bracelets clattered furiously as she shuffled papers. Finding what she wanted, she said brightly: 'You are Mr Alonzo Garcia, and you come from the Argentine, yes?'

I shook my head.

Disconcerted, she scrabbled again amongst the piles of paper. Then, seizing a sheet with obvious relief, she said triumphantly: 'You are Mr Anthony Aspinall and you come from England?'

I admitted this was so.

She continued to peruse the typescript. 'The welfare staff here have recommended you should be sent to a prison in the province of Groningen. It will be a modern prison with all the privileges you have here in the *Schouw*. You will agree, yes?'

She gazed at me, expectantly.

'Is it necessary for me to be sent so far away?' I asked. 'My friends in Amsterdam come to see me quite often. If I'm sent up to Groningen, it will take them a whole day to get there and back. Obviously I shan't see much of them. Is there nothing nearer?'

She pushed the rattling, grey metal up her forearms and extracted what looked like a nominal roll from another pile. After studying it intently, she said: 'There may be a vacancy shortly at Alkmaar. That might suit you better. The journey from Amsterdam is only one half-hour. A small prison – very nice.'

I agreed it sounded better.

'Then I will recommend you to be sent there.' As she took up her pen, she spied something on the paper that made her frown. 'Oh, I see medical treatment you are having from the *huidarts*?'

'It hasn't yet started,' I said.

'No matter. You will not be moved from here until it is completed. No move – until you are well.'

The interview was over. I thanked her and left the office relieved I was not to be thrown immediately out of my comfortable eyrie. Subsequently, I was to discover that Alkmaar would not have been at all a good thing. It was an old prison and had most of the disadvantages of the Hague, but on a smaller scale.

As so often happens in early January, Amsterdam became embedded in ice. The snowfall this year was not excessive, just enough to convert the view from my cell into a Christmas-card landscape; but the temperature dropped to well below freezing and remained there.

Exercise in the open air was voluntary. If you preferred to stay in your warm cell, you could without being criticised.

I always preferred to go out. In bad weather, there were only a few of us. Sometimes, if it was bitterly cold, I was alone, especially if the exercise period was at 8 AM. This was not due to any frantic desire to keep fit, but merely to rid myself of the feeling of dehydration caused by the air-conditioning.

Unfortunately for the staff, it was necessary, under regulations, for two of them to accompany me; and while I, clad in a warm sheepskin jacket, could walk quickly round our yard-garden, enjoying the ringing of frozen flag-stones under my shoes, they had to remain like sentries trying to keep their circulation moving by stamping their feet and clapping their gloved hands. They became increasingly blue in the biting, north-easterly wind, while I was hurrying around the snow-covered shrubs, under walls partly concealed by winter jasmine and cascades of vividly crimson pyrrhus-japonica, enjoying every moment.

After half an hour I sometimes felt it was too unkind to compel them – young as they were – to go on freezing, and would allow myself to be escorted inside with relieved smiles and chattering teeth.

The skin specialist and his motherly wife returned as appointed; the biopsy showed me to be suffering, once again, from the type of skin cancer they described as basel cell carcinoma. I was told its reappearance demonstrated that it could no longer be treated successfully with a chemical paste. My notes had been sent to Amsterdam's University Hospital. I was to become an out-patient of their skin clinic. A few days later two guards took me by taxi on the first of many visits to this large hospital on the southern outskirts, close to the residential suburb of Amstelveen.

It is not the most modern of Amsterdam's hospitals, although many new buildings have been added to it. The complex is linked by paths and private roads, bordered by shrubs and trees. For my first few visits, I was shuttled to and fro between the skin clinic, in a comparatively new, white edifice, and the main hospital a quarter of a mile away. I was examined, alternately, by a fair-haired, boyish doctor in one of the clinic's small surgeries, which had a French window overlooking a formal garden; and by a much older, urbane consultant in all types of cancer who functioned on the second floor of the main building. Access to his impressive consulting room was by a lift so small it resembled a child's pencil-box on a string.

While waiting to see the great man, I would be closeted with half-a-dozen patients plainly suffering from more serious cancers. Skeletally thin, with skin like old parchment, varying from pale grey to blue-white, their eyes expressed the resignation often seen in animals who know they are about to die. I felt myself to be in the very anteroom of death.

After a good deal of discussion, I was made to submit to yet another biopsy. Apparently no medical authority willingly accepts a diagnosis made by another member of the profession.

A further two weeks elapsed before I was summoned to hear the verdict. I was from now onwards accompanied by only one guard. The directors of the *Schouw* had clearly decided I was unlikely to complicate my life – and theirs – by absconding. I always enjoyed my walks in the hospital grounds. I was never handcuffed, but allowed to stroll about unfettered, usually with a different guard each visit. All were friendly young men who had, doubtless, decided that I was unlikely to make any attempt to escape, and were confident of their ability to grab me if I did.

I was taken directly to the consultant: the young doctor from the clinic was with him. The older man gave me a summary of the methods that could be used to remove the cancer. But first he asked if I appreciated my luck in having acquired only a basel cell carcinoma.

I asked what was lucky about it.

'Because,' he said, 'basel cell means it's a form of cancer that doesn't spread throughout the body. Apart from this trouble beneath your eye, you're an exceptionally healthy old man. We don't have to look for what we call secondaries elsewhere.'

This was good news I had not previously appreciated.

He went on to describe the three types of treatment available and their various disadvantages. Ray treatment was a possibility, but would leave deep scars. The cancer could be excised surgically, and a skin-graft substituted, but the risk of damaging a tear-duct was high, which would leave me with a continuously weeping left eye. A third choice was something called cryo-surgery: this was an application to the affected spot of a forceful jet of vapour from liquid nitrogen, which would burn away the cancer and leave some scarring, but not as much as ray treatment.

It was obvious that the consultant and the expert from the clinic favoured cryo-surgery. As I instinctively trusted both men, I had no hesitation in accepting their advice. An appointment was made for the operation to take place in the skin clinic the next week.

I arrived punctually and was directed to lie on a white, plastic-covered couch in the young doctor's surgery. A stainless-steel object, about four feet high, resembling a cross between a dalek and an old-fashioned milk churn was wheeled in. From its centre emerged a length of flexible metal tubing, ending in a small nozzle.

While a nurse draped a green sheet over my shirt and around my neck, dazzling lights above me were switched on and I hastily closed my eyes against the glare.

The specialist and the consultant experimented for some minutes with various methods of protecting my eye from the nitrogen vapour. Eventually they seemed satisfied with their precautions, and the young doctor murmured in my ear: 'I'm going to give you a local anaesthetic. The face is a sensitive area and I'm afraid it will be painful.'

I gritted my teeth as something that looked like a fine needle – but felt like a hatpin – punctured my cheek again and again over a

387

wide space below the eye. Gradually all feeling disappeared from that side of my face.

My left eye was now covered by a steel shade and, as the hissing nozzle of the tubing was brought close to my head, I closed my other eye, tensing for the moment when the jet would start to bore into my skin. I was surprised to feel nothing, except steadily increasing pressure.

The whistling from the thrusting stream of vapour changed slightly in pitch as the young doctor constantly altered the angle of the jet. This assault went on for longer than I expected and I began to wonder how much of my epidermis was being scorched away. Every few minutes the dalek would be switched off and the nurse would swab my cheek and neck very gently. Although I still felt nothing, I was obviously bleeding profusely. When I thanked her, apologising for my inadequate Dutch, she said: 'Don't give it a thought, honey – I'm an American!'

So determined was the doctor to do a thorough job that the anaesthetic slowly began to lose effect. The block of ice that had been my face started to soften, and the pain increased so much, I found it difficult not to squirm away from the implacable, hissing jet.

I heard the consultant say: 'He's beginning to feel it.'

'I know,' was the young man's reply. To me, he said urgently: 'Give me one more minute and it will be over – please, just sixty seconds … '

Never had I known seconds to tick away more slowly until the noise of the jet ceased and the pain, that had been excruciating, became bearable.

Both doctors drew back to allow the nurse to clean me up. She removed the covering from my eye and mopped up the blood which had, in places, soaked through the protective sheet. She laid absorbent material lightly over the wound. A clean pillow was inserted under my head and I was told to lie quietly for half an hour.

The consultant offered me a pain-killing injection which I declined.

'I thought you were in favour of drugs,' he said, smiling.

'Not if taken intravenously,' I snapped.

He laughed, saying I would be given plenty of tablets to take away.

The trio now left, the consultant saying he would be examining me again within a few days.

As I lay looking at the ceiling (they had dimmed those awful lights) I wondered if I had been wise to decline the injection. The anaesthetic had now completely worn off and my left cheek felt as if it had been assaulted by a red-hot poker.

I heard the door behind me open and shut. This puzzled me because only a few minutes had elapsed since I had been left alone and I had not pressed the bell beside me. The anxious face of the guard who had brought me to the hospital looked down at me.

Was I all right? Would I like some coffee?

I refused, saying I could drink nothing without disturbing the swabs precariously balanced over my cheek.

The guard, Henk, was from my own pavilion. He was tall, very slim, with red hair, many freckles and pale eyes. He noticed that the French window had been left slightly open. The sight made him grin at me: 'Straight out of here you could have walked at any time in the last few minutes!'

'I wonder how far I'd have got – looking like this.'

'You don't look too bad – apart from the *verbanden* on your face and the blood on your collar and shirt.'

He made no attempt to close the window but asked if I wanted to be left alone.

I told him I would be glad of his company, but surely he would be much happier chatting up the pretty nurses.

'They are too busy for chat – and, anyway, I am a serious man with a wife and three children.'

I encouraged him to tell me about his family and his home which, I knew, was in an outlying suburb where I had friends. He spoke proudly of his eldest boy's successes at school and of his anxiety about the frequent illness of his youngest, a daughter who was obviously very important to him. My bachelor's antennae noticed that he implied, rather than stated, that he and his wife did not see eye to eye.

Doctor and nurse returned and asked Henk to ring for a taxi. The nurse removed the swabs, telling me, with approval, that my blood was clotting beautifully. She then swathed my head in bandages, allowing freedom only to my mouth, nostrils and right eye, assuring me this was necessary because of the position of the wound.

When Henk returned he was given a box of tablets to hand to the *Schouw*'s nursing orderlies, who were to dole them out to me, four per day. I was given two on the spot, with an order to take them before going to bed. I was to be brought back the following afternoon for a check-up and fresh dressings.

Henk should have gone off duty as soon as we got back, but he insisted on accompanying me up to pavilion 5. The evening meal was being circulated.

I could only eat a few mouthfuls. When Khan came to collect my tray, he reminded me there was a film that evening in the gymnasium. The whole pavilion would be attending – did I wish to go? All I wanted was to swallow my tablets and fall into bed.

He looked at me with large, anxious dark eyes saying: 'You realise you will be quite alone in the pavilion? There is no one we can delegate to look after you.'

'I don't need looking after,' I said. 'My only need is for my carton of grapefruit juice from the prisoners' fridge. If you could bring it before going to the flicks, I'd be glad.' He did as I asked, but still looked concerned when saying good night.

As I got into bed, everyone was let out of their cells and milled around waiting for the lifts. Many seemed touchingly anxious to know how the old Englishman had survived his visit to the hospital and a queue must have formed outside my cell. Face after face appeared at the little window, expressing concern at the spectacle of the figure with the dramatically bandaged head. I had only just enough energy to raise my thumb repeatedly, and hoped this would signal I was on the road to recovery.

I was still awake when the mob returned two hours later. This time they left me alone but I was conscious, just before the staff went off-duty, of the flap over my spy-window being raised and Khan gazing at me. I had turned out my bedside lamp and was too weary to make facetious signals. He obviously assumed I must be asleep.

In spite of the tablets, I slept badly and, at about 6 AM, got up for a drink of water: the pain-killers had made me desperately thirsty. As I stretched out for the tooth-glass, I caught sight of myself in the mirror above the basin and recoiled with shock. Overnight, I had become a gargoyle. The glands on my neck had swollen into an array of scarlet balloons, streaked with purple. Beneath my chin an object like a giant goitre wobbled obscenely. Had I been frozen into stone, I would have resembled one of the gutter-spouts high up on the western façade of Notre Dame de Paris. I made an abortive attempt to shave the small areas of face between bandages.

When I heard the staff approaching with the coffee I wondered if they would wince away from me or burst out laughing. They merely gazed silently until one said: 'God! Is it as painful as it looks?'

I was able to tell them it was only the glands – now rock-hard in the back of my neck – and the hole in my cheek, that really hurt. The highly coloured excrescences under my chin were comparatively painless.

The programme for my day was a working morning and the hospital in the afternoon. I was told I could go sick from work if I wished. I decided to carry on as usual and was relieved when everybody, once they had got over the initial shock, accepted the gargoyle without complaint. They made it easier for me by joking, saying I looked like a character from outer space.

At the clinic the doctor tore off my bloodstained bandages with such practised fingers, I scarcely felt anything. He examined my cheek for a long time, touching it lightly once or twice. 'I'm pleased with my handiwork,' he said at last.

'Can I look?' I asked. There was a mirror on the wall.

I was appalled by my reflection. Under my left eye was a crimson crater, big enough to bury the bowl of a large dessert spoon.

Sensing what was going through my mind, the doctor said: 'When it heals you'll hardly notice it.'

'But will it ever heal?' I was badly shaken by the depth of the hole.

'Of course it will,' he said confidently. 'Now come and sit down while I fix you up.'

He placed surgical gauze gently over the wound and fixed it into position with adhesive tape. It was a relief to know I would not again have to have my head encircled in yards of bandaging. I asked how long it would be before my glands reverted to normal and was told it would take some days.

The doctor said he would be telephoning the director of the *Schouw* to say it was imperative my dressings should be changed daily and I must be brought back to the clinic each week to be examined for a minimum of four weeks; after that it would be fortnightly, then monthly.

This was good news; it meant I should be remaining in the *Schouw* until the end of my sentence. I would not be transferred to Alkmaar and have to undergo the strain of new conditions and friends.

The tower's two young medical orderlies conscientiously carried out the instructions about my dressings. At the beginning, when my face was still raw, they tried hard not to hurt me, and I, in turn, felt impelled not to flinch unnecessarily.

There can be no doubt that I owe a considerable debt to all the staff of the detention centre with whom I came in contact, not forgetting those in charge of security. Judging from what one sees on television and reads in the newspapers, the Dutch prison officer differs considerably from the British.

Men and women accepted into the Netherlands prison service must have achieved high educational standards and are required to undergo months of special training before they ever set eyes on a prisoner. The result is a corps that resembles a team of social workers rather than mere custodians.

When first appointed to a prison or remand centre, they are provided with a 'minder' – a senior guard, who takes them under his or her wing, and without whom they are not allowed to give orders or take any action for five or six weeks. And their training seems to continue, intermittently, throughout their careers. Even guards with years of experience are regularly sent on courses.

They wear uniform, but of a pleasantly casual type. The men wear pale blue shirts, dark blue ties, navy-blue blazers with an insignia embroidered on the breast pocket; dark grey trousers and light-weight, slip-on, black shoes. The women wear pale blue blouses instead of shirts, and the majority seem to prefer dark grey skirts to slacks of the same material.

Apart from in the tower for women prisoners, it was rare for more than one woman to be attached to any pavilion. During the eleven and a half months I spent in the *Schouw*, only two women were appointed to pavilion 5 and neither remained for long. One was comparatively senior in the service; a plump, motherly creature in her late forties with a quiet voice and gentle manner whom all of us liked and who could calm the most churlish prisoner with a soothing word. Unfortunately, she suffered from high blood-pressure and was advised by her doctor to resign. We were sorry to see her go.

The other was much younger; blonde, shrill and unnecessarily bossy when a touch of diplomacy would have been preferable. She had, however, a china-doll prettiness, plus a good figure, and I assumed the younger generation of residents would consider her temptingly sexy. I was mistaken. They all hated her. It was perhaps as well that she was shifted fairly soon.

As for the male guards, they were a remarkable collection of men whose courtesy and good humour never faltered under the severest provocation. All treated me with a politeness I found astonishing. They never gave me a direct order. I was always addressed as Mr Aspinall. 'Will you please, Mr Aspinall, do this, that or the other,' and yet, like everybody else, I called each by his Christian name.

I was, of course, probably less of a nuisance than some. I looked upon myself as a gambler who had lost a 'coup' and was paying his debts. As a criminal I knew I was a rank amateur. I could not regard prison staff as natural enemies to be harassed and provoked as much as possible. The kindly but irascible Ian may have summed up the situation accurately when he said: 'You're the screws' pet, Tony, because your door is the only one in the whole bloody pavilion they can open and be confident of *not* receiving a complaint, a wail of self-pity or an abusive shout. No wonder they love you!'

Love me or not, their kindness and consideration gave me a standard for human behaviour from which I shall never wish to escape.

They were frequently astonished by the behaviour of their British counterparts as portrayed on television – Dutch TV takes a good deal of its material from the BBC and ITV. I was often asked why the British prison officers (*bewaarder*) wanted to pretend they were soldiers? Why all that parade-ground stamping of heavy boots? Why all the shouting and sweating in thick uniforms – and those caps! It was the caps, glued to their heads night and day, indoors and out that amazed the Dutchmen. 'Do they wear them in bed?' they would ask. 'We find it strange you British are still so militaristic when even the Germans have given up such behaviour.'

The Dutch male can be tough but is not addicted to spit and polish. In appearance, their army is just a little bit casual. Hair is allowed to be long and rings are permitted in the ear. I once heard an Englishman in the exercise yard refer contemptuously to these habits, only to be squelched by two Israelis who quarrelled frequently with each other but joined forces to point out that Israel's army also allowed long hair and ear-rings: 'And if you think we can't fight just send us a few of your short-back-and-sides to find out!' they roared in anger.

Soon it was April and I settled down to a quiet life watching the foliage in the Juliana Park growing greener, and the commercial craft on the Weesper Canal being outnumbered by small white yachts.

I was still being taken every two weeks to the skin clinic, by taxi with a single guard. I shall not forget the beginning of one trip when we had settled in the back of the usual Mercedes diesel taxi in the garage. My keeper realised he had forgotten his cigarettes and leapt away upstairs to collect them. It was some time before he returned; the taxi-driver and I gossiped. Eventually, he looked anxiously at the dashboard clock, saying: 'I hope your colleague won't be much longer. I've another customer to collect in half an hour.' He looked at me. 'I understand we're taking a prisoner to hospital?'

'You've already got him,' I said.

His round, good-natured face registered amazement. 'Not you – surely?' he stuttered.

'Yes, me. Who did you think I was?'

Absurdly embarrassed, he said: 'I thought you must be an English official visiting a new Dutch prison!' After my recent ups and downs, I was surprised I still gave an impression of respectability.

The deep hole under my eye had now filled up with new pink flesh. The dressings were no longer necessary and I was, at first, dreadfully conscious of the crimson scar. There was also a slight distortion of the eyelid, caused by the shrinkage of the skin under the burning vapour. I was assured both these minor disfigurements would lessen with time. Now, four years later, neither the scarring nor the distortion have entirely disappeared, but both, I am told, are hardly noticeable and no longer cause me concern. More important – there has been no recurrence of the cancer.

During my last two months in the *Schouw*, apart from two Dutch prisoners who were waiting for appeals, I had been longer in pavilion 5 than anyone else. Among those who arrived during my final months were the two Israelis. I found them to be a fascinating contrast. Karl, Austrian by birth, had emigrated to Israel in his early twenties. He was now forty-eight and had resettled in the Middle West of the United States, because of his ever-increasing disenchantment with the State of Israel. He had, he said, gone out to Tel-Aviv in a mood of youthful idealism at becoming a citizen of a Jewish homeland. He now denounced almost every Israeli political party, accusing them of having turned the so-called homeland into a greedy, imperialist power, based on a reservoir of cheap Arab labour.

These opinions aroused the wrath of the other Israeli, whose ancestral roots had not been in a Viennese suburb but in the Mellah of Marrakech. Benyamin – known to all as Benny – was not yet thirty; a diamond-cutter by trade who had made a brief but unlucky incursion into the hard drug scene, he was now awaiting extradition to Belgium. Benny believed implicitly in the superiority of the Jewish race and considered the Arabs ought to be grateful for being dragged — even if a trifle roughly — into the twentieth century. All they had ever done, he insisted, before the Jews returned to their rightful home, was to sit on their flea-bitten bottoms in waterless deserts.

These savagely divided opinions led to violent slanging matches between them, Benny accusing Karl of being a traitor to his race, Karl counter-charging that Benny was the sort of unimaginative lout whose attitude was almost certain to provoke a third world war.

I succeeded in keeping on friendly terms with both. Karl was typically Viennese in his enthusiasm for serious music and I was happy to listen to his amusing gossip about central European orchestras and the often outrageous behaviour of famous soloists and conductors. He, in turn, showed a surprising interest in my recollections of musical events in Salzburg and Vienna long before he was born.

He had been convicted of possessing a hundred kilos of cannabis, for which he had been sentenced to four months. This was not a new experience for him. He had done time for the same offence in Greece and Spain. For the Greeks he had nothing but praise, but Spanish prison conditions, he insisted, were still in the Middle Ages.

It amused me to learn that, in spite of these European disincentives, he always managed to maintain a flow of soft drugs into the United States. With his wife and a younger brother, he had set up an establishment to provide well-trained guard-dogs for the private houses of the rich, and for business premises, in the Ohio city where he lived. They specialised in German shepherd dogs, imported from some of the best kennels in the Rhineland.

Such dogs, if imported by air, have to travel in a special crate provided by the airline. These crates may be obtained some days in advance of the flight. You just tell the air-freight department that you wish the dog to become accustomed to sleeping and eating inside the wooden cage before it is thrust into the aircraft hold. You refrain from mentioning that certain changes will be made to the sides and base of the crate: what was previously hollow will have a solid centre of cannabis.

Flying at high altitudes for eight hours has a disturbing effect on the temper of even the gentlest dogs and customs officers are understandably reluctant to allow their hands to be torn to shreds by an enraged Alsatian.

Benny was a complete contrast. If he had any interest in music it was confined to pop. He was exceptionally handsome, dark-skinned and glossy-haired, and exuded sex-appeal from every pore in his massive body. This was confirmed by the number of letters he received from girlfriends all over Western Europe. Unable to read French or English, he often asked me to translate. His spoken English, unlike Karl's, had been picked up listening to the disc jockeys of the American Forces Network. Most of the letters were startlingly frank and dwelt nostalgically on Benny's physical attributes, his insatiable performances in bed and how much they missed him. He encouraged me to read aloud my on-the-spot translations of these effusions in purple ink, while he preened like a randy parrot, saying things like: 'Wow, man! She must be the broad I picked up in that bar on the Reguliers Gracht – a real doll!'

It surprised me that the three Arabs in the pavilion were much friendlier towards him than they ever were to Karl. They apparently felt a natural kinship with a Jew whose ancestors had lived under the protection of a Moroccan sultan and very little with one from a cultivated, middle-class, central European background, and who was prepared to speak out in defence of their own race under Israeli domination.

For some time after the irrepressible, motorbike loving Pieter had left us, his cell next to mine was occupied by a middle-aged Pakistani, a lean brown man, with mournful eyes and gentle manner. His hair was heavily flecked with grey, making him look older than his forty-six years. Possibly the strain of numerous children contributed to this. He had lived for years in Amsterdam and was a prosperous shopkeeper with a large emporium in an outer suburb, specialising in women's clothing from the Indian continent. He had many relations who had established themselves, not only in the Netherlands, but also in the north of England.

He showed a touching concern about my future, urging me, if I were ever in need, to go at once to any of his brothers – he had an astonishing number. All I needed to do, he assured me, was mention his name and where we had met. I would be given shelter and put financially on my feet. I found it difficult to understand the reason for this extraordinarily generous suggestion to an old Englishman he barely knew. In the end I decided it could only be due to sheer goodness. It was not easy to reconcile this with the reason for his imprisonment. One of his brothers had been accused of killing a teenaged daughter who had brought disgrace upon the family by becoming pregnant. My neighbour was charged with complicity by supplying the fuel for the burning of his niece's body. He pleaded that he had not known the intended purpose of the jerry-can of petrol. Both were found guilty and sentenced to ten years apiece.

The next occupant of that cell was a tall, pale, shortsighted Dutchman of about twenty who, with the help of contact lenses, showed outstanding ability at all outdoor games. Well educated, he spoke exceptionally good English and was as interested in vintage, or veteran, motor cars as young Pieter had been in up-to-date motorbikes.

As I belong to the same generation as these old crocks and, half a century before, had owned several and driven many, he regarded me as a kind of mobile encyclopaedia on his favourite subject. It was doubtless for this reason and also because he wanted to practise his English, that he followed me around like Mary's little lamb during free association.

However, a few days after his arrival a guard asked me if I had noticed a case involving the rape and murder of several elderly women in Amsterdam. The popular press were referring to the killer as the Netherlands version of the Yorkshire Ripper. I had noticed the case; it was achieving the sort of notoriety that made it impossible to avoid.

'You know the police have caught the man they believe to be responsible?'

I admitted I had read this about ten days ago.

'You remember the description of the killer?'

'A student at a local polytechnic, wasn't it? Impeccable family background – twenty years of age … ' I knew what the guard was going to tell me.

He jerked his head towards my neighbour's cell. 'He's next door to you.'

I think I said 'Good God!' and then asked why the boy had not been sent to the psychiatric tower.

'Presumably because the doctors feel he will have a better chance of recovery if he is kept amongst ordinary people.'

That his rehabilitation should already have become a number one priority was, I felt, typical of the Dutch penal system.

'We've noticed,' said the guard, 'that, towards you, he seems most friendly.'

'He likes to ask me questions about old-fashioned motor cars.'

'For whatever reason it is your company he seems to seek during free association and we want you to be careful.'

'Careful of what?'

'Careful – because he's been accused of raping and killing women of your age and even older.'

'And, in the absence of old women, you feel he might switch to old men?'

My brusqueness made him turn pink. 'We think there is no real danger – but, because of your age, we have to caution you.'

Although no other prisoner was given an official warning, his identity did not remain secret long. The revelation at first produced shivers of abhorrence, especially among the younger prisoners. But they never abused him, they just ignored him. This was particularly noticeable in the exercise yard: they would do their best to avoid walking with him. However, as the weeks went by these feelings of repugnance became less intense and, eventually, everyone was able to accept him without visibly recoiling.

While awaiting trial, he became a temporary patient in a high-security psychiatric hospital near Utrecht. A week or so before going to court he was back in pavilion 5. As he had never shown any symptoms we could recognise as psychopathic, we were unable to detect if his time in hospital had done him good. He was full of praise for the staff and appeared to have enjoyed himself. His only complaint was of the noise of trains from a nearby railway line.

Outwardly, he was a perfectly normal, slightly boring young man of average intelligence who was good at games and showed few signs of internal conflict. His parents came regularly to see him, also a married sister. His brother-in-law did not, which was obviously much resented. His mother and father had always been enthusiastic voluntary social workers, concentrating on the housebound and elderly. It was from these geriatrics that their son had chosen his victims. The police had suspected, from the first rape and murder, that the killer had been known and trusted by his prey, because there was never any sign of forced entry into their homes. The psychiatrists who gave evidence at his trial advanced the theory that his impulse to kill sprang from a psychopathic resentment of the care and affection bestowed upon these underprivileged old women by his parents.

The court sentenced him to ten years – to be served under close psychiatric supervision. This meant he would be free in just over six years. Some of us wondered if the 'head shrinkers' could make him sufficiently safe to be let loose by then.

The sentence was shorter than the young man expected and, naturally, he was delighted. But his pleasure was short-lived, because the public prosecutor swiftly made use of his own right of appeal – presumably he felt the sentence was too lenient and might endanger more innocent lives. The news of the prosecutor's decision was brought to the youngster by his lawyer and triggered off an outburst of fury. For the first time we realised the potential for violence beneath his bland exterior.

I had left the Netherlands some months before the appeal came up. I was never told of the result, nor did I see it reported.

It was a pleasant contrast to seek out the pavilion's trio of conscientious objectors, young Dutchmen who had refused to do national service. When offered the usual alternative of working as medical orderlies, they had turned that down as well. In the Netherlands, these more extreme types of objector to conscription are chucked into prison for the time they would have spent in the forces.

Our pacifists were not popular with the staff and were especially disliked by the hierarchy in the base of the tower: the director and his deputies. This was understandable, for they were an exceptionally bright triumvirate of natural-born rebels against authority. Two were studying law, the third medicine. All had made themselves familiar with the fine print of every instruction issued by the Ministry of Justice on the subject of prison and prisoners. If any of the staff infringed, by a hair's breadth, a ruling that might be to a prisoner's advantage, they would rush immediately – and most eloquently – to the man's defence, showing every sign of enjoyment. Occasionally they went too far in their concern for the underdog and delight in cocking snooks at authority, and were whisked to the tower's attic to those bare cells, furnished only with a mattress, for twenty-four hours – sometimes longer.

The younger embryo lawyer made no secret of being gay. This, in a country which permits its army to have an official Gay Support Group, was never the cause of a single eyebrow being raised and was regarded as being of no more importance than the colour of his eyes: large, blue and extremely mischievous.

Alan Reeve was allowed to mix with the rest of us during my last months. He was lean and tall with splendid honey-pale hair brushed straight back from a high forehead. I felt he would have made an admirable stand in for the late Johnny Weismuller, the original Hollywood Tarzan. I was amused to see he was treated with noticeable deference by most other prisoners. They plainly looked upon him as the supreme aristocrat of crime and tended to be more than a little obsequious. This attitude had, I think, been exacerbated by his long isolation, which had given him the status of a *monstre sacré*.

He retained an aura of a man apart, even after his transfer to the *Schouw*, where he was treated as a normal prisoner.

We met occasionally, in the library and at cinema shows; from time to time we exchanged books and magazines. He never joined us in the workshops, occupying himself by writing articles for left-wing weeklies. His account of his unhappy years in Broadmoor was published several years ago under the title *Notes from a Waiting Room*.

At his trial the prosecution asked for a sentence of twenty years; the court imposed a penalty of fifteen: one of the longest promulgated in a Dutch court in recent years.

We last met shortly before my release when we found ourselves side by side in the English section of the library. We exchanged the usual polite enquiries about health. Usually he seemed coolly indifferent to everything around him which, in view of his history, I found surprising. On this occasion, however, his last words were fervent thanks that he was no longer a prisoner in England.

Months later, I read that he had been moved to the stale-smelling old prison in the Hague, where he had gone on hunger strike for what he believed to be unfair treatment. Dinos had by then been transferred to a modern prison near the German frontier, so I no longer received an 'off the record' account of Reeve's difficulties at the Hague.

As the date of my release grew nearer, I made plans for disposing of the books and clothes that had been stored in my lawyer's attic. Early in June, Jan Drukker had told me the premises had been burgled and, to everyone's amazement, the thieves appeared to have been interested only in my luggage. The suitcases had been broken open, but nothing, so far as he could tell, had been stolen.

The reason for this extraordinary break-in remains a mystery. Some say it was a clandestine operation conducted by the DEA in a ham-fisted attempt to find evidence (drugs) that would have embarrassed the law firm. I find this theory a bit too Machiavellian.

I was naturally anxious to check for myself at the first opportunity, and to select the articles I wanted, for my release would coincide with a deportation order.

The procedure for release required the Ministry of Justice to confirm, after consulting the *Schouw*'s director and Françoise, that six months' remission had been granted, and I would be free precisely one year from the date of arrest. But, as a foreigner, it would be a qualified sort of freedom.

A Dutchman could walk out of the Bijlmer *penitentaire inrichting* on the morning he was discharged and pick up the metro at the Spaklerweg station, or ring for a taxi if he could afford it; often a girlfriend would be waiting with a car. But these privileges were not available to foreigners.

The Dutch, understandably, had become tired of having so many criminals among the alien hordes in their principal cities and were doing their best to rid themselves of those they had successfully prosecuted.

The drill was to hand us over to a special police unit that operated from its own headquarters close to the Waterlooplein. They were said to function under the feather-light control of the Ministry of Justice in the Hague and were considered very much a law unto themselves. Everybody referred to them as the 'foreign' police; officially, they were known by initials that seemed to have no bearing on their functions – which included responsibility for newly-discharged foreign prisoners. Its staff were notorious for making capricious decisions from which there was no appeal. Not only foreign prisoners, but many Dutch lawyers and probation officers were distinctly nervous of them, admitting that no court could bring them to heel. They were, so it was said, almost a state within a state.

Frontier control inside Benelux being light, it was their habit to take all foreign prisoners, under escort,and deport them outside this area within a few hours of their release. The British, in handcuffs, were usually driven to Schiphol to be put on a flight to the United Kingdom, or down to the Hook of Holland to board a car-ferry to

Harwich: the 'bracelets' not being removed until they had their feet on the gangway.

Knowing the 'foreign' police would decide if I could have time to pack some belongings and get rid of the rest, I begged Françoise and Jan Drukker to make a personal approach to them. They nobly agreed, but warned it was unlikely to have much effect on this most autocratic of units.

On the day before my release I was taken to the University Hospital for a final check-up. In the evening, the bulletin listing those appearing in court or due to be released the following day, was pinned to the noticeboard. There were three names under 'To be discharged'; two were Dutch; the third was my own, to which had been added the ominous tailpiece: that I was to be paroled at 10 AM into the custody of the string of initials which shrouded the identity of the 'foreign' police.

Those prisoners I would not see in the morning came to say goodbye. Although glad freedom was so close, I liked most of them well enough to feel saddened that we should probably never meet again. Those guards not on duty the following morning also gave me their good wishes. Several had accompanied me to the hospital and I told them it might be a long time before I became accustomed to looking after myself.

In the morning, I finished my muesli with my early coffee. My door had been left open – a sign of impending freedom – so I collected a trolley from outside the lifts and began loading all my gear.

The landing were released for their morning work and crowded around to say goodbye; the Arabs kissing me on both cheeks, the Surinamers, Germans, French and Dutch shaking me frantically by the hand and slapping me on the back.

When they had been hustled into the lifts, the guards took an inventory of everything in my cell. Having made sure nothing had been broken or stolen, they left me to kick my heels until a few minutes before ten, when the chief guard shouted it was time for me to get going. As I pushed my trolley into the lift there were more goodbyes to the guards who rushed out of the office. As the lift descended, I could still hear them shouting good wishes.

I flashed my identity card at the control-room window for the last time, surrendering it as I entered the admin block. In the clothing-store my suitcase and shoulder-bag had been put ready on a counter. When I had repacked the contents and added what I had brought on the trolley, I dumped the bags against the wall while I went to the bank and withdrew all the money in my account.

I was now ready to leave but there was no sign of the 'foreign' police. There were no chairs, either, so I just leaned against the wall. I had to lean for quite a long time. It was nearly eleven-thirty before two self-important men in rumpled suits turned up.

They were given documentary proof of my identity, and I was led downstairs (no handcuffs) to a two-door Opel; the younger policeman carried my suitcase, for which I was grateful. I was politely but firmly pushed on to the back seat – presumably to thwart any attempt to escape from their clutches.

Their offices were in the city centre, in a converted warehouse overlooking the River Amstel. We entered a sort of general office where half-a-dozen young men in plain clothes – most in shirtsleeves – sat at desks. Some were talking to visitors or telephoning, others laboriously using old-fashioned manual typewriters. The sun was shining through large windows overlooking the river. No one appeared to notice our arrival. My escorts pointed me to a chair in a corner, put my luggage beside me and disappeared.

I remained apparently invisible for about a quarter of an hour. Suddenly, a shirtsleeved policeman, older than most of them, waved a commanding hand in my direction, summoning me in front of him.

I obeyed, wondering nervously what he was going to say. For a long minute he said nothing – just looked at me while pushing back a grey forelock.

'Mr Aspinall,' he said at last in a bored tone, 'we understand you wish to have your deportation from the Netherlands deferred while you dispose of the contents of your former apartment?'

I admitted this was so.

'It is unfortunate that Inspector van den Bruin, who has a special authority over people like yourself, will be away until Monday.'

My spirits sank. Today was Friday. Would I be locked up over the weekend or would I, perhaps, be kicked out of the country right away?

As I was about to ask, the policeman forestalled me by saying, casually: 'We've therefore decided to release you, temporarily, into the city. You must return here on Monday at eleven o'clock to see the inspector. Meanwhile you may stay with friends or go to an hotel. We understand you have more than enough money to cover your expenses?'

For a moment I was speechless. I just nodded dumbly, hardly believing my ears. Could this be the dreaded 'foreign' police, or was I dreaming?

'There is something else you must do,' he continued, 'before your interview with the inspector. You must get yourself a one-way ticket to England – by air or sea, the route doesn't matter. It will be for Inspector van den Bruin to decide how long you may remain here, so the ticket should not be dated. You understand?'

I nodded.

'We shall, of course, keep your passport for the time being.'

'How can I register in a hotel without it?' I asked.

He opened a drawer and took out the sort of card travellers have to fill in before entering a foreign country. He wrote my full name and passport number on it and signed it with a flourish. Handing it to me, he said: 'This merely states your passport has been mislaid and its loss is being investigated. It doesn't label you as a criminal, so don't worry.' He dismissed me, saying: 'That's all. Remember to be punctual for the inspector on Monday. I can't tell you how long he will let you stay in Amsterdam – he may throw you out immediately – that is for him to decide. Now you had better get going. You'll find a taxi outside – I ordered it before I spoke to you.'

I thanked him, seized my luggage and almost ran down the stairs. I threw my stuff into the taxi beside the driver, naming a small hotel on the Kaisersgracht where I had stayed before. The sun was high in the heavens and I felt jubilant.

My first action after I had settled into the hotel was to ring up friends, not only in Amsterdam but also in France and England, to tell them I was 'out'. Then a ten-minute walk to the Dam Square brought me to what is often described as the Harrods of this great city: a department store called the Bijenkorf, where I ate lunch in the self-service restaurant. I had no complaints about the food in the *Schouw*, but it was wonderful to be able to choose what I really wanted and to pick up a carafe of good red wine to drink with it.

Happily replete, I walked to my lawyer's office, close to the law courts. Jan Drukker was, I knew, on holiday but Cornelius van Akker saw me at once.

He was able to reassure me about Monday's interview, saying I would never have been released into Amsterdam so casually if there was any intention of throwing me out of the country when the weekend was over.

Guessing I wanted to check my stuff he took me up to the attic. He advised me just to take a cursory look and then go off to enjoy my first weekend of freedom. Saying he had to be in court within the next quarter of an hour, he gave me the attic key, asking me to give it to his secretary when I had finished. 'Don't get really stuck in until Monday afternoon,' he advised, as he disappeared, taking two steps at a time.

My small library of forty to fifty hardback books was missing, also an exceptionally large collection of road maps covering the whole of Europe, North Africa, the Middle East and much of South America had disappeared. It was some time before I realised a favourite piece of luggage – a canvas and leather bag that held a lot and yet would fit under the seat of any aircraft – was also missing. Perhaps it had been used to carry away the books and maps? Paperbacks were apparently of no interest to the thief.

Whoever it was had entered, and left, the firm's premises by the double front doors onto the Prinsengracht. To do this he must have procured duplicate keys, which could not have been easy and were probably expensive. To go to all this trouble for books by present-day English and American writers was plainly absurd. They were first editions – biographies, travels and novels – that, in time, might have acquired some value, but not for years. The thief was obviously looking for something more important – presumably drugs – to embarrass me and those who had defended me. Malice on the part of the DEA, who were said to be livid with the Dutch authorities for blocking their attempt to snoop on pot-smoking GIs on leave in the Netherlands? I often wonder. Whoever it was, he was clearly well-read and, I suspect, American.

As I walked back to my hotel, I stopped at a travel agent and bought a single, open ticket to London via the Hook to Harwich route. Knowing my luggage would be heavy, I had decided to travel by sea. Having so often paid astronomical sums for overweight when travelling by air (hashish can be very heavy) I felt it was time to begin economising.

I settled down at a desk at my bedroom window, overlooking the canal. I wanted to write a 'bread and butter' letter to the guards of pavilion 5 to thank them for their many acts of kindness. I looked hopefully for writing paper, but it was not that sort of hotel. However, I did find an extra-large, highly coloured postcard of red roses and decided this would have to do as a stop-gap.

I decided to eat that evening at a Greek restaurant I had frequented when I was feeling too lazy to cook. The staff recognised me with cries of: 'It's been so long since we've seen you! Where have you been?' I murmured something about South America – after all, I had been to Peru since I last saw them – which made them say how nice it must be to travel. My reply had been: 'Well … sometimes!'

After dinner I strolled about the city alone, enjoying the sensation of being a free man. It was a warm evening and the willow trees lining some of the canals were trailing their leaf-laden branches in the water. My route took me through the centre. The streets were ablaze with light, there were lots of people about and I was happy to walk anonymously among them. All along the Damrack – the wide thoroughfare that links the Central Station to the Dam Square, with its incessant cavalcade of bell-ringing, yellow trams – I watched a score of young Surinamers, darting like tropical fish in and out of the crowds, mouthing, 'Hash?' at anyone who looked like a customer. They ignored me, as always, which I found amusing. It is only in Arab countries and in South America that pot-smoking is regarded as an old man's hobby.

After a while I began to feel pleasantly tired and returned to my hotel. I sat for half an hour, slowly sipping a *Genever*, on its narrow terrace overlooking the canal. The Dutch seldom draw their curtains at night and the light from the windows of the seventeenth- and eighteenth-century houses, reflected in the water, adds greatly to the city's charm. Now hardly able to keep my eyes open, I went up to my room and, after a warm shower, fell into bed and slept dreamlessly.

I spent the next days with friends whose homes were in or near Amsterdam. They were all employed in publishing, journalism or television: none had any connection with the world of narcotics. Several lived in the Bijlmermeer, and each time my train stopped in the Spaklerweg station I would look up at the white tower-blocks of the remand centre with a slight feeling of genuine nostalgia. I gazed at the top-floor windows of the *Schouw*, wondering what changes had taken place since my departure. I cannot imagine any ex-prisoner looking at the exterior of a British jail with similar emotions.

On Monday morning I ate a leisurely breakfast – the usual Dutch morning meal: a platter of cold meats; slices of Edam and Gouda cheese; a basket of white, brown and black bread; a small mountain of butter and the inevitable boiled egg – always much too lightly cooked for my taste, and with a tiresome white plastic teaspoon with which to eat it.

The dining-room was as typically Dutch as the breakfast. Dark red wallpaper; chiffoniers in the darkest of dark oak; a great many silk, bell-shaped lampshades in a brown and red pattern, edged with velvet bobbles. Every available space was, of course, filled to capacity with pot-plants whose foliage had climbed up the walls like lianas in a jungle. Some visitors to the Netherlands find this nineteenth-century type of interior decoration depressing. To me, it is pleasantly soothing.

I decided I would walk to my rendezvous. It was a delightful sunny morning with a fresh breeze sweeping across from the North Sea. The bells of the Munt Tower were chiming half-past ten as I passed by and continued beside the rippling water of the Amstel until, dodging a couple of trams, I crossed over the Blaubrug and made my way around the vast open space of the Waterlooplein – at that moment being dug up to prepare for the construction of a new Stadhuis and opera house.

I arrived at my destination at ten minutes to eleven. Deciding it would do no harm to be early, I went straight in and enquired at reception where I could find Inspector van den Bruin. The clerk pointed to the open plan, polished-wood staircase: 'First floor – office at the end of the corridor.'

The nervous tension I had felt ever since waking increased as I mounted the stairs. The corridor was short and the door at the end wide open.

I stood silently on the threshold of a small office. Its only occupant was a pink-cheeked young man at a desk, writing in a large notebook. I could only see his profile and this looked familiar. As I watched, he threw down his pen and swivelled round to gaze directly at me. What he saw seemed to amuse him. Without getting up, he held out a welcoming hand, saying, with a broad grin: 'So it *is* you! I knew at once your name was familiar!'

I shook the hand, realising where we had met. He had been one of the posse who burst into Dinos' flat to arrest us. During my time at the central police station he had become a familiar figure in the anti-narcotics brigade office, although we had never exchanged a word.

Still amused, he said: 'So they've let you out already? This is terrible – makes it hardly worth the trouble we took to catch you! You remember me?'

'Of course. But I hadn't expected to find you here.'

'I've been promoted.' He sounded despondent and the bright smile faded a bit.

'Congratulations.'

'Thank you. Actually, I would much rather have stayed where I was – plenty of action, which I enjoyed. Now I'm tied to a desk.'

'Making decisions about what should be done with people like myself?'

'Exactly.' He pointed to some papers. 'I've just been reading some letters about you. I gather you want to get rid of the contents of your former apartment before we deport you. Now tell me, honestly, how much time d'you really need?'

There was a pause that seemed to go on forever. I was tempted to ask for a week's grace, but wondered if I could complete the job in that time. On the other hand, if I were to ask for longer, might he not consider it impertinence and have me put on the boat train that very evening?

He broke the silence. 'Would a month be enough?' he asked, quite seriously.

For a moment surprise deprived me of speech. I managed to find enough breath to say: 'Oh yes – more than enough!'

'All right,' he said, briskly, 'we'll give you a month to settle your affairs.' He produced my battered passport. 'Have you got your ticket with you?' he asked.

I handed the Sealink ticket to him. He glanced at it and took an official-looking, printed postcard from the drawer and waved it at me, saying: 'Give this to passport control at the Hook when you leave. They'll send it back to us, and we'll know you've gone and the date you left.' He put the card and the ticket in the passport and handed it to me.

'Where are you staying at present?' was his next question, which surprised me. I had assumed my taxi driver of Friday to be a copper's nark who would have reported where he had driven me. Perhaps he had, but the query sounded genuine.

'A small hotel on the Kaisersgracht,' I said, giving its name.

'Not far from where you used to live,' he commented. 'Will you be staying there until you go?'

'I think so. I've had several invitations from friends but, at the moment, I'd rather be on my own.'

'Because it gives you a greater feeling of freedom, and that's important to you?'

'Very important.'

'In that case I won't keep you from it any longer!' He got to his feet and I realised his height was one of my reasons for remembering him. His six feet seven inches towered over my mere six feet.

As we shook hands, I tried to thank him adequately for what seemed an astonishing concession, but he interrupted, saying: 'Of course I know I'm taking a chance on you, but I don't think I'll regret it. You're an Englishman – a race that seldom gives us much trouble. The ones who do are mostly your yobbish football supporters – and you're hardly that type, or, for that matter, their age!'

I left the building feeling as if I were walking on air.

Early that afternoon I was back in my law firm's attic, sorting out the clutter I had collected during the last ten years. My suitcases were crammed to bursting with clothes I had bought for trips to Canada in winter, to South America in summer, to Greece, Turkey and the Middle East at all times of the year. There were countless paperbacks, great quantities of photographs I had always intended to stick into albums. Nothing of mine had, it seemed, escaped the eye of my good landlord; everything was there, from old letters to dried-up shoe polish.

During the next few days, I gradually built up three separate piles. Pile number 1 consisted of what I intended to take to England. Pile number 2 comprised those objects I hoped to be able to leave with friends in Amsterdam, to be collected later, or sent on when I had settled somewhere. Pile number 3, which quickly became the largest, included everything to be given to some charitable organisation or thrown away. I rented a small car and delivered pile number 2 to long-suffering friends.

The disposal of what I hoped to give away posed an unexpected problem. I called on various charities and telephoned even more; none showed the slightest interest in the discarded contents of an old Englishman's wardrobe, although everything was in good condition. The Dutch standard of living is exceptionally high. Most people when they tire of anything, just throw it away and buy new.

Eventually, and with some reluctance, I offered it all to the Salvation Army who, to my relief, accepted enthusiastically. My hesitation was due to this organisation's openly expressed antagonism towards homosexuals, whom they appear to regard as emissaries of Satan. As they took away a small truck-load of my old clothes with many expressions of gratitude, I felt strongly tempted to tell them they would be equipping Amsterdam's down-and-outs with the cast-offs of an unrepentant sodomite. But tact, plus my anxiety to get rid of the stuff, made me refrain.

Eleven days after my release the job was finished. The attic was empty – although its dustbins were decidedly overfull. I had said my goodbyes and was ready to leave.

The following morning, I went by taxi to the station, carrying my faithful shoulder-bag and an enormous canvas and leather suitcase almost as heavy as the wardrobe-trunks of bygone generations.

Amsterdam's Central Station, a splendid nineteenth-century red-brick pile designed by the same architect as the Rijksmuseum, belongs to the era when all railway termini were staffed by a superabundance of porters, eager to carry luggage. In the present democratic age where passengers have to hump their own belongings, even the trolleys are virtually useless in this station, because access to all platforms is only possible from two cavernous underpasses and up flights of thirty or more steps, and the only possible means of getting one's luggage on to the platform is by manhandling it oneself.

It was getting towards the end of the morning rush-hour, but commuters were still streaming into the subways from suburban lines.

With my shoulder-bag around my neck and using both hands to hold my vast suitcase (unfortunately, it lacked wheels) I pushed my way along one of the underpasses against the tide of humanity hurrying towards the exit.

When I reached the staircase up to the boat-train I was sadly out of breath and decided to take a short rest before attempting the climb. I dropped the suitcase and, panting like an old dog, leaned against the wall, endeavouring to keep out of the way of the descending crowd.

I suddenly remarked a noticeably upper-class young Dutchman amongst those hurrying down the steps. I remember thinking he was the Netherlands equivalent of what, in present-day vernacular, would be described in England as a Sloane Ranger and in America as an Ivy Leaguer; a suit built on him, probably in Savile Row, and splendidly polished, obviously handmade shoes. To my surprise, he stopped in front of me and, with what sounded like a murmur of apology, picked up my suitcase and started, quickly, to retrace his steps up to the plat-form while I, vainly, tried to keep up, breathlessly protesting that he was risking a double-rupture and should drop it at once. He ignored me and hurried along the boat-train until he reached a first-class coach where he put down the suitcase. I had not the heart to tell him I was travelling second.

'Much too heavy for someone of your age,' he said, waving away my thanks. 'Glad to have been of help. Have a good journey!' With these words he sped away down the steps.

I felt the Netherlands were expelling an undesirable criminal with astonishing courtesy. I wondered how many elderly Dutchmen would receive similar help in London or New York.

The sun continued to shine as the immaculate boat-train (all Dutch trains are immaculate) trundled through the province of North Holland to the outer Rotterdam suburb of Schiedam where, after a brief halt, it reversed towards the Hoek van Holland, along the banks of the wide River Maas with its multitude of cranes, surrounding the docks of the great Europort, silhouetted against the sky on the far side of this great expanse of shimmering water. A light swell was rolling in from the North Sea and I could taste the salt in the air.

There were plenty of trolleys at the Hook and no steps. My trolley had the usual habit of preferring to move like a crab, but thwarting this tendency was a good deal less exhausting than carrying the stuff.

Passport control was in a single-storey building, close to the edge of the quay. Several officials in blue were sitting in a row of open-fronted booths, paying little attention to the passengers walking past, most of whom were members of the EEC whose passports did not require stamping.

Conscious of being in a different category, I halted in front of a Paul Newman look-alike and handed him the printed postcard from Inspector van den Bruin, together with my passport.

The young official looked surprised, so I felt some explanation was necessary. 'The Amsterdam "foreign" police asked me to give you this card,' I said. 'They want it sent back to them – evidence that I've left the country.'

He looked carefully at both sides of the postcard and then gave me a grin in which amusement and sympathy seemed equally mixed. 'Thank you,' he said, 'I'll see it's sent off today.' He gave me back the passport without stamping it. As I moved towards the ship, he called out, in a tone that sounded as if he really meant it: 'I hope you have a good journey!'

I left my luggage at the top of the companionway to the main saloon and went up to the boat deck. A flock of gulls were circling the ship; occasionally, one would peel off from the rest and dive like a Stuka towards the ruffled waters of the Maas to scoop up a morsel of fish-offal while still in flight. The sight made me feel that if it were not possible to be a human being I would rather be a gull than any other form of creation.

The hawsers were lifted off their bollards by huge Dutch long-shoremen with vast beer-bellies and winched slowly inboard. The space between us and the landing-stage gradually widened and the *Konigen Juliana* moved slowly forward between the long breakwaters that jut into the North Sea from the shining clean, but ugly, harbour installations that line the northern shore of this estuary. The only beautiful things to be seen were the gulls who continued to circle overhead, presumably in the hope of tit-bits from the galley.

As we increased speed, I hung over the rail looking at the undulating sand dunes of the Netherlands coastline towards Scheveningen, and felt close to tears. If the appeal Jan Drukker was going to make against my deportation failed, this might be the last glimpse I would ever have of a country I loved deeply and whose nationals, white, brown and black, had always treated me with a kindness I never deserved, right up to the moment of my final embarkation.

I knew, as I watched the faint outline of the Hook's breakwaters disappearing into the summer haze that, as far as I was concerned, the Dutch habit of treating convicted criminals with what other countries considered shocking leniency was, in my case, going to work.

In spite of offers made through the prison's international grape-vine from a disorganised Marseille *milieu* to re-establish their lines of communication with several Canadian provinces, I knew I would now give up all involvement with narcotics. The Dutch had given me hardly more than a tap on the wrist in reproof, and had done so without a trace of smug moralising: they had shown none of the vengeful hysteria that seemed to prevail in British and American courts. In return, I intended to sever my connection with the drug scene. This was no sudden death-bed conversion, it was a point of view that had grown stronger with each month I had spent in the *Schouw*.

It seemed a pity that so many countries had not heeded the advice of the American novelist and essayist, Gore Vidal, who had written, a long time ago: 'Fighting drugs is nearly as big a business as pushing them. Since the combination of sin and money is irresistible (particularly to the professional politician), the situation will clearly grow worse.'

I had no idea of what the future would hold for me. Conscious that I would shortly be pushing eighty yet, with an inborn streak of anarchy still very much alive, I was hopeful of evading most aspects of conventional respectability until my last breath. And, with these thoughts in mind, I went below to lunch.